# BARRON'S

# BASIC TIPS

## ON THE

*

## SCHOLASTIC APTITUDE TEST

## Fifth Edition

**Samuel C. Brownstein**
Formerly Chairperson, Science Department
George W. Wingate High School, Brooklyn, New York

**Mitchel Weiner**
Formerly Member, Department of English
James Madison High School, Brooklyn, New York

**Sharon Weiner Green**
Adjunct Lecturer in English
College of Staten Island, City University of New York
Staten Island, New York

**Barron's Educational Series, Inc.**
New York • London • Toronto • Sydney

The sample SAT questions in Chapter 2 are reprinted by permission of Educational Testing Service, the copyright owner of the test questions. SAT questions selected from *10 SATs* (2nd and 3rd editions) and *Taking the SAT* (1988–1989 edition), College Entrance Examination Board, 1986, 1988. Permission to reprint the SAT material does not constitute review or endorsement by Educational Testing Service or the College Board of this publication as a whole or of any other testing information it may contain.

International Standard Book No. 0-8120-4186-0

**Library of Congress Cataloging-in-Publication Data**

Brownstein, Samuel C.
  Barron's basic tips on the SAT, scholastic aptitude test / Samuel C. Brownstein, Mitchel Weiner, Sharon Weiner Green. —5th ed.
  p. cm.
  Rev. ed. of: Basic tips on the scholastic aptitude test, SAT. 4th ed. c1986.
  Summary: Drill material and review in word study, reading comprehension, standard written English, and mathematics. Also includes a complete simulated test with correct answers explained.
  ISBN 0-8120-4186-0
  1. Scholastic aptitude test—Study guides.   2. Universities and colleges—United States—Examinations—Study guides.
[1. Scholastic aptitude test—Study guides.   2. Universities and colleges—Examinations—Study guides.]   I. Weiner, Mitchel.
II. Green, Sharon.   III. Brownstein, Samuel C. Basic tips on the SAT, scholastic aptitude test.   IV. Brownstein, Samuel C. Basic tips on the scholastic aptitude test, SAT.   V. Title.   VI. Title: Barron's basic tips on the scholastic aptitude test, SAT.
LB2353.57.B763      1989      89-6847
378.1'664—dc20                                        CIP
AC

PRINTED IN THE UNITED STATES OF AMERICA

01    5500    987654321

# Contents

Preface   **v**

Timetable for the SAT   **vi**

SAT Test Dates   **vii**

**1   About the SAT**   **1**
    Commonly Asked Questions About the SAT   1
    Tips and Strategies for the SAT   4

**2   Sample SAT Questions**   **8**
    Verbal Questions   8
    Mathematics Questions   14
    Test of Standard Written English (TSWE)   20
    Answer Key   23

**3   Building Your Vocabulary**   **24**
    SAT High-Frequency Word List   25
    Long-Range Strategy   30
    Basic Word List *with Etymologies and Synonym*
      *and Antonym Tests*   32
    Answer Key   162

**4   The Verbal Sections: Strategies, Tips, and Practice**   **166**
    Long-Range Strategy   166
    General Tips for Answering Verbal Questions   166
    The Antonym Question   167
    The Analogy Question   176
    The Sentence Completion Question   187
    The Reading Comprehension Question   200

| 5 | **The Test of Standard Written English** | **226** |
|---|---|---|
| | Long-Range Strategy | 226 |
| | Tips to Help You Cope | 228 |
| | Practice Exercise | 230 |
| | Answer Key | 234 |

| 6 | **The Mathematics Sections: Strategies, Tips, and Practice** | **235** |
|---|---|---|
| | General Tips for Answering Mathematics Questions | 235 |
| | Long-Range Strategy | 237 |
| | Mathematics Review | 238 |
| | The Standard Multiple-Choice Question | 246 |
| | The Quantitative Comparison Question | 274 |

| 7 | **Practice SAT Exam** | **293** |
|---|---|---|
| | Test | 301 |
| | Answer Key | 360 |
| | Answer Explanations | 362 |

# Preface

You have in your hands Barron's *Basic Tips on the SAT*, the compact version of Barron's classic *How to Prepare for the SAT*. Small enough to fit in your pocket, portable enough to read on the bus, this short course in SAT preparation provides you with the basic tips and strategies you need to cope with the SAT.

If you feel unready for the SAT, if you don't quite know what to expect on it, *Basic Tips* may be just the eye-opener you need.

It provides you with actual sample questions from the SAT—antonyms, analogies, sentence completions, reading comprehension questions, standard multiple-choice math questions, and quantitive comparisons.

It offers you dozens of specific tips that will help you attack every type of SAT question, and provides you with practice exercises.

It offers you Barron's abridged Basic Word List, your best chance to acquaint yourself with the college-level vocabulary you will face on the SAT.

It offers you the brand-new, exclusive SAT High-Frequency Word List, words that have been shown by computer analysis to occur and reoccur on actual published SATs.

Best of all, it offers you the chance to take a complete practice SAT—three hours straight spent answering questions that correspond to actual SAT questions in content, format, and level of difficulty.

Read the tips. Go over the strategies. Do the practice exercises. *Then* take the practice SAT and see how you score. Study the answer explanations, especially those for questions you were unsure of or answered incorrectly. You'll come out feeling far more secure about what it will be like to take the SAT.

# Timetable for the SAT*    Total Time:   3 Hours

| | | |
|---|---|---|
| **9:00** to **9:30** | Section 1 **Verbal** | 15 Antonym Questions |
| | | 10 Analogy Questions |
| | | 10 Sentence Completion Questions |
| | | 10 Reading Comprehension Questions |
| **9:30** to **10:00** | Section 2 **Mathematics** | 25 Standard Multiple-Choice Questions |
| **10:00** to **10:05** | BREAK | |
| **10:05** to **10:35** | Section 3 **Test of Standard Written English** | 35 Usage Questions |
| | | 15 Sentence Correction Questions |
| **10:35** to **11:05** | Section 4 **Verbal** | 10 Antonym Questions |
| | | 10 Analogy Questions |
| | | 5 Sentence Completion Questions |
| | | 15 Reading Comprehension Questions |
| **11:05** to **11:10** | BREAK | |
| **11:10** to **11:40** | Section 5 **Mathematics** | 15 Standard Multiple-Choice Questions |
| | | 20 Quantitative Comparison Questions |
| **11:40** to **12:10** | Section 6 **Verbal** | 40 or 45 Questions |
| | | or |
| | **Mathematics** | 25 or 35 Questions |
| | | or |
| | **Test of Standard Written English** | 50 Questions |

*Actual times will vary in accordance with the time the proctor takes to complete the preliminary work and begin the actual test. Format and timing are subject to change.

# SAT Test Dates

| Test Dates | Registration Deadlines | |
|---|---|---|
| National | Regular | Late |
| **1989** | | |
| *October 14 | September 22 | September 22 |
| November 4 | September 29 | October 6 |
| December 2 | October 27 | November 3 |
| **1990** | | |
| January 27 | December 22 | December 29 |
| March 31 | February 23 | March 2 |
| May 5 | March 30 | April 6 |
| June 2 | April 27 | May 4 |

*Only given in California, Florida, Georgia, Hawaii, Illinois, North Carolina, South Carolina, and Texas.

# 1 About the SAT

## COMMONLY ASKED QUESTIONS ABOUT THE SAT

### What Is the Scholastic Aptitude Test (SAT)?

The SAT is a three-hour test of multiple-choice questions designed to measure your ability to do college work. Part of the test deals with verbal skills, including the ability to read with understanding and to use words correctly. The verbal sections of the SAT measure the extent of your vocabulary, your ability to interpret and relate ideas, and your ability to reason logically and draw conclusions correctly. The mathematics sections measure your ability to use and reason with numbers or mathematical concepts. These sections test your ability to handle general number concepts rather than specific achievement in mathematics.

There are six sections on the test. Thirty minutes are allowed for each section. Two sections test verbal ability with questions on antonyms, analogies, sentence completion, and reading comprehension. Two sections test quantitive thinking with mathematics questions. One section, known as the Test of Standard Written English (TSWE), has questions on grammar, usage, and sentence structure. (The result of the TSWE does not affect your SAT score. The main purpose of this section is to help the college determine which freshman English class will be right for you.) Finally, one section of the SAT is an experimental section (verbal, mathematics, or TSWE) with questions that the examiners are trying out for possible use in future tests. Your performance on this section will not affect your SAT score. However, you probably won't be able to recognize the experimental section, and so you had better try to do your best on the entire test.

### How Do I Register for the SAT?

If a registration form is not available at your school, request one by mail. You can obtain a form from the College Entrance Examination Board, Box 6200, Princeton, New Jersey 08451 or Box 1025, Berkeley, California 94701.

### What Are the Fees for the SAT?

The fee for the SAT is $13 nationally ($14 in New York State). If you feel you cannot afford this fee, consult your school guidance counselor.

### When Is the SAT Given?

The SAT is given in January, March or April, May, June, October (only in some states), November, and December. The regularly scheduled dates fall on Saturdays, but applicants who, for religious reasons, do not wish to appear on these dates may apply for testing on the Sunday following the regularly scheduled day. (In New York there are now equal numbers of Saturday and Sunday test dates.)

### How Is the Test Scored?

The SAT is scored on a scale that ranges from 800, the highest possible grade, to 200, the lowest possible grade. You will get separate grades for the mathematics and verbal sections of the test. The TSWE is scored on a scale that ranges from 60 down to 20 and is entirely separate.

Your score is based on the number of questions you answered correctly, minus points for those you answered incorrectly. Wrong answers on five-choice questions subtract ¼ point from your raw score. Wrong answers on the four-choice quantitative comparison questions subtract ⅓ of a point from your score. The raw score is then scaled. The scale varies slightly from year to year. Answering 45 of the 60 mathematics questions correctly might give you a score of 650 one year and 660 another year.

You should not expect to answer all the questions correctly. Very few people ever do. You may go through your entire life and never meet anyone who scored 800 on the SAT. In fact, half the people who take the SAT answer fewer than half the questions correctly. Median SAT scores in recent years have been in the low to mid 400s. Answering half the verbal questions correctly will usually give you a score around 490. Answering half the mathematics questions correctly will give you a score around 530.

### How Important Are SAT Scores?

Most colleges will hesitate to officially announce any cutoff points for SAT scores. They feel that announcing such scores would discourage otherwise potential candidates for admission. Most schools consider far more than these scores when making their admissions decisions. You should bear in mind, however, that a poor score on the examination, even if accompanied by a fairly good high school record, may make a college think twice about accepting you. On the other hand, a good college entrance examination score with an accompanying mediocre high school record is not uncommon. Since the scores are a sign you have good potential, admissions officers may spend some time going over the reasons your grades were only so-so.

The results of college entrance examinations are important because they are a scientific way of comparing all candidates in regard to their abilities to do college work. A high school record alone cannot be a yardstick of academic promise. Marking standards differ among high schools. Class standing in a small high school is not as significant as it is in a large city school. The standing in a specialized school is of little significance except for those at the very top. Entrance examinations afford equal opportunity to every one of you.

### How Can This Book Help You Score High on the College Boards?

Obviously no book used for a few months in the sophomore or junior year of high school is the complete answer to superior SAT scores. As one admissions officer has put it, the books in the home of the kindergarten child are more important than the books in the hands of the high school junior. The home environment and the emphasis on in-school and outside-school educational and cultural agencies throughout a child's formative years are the most important reasons for high scores on these examinations, which measure general background as well as specific subject abilities.

This book will help the superior, the average, and the below-average student to achieve better scores. Throughout, it stresses test-taking strategies and offers exercises in the format of actual examination questions. It concludes with a full-length practice SAT, with all answers completely explained.

Study the tips and strategies that follow to start you on your way toward a high SAT score.

---

# TIPS AND STRATEGIES FOR THE SAT

The easiest way to answer a question correctly is to know the answer. If you know what all the words mean in an antonym question, you won't have any trouble choosing the right answer. If you know exactly how to solve a mathematics question and don't make any mistakes in arithmetic, you won't have any trouble choosing the right answer. But you won't always be absolutely sure of the right answer. Here are some suggestions that may help you. (You'll find specific strategies and tips for each type of question in later chapters of the book.)

## Guessing

Since wrong answers count against you on the SAT, you may think that you should never guess if you aren't sure of the right answer to a question. But even if you guessed wrong four times for every time you guessed right, you would still come out even. A wrong answer costs you only ¼ of a point (⅓ on the quantitative comparison questions). The most usual advice is to guess if you can eliminate one or two of the answers. You have a better chance of hitting the right answer when you make this sort of "educated" guess.

### Timing

You have only a limited amount of time in which to complete each section of the test, and you don't want to waste any of it. So here are two suggestions.

1. By the time you get to the actual SAT, you should have a fair idea of how much time to spend on each question. If a question is taking too long, leave it and go on to the next question. This is no time to try to show the world that you can stick to a job no matter how long it takes. All the machine that grades the test will notice is that you didn't have any correct answers after question 17.

2. Memorize the directions for each type of question. They are given in the next chapter and they appear in the practice test. They are exactly the same directions that will appear on the SAT. However, the time you spend reading them at the SAT is test time. If you don't have to read the directions, you have that much more time to answer the questions.

### The SAT as a Whole

1. The best way to prepare for any test you ever take is to get a good night's sleep before the test so you are well rested and alert.

2. Allow plenty of time for getting to the test site. Taking a test is pressure enough. You don't need the extra tension that comes from worrying about whether you will get there on time.

3. Remember that you are allowed to write in the test book. You can write anything you want in the test book. You can and should do your mathematics computations in the booklet. There is absolutely no need to try to do them in your head. You should also circle any questions that you're not sure of. Then if you have time at the end of the test, you will be able to locate them quickly. And if it helps you to doodle while you think, then doodle away. What is written in the test booklet does not matter to anyone.

4. What is written on the answer sheet does matter. Be very careful not to make any stray marks on it. This test is graded by a machine, and a machine cannot tell the difference between an accidental mark and a filled-in answer. When the machine sees two marks, it calls the answer wrong.

5. Check frequently to make sure you are answering the questions in the right spots. No machine is going to notice that you made a mistake early in the test, answered question 4 in the space for question 5, and put all your following answers in the wrong place.

6. Know what to expect. By the time you have finished with this book, you will be familiar with all the kinds of questions that are going to appear on the SAT. You should also be aware of how long it is going to take. There are six sections on the test. Each one is a half-an-hour long, and there is supposed to be a five-minute break between sections. If you are scheduled to start the SAT at 9 a.m., do not make a dentist appointment for noon. You can't possibly get there on time, and you'll just spend the last two sections of the test worrying about it.

7. The College Board tells you to bring two sharpened number 2 pencils to the test. Bring four. They don't weigh much, and this might be the one day in the decade when two pencil points decide to break. And bring full-size pencils, not little stubs. They are easier

to write with, and you might as well be comfortable.

8. Speaking of being comfortable, wear comfortable clothes. This is a test, not a fashion show. And bring a sweater. The test room may be hot, or it may be cold. You can't change the room, but you can put on a sweater.

9. Bring an accurate watch. The room in which you take the test may not have a clock, and some proctors are not very good about posting the time on the blackboard. Each time you begin a test section, write down in your booklet the time according to your watch. That way you will always know how much time you have left.

10. The questions in each segment of the test get harder as you go along (except the reading comprehension questions). But each new segment starts with easy questions. So don't get bogged down on a difficult antonym question when only three questions away the easy sentence completion questions begin.

11. Read the question. Answer the one that was asked, not the one you thought was going to be asked.

12. Eliminate as many wrong answers as you can. Deciding between two choices is easier than deciding among five.

# 2  Sample SAT Questions*

The purpose of this chapter is to familiarize you with the kinds of questions that appear on the SAT. Knowing what to expect when you take the examination is an important step in preparing for the test and succeeding on it. For this reason we are providing you with sample questions taken from actual, current SATs.

The sample questions that follow illustrate the kinds of questions you will find in the verbal and mathematical sections of the SAT and on the Test of Standard Written English.

## VERBAL QUESTIONS

Your SAT verbal score is based on how well you do on 85 questions: 25 antonyms, 20 analogies, 15 sentence completions, and 25 reading comprehension questions. Your college success will be closely bound up with your verbal abilities—especially your ability to understand what you read. This often means your ability to understand the words you read: your vocabulary. The SAT tests these verbal skills of yours in several different ways, but throughout the test the emphasis is on the formal written language, rather than on the casual English you might speak.

### Antonyms

These are the most straightforward vocabulary questions on the test. You are given a word and must choose, from the five

*SAT questions selected from *10 SATs* (2nd and 3rd editions) and *Taking the SAT* (1988–1989 edition). College Entrance Examination Board, 1986, 1988. Reprinted by permission of Educational Testing Service, the copyright owner of the test questions.
Permission to reprint the SAT material does not constitute review or endorsement by Educational Testing Service or the College Board of this publication as a whole or of any other testing information it may contain.

choices that follow it, the best antonym. The vocabulary in this section includes words that you have probably seen in your reading, although you may never have used or even heard many of them in everyday conversations.

Here are the directions for the antonym questions and 3 sample questions from recent SATs.

---

Each question below consists of a word in capital letters, followed by five lettered words or phrases. Choose the word or phrase that is most nearly <u>opposite</u> in meaning to the word in capital letters. Since some of the questions require you to distinguish fine shades of meaning, consider all the choices before deciding which is best.

Example:

GOOD: (A) sour  (B) bad  (C) red
(D) hot  (E) ugly          (A) ● (C) (D) (E)

---

1. HARBOR:   (A) enlighten   (B) burden   (C) permit
   (D) prepare for   (E) turn away

2. BANEFUL:   (A) brilliant   (B) beneficial   (C) mysterious
   (D) rough   (E) careful

3. UNDERMINE:   (A) entangle   (B) parch   (C) overwork
   (D) enter   (E) support

## Sentence Completion

The sentence completion questions ask you to choose the best way to complete a sentence from which one or two words have been omitted. These questions test a combination of reading comprehension skills and vocabulary. You must be able to recognize the logic, style, and tone of the sentence, so that you will be able to choose the answer that makes sense in this context. You must also be able to recognize the way words are normally used. At some time in your schooling, you have probably had a vocabulary assignment in which you were asked to define a word and use it in a sentence. In this part of the SAT, you have to fit words in sentences. Once you understand the implications of the sentence, you should be able to choose the answer that will make the sentence clear, logical, and stylistically consistent. The sentences cover a wide variety of topics of the sort you have probably encountered in your general reading. However, this is not a test of your general knowledge. You may feel more comfortable if you are familiar with the topic the sentence is discussing, but you should be able to handle any of the sentences using your understanding of the English language.

Here are the directions for sentence completion questions and 3 sample questions from recent SATs.

---

Each sentence below has one or two blanks, each blank indicating that something has been omitted. Beneath the sentence are five lettered words or sets of words. Choose the word or set of words that <u>best</u> fits the meaning of the sentence as a whole.

Example:

Although its publicity has been ----, the film itself is intelligent, well-acted, handsomely produced, and altogether ----.

(A) tasteless..respectable    (B) extensive..moderate

  (C) sophisticated..amateur    (D) risqué..crude

    (E) perfect..spectacular

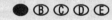

---

4. It is inaccurate to describe Hopkins as a crusader for progressive reforms, for, although he debunks certain popular myths, he is not really ---- of change

    (A) an advocate    (B) a censor    (C) an adversary
        (D) a caricature    (E) a descendant

5. The reef's fragile surface of living polyps is probably more ---- to wounds and infection than a child's skin; indeed, merely brushing against living coral ---- its delicate protoplasm.

    (A) resistant..revives    (B) susceptible..enhances
        (C) immune..imperils    (D) vulnerable..damages
        (E) attractive..impairs

**6.** He had a delightfully indulgent way of showing his ---- for his friends; these actions in themselves ---- a kind heart.

   (A) respect..contradicted     (B)  concern..deprecated
      (C) disdain..established      (D) intolerance..denoted
       (E)  fondness..betokened

### Analogies

These are the questions that people seem to think of most often when they think about the SAT. Analogies may well be the most difficult kind of question on the test, but they aren't impossible, and at least some of them will be fairly easy. Questions of this kind test your understanding of the relationships among words and ideas. You are given one pair and must choose another pair that is related in the same way. Many relationships are possible. The two terms in the pair can be synonyms; one term can be a cause, the other the effect; one can be a tool, the other the user. Consider the first pair in each question carefully, and try to make a brief sentence using the two terms. Then look at the other pairs. It should be possible to substitute the correct answer (and only the correct answer) into your sentence and still have the sentence make sense.

Here are the directions for the analogy questions and 3 sample questions from recent SATs.

---

Each question below consists of a related pair of words or phrases, followed by five lettered pairs of words or phrases. Select the lettered pair that <u>best</u> expresses a relationship similar to that expressed in the original pair.

Example:
  YAWN : BOREDOM :: (A) dream : sleep
  (B) anger : madness      (C) smile : amusement
   (D) face : expression      (E) impatience : rebellion

---

7. GIBE : SCORN :: (A) confess : punishment (B) smile : awe (C) rebuff : friendship (D) twitch : fury (E) chortle : exultation

8. ISLAND : ARCHIPELAGO :: (A) castle : moat (B) star : galaxy (C) river : delta (D) bay : peninsula (E) earth : hemisphere

9. PERFUNCTORY : ENTHUSIASM :: (A) hostile : animosity (B) submissive : defiance (C) flagrant : criticism (D) solitary : conviction (E) honorary : admiration

## Reading Comprehension

These questions test your ability to understand and interpret what you read. This is probably the most important ability you will need in college and afterward. It's the ability you are using right now, when you are reading about the SAT.

There will be several reading passages on the SAT, of varying length. The shorter passages may have only two or three questions, and the longer passages may have five questions. The passages may be about any subject matter. However, you do not need to know anything about the subject discussed in the passage. The purpose of these questions is to test your reading ability, not your knowledge of history or science. Some of the questions will be factual, asking you about specific details in the passage. Others will ask you to interpret the passage, to make judgments about it.

Here are the directions for the reading comprehension questions and 3 sample questions from recent SATs.

Each passage below is followed by questions based on its content. Answer all questions following a passage on the basis of what is stated or implied in that passage.

In the early years of the Third French Republic (1870–1940), an urgent need was felt for an adequate patron, preferably drawn from the great leaders of the First Republic. Danton seemed promising material and, after a band of official

*(5)* historians had gotten to work on him, his statue glared forth
with audacity from its pedestal. Respected historian Albert
Mathiez, however, set to work to attack this new idol and, after
twenty-four years of research, made it pretty clear that Danton
was unprincipled, venal, implicated in treasonable negotiations,
*(10)* by no means an ardent republican, and, with all this, not a
very influential politician after all.

Needless to say, in spite of Mathiez' work, Danton's statue
is still firm on its pedestal, his reputation spotless in the
school books of France today. The Third Republic properly
*(15)* made Danton great: in its amoral complacency, he would have
been quite at home. Danton always believed that a popular
system of government for his country was absurd; that the
people were too ignorant, too inconsistent, and too corrupt to
support a legal administration; that, habituated to obey, they
*(20)* required a master. His conduct was in perfect unison with
those beliefs when he acted, but he was too voluptuous for his
ambition, too indolent to acquire supreme power. Moreover,
his objective seems to have been great wealth rather than
great fame.

**10.** The author's primary purpose in this passage is to

   (A) describe and assess the reputation and character of Danton
   (B) denounce Danton as one chiefly concerned with enhancing his
       own notoriety
   (C) show the impossibility of drawing an accurate historical picture of
       a figure like Danton
   (D) expose the government leaders' exploitation of Danton's
       reputation for personal gain
   (E) explore the influence of the First French Republic on the Third

**11.** The tone of the first two sentences of the second paragraph (lines
12–16) can best be described as

   (A) honest and straightforward
   (B) scholarly
   (C) indifferent
   (D) ironic
   (E) sensational and melodramatic

12. It can be inferred from the passage that Mathiez' findings about Danton were

    (A) accepted by the public as accurate
    (B) refuted by later writers
    (C) largely ignored
    (D) attacked as an attempt to embarrass the government
    (E) the cause of continuing controversy and debate

---

# MATHEMATICS QUESTIONS

Your SAT math score is based on how well you do on 60 mathematics questions: 40 standard multiple-choice math questions and 20 quantitative comparison questions. These questions assume that you have had, and remember, elementary algebra and geometry. You do not need to know any more advanced mathematics. You will be asked to use graphic, spatial, numerical, and symbolic techniques in a variety of problems. Many will be similar to the kinds of problems you had in your textbooks; others will not. The questions are intended to show how well you understand elementary mathematics, how well you can apply your knowledge to solve problems, and how good your mathematical instincts are—how well you can use nonroutine ways of thinking. What do we mean by "mathematical instincts" or "nonroutine ways of thinking"? In one sense, you need some insight to spot the right approach for solving any mathematical question. More important, on the SAT, is the ability to see which answer must be correct, or at least which answers are impossible, without actually solving the problem. This is basically the ability to apply mathematical rules and principles that you already know. For example, imagine that you are asked to multiply $27,654 \times 3042$. You should see right away that the answer will have to end in 8. When the multiplicand ends in a 4 and the multiplier ends in a 2, then the product must end with an 8. This is a typical illustration of saving time with insight rather than doing lengthy, time-consuming computation, which, incidentally, may lead to computational errors. So not only is it a time-saver, it may also be an error-saver.

### Standard Multiple-Choice

These will cover a wide range of topics in arithmetic, elementary algebra, and plane geometry. They are like the questions you're used to seeing in your math textbooks and on math tests in school.

Here are the directions for these questions and 10 sample questions from recent SATs.

---

In this section solve each problem, using any available space on the page for scratchwork. Then decide which is the best of the choices given and blacken the corresponding space on the answer sheet.

---

The following information is for your reference in solving some of the problems.

Circle of radius $r$: Area = $\pi r^2$; Circumference = $2\pi r$

The number of degrees of arc in a circle is 360. The measure in degrees of a straight angle is 180.

Definitions of symbols:

| | |
|---|---|
| = is equal to | ≤ is less than or equal to |
| ≠ is unequal to | ≥ is greater than or equal to |
| < is less than | ‖ is parallel to |
| > is greater than | ⊥ is perpendicular to |

Triangle: The sum of the measures in degrees of the angles of a triangle is 180.

If $\angle CDA$ is a right angle, then

(1) area of $\triangle ABC = \dfrac{AB \times CD}{2}$

(2) $AC^2 = AD^2 + DC^2$

<u>Note</u>: Figures that accompany problems in this test are intended to provide information useful in solving the problems. They are drawn as accurately as possible EXCEPT when it is stated in a specific problem that its figure is not drawn to scale. All figures lie in a plane unless otherwise indicated. All numbers used are real numbers.

1. How many more boxes would be needed to package 1,200 magazines in boxes of 10 than in boxes of 12?

   (A) 2
   (B) 10
   (C) 20
   (D) 100
   (E) 200

---

2. If $\frac{4}{3} = \frac{12}{x}$, then $x =$

   (A) 1
   (B) 9
   (C) 11
   (D) 12
   (E) 16

---

3. If $2y = 3$, then $3(2y)^2 =$

   (A) $\frac{27}{4}$
   (B) 18
   (C) $\frac{81}{4}$
   (D) 27
   (E) 81

---

4. The number $n - 3$ is how much less than $n + 3$?

   (A) 3
   (B) 6
   (C) $n - 6$
   (D) $n - 3$
   (E) $2n$

5.  How many odd positive integers are less than 36?

    (A)  16
    (B)  17
    (C)  18
    (D)  19
    (E)  35

___

6.  The ratio of the lengths of the sides of two squares is 1:3. What is the ratio of their areas?

    (A)  1:9
    (B)  1:6
    (C)  1:4
    (D)  1:3
    (E)  2:3

___

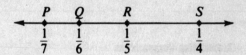

| $P$ | $Q$ | $R$ | $S$ |
|---|---|---|---|
| $\dfrac{1}{7}$ | $\dfrac{1}{6}$ | $\dfrac{1}{5}$ | $\dfrac{1}{4}$ |

7.  On the number line above, where does the number 0.13 lie?

    (A)  To the right of point $S$      (D)  Between points $P$ and $Q$
    (B)  Between points $R$ and $S$     (E)  To the left of point $P$
    (C)  Between points $Q$ and $R$

___

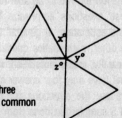

8.  In the figure above, if the three equilateral triangles have a common vertex, then $x + y + z =$

    (A)  90      (B)  120      (C)  180      (D)  360
    (E)  It cannot be determined from the information given.

9. Paul caught exactly 3 times as many fish as Eric and exactly 4 times as many as Steve. If they caught less than 100 fish altogether, what is the greatest number of fish that Paul could have caught?

   (A) 72
   (B) 66
   (C) 60
   (D) 50
   (E) 48

---

10. If $\otimes$ represents $\pi x^4$, then the area of a circle of radius 4 is represented by

   (A) ②  (B) ④  (C) ⑧  (D) ⑯  (E) ⑯π

## Quantitative Comparisons

You may never have seen questions like these before, so they require some explanation. You will be given two quantities. Sometimes you will also be given information about one or both of them. Then you must decide whether one of the quantities is greater than the other, or whether they are equal. Sometimes there will not be enough information for you to be able to make a decision.

These questions emphasize the concepts of equalities, inequalities, and estimation. In general, these questions require less time than the other mathematics questions, since they require less reading and, usually, less computation. These are the only questions on the SAT that have only four answer choices.

Here are the directions for the quantitative comparison questions and 5 sample questions from a recent SAT.

Questions 11-15 each consist of two quantities, one in Column A and one in Column B. You are to compare the two quantities and on the answer sheet blacken space

    A  if the quantity in Column A is greater:

    B  if the quantity in Column B is greater;

    C  if the two quantities are equal;

    D  if the relationship cannot be determined from the information given.

**AN E RESPONSE WILL NOT BE SCORED.**

Notes:

1. In certain questions, information concerning one or both of the quantities to be compared is centered above the two columns.
2. In a given question, a symbol that appears in both columns represents the same thing in Column A as it does in Column B.
3. Letters such as $x$, $n$, and $k$ stand for real numbers.

---

### EXAMPLES

| | Column A | Column B | Answers |
|---|---|---|---|
| E1. | $2 \times 6$ | $2 + 6$ | ⬤ Ⓑ Ⓒ Ⓓ Ⓔ |

| | | | |
|---|---|---|---|
| E2. | $180 - x$ | $y$ | Ⓐ Ⓑ ⬤ Ⓓ Ⓔ |
| E3. | $p - q$ | $q - p$ | Ⓐ Ⓑ Ⓒ ⬤ Ⓔ |

|  | Column A | Column B |
|---|---|---|

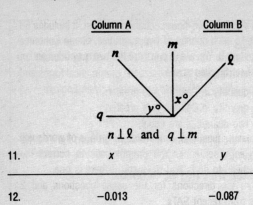

$n \perp \ell$ and $q \perp m$

| 11. | $x$ | $y$ |
|---|---|---|

| 12. | $-0.013$ | $-0.087$ |
|---|---|---|

$$x \neq 0$$

| 13. | $3x^2$ | $(3x)^2$ |
|---|---|---|

$$p > q > r > 0$$

| 14. | $p^2 + q^2$ | $pq + qr$ |
|---|---|---|

### TELEPHONE RATES

| From P to | First 3 Minutes | Each Additional Minute |
|---|---|---|
| Q | 45¢ | 10¢ |
| S | 15¢ | 5¢ |

| 15. | The cost of a 20-minute call from P to S | $1.00 |
|---|---|---|

## TEST OF STANDARD WRITTEN ENGLISH (TSWE)

This test is not really part of the SAT. It is graded separately and is intended to help colleges place students in composition courses. There is only one half-hour section to this test. It includes 50 questions. Of these, 35 are usage questions and 15 are sentence correction questions. You do not have to write anything yourself on this test, but you are expected to recognize the grammatical forms and usage that are considered acceptable in formal written English.

### Usage

In the usage questions, four words or groups of words will be underlined in each sentence. You do not have to correct the sentence. All you need to do is find the error, if there is one.

Here are the directions for the usage questions and 2 sample questions from recent SATs.

---

<u>Directions:</u>The following sentences contain problems in grammar, usage, diction (choice of words), and idiom.

Some sentences are correct.

No sentence contains more than one error.

You will find that the error, if there is one, is underlined and lettered. Assume that elements of the sentence that are not underlined are correct and cannot be changed. In choosing answers, follow the requirements of standard written English.

If there is an error, select the <u>one underlined part</u> that must be changed to make the sentence correct and blacken the corresponding space on your answer sheet.

If there is no error, blacken answer space Ⓔ.

EXAMPLE:

The region has a climate <u>so severe that</u> plants
                       **A**

<u>growing there</u> rarely <u>had been</u> more than twelve inches
  **B**            **C**

<u>high</u>. <u>No error</u>
 **D**   **E**

SAMPLE ANSWER

1.  <u>Whenever</u> we hear of a natural disaster, <u>even in</u> a distant part of the
    A                                          B

    world, <u>you</u> <u>feel sympathy</u> for the people affected. <u>No error</u>
           C      D                                            E

2.  The energy question, along with <u>several other</u> issues, <u>are going</u>
                                     A                        B

    <u>to be discussed</u> <u>at</u> the next meeting of the state legislature. <u>No error</u>
    C               D                                                    E

### Sentence Correction

For these questions you have to do more than just spot the error. You have to find the correction as well. These questions give you sentences in which one section is underlined. The answer choices repeat the underlined section and give you four other versions of the same section. You must decide which version is best. Since these questions can deal with large sections of a sentence, many of them cover errors in the structure or logic of a sentence.

Here are the directions for the sentence correction questions and 2 sample questions from recent SATs.

---

<u>Directions:</u> In each of the following sentences, some part or all of the sentence is underlined. Below each sentence you will find five ways of phrasing the underlined part. Select the answer that produces the most effective sentence, one that is clear and exact, without awkwardness or ambiguity, and blacken the corresponding space on your answer sheet. In choosing answers, follow the requirements of standard English. Choose the answer that best expresses the meaning of the original sentence.

Answer (A) is always the same as the underlined part. Choose answer (A) if you think the original sentence needs no revision.

EXAMPLE:

Laura Ingalls Wilder published her first book <u>and she was</u> <u>sixty-five years old then</u>.

(A)  and she was sixty-five years old then
(B)  when she was sixty-five years old

(C) at age sixty-five years old
(D) upon reaching sixty-five years
(E) at the time when she was sixty-five

SAMPLE ANSWER

(A) ● (C) (D) (E)

3. Consumers are beginning to take notice of electric cars because they are quiet, cause no air pollution, and gasoline is not used.

(A) cause no air pollution, and gasoline is not used
(B) air pollution is not caused, and gasoline is not used
(C) cause no air pollution, and use no gasoline
(D) causing no air pollution, and using no gasoline
(E) air pollution is not caused, and no gasoline is used

4. Joseph Conrad was born and educated in Poland and he wrote all of his novels in English.

(A) Joseph Conrad was born and educated in Poland and he
(B) Joseph Conrad, being born and educated in Poland,
(C) Although being born and educated in Poland, Joseph Conrad
(D) Although Joseph Conrad was born and educated in Poland, he
(E) Being from Poland, where he was born and educated, Joseph Conrad

## Answer Key

**Verbal**

| | | |
|---|---|---|
| 1. **E** | 5. **D** | 9. **B** |
| 2. **B** | 6. **E** | 10. **A** |
| 3. **E** | 7. **E** | 11. **D** |
| 4. **A** | 8. **B** | 12. **C** |

**Mathematics**

| | | |
|---|---|---|
| 1. **C** | 6. **A** | 11. **C** |
| 2. **B** | 7. **E** | 12. **A** |
| 3. **D** | 8. **C** | 13. **B** |
| 4. **B** | 9. **C** | 14. **A** |
| 5. **C** | 10. **A** | 15. **C** |

**Test of Standard Written English**

1. **C**    2. **B**    3. **C**    4. **D**

# 3 Building Your Vocabulary

Recognizing the meaning of words is essential to comprehending what you read. The more you stumble over unfamiliar words in a text, the more you have to take time out to look up words in your dictionary, the more likely you are to wind up losing track of what the author has to say.

To succeed in college, you must develop a college-level vocabulary. The time you put in now learning vocabulary-building techniques for the SAT will pay off later, and not just on the SAT. In this chapter you'll find two word lists that will help you build your vocabulary: the SAT High-Frequency Word List and the Basic Word List.

No matter how little time you have before you take the SAT, you can familiarize yourself with the sort of vocabulary you will be facing on the test. First, look over the words on our SAT High-Frequency Word List: each of these words, ranging from everyday words such as *abstract* and *objective* to less commonly known ones such as *chimerical* and *quandary,* has appeared (as answer choices or as question words) at least four times in SATs published in the 1980s. All of them appear, defined and accompanied with illustrative sentences to clarify their meaning, later in the chapter in the Basic Word List.

Not only will looking over the SAT High-Frequency Word List reassure you that you *do* know some SAT-type words, but also it may well help you on the actual day of the test. These words have turned up on recent tests: some of them may turn up on the test you take. Look over these words. Review any of them that are unfamiliar to you. Try using them on your parents and friends. Then, if they do turn up on your test, feel confident: your knowledge of them will help you come up with the correct answer or eliminate an incorrect answer choice.

## SAT HIGH-FREQUENCY WORD LIST

abstract
acquiesce
adroit
adversary
advocate
aesthetic
affirmation
alienate
aloof
altruistic
amass
ambiguous
ambivalence
ameliorate
amend
amity
amorphous
analogous
anarchist
antagonistic
antithesis
apathy
appease
apprehension
arbitrary
arrogance
articulate
ascendancy
ascetic
assessment
assuage
astute
asylum

atrophy
augment
austerity
banal
belittle
belligerent
benevolent
benign
blasphemous
blithe
bolster
brevity
candor
capricious
caustic
censorious
censure
charlatan
chimerical
clamor
clemency
coalesce
coerce
collaborate
compatible
complacent
compliance
comprehensive
concede
conciliatory
concise
concur
condescend

condone

conspicuous

contempt

contrite

conviction

crass

credulity

criterion

cynical

decadence

defamation

deference

deleterious

deliberate

delineate

denounce

depict

deplete

depravity

deprecate

derivative

despondent

detached

deterrent

detrimental

deviate

didactic

diligence

diminution

discerning

discordant

discretion

discriminating

discursive

disdain

disinclination

disparage

disparity

dispassionate

dispel

disperse

disputatious

disseminate

dissent

dissonance

diverge

diverse

diversion

document

dogmatic

dubious

eccentric

effervescence

elaboration

elated

eloquence

elusive

endorse

engender

enhance

enigma

ephemeral

equivocal

erratic

erroneous

esteem

evasive

exacerbate

exalt

execute

| | |
|---|---|
| exhaustive | immutable |
| expedient | impartial |
| expedite | implication |
| explicit | impoverished |
| exploit | inadvertently |
| extol | inane |
| extraneous | incidental |
| extricate | incite |
| exuberance | incompatible |
| facilitate | incongruity |
| fallacious | inconsequential |
| fanaticism | incorrigible |
| fastidious | indict |
| fervor | indifferent |
| fickle | indiscriminate |
| flagrant | indolence |
| fledgling | indulgent |
| fluctuate | inevitable |
| foresight | infallible |
| frivolity | infamous |
| furtive | infer |
| garbled | inhibit |
| glutton | initiate |
| grandiose | injurious |
| gravity | innate |
| grudging | innocuous |
| guile | innovation |
| gullible | insipid |
| hamper | insolvent |
| haphazard | instigate |
| haughtiness | insurgent |
| heed | interminable |
| hindrance | intricate |
| humility | ironic |
| hypocritical | irresolute |
| hypothetical | kindle |
| illusory | languish |

laudatory

legacy

lethargic

levity

listless

lofty

lucid

magnanimous

malicious

marred

meager

meander

methodical

meticulous

minute

miserly

mitigate

morose

muted

novelty

objective

obliterate

oblivion

obscure

obsolete

obstinate

ominous

opaque

opportunist

optimist

painstaking

parochial

partial

partisan

paucity

pedantic

peripheral

pessimism

petty

phenomena

pious

placate

plausible

pomposity

potent

preclude

predecessor

pretentious

prodigal

prodigious

profound

profusion

prolific

provincial

provoke

prudent

qualified

quandary

ratify

rebuttal

rectify

redundant

refute

relegate

remorse

renounce

reprehensible

reproach

reprove

repudiate

rescind

reserved

resigned

resolution

respite
restraint
retaliate
reticence
revere
rhetorical
sanction
satirical
saturate
scanty
scrupulous
scrutinize
seclusion
servile
shrewd
skeptic
slander
solemnity
sporadic
squander
stagnant
stanza
static
steadfast
stoic
subtlety
superficial
superfluous
suppress
surpass

surreptitious
swindler
sycophant
symmetry
taciturn
tedious
tentative
terse
thrifty
tirade
trepidation
trivia
turbulence
tyranny
undermine
uniformity
unobtrusive
vacillation
venerate
verbose
viable
vigor
vilify
virtuoso
virulent
volatile
vulnerable
whimsical
wither
zealot

**Long-Range Strategy:** There is only one effective long-range strategy for vocabulary building: READ. Read widely and well. Sample different fields—physics, art history, political science, geology—and different styles. Extensive reading is the one sure way to make your vocabulary grow.

As you read, however, take some time to acquaint yourself specifically with the sorts of words you must know to do well on the SAT. To get an idea of the level of vocabulary you must master, look over the Basic Word List on the following pages. *Do not let this list overwhelm you.* You do not need to memorize every word.

For those of you who wish to work your way through the word list and feel the need for a plan, we recommend that you follow the procedures described below in order to use the lists and the exercises most profitably:

1. Allot a definite time each day for the study of a list.

2. Devote at least one hour to each list.

3. First go through the list looking at the flagged High-Frequency words and the short, simple-looking words (6 letters at most). Mark those you don't know. In studying, pay particular attention to them.

4. Go through the list again looking at the longer words. Pay particular attention to words with more than one meaning and familiar-looking words that have unusual definitions that come as a surprise to you. Many tests make use of these secondary definitions.

5. List unusual words on index cards that you can shuffle and review from time to time. (Study no more than 5 cards at a time.)

6. Use the illustrative sentences in the list as models and make up new sentences of your own.

7. Take the test that follows each list at least one day after studying the words. In this way, you will check your

ability to remember what you have studied. (An answer key for all the Word List Tests is at the end of this chapter.)

8. If you can answer correctly 15 of the 20 questions in the test, you may proceed to the next list; if you cannot, restudy the list.

9. Keep a record of your guesses and of your success as a guesser.

For each word, the following is provided:

1. The word (printed in heavy type).
2. Its part of speech (abbreviated).
3. A brief definition.
4. A sentence illustrating the word's use.
5. Whenever appropriate, related words are provided, together with their parts of speech.
6. Following each word list will be a group of common prefixes, suffixes and roots.

The 30 word lists are arranged in strict alphabetical order. In each word list, High-Frequency words are marked with a square bullet (■).

# BASIC WORD LIST

### Word List 1   abase - allegory

**abase** V. lower; humiliate. His refusal to *abase* himself in the eyes of his followers irritated the king, who wanted to humiliate the proud leader.

**abate** V. subside or moderate. Rather than leaving immediately, they waited for the storm to *abate*. abatement, N.

**abbreviate** V. shorten. Because we were running out of time, the lecturer had to *abbreviate* her speech.

**abdicate** V. renounce; give up. When Edward VIII *abdicated* the British throne, he surprised the entire world.

**abet** V. aid, usually in doing something wrong; encourage. She was unwilling to *abet* him in the swindle he had planned. abettor, N.

**abeyance** N. suspended action. The deal was held in *abeyance* until his arrival.

**abhor** V. detest; hate. He *abhorred* all forms of bigotry. abhorrence, N.

**abominate** V. loathe; hate. Moses scolded the idol worshippers in the tribe because he *abominated* the custom.

**abortive** ADJ. unsuccessful; fruitless. We had to abandon our *abortive* attempts.

**absolve** V. pardon (an offense). The father confessor *absolved* him of his sins. absolution, N.

**abstemious** ADJ. temperate; sparing in drink, etc. The drunkards mocked him because of his *abstemious* habits.

**abstinence** N. restraint from eating or drinking. The doctor recommended total *abstinence* from salted foods. abstain, V., abstinent, ADJ.

■ **abstract** ADJ. theoretical; not concrete; nonrepresentational. To him, hunger was an *abstract* concept; he had never missed a meal.

**abstruse** ADJ. obscure; profound; difficult to understand. He read *abstruse* works in philosophy.

**accelerate** V. move faster. In our science class, we learn how falling bodies *accelerate*.

**accessory** N. additional object; useful but not essential thing. The *accessories* she bought cost more than the dress. also ADJ.

**acclaim** V. applaud; announce with great approval. The NBC sportscasters *acclaimed* every American victory in the Olympics and decried every American defeat. also N.

**accolade** N. award of merit. In Hollywood, an "Oscar" is the highest *accolade*.

**accomplice** N. partner in crime. Because he had provided the criminal with the lethal weapon, he was arrested as an *accomplice* in the murder.

**accord** N. agreement. He was in complete *accord* with the verdict.

**accost** V. approach and speak first to a person. When the two young men *accosted* me, I was frightened because I thought they were going to attack me.

**accrue** V. come about by addition. You must pay the interest which has *accrued* on your debt as well as the principal sum. accrual, N.

**acknowledge** V. recognize; admit. When pressed for an answer, he *acknowledged* the existence of another motive for the crime.

**acme** N. top; pinnacle. His success in this role marked his *acme* as an actor.

**acoustics** N. science of sound; quality that makes a room easy or hard to hear in. Carnegie Hall is liked by music lovers because of its fine *acoustics*.

■ **acquiesce** V. assent; agree without protesting. When we asked her to participate in the play, she immediately *acquiesced*.

**acquittal** N. deliverance from a charge. Her *acquittal* by the jury surprised those who had thought her guilty. acquit, V.

**acrid** ADJ. sharp; bitterly pungent. The *acrid* odor of burnt gunpowder filled the room after the pistol had been fired.

**acrimonious** ADJ. stinging; caustic. His tendency to utter *acrimonious* remarks alienated his audience, acrimony, N.

**acumen** N. mental keenness. Her business *acumen* helped her to succeed where others had failed.

**adage** N. wise saying; proverb. There is much truth in the old *adage* about fools and their money.

**adamant** ADJ. hard; inflexible. She was *adamant* in her determination to punish the wrongdoer. adamantine, ADJ.

**adapt** V. alter; modify. Some species of animals have become extinct because they could not *adapt* to a changing environment.

**addiction** N. compulsive, habitual need. His *addiction* to drugs caused his friends much grief.

**adept** ADJ. expert at. He was *adept* at the fine art of irritating people. also N.

**adhere** V. stick fast to. I will *adhere* to this opinion until proof that I am wrong is presented. adhesion, N.

**admonish** V. warn; reprove. He *admonished* his listeners to change their wicked ways. admonition, N.

■ **adroit** ADJ. skillful. Her *adroit* handling of the delicate situation pleased her employers.

**adulation** N. flattery; admiration. He thrived on the *adulation* of his henchmen.

**adulterate** V. make impure by mixing with baser substances. It is a crime to *adulterate* foods without informing the buyer.

■ **adversary** N. opponent; enemy. The young wrestler struggled to defeat his *adversary*.

**adverse** ADJ. unfavorable; hostile. *Adverse* circumstances compelled him to close his business.

**adversity** N. poverty; misfortune. We must learn to meet *adversity* gracefully.

■ **advocate** V. urge; plead for. The abolitionists *advocated* freedom for the slaves. also N.

■ **aesthetic** ADJ. artistic; dealing with or capable of appreciation of the beautiful. Because of his *aesthetic* nature, he was emotionally disturbed by ugly things. aesthete, N.

**affable** ADJ. courteous. Although he held a position of responsibility, he was an *affable* individual and could be reached by anyone with a complaint.

**affected** ADJ. artificial; pretended. His *affected* mannerisms irritated many of us who had known him before his promotion. affectation, N.

**affiliation** N. joining; associating with. His *affiliation* with the political party was of short duration for he soon disagreed with his colleagues.

**affinity** N. kinship. He felt an *affinity* with all who suffered; their pains were his pains.

■ **affirmation** N. solemn pledge by one who refuses to take an oath. The Constitution of this country provides for oath or *affirmation* by officeholders. affirm, V.

**affluence** N. abundance; wealth. Foreigners are amazed by the *affluence* and luxury of the American way of life. affluent, ADJ.

**agape** ADJ. openmouthed. He stared, *agape*, at the many strange animals in the zoo.

**agenda** N. items of business at a meeting. We had so much difficulty agreeing upon an *agenda* that there was very little time for the meeting.

**aggrandize** V. increase or intensify. The history of the past quarter century illustrates how a President may *aggrandize* his power to act aggressively in international affairs without considering the wishes of Congress.

**aggregate** ADJ. sum; total. The *aggregate* wealth of this country is staggering to the imagination. also V.

**aghast** ADJ. horrified. He was *aghast* at the nerve of the speaker who had insulted his host.

**agility** N. nimbleness. The *agility* of the acrobat amazed and thrilled the audience.

**agitate** V. stir up; disturb. His fiery remarks *agitated* the already angry mob.

**alacrity** N. cheerful promptness. He demonstrated his eagerness to serve by his *alacrity* in executing the orders of his master.

**alias** N. an assumed name. John Smith's *alias* was Bob Jones. also ADV.

■ **alienate** V. make hostile; separate. Her attempts to *alienate* the two friends failed because they had complete faith in one another.

**allay** V. calm; pacify. The crew tried to *allay* the fears of the passengers by announcing that the fire had been controlled.

**allege** V. state without proof. It is *alleged* that he had worked for the enemy. allegation, N.

**allegory** N. story in which characters are used as symbols; fable. *Pilgrim's Progress* is an *allegory* of the temptations and victories of man's soul. allegorical, ADJ.

---

## ETYMOLOGY 1

AB, ABS (from, away from) prefix

    **abduct**   lead away, kidnap

    **abjure**   renounce (swear away from)

    **abscond**   depart secretly and hide

ABLE, IBLE (capable of) adjective suffix

    **portable**   able to be carried

    **legible**   able to be read

    **interminable**   unable to be ended

AC, ACR (sharp)

    **acrimonious**   bitter

    **acerbity**   bitterness of temper

    **acidulate**   make somewhat acidic or sour

AD (to, forward) prefix

    **adjure**   request earnestly

    **admit**   allow entrance

    **Note:**   By assimilation, the AD prefix is changed to

            AC   in accord

            AF   in affliction

            AG   in aggregation

            AN   in annexation

            AP   in apparition

            AR   in arraignment

            AS   in assumption

            AT   in attendance

AG, ACT (to do)

    **act**   deed

    **agent**   doer

**retroactive** having a backward or reversed action

ALI (another)

**alias** assumed (another) name
**alienate** estrange (divert from another)
**inalienable** unable to be diverted from another

---

## TEST — Word List 1 — Synonyms

Each of the questions below consists of a word printed in italics, followed by five words or phrases numbered 1 to 5. Choose the numbered word or phrase which is most nearly similar in meaning to the word in italics and write the number of your choice on your answer paper.

1. *accessory* 1 first designs 2 absolutions 3 finales 4 concepts 5 additional object
2. *abeyance* 1 obedience 2 discussion 3 excitement 4 suspended action 5 editorial
3. *abate* 1 discuss 2 subside 3 run off secretly 4 perjure 5 project
4. *accord* 1 censure 2 forgiveness 3 mutiny 4 survival 5 agreement
5. *abortive* 1 unsuccessful 2 consuming 3 financing 4 familiar 5 fruitful
6. *abasement* 1 incurrence 2 taxation 3 ground floor 4 humility 5 humiliation
7. *abettor* 1 conception 2 one who wagers 3 encourager 4 evidence 5 protection
8. *abstruse* 1 profound 2 irrespective 3 suspended 4 protesting 5 not thorough
9. *adage* 1 index 2 report 3 proverb 4 character 5 negotiator
10. *admonish* 1 compromise 2 reprove 3 revise 4 encounter 5 visit
11. *accrue* 1 come about by addition 2 reach summit 3 create a crisis 4 process 5 educate
12. *accretion* 1 mayonnaise 2 ban 3 increase 4 protection 5 ceremony
13. *acme* 1 pinnace 2 skin disease 3 basement 4 congestion 5 pinnacle
14. *abstruse* 1 recommended 2 witty 3 realistic 4 obscure 5 very generous
15. *abstinence* 1 restrained eating or drinking 2 vulgar display 3 deportment 4 reluctance 5 population
16. *acrid* 1 sour 2 bitterly pungent 3 sweetish 4 slightly acid 5 very hard
17. *adamant* 1 sandy 2 round 3 hard 4 alkali 5 egocentric
18. *affable* 1 incidental 2 happy 3 courageous 4 courteous 5 foretelling
19. *affluence* 1 wealth 2 fear 3 persuasion 4 consideration 5 neglect
20. *allegory* 1 fable 2 poem 3 essay 4 anecdote 5 novel

### Word List 2 alleviate - aptitude

**alleviate** V. relieve. This should *alleviate* the pain; if it does not, we shall have to use stronger drugs.

**allocate** V. assign. Even though the Red Cross had *allocated* a large sum for the relief of the sufferers of the disaster, many people perished.

**alloy** N. a mixture as of metals. *Alloys* of gold are used more frequently than the pure metal.

**allude** V. refer indirectly. Try not to *allude* to this matter in his presence because it annoys him to hear of it. allusion, N.

■ **aloof** ADJ. apart; reserved. He remained *aloof* while all the rest conversed.

**altercation** N. wordy quarrel. Throughout the entire *altercation*, not one sensible word was uttered.

■ **altruistic** ADJ. unselfishly generous; concerned for others. In providing tutorial assistance and college scholarships for hundreds of economically disadvantaged youths, Eugene Lang performed a truly *altruistic* deed. altruism, N.

**amalgamate** V. combine; unite in one body. The unions will attempt to *amalgamate* their groups into one national body.

■ **amass** V. collect. The miser's aim is to *amass* and hoard as much gold as possible.

■ **ambiguous** ADJ. unclear or doubtful in meaning. His *ambiguous* instructions misled us; we did not know which road to take. ambiguity, N.

■ **ambivalence** N. the state of having contradictory or conflicting emotional attitudes. Torn between loving her parents one minute and hating them the next, she was confused by the *ambivalence* of her feelings. ambivalent, ADJ.

**amble** N. moving at an easy pace. When she first mounted the horse, she was afraid to urge the animal to go faster than a gentle *amble*.

**ambulatory** ADJ. able to walk. He was described as an *ambulatory* patient because he was not confined to his bed.

■ **ameliorate** V. improve. Many social workers have attempted to *ameliorate* the conditions of people living in the slums.

**amenable** ADJ. readily managed; willing to be led. He was *amenable* to any suggestions which came from those he looked up to; he resented advice from his inferiors.

■ **amend** V. correct; change, generally for the better. Hoping to *amend* his condition, he left Vietnam for the United States. amendment, N.

**amiable** ADJ. agreeable; lovable. Her *amiable* disposition pleased all who had dealings with her.

**amicable** ADJ. friendly. The dispute was settled in an *amicable* manner with no harsh words.

**amnesia** N. loss of memory. Because she was suffering from *amnesia*, the police could not get the young girl to identify herself.

**amnesty** N. pardon. When his first child was born, the king granted *amnesty* to all in prison.

■ **amity** N. friendship. Student exchange programs such as the Experiment in International Living were established to promote international *amity*.

■ **amorphous** ADJ. shapeless. She was frightened by the *amorphous* mass which had floated in from the sea.

**amphibian** ADJ. able to live both on land and in water. Frogs are classified as *amphibian*. also N.

**amphitheater** N. oval building with tiers of seats. The spectators in the *amphitheater* cheered the gladiators.

**ample** ADJ. abundant. He had *ample* opportunity to dispose of his loot before the police caught up with him.

**amplify** V. enlarge. His attempts to *amplify* his remarks were drowned out by the jeers of the audience.

**amputate** V. cut off part of body; prune. When the doctors decided to *amputate* his leg to prevent the spread of gangrene, he cried that he preferred death to incapacity.

**amuck** ADV. in a state of rage. The police had to be called in to restrain him after he ran *amuck* in the department store.

**amulet** N. charm; talisman. Around his neck he wore the *amulet* which the witch doctor had given him.

■ **analogous** ADJ. comparable. She called our attention to the things that had been done in an *analogous* situation and recommended that we do the same.

**analogy** N. similarity; parallelism. Your *analogy* is not a good one because the two situations are not similar.

■ **anarchist** N. person who advocates abolishing governments. I am not an *anarchist*; I wish to change our system of government, not to put an end to government.

**anarchy** N. absence of governing body; state of disorder. The assassination of the leaders led to a period of *anarchy*.

**anchor** V. secure or fasten firmly; be fixed in place. We set the pot in concrete to *anchor* it in place. anchorage, N.

**ancillary** ADJ. serving as an aid or accessory; auxiliary. In an *ancillary* capacity he was helpful; however, he could not be entrusted with leadership. also N.

**anemia** N. condition in which blood lacks red corpuscles. The doctor ascribes his tiredness to *anemia*. anemic, ADJ.

**anesthetic** N. substance that removes sensation with or without loss of consciousness. His monotonous voice acted like an *anesthetic;* his audience was soon asleep. anesthesia, N.

**angular** ADJ. sharp-cornered; stiff in manner. His features, though *angular*, were curiously attractive.

**animated** ADJ. lively. Her *animated* expression indicated a keenness of intellect.

**animosity** N. active enmity. He incurred the *animosity* of the ruling class because he advocated limitations of their power.

**annihilate** V. destroy. The enemy in its revenge tried to *annihilate* the entire population.

**annul** V. make void. The parents of the eloped couple tried to *annul* the marriage.

**anomalous** ADJ. abnormal; irregular. She was placed in the *anomalous* position of seeming to approve procedures which she despised.

**anomaly** N. irregularity. A bird that cannot fly is an *anomaly*.

**anonymous** ADJ. having no name. He tried to ascertain the identity of the writer of the *anonymous* letter.

■ **antagonistic** ADJ. hostile; actively resisting. The negotiators tried to reconcile the two *antagonistic* parties.

**antecede** V. precede. The invention of the radiotelegraph *anteceded* the development of television by a quarter of a century. antecedent, N.

**antediluvian** ADJ. antiquated; ancient. The *antediluvian* customs had apparently not changed for thousands of years. also N.

**anthropologist** N. a student of the history and science of mankind. *Anthropologists* have discovered several relics of prehistoric man in this area.

**anticlimax** N. letdown in thought or emotion. After the fine performance in the first act, the rest of the play was an *anticlimax*. anticlimactic, ADJ.

**antipathy** N. aversion; dislike. His extreme *antipathy* to dispute caused him to avoid argumentative discussions with his friends.

**antiseptic** N. substance that prevents infection. It is advisable to apply an *antiseptic* to any wound, no matter how slight or insignificant. also ADJ.

■ **antithesis** N. contrast; direct opposite of or to. This tyranny was the *antithesis* of all that he had hoped for, and he fought it with all his strength.

■ **apathy** N. indifference; lack of concern. A firm believer in democratic government, she could not understand the *apathy* of people who never bothered to vote. apathetic, ADJ.

**aperture** N. opening; hole. He discovered a small *aperture* in the wall, through which the insects had entered the room.

**apex** N. tip; summit; climax. He was at the *apex* of his career.

**aphorism** N. pithy maxim. An *aphorism* differs from an adage in that it is more philosophical or scientific. aphoristic, ADJ.

**apocryphal** ADJ. not genuine; sham. Her *apocryphal* tears misled no one.

**apotheosis** N. deification; glorification. The *apotheosis* of a Roman emperor was designed to insure his eternal greatness.

**apparition** N. ghost; phantom. Hamlet was uncertain about the identity of the *apparition* that had appeared and spoken to him.

■ **appease** V. pacify; soothe. We have discovered that, when we try to *appease* our enemies, we encourage them to make additional demands.

**appellation** N. name; title. He was amazed when the witches hailed him with his correct *appellation*.

**append** V. attach. I shall *append* this chart to my report.

**appraise** V. estimate value of. It is difficult to *appraise* the value of old paintings; it is easier to call them priceless. appraisal, N.

**apprehend** V. arrest (a criminal); dread; perceive. The police will *apprehend* the culprit and convict him before long.

■ **apprehension** N. fear; discernment. His nervous glances at the few passersby on the dim-lit street revealed his *apprehension* that he might be mugged. apprehensive, ADJ.

**apprise** V. inform. When he was *apprised* of the dangerous weather conditions, he decided to postpone his trip.

**approbation** N. approval. She looked for some sign of *approbation* from her parents.

**appropriate** V. acquire; take possession of for one's own use. The ranch owners *appropriated* the lands that had originally been set aside for the Indians' use.

**appurtenances** N. subordinate possessions. He bought the estate and all its *appurtenances*.

**aptitude** N. fitness; talent. The counselor gave him an *aptitude* test before advising him about the career he should follow.

---

## ETYMOLOGY 2

AMBI (both) prefix
    **ambidextrous**   skillful with both hands
    **ambiguous**   of double meaning
    **ambivalent**   possessing conflicting (both) emotions
AN (without) prefix
    **anarchy**   lack of government
    **anemia**   lack of blood
    **anesthetize**   deprive of feeling

ANTE (before) prefix
        **antecedent**   preceding event or word
        **antediluvian**   ancient (before the flood)
        **ante-nuptial**   before the wedding
ANTHROP (man)
        **anthropology**   study of man
        **misanthrope**   recluse (hater of mankind)
        **philanthropy**   love of mankind; charity

---

## TEST — Word List 2 — Antonyms

Each of the questions below consists of a word printed in italics, followed by five words or phrases numbered 1 to 5. Choose the numbered word or phrase which is most nearly opposite in meaning to the word in italics and write the number of your choice on your answer paper.

21. *alleviate*  1 endure 2 worsen 3 enlighten 4 maneuver 5 humiliate
22. *amalgamate*  1 equip 2 separate 3 generate 4 materialize 5 repress
23. *amass*  1 concentrate 2 rotate 3 concern 4 separate 5 recollect
24. *antediluvian*  1 transported 2 subtle 3 isolated 4 celebrated 5 modern
25. *antipathy*  1 profundity 2 objection 3 willingness 4 abstention 5 fondness
26. *appease*  1 agitate 2 qualify 3 display 4 predestin 5 interrupt
27. *analogous*  1 dissimilar 2 diagonal 3 exponential 4 unobtrusive 5 discouraging
28. *apprehend*  1 obviate 2 set free 3 shiver 4 understand 5 contrast
29. *aloof*  1 triangular 2 gregarious 3 comparable 4 honorable 5 savory
30. *amicable*  1 penetrating 2 compensating 3 unfriendly 4 zig-zag 5 unescapable
31. *amorphous*  1 nauseous 2 obscene 3 providential 4 definite 5 happy
32. *amplify*  1 distract 2 infer 3 publicize 4 decrease 5 pioneer
33. *antithesis*  1 velocity 2 maxim 3 similarity 4 acceleration 5 reaction
34. *anomaly*  1 desperation 2 requisition 3 registry 4 regularity 5 radiation
35. *aptitude*  1 sarcasm 2 inversion 3 adulation 4 lack of talent 5 gluttony
36. *ameliorate*  1 locate 2 deceive 3 regulate 4 radiate 5 exacerbate
37. *altruism*  1 good nature 2 height 3 descent 4 modernity 5 miserliness
38. *ambiguous*  1 salvageable 2 corresponding 3 responsible 4 clear 5 auxiliary
39. *anemic*  1 pallid 2 cruel 3 red-blooded 4 ventilating 5 hazardous
40. *anonymous*  1 desperate 2 signed 3 defined 4 expert 5 written

## Word List 3   aquiline - bantering

**aquiline** ADJ. curved, hooked. He can be recognized by his *aquiline* nose, curved like the beak of the eagle.

**arable** ADJ. fit for plowing. The land was no longer *arable;* erosion had removed the valuable topsoil.

■ **arbitrary** ADJ. fixed or decided; despotic. Any *arbitrary* action on your part will be resented by the members of the board whom you do not consult.

**archaeology** N. study of artifacts and relics of early mankind. The professor of *archaeology* headed an expedition to the Gobi Desert in search of ancient ruins.

**archaic** ADJ. antiquated. "Methinks," "thee," and "thou" are *archaic* words which are no longer part of our normal vocabulary.

**archipelago** N. group of closely located islands. When he looked at the map and saw the *archipelagoes* in the South Seas, he longed to visit them.

**ardor** N. heat; passion; zeal. His *ardor* was contagious; soon everyone was eagerly working.

**arduous** ADJ. hard; strenuous. His *arduous* efforts had sapped his energy.

**arid** ADJ. dry; barren. The cactus has adapted to survive in an *arid* environment.

**aromatic** ADJ. fragrant. Medieval sailing vessels brought *aromatic* herbs from China to Europe.

**arraign** V. charge in court; indict. After his indictment by the Grand Jury, the accused man was *arraigned* in the County Criminal Court.

■ **arrogance** N. haughtiness. The *arrogance* of the nobility was resented by the middle class.

■ **articulate** ADJ. expressing oneself, or expressed, readily, clearly, or effectively. Her *articulate* presentation of the advertising campaign impressed her employers. also V.

**artifacts** N. products of primitive culture. Archaeologists debated the significance of the *artifacts* discovered in the ruins of Asia Minor and came to no conclusion.

**artifice** N. deception; trickery. The Trojan War proved to the Greeks that cunning and *artifice* were often more effective than military might.

**artisan** N. a manually skilled worker. Artists and *artisans* alike are necessary to the development of a culture.

■ **ascendancy** N. controlling influence. I often wonder how leaders of religious cults maintain their *ascendancy* over their followers. ascend, V.

**ascertain** V. find out for certain. Please *ascertain* his present address.

■ **ascetic** ADJ. practicing self-denial; austere. The cavalier could not understand the *ascetic* life led by the monks. also N.

**ascribe** V. refer; attribute; assign. I can *ascribe* no motive for his acts.

**ashen** ADJ. ash-colored. His face was *ashen* with fear.

**aspirant** N. seeker after position or status. Although I am an *aspirant* for public office, I am not willing to accept the dictates of the party bosses. also ADJ.

**aspiration** N. noble ambition. Man's *aspirations* should be as lofty as the stars.

**assail** V. assault. She was *assailed* with questions after her lecture.

■ **assessment** N. evaluation; judgment. Your SAT score plays a part in the Admission Committee's *assessment* of you as an applicant.

**assiduous** ADJ. diligent. His employer praised him for his *assiduous* work. assiduity, N.

■ **assuage** V. ease; lessen (pain). Your messages of cheer should *assuage* her suffering. assuagement, N.

**asteroid** N. small planet. *Asteroids* have become commonplace to the readers of interstellar travel stories in science fiction magazines.

**astronomical** ADJ. enormously large or extensive. The government seems willing to spend *astronomical* sums on weapons development.

■ **astute** ADJ. wise; shrewd. That was a very *astute* observation. I shall heed it.

■ **asylum** N. place of refuge; safety. Fleeing persecution, the political refugee sought *asylum* in the United States.

**atheistic** ADJ. denying the existence of God. His *atheistic* remarks shocked the religious worshippers.

**atrocity** N. brutal deed. In time of war, many *atrocities* are committed by invading armies.

■ **atrophy** N. wasting away. Polio victims need physiotherapy to prevent the *atrophy* of affected limbs. also V.

**attest** V. testify, bear witness. Having served as a member of the Grand Jury, I can *attest* that our system of indicting individuals is in need of improvement.

**attribute** N. essential quality. His outstanding *attribute* was his kindness.

**attrition** N. gradual wearing down. They decided to wage a war of *attrition* rather than to rely on an all-out attack.

**atypical** ADJ. not normal. You have taken an *atypical* case. It does not prove anything.

**audacity** N. boldness. His *audacity* in this critical moment encouraged us.

**audit** N. examination of accounts. When the bank examiners arrived to hold their annual *audit*, they discovered the embezzlements of the chief cashier. also V.

■ **augment** V. increase. How can we hope to *augment* our forces when our allies are deserting us?

**auspicious** ADJ. favoring success. With favorable weather conditions, it was an *auspicious* moment to set sail.

■ **austerity** N. sternness; severity. The *austerity* and dignity of the court were maintained by the new justices. austere, ADJ.

**authenticate** V. prove genuine. An expert was needed to *authenticate* the original Van Gogh painting from its imitation.

**authoritative** ADJ. having the weight of authority; dictatorial. We accepted her analysis of the situation as *authoritative*.

**autocrat** N. monarch with supreme power. The nobles tried to limit the powers of the *autocrat* without success. autocracy, N.; autocratic, ADJ.

**automaton** N. mechanism which imitates actions of humans. Long before science fiction readers became aware of robots, writers were presenting stories of *automatons* who could outperform men.

**autonomous** ADJ. self-governing. This island is a colony; however, in most matters, it is *autonomous* and receives no orders from the mother country. autonomy, N.

**autopsy** N. examination of a dead body; post-mortem. The medical examiner ordered an *autopsy* to determine the cause of death. also V.

**auxiliary** ADJ. helper, additional or subsidiary. To prepare for the emergency, they built an *auxiliary* power station. also N.

**avarice** N. greediness for wealth. King Midas's *avarice* has been famous for centuries. avaricious, ADJ.

**aver** V. state confidently. I wish to *aver* that I am certain of success.

**averse** ADJ. reluctant. He was *averse* to revealing the sources of his information.

**aversion** N. firm dislike. Their mutual *aversion* was so great that they refused to speak to one another.

**avid** ADJ. greedy; eager for. He was *avid* for learning and read everything he could get. avidity, N.

**avow** V. declare openly. I must *avow* that I am innocent.

**awe** N. solemn wonder. The tourists gazed with *awe* at the tremendous expanse of the Grand Canyon.

**awry** ADV. distorted; crooked. He held his head *awry*, giving the impression that he had caught cold in his neck during the night. also ADJ.

**axiom** N. self-evident truth requiring no proof. Before a student can begin to think along the lines of Euclidean geometry, he must accept certain principles or *axioms*.

**babble** V. chatter idly. The little girl *babbled* about her doll. also N.

**badger** V. pester; annoy. She was forced to change her telephone number because she was *badgered* by obscene phone calls.

**baffle** V. frustrate; perplex. The new code *baffled* the enemy agents.

**baleful** ADJ. deadly; destructive. The drought was a *baleful* omen.

**balk** v. foil. When the warden learned that several inmates were planning to escape, he took steps to *balk* their attempt.

**balmy** ADJ. mild; fragrant. A *balmy* breeze refreshed us after the sultry blast.

■ **banal** ADJ. hackneyed; commonplace; trite. His frequent use of clichés made his essay seem *banal*. banality, N.

**baneful** ADJ. ruinous; poisonous. His *baneful* influence was feared by all.

**bantering** ADJ. good-natured ridiculing. They resented his *bantering* remarks because they thought he was being sarcastic.

---

## ETYMOLOGY 3

ARCH (chief, first) prefix
> **archetype**   original model
> **archbishop**   chief bishop
> **archaeology**   study of antiquities (study of first things)

ARCH (government, ruler, first)
> **monarch**   sole ruler
> **anarchy**   lack of government
> **oligarchy**   government by the few

ASTER, ASTR (star)
> **astronomy**   study of the stars
> **asterisk**   starlike type character (*)
> **disaster**   catastrophe (contrary star)

AUD, AUDIT (to hear)
> **audible**   able to be heard
> **auditorium**   place where people may be heard
> **audience**   hearers

AUTO (self)
> **autocracy**   rule by self (one person)
> **automobile**   vehicle that moves by itself
> **autobiography**   story of a person's life written by himself

---

## TEST — Word List 3 — Synonyms and Antonyms

Each of the following questions consists of a word printed in italics, followed by five words or phrases numbered 1 to 5. Choose the numbered word or phrase which is most nearly the same as or the opposite of the word in italics and write the number of your choice on your answer paper.

41. *aquiline* 1 watery 2 hooked 3 refined 4 antique 5 rodentlike
42. *archaic* 1 youthful 2 cautious 3 antiquated 4 placated 5 buttressed
43. *ardor* 1 zeal 2 paint 3 proof 4 group 5 excitement
44. *artifice* 1 spite 2 exception 3 anger 4 candor 5 loyalty
45. *artisan* 1 educator 2 decider 3 sculptor 4 discourser 5 unskilled laborer
46. *ascertain* 1 amplify 2 master 3 discover 4 retain 5 explode
47. *asteroid* 1 Milky Way 2 radiance 3 large planet 4 rising moon 5 setting moon
48. *austerity* 1 anguish 2 absence 3 innuendo 4 sternness 5 legality
49. *assuage* 1 stuff 2 describe 3 wince 4 worsen 5 introduce
50. *astute* 1 sheer 2 noisy 3 astral 4 unusual 5 foolish
51. *atrocity* 1 endurance 2 fortitude 3 session 4 heinous act 5 hatred
52. *atypical* 1 superfluous 2 booming 3 normal 4 clashing 5 lovely
53. *audacity* 1 boldness 2 asperity 3 strength 4 stature 5 anchorage
54. *avarice* 1 anxiety 2 generosity 3 statement 4 invoice 5 power
55. *balmy* 1 venturesome 2 dedicated 3 mild 4 fanatic 5 memorable
56. *awry* 1 recommended 2 commiserating 3 startled 4 straight 5 psychological
57. *banal* 1 philosophical 2 original 3 dramatic 4 heedless 5 discussed
58. *baleful* 1 doubtful 2 virtual 3 deadly 4 conventional 5 virtuous
59. *auxiliary* 1 righteous 2 prospective 3 assistant 4 archaic 5 mandatory
60. *baneful* 1 intellectual 2 thankful 3 decisive 4 nonpoisonous 5 remorseful

---

### Word List 4    barb - cadaverous

**barb** N. sharp projection from fishhook, etc. The *barb* from the fishhook caught in his finger as he grabbed the fish. barbed, ADJ.

**baroque** ADJ. highly ornate. They found the *baroque* architecture amusing.

**beguile** V. delude; cheat; amuse. He *beguiled* himself during the long hours by playing solitaire.

**belabor** V. beat soundly; assail verbally. He was *belaboring* his opponent.

**belated** ADJ. delayed. He apologized for his *belated* note of condolence to the widow of his friend and explained that he had just learned of her husband's untimely death.

■ **belittle** V. disparage; depreciate. Parents should not *belittle* their children's early attempts at drawing, but should encourage their efforts.

**bellicose** ADJ. warlike. His *bellicose* disposition alienated his friends.

■ **belligerent** ADJ. quarrelsome. Whenever he had too much to drink, he became *belligerent* and tried to pick fights with strangers. belligerence, N.

**benediction** N. blessing. The appearance of the sun after the many rainy days was like a *benediction.*

**benefactor** N. gift giver; patron. Scrooge later became Tiny Tim's *benefactor.*

■ **benevolent** ADJ. generous; charitable. His *benevolent* nature prevented him from refusing any beggar who accosted him.

■ **benign** ADJ. kindly; favorable; not malignant. The old man was well liked because of his *benign* attitude toward friend and stranger alike.

**berate** V. scold strongly. He feared she would *berate* him for his forgetfulness.

**bereft** ADJ. deprived of; lacking. The foolish gambler soon found himself *bereft* of funds.

**berserk** ADV. frenzied. Angered, he went *berserk* and began to wreck the room.

**bestow** V. confer. She wished to *bestow* great honors upon the hero.

**bicameral** ADJ. two-chambered, as a legislative body. The United States Congress is a *bicameral* body.

**biennial** ADJ. every two years. The plant bore *biennial* flowers. also N.

**bigotry** N. stubborn intolerance. Brought up in a democratic atmosphere, the student was shocked by the *bigotry* and narrowness expressed by several of his classmates.

**bizarre** ADJ. fantastic; violently contrasting. The plot of the novel was too *bizarre* to be believed.

**bland** ADJ. soothing; mild. She used a *bland* ointment for her sunburn.

**blandishment** N. flattery. Despite the salesperson's *blandishments,* the customer did not buy the outfit.

■ **blasphemous** ADJ. profane; impious. The people in the room were shocked by her *blasphemous* language. blasphemy, N.

**blatant** ADJ. loudly offensive. I regard your remarks as *blatant* and ill-mannered. blatancy, N.

**bleak** ADJ. cold; cheerless. The Aleutian Islands are *bleak* military outposts.

**blighted** ADJ. suffering from a disease; destroyed. The extent of the *blighted* areas could be seen only when viewed from the air.

■ **blithe** ADJ. gay; joyous. Shelley called the skylark a *"blithe* spirit" because of its happy song.

**bloated** ADJ. swollen or puffed as with water or air. The *bloated* corpse was taken from the river.

**bludgeon** N. club; heavy-headed weapon. His walking stick served him as a *bludgeon* on many occasions. also V.

**bode** V. foreshadow; portend. The gloomy skies and the sulphurous odors from the mineral springs seemed to *bode* evil to those who settled in the area.

**bogus** ADJ. counterfeit; not authentic. The police quickly found the distributors of the *bogus* twenty-dollar bills.

**boisterous** ADJ. violent; rough; noisy. The unruly crowd became even more *boisterous* when he tried to quiet them.

■ **bolster** V. support; prop up. I do not intend to *bolster* your hopes with false reports of outside assistance; the truth is that we must face the enemy alone. also N.

**bombastic** ADJ. pompous; using inflated language. The orator spoke in a *bombastic* manner. bombast, N.

**bountiful** ADJ. generous; showing bounty. She distributed gifts in a *bountiful* and gracious manner.

**bourgeois** N. middle class. The French Revolution was inspired by the *bourgeois*. also ADJ.

**braggadocio** N. boasting. He was disliked because his manner was always full of *braggadocio*.

**braggart** N. boastful person. I wouldn't mind his being such a *braggart* if I felt he'd done anything worth bragging about.

**bravado** N. swagger; assumed air of defiance. The *bravado* of the young criminal disappeared when he was confronted by the victims of his brutal attack.

**brazen** ADJ. insolent. Her *brazen* contempt for authority angered the officials.

**breach** N. breaking of contract or duty; fissure; gap. They found a *breach* in the enemy's fortifications and penetrated their lines. also V.

■ **brevity** N. conciseness. *Brevity* is essential when you send a telegram or cablegram; you are charged for every word.

**bristling** ADJ. rising like bristles; showing irritation. The dog stood there, *bristling* with anger.

**broach** V. open up. He did not even try to *broach* the subject of poetry.

**brocade** N. rich, figured fabric. The sofa was covered with expensive *brocade*.

**brochure** N. pamphlet. This *brochure* on farming was issued by the Department of Agriculture.

**brusque** ADJ. blunt; abrupt. She was offended by his *brusque* reply.

**buffoonery** N. clowning. Steve Martin's *buffoonery* was hilarious.

**bullion** N. gold and silver in the form of bars. Much *bullion* is stored in the vaults at Fort Knox.

**bulwark** N. earthwork or other strong defense; person who defends. The navy is our principal *bulwark* against invasion.

**bungle** V. spoil by clumsy behavior. I was afraid you would *bungle* this assignment but I had no one else to send.

**bureaucracy** N. government by bureaus. Many people fear that the constant introduction of federal agencies will create a government by *bureaucracy*.

**burgeon** V. grow forth; send out buds. In the spring, the plants that burgeon are a promise of the beauty that is to come.

**burlesque** V. give an imitation that ridicules. In his caricature, he *burlesqued* the mannerisms of his adversary. also N.

**burnish** V. make shiny by rubbing; polish. The *burnished* metal reflected the lamplight.

**buttress** N. support or prop. The huge cathedral walls were supported by flying *buttresses*. also V.

**buxom** ADJ. plump; vigorous; jolly. The soldiers remembered the *buxom* nurse who had always been so pleasant to them.

**cabal** N. small group of persons secretly united to promote their own interests. The *cabal* was defeated when their scheme was discovered.

**cache** N. hiding place. The detectives followed the suspect until he led them to the *cache* where he had stored his loot. also V.

**cacophony** N. discord. Some people seem to enjoy the *cacophony* of an orchestra that is tuning up.

**cadaver** N. corpse. In some states, it is illegal to dissect *cadavers*.

**cadaverous** ADJ. like a corpse; pale. By his *cadaverous* appearance, we could see how the disease had ravaged him.

---

## ETYMOLOGY 4

BELLI (war)

    **bellicose**   inclined to fighting

    **belligerent**   engaged in war

    **rebellious**   warring against authority

BEN, BON (well, good) prefix

    **benefactor**   one who does good

    **benevolence**   charity (wishing good)

    **bonus**   something extra above regular pay

BI (two) prefix

    **bicameral**   legislature consisting of two houses

    **biennial**   every two years

    **bicycle**   two-wheeled vehicle

BIBLI (book)

    **bibliography**   list of books

    **bibliophile**   lover of books

    **Bible**   the sacred scriptures ("The Book")

BIO (life)

    **biology**   study of living things

    **biography**   writing about a person's life

    **biochemist**   a student of the chemistry of living things

BREV, BREVE (short)
>    **brevity** briefness
>    **abbreviate** shorten
>    **breve** mark placed over a vowel to indicate that it is short (ă
>    as in *hăt*)

---

## TEST — Word List 4 — Synonyms

Each of the questions below consists of a word printed in italics,
followed by five words or phrases numbered 1 to 5. Choose the
numbered word or phrase which is most nearly similar in meaning
to the word in italics and write the number of your choice on your
answer paper.

61. *baroque* 1 polished 2 constant 3 transformed 4 highly ornate 5 aglow
62. *benign* 1 tenfold 2 peaceful 3 blessed 4 wavering 5 favorable
63. *boisterous* 1 conflicting 2 noisy 3 testimonial 4 grateful 5 adolescent
64. *brazen* 1 shameless 2 quick 3 modest 4 pleasant 5 melodramatic
65. *belittle* 1 shrink 2 confine 3 disparage 4 distress 5 dissect
66. *biennial* 1 yearly 2 every two years 3 favorable 4 impressive 5 celebrated
67. *bombastic* 1 sensitive 2 pompous 3 rapid 4 sufficient 5 expensive
68. *beneficial* 1 expensive 2 cautious 3 helpful 4 proper 5 synthetic
69. *belated* 1 gloomy 2 unwilling 3 unattractive 4 delayed 5 fatal
70. *bigotry* 1 arrogance 2 approval 3 mourning 4 promptness 5 intolerance
71. *bolster* 1 confuse 2 invigorate 3 divert 4 support 5 evaluate
72. *buxom* 1 voluminous 2 indecisive 3 convincing 4 plump 5 bookish
73. *barren* 1 unhappy 2 unproductive 3 inactive 4 unacceptable 5 inedible
74. *bland* 1 mild 2 meager 3 soft 4 uncooked 5 helpless
75. *braggadocio* 1 distress 2 boasting 3 skirmish 4 encounter 5 position
76. *cache* 1 lock 2 hiding place 3 tide 4 automobile 5 grappling hook
77. *bellicose* 1 warlike 2 naval 3 amusing 4 piecemeal 5 errant
78. *blithe* 1 spiritual 2 profuse 3 gay 4 hybrid 5 comfortable
79. *brochure* 1 opening 2 pamphlet 3 censor 4 bureau 5 pin
80. *cacophony* 1 discord 2 dance 3 applause 4 type of telephone 5 rooster

---

### Word List 5    cajole - churlish

**cajole** v. coax; wheedle. I will not be *cajoled* into granting you your wish.

**caliber** N. ability; capacity. A man of such *caliber* should not be assigned
such menial tasks.

**callous** ADJ. hardened; unfeeling. He had worked in the hospital for so many
years that he was *callous* to the suffering in the wards. callus, N.

**calorific** ADJ. heat-producing. Coal is much more *calorific* than green wood.

**calumny** N. malicious misrepresentation; slander. He could endure his financial failure, but he could not bear the *calumny* that his foes heaped upon him.

**cameo** N. shell or jewel carved in relief. Tourists are advised not to purchase *cameos* from the street peddlers of Rome who sell poor specimens of the carver's art.

■ **candor** N. frankness. The *candor* and simplicity of her speech impressed us all; it was clear she held nothing back. candid, ADJ.

**canker** N. any ulcerous sore; any evil. Poverty is a *canker* in the body politic; it must be cured.

**canny** ADJ. shrewd; thrifty. The *canny* Scotsman was more than a match for the swindlers.

**cant** N. jargon of thieves; pious phraseology. Many listeners were fooled by the *cant* and hypocrisy of his speech.

**cantankerous** ADJ. ill humored; irritable. Constantly complaining about his treatment and refusing to cooperate with the hospital staff, he was a *cantankerous* patient.

**cantata** N. story set to music, to be sung by a chorus. The choral society sang the new *cantata* composed by its leader.

**canter** N. slow gallop. Because the racehorse had outdistanced its competition so easily, the reporter wrote that the race was won in a *canter*. also V.

**canto** N. division of a long poem. In *The Man without a Country*, Philip Nolan is upset when he reads one of Sir Walter Scott's *cantos*.

**canvass** V. determine votes, etc. After *canvassing* the sentiments of his constituents, the congressman was confident that he represented the majority opinion of his district. also N.

**capitulate** V. surrender. The enemy was warned to *capitulate* or face annihilation.

■ **capricious** ADJ. fickle; incalculable. The storm was *capricious* and changed course constantly. caprice, N.

**caption** N. title; chapter heading; text under illustration. I find the *captions* which accompany these cartoons very clever and humorous. also V.

**caricature** N. distortion; burlesque. The *caricatures* he drew always emphasized a personal weakness of the people he burlesqued. also V.

**carnivorous** ADJ. meat-eating. The lion is a *carnivorous* animal. carnivore, N.

**carping** ADJ. finding fault. A *carping* critic disturbs sensitive people.

**cascade** N. small waterfall. We could not appreciate the beauty of the many *cascades* as we were forced to make detours around each of them. also V.

**castigate** V. punish. He decided to *castigate* the culprit personally.

**casualty** N. serious or fatal accident. The number of *casualties* on this holiday weekend was high.

**cataclysm** N. deluge; upheaval. A *cataclysm* such as the French Revolution affects all countries. cataclysmic, ADJ.

**catalyst** N. agent which brings about a chemical change while it remains unaffected and unchanged. Many chemical reactions cannot take place without the presence of a *catalyst.*

**catapult** N. slingshot; a hurling machine. Airplanes are sometimes launched from battleships by *catapults.* also V.

**catastrophe** N. calamity. The Johnstown flood was a *catastrophe.*

**catechism** N. book for religious instruction; instruction by question and answer. He taught by engaging his pupils in a *catechism* until they gave him the correct answer.

**catholic** ADJ. broadly sympathetic; liberal. He was extremely *catholic* in his reading tastes.

■ **caustic** ADJ. burning; sarcastically biting. The critic's *caustic* remarks angered the hapless actors who were the subjects of his sarcasm.

**cauterize** V. burn with hot iron or caustic. In order to prevent infection, the doctor *cauterized* the wound.

**cavalcade** N. procession; parade. As described by Chaucer, the *cavalcade* of Canterbury pilgrims was a motley group.

**cavil** V. make frivolous objections. I respect your sensible criticisms, but I dislike the way you *cavil* about unimportant details. also N.

**cede** V. transfer; yield title to. I intend to *cede* this property to the city.

**celestial** ADJ. heavenly. He wrote about the music of *"celestial* spheres."

**celibate** ADJ. unmarried; abstaining from sexual intercourse. He vowed to remain *celibate.* celibacy, N.

**censor** N. overseer of morals; person who reads to eliminate inappropriate remarks. Soldiers dislike having their mail read by a *censor* but understand the need for this precaution. also V.

■ **censorious** ADJ. critical. *Censorious* people delight in casting blame.

■ **censure** V. blame; criticize. He was *censured* for his ill-advised act. also N.

**centigrade** ADJ. measure of temperature used widely in Europe. On the *centigrade* thermometer, the freezing point of water is zero degrees.

**centrifugal** ADJ. radiating; departing from the center. Many automatic drying machines remove excess moisture from clothing by *centrifugal* force.

**cerebral** ADJ. pertaining to the brain or intellect. The content of philosophical works is *cerebral* in nature and requires much thought.

**cerebration** N. thought. Mathematics problems sometimes require much *cerebration.*

**cessation** N. stopping. The workers threatened a *cessation* of all activities if their demands were not met. cease, V.

**cession** N. yielding to another; ceding. The *cession* of Alaska to the United States is discussed in this chapter.

**chafe** V. warm by rubbing; make sore by rubbing. The collar *chafed* his neck. also N.

**chaffing** ADJ. bantering; joking. Sometimes his flippant and *chaffing* remarks annoy us.

**chagrin** N. vexation; disappointment. Her refusal to go with us filled us with *chagrin.*

**chameleon** N. lizard that changes color in different situations. Like the *chameleon,* he assumed the political thinking of every group he met.

**champion** V. support militantly. Martin Luther King, Jr., won the Nobel Peace Prize because he *championed* the oppressed in their struggle for equality.

**chaotic** ADJ. in utter disorder. She tried to bring order into the *chaotic* state of affairs. chaos, N.

**charisma** N. divine gift; great popular charm or appeal of a political leader. Political commentators have deplored the importance of a candidate's *charisma* in these days of television campaigning.

■**charlatan** N. quack; pretender to knowledge. Because he was unable to substantiate his claim that he had found a cure for the dread disease, he was called a *charlatan* by his colleagues.

**chary** ADJ. cautiously watchful. She was *chary* of her favors.

**chasm** N. abyss. They could not see the bottom of the *chasm.*

**chassis** N. framework and working parts of an automobile. Examining the car after the accident, the owner discovered that the body had been ruined but that the *chassis* was unharmed.

**chaste** ADJ. pure. Her *chaste* and decorous garb was appropriately selected for the solemnity of the occasion. chastity, N.

**chastise** V. punish. I must *chastise* you for this offense.

**chauvinist** N. blindly devoted patriot. A *chauvinist* cannot recognize any faults in his country, no matter how flagrant they may be.

**checkered** ADJ. marked by changes in fortune. During his *checkered* career he had lived in palatial mansions and in dreary boarding-houses.

**chicanery** N. trickery. Your deceitful tactics in this case are indications of *chicanery.*

**chide** V. scold. Grandma began to *chide* Steven for his lying.

■**chimerical** ADJ. fantastic; highly imaginative. Poe's *chimerical* stories are sometimes too morbid for reading in bed. chimera, N.

**choleric** ADJ. hot-tempered. His flushed, angry face indicated a *choleric* nature.

**chronic** ADJ. long established as a disease. The doctors were able finally to attribute his *chronic* headaches and nausea to traces of formalde-hyde gas in his apartment.

**churlish** ADJ. boorish; rude. Dismayed by his *churlish* manners at the party, the girls vowed never to invite him again.

---

## ETYMOLOGY 5

CAP, CAPT, CEP, CIP (to take)
  **participate** take part
  **precept** a wise saying (originally, a command)
  **capture** seize

CAP (head)
  **decapitate** behead
  **captain** chief
  **capital** major city or site; first-rate

CED (to yield, to go)
  **recede** go back, withdraw
  **antecedent** that which goes before
  **concede** yield, agree with

CENT (one hundred)
  **century** one hundred years
  **centennial** hundredth anniversary

CHRONOS (time)
  **chronology** timetable of events
  **anachronism** a thing out of time sequence, as Shakespeare's reference to clocks in *Julius Caesar*
  **chronicle** register events in order

---

## TEST — Word List 5 — Antonyms

Each of the questions below consists of a word printed in italics, followed by five words or phrases numbered 1 to 5. Choose the numbered word or phrase which is most nearly opposite in meaning to the word in italics and write the number of your choice on your answer paper.

81. *candid* 1 vague 2 secretive 3 experienced 4 anxious 5 sallow
82. *carnivorous* 1 gloomy 2 tangential 3 productive 4 weak 5 vegetarian
83. *celibate* 1 investing 2 married 3 retired 4 commodious 5 dubious
84. *chimerical* 1 developing 2 wonderful 3 disappearing 4 economical 5 realistic
85. *censorious* 1 warlike 2 cordial 3 curious 4 not critical 5 not capable
86. *chagrin* 1 indifference 2 pleasure 3 tension 4 caution 5 frown
87. *censure* 1 process 2 enclose 3 interest 4 praise 5 penetrate
88. *choleric* 1 irascible 2 episodic 3 coolheaded 4 global 5 seasonal
89. *capricious* 1 satisfied 2 insured 3 photographic 4 scattered 5 steadfast
90. *catholic* 1 religious 2 pacific 3 narrow 4 weighty 5 funny
91. *cessation* 1 premium 2 gravity 3 beginning 4 composition 5 stoppage
92. *churlish* 1 marine 2 economical 3 polite 4 compact 5 young
93. *chaotic* 1 orderly 2 capable 3 frivolous 4 victorious 5 memorable
94. *capitulate* 1 behead 2 invest 3 abbreviate 4 resist 5 donate
95. *chaste* 1 clean 2 clear 3 curt 4 wanton 5 outspoken
96. *chaffing* 1 achieving 2 serious 3 capitalistic 4 sneering 5 expensive
97. *caustic* 1 impressive 2 minute 3 soothing 4 actual 5 private
98. *centrifugal* 1 centripetal 2 ephemeral 3 lasting 4 barometric 5 algebraic
99. *chide* 1 unite 2 fear 3 record 4 skid 5 praise
100. *carping* 1 acquiescent 2 mean 3 limited 4 farming 5 racing

---

## Word List 6    circuitous - concise

**circuitous** ADJ. roundabout. Because of the traffic congestion on the main highways, he took a *circuitous* route. circuit, N.

**circumlocution** N. indirect or roundabout expression. He was afraid to call a spade a spade and resorted to *circumlocutions* to avoid direct reference to his subject.

**circumscribe** V. limit; confine. Although I do not wish to *circumscribe* your activities, I must insist that you complete this assignment before you start anything else.

**circumspect** ADJ. prudent; cautious. Investigating before acting, she tried always to be *circumspect*.

**circumvent** V. outwit; baffle. In order to *circumvent* the enemy, we will make two preliminary attacks in other sections before starting our major campaign.

**citadel** N. fortress. The *citadel* overlooked the city like a protecting angel.

**cite** V. quote; commend. He could *cite* passages in the Bible from memory. citation, N.

**clairvoyant** ADJ., N. having foresight; fortuneteller. Cassandra's *clairvoyant* warning was not heeded by the Trojans. clairvoyance, N.

■**clamor** N. noise. The *clamor* of the children at play outside made it impossible for her to take a nap. also V.

**clandestine** ADJ. secret. After avoiding their chaperon, the lovers had a *clandestine* meeting.

**claustrophobia** N. fear of being locked in. His fellow classmates laughed at his *claustrophobia* and often threatened to lock him in his room.

**cleave** V. split asunder. The lightning *cleaves* the tree in two. cleavage, N.

**cleft** N. split. There was a *cleft* in the huge boulder. also ADJ.

■**clemency** N. disposition to be lenient; mildness, as of the weather. The lawyer was pleased when the case was sent to Judge Smith's chambers because Smith was noted for her *clemency* toward first offenders.

**cliché** N. phrase dulled in meaning by repetition. High school compositions are often marred by such *clichés* as "strong as an ox."

**climactic** ADJ. relating to the highest point. When he reached the *climactic* portions of the book, he could not stop reading. climax, N.

**clique** N. small exclusive group. He charged that a *clique* had assumed control of school affairs.

**cloister** N. monastery or convent. The nuns lived in the *cloister*.

■**coalesce** V. combine; fuse. The brooks *coalesce* into one large river.

■**coerce** V. force; repress. Do not *coerce* me into doing this; I hate force. coercion, N.

**cog** N. tooth projecting from a wheel. On steep slopes, *cog* railways are frequently used to prevent slipping.

**cogent** ADJ. convincing. She presented *cogent* arguments to the jury.

**cogitate** V. think over. *Cogitate* on this problem; the solution will come.

**cognate** ADJ. allied by blood; of the same or kindred nature. In the phrase "die a thousand deaths," the word "death" is a *cognate* object.

**cognizance** N. knowledge. During the election campaign, the two candidates were kept in full *cognizance* of the international situation.

**cohere** V. stick together. Solids have a greater tendency to *cohere* than liquids. coherent, ADJ.

**cohesion** N. force which keeps parts together. In order to preserve our *cohesion*, we must not let minor differences interfere with our major purposes.

**coincident** ADJ. occurring at the same time. Some people find the *coincident* events in Hardy's novels annoying.

■**collaborate** V. work together. Two writers *collaborated* in preparing this book.

**colloquial** ADJ. pertaining to conversational or common speech. Your use of *colloquial* expressions in a formal essay such as the one you have presented spoils the effect you hope to achieve.

**collusion** N. conspiring in a fraudulent scheme. The swindlers were found guilty of *collusion*.

**colossal** ADJ. huge. Radio City Music Hall has a *colossal* stage.

**combustible** ADJ. easily burned. After the recent outbreak of fires in private homes, the fire commissioner ordered that all *combustible* materials be kept in safe containers. also N.

**commandeer** V. to draft for military purposes; to take for public use. The policeman *commandeered* the first car that approached and ordered the driver to go to the nearest hospital.

**commensurate** ADJ. equal in extent or size; proportionate. Your reward will be *commensurate* with your effort.

**commiserate** V. feel or express pity or sympathy for. Her friends *commiserated* with the widow.

**commodious** ADJ. spacious and comfortable. After sleeping in small roadside cabins, they found their hotel suite *commodious.*

**compact** N. agreement; contract. The signers of the Mayflower *Compact* were establishing a form of government.

■ **compatible** ADJ. harmonious; in harmony with. They were *compatible* neighbors, never quarreling over unimportant matters.

**compilation** N. listing of statistical information in tabular or book form. The *compilation* of available scholarships serves a very valuable purpose.

■ **complacent** ADJ. self-satisfied. There was a *complacent* look on his face as he examined his paintings. complacency, N.

**complement** N. that which completes. A predicate *complement* completes the meaning of the subject. also V.

■ **compliance** N. readiness to yield; conformity in fulfilling requirements. When I give an order, I expect *compliance,* not defiance. compliant, ADJ.; comply, V.

■ **comprehensive** ADJ. thorough; inclusive. This book provides a *comprehensive* review of verbal and math skills for the SAT.

**compunction** N. remorse. The judge was especially severe in his sentencing because he felt that the criminal had shown no *compunction* for his heinous crime.

**compute** V. reckon; calculate. She failed to *compute* the interest.

■ **concede** V. admit; yield. Despite all the evidence Monica had assembled, Mark refused to *concede* that she was right.

**conception** N. beginning; forming of an idea. At the first *conception* of the work, she was consulted. conceive, V.

■ **conciliatory** ADJ. reconciling; appeasing; amiable. Hoping to end the coldness that had grown between them, she wrote a *conciliatory* note. conciliate, V.

■ **concise** ADJ. brief and compact. When you define a new word, be *concise:* the shorter the definition, the easier it is to remember.

## ETYMOLOGY 6

CID, CIS (to cut, to kill)
        **incision**   a cut (surgical)
        **homicide**   killing of a man
        **fratricide**   killing of a brother

CIRCUM (around) prefix
        **circumnavigate**   sail around the world
        **circumspect**   cautious (looking around)
        **circumscribe**   place a circle around

CIVI (citizen)
        **civilization**   society of citizens, culture
        **civilian**   member of a community
        **civil**   courteous

CLAUD, CLAUS, CLOS, CLUD (to close)
        **claustrophobia**   fear of close places
        **enclose**   close in
        **conclude**   finish

COGNOSC, COGNIT (to learn)
        **agnostic**   lacking knowledge, skeptical
        **incognito**   traveling under an assumed identity (without knowledge)
        **cognition**   knowledge

COM (with, together) prefix
        **combine**   merge with
        **commerce**   trade with
        **communicate**   correspond with
        **Note:** By assimilation,
        **coeditor**   associate editor
        **collateral**   connected
        **conference**   meeting
        **corroborate**   confirm

COMP (to fill)
        **complete**   filled out
        **complement**   that which completes something
        **comply**   fulfill

## TEST — Word List 6 — Synonyms and Antonyms

Each of the following questions consists of a word printed in italics, followed by five words or phrases numbered 1 to 5. Choose the numbered word or phrase which is most nearly the same as or the opposite of the word in italics and write the number of your choice on your answer paper.

101. *clandestine* 1 abortive 2 secret 3 tangible 4 doomed 5 approved
102. *citadel* 1 fortress 2 dwarf 3 suspicion 4 kind of railway 5 accomplice
103. *combustible* 1 flammable 2 industrious 3 waterproof 4 specific 5 plastic
104. *compliant* 1 numerous 2 veracious 3 soft 4 adamant 5 livid
105. *circumspect* 1 abstract 2 swift 3 early 4 constructed 5 imprudent
106. *cleft* 1 split 2 waterfall 3 assembly 4 parfait 5 surplus
107. *cohesion* 1 independence 2 pedestrian 3 shift 4 pharmacy 5 climbing
108. *cogent* 1 vigorous 2 convincing 3 liquid 4 beautiful 5 circumvented
109. *circuitous* 1 direct 2 complete 3 obvious 4 aware 5 tortured
110. *cliché* 1 increase 2 vehicle 3 morale 4 original 5 pique
111. *coincidental* 1 simultaneous 2 changing 3 fortuitous 4 startling 5 trivial
112. *clemency* 1 acme 2 emphasis 3 distillery 4 spree 5 mildness
113. *claustrophobia* 1 lack of confidence 2 fear of spiders 3 love of books 4 fear of grammar 5 fear of closed places
114. *cite* 1 galvanize 2 visualize 3 locate 4 quote 5 signal
115. *coerce* 1 recover 2 total 3 force 4 license 5 ignore
116. *cognizance* 1 policy 2 ignorance 3 advance 4 omission 5 examination
117. *colloquy* 1 dialect 2 diversion 3 announcement 4 discussion 5 expansion
118. *conciliate* 1 defend 2 activate 3 integrate 4 quarrel 5 react
119. *commiserate* 1 communicate 2 expand 3 repay 4 diminish 5 sympathize
120. *commodious* 1 numerous 2 accommodating 3 leisurely 4 limited 5 expensive

---

## Word List 7    conclave - crux

**conclave** N. private meeting. He was present at all their *conclaves* as a sort of unofficial observer.

**conclusive** ADJ. convincing; decisive. We have *conclusive* evidence that proves his guilt.

**concoct** V. prepare by combining; make up in concert. How did you ever *concoct* such a strange dish? concoction, N.

■ **concur** V. agree in opinion. Justice Brennan wrote a minority opinion because he did not *concur* with his fellow justices.

**concurrent** ADJ. happening at the same time. In America, the colonists were resisting the demands of the mother country; at the *concurrent* moment in France, the middle class was sowing the seeds of rebellion.

■ **condescend** v. bestow courtesies with a superior air. The king *condescended* to grant an audience to the friends of the condemned man. condescension, N.

**condole** v. express sympathetic sorrow. His friends gathered to *condole* with him over his loss. condolence, N.

■ **condone** v. overlook; forgive. We cannot *condone* your recent criminal cooperation with the gamblers.

**confiscate** v. seize; commandeer. The army *confiscated* all available supplies of uranium.

**conflagration** N. fire. In the *conflagration* that followed the 1906 earthquake, much of San Francisco was destroyed.

**conformity** N. harmony; agreement. In *conformity* with our rules and regulations, I am calling a meeting of our organization.

**congeal** v. freeze; coagulate. His blood *congealed* in his veins as he saw the dread monster rush toward him.

**congenial** ADJ. pleasant; friendly. My father loved to go out for a meal with *congenial* companions.

**conglomeration** N. mass of material sticking together. In such a *conglomeration* of miscellaneous statistics, it was impossible to find a single area of analysis.

**conjecture** N. surmise; guess. I will end all your *conjectures;* I admit I am guilty as charged. also v.

**conjugal** ADJ. pertaining to marriage. Their dreams of *conjugal* bliss were shattered as soon as their temperaments clashed.

**conjure** v. summon a devil; practice magic; imagine; invent. He *conjured* up an image of a reformed city and had the voters completely under his spell.

**connivance** N. pretense of ignorance of something wrong; assistance; permission to offend. With the *connivance* of her friends, she plotted to embarrass the teacher. connive, v.

**connoisseur** N. person competent to act as a judge of art, etc.; a lover of an art. He had developed into a *connoisseur* of fine china.

**connotation** N. suggested or implied meaning of an expression. Foreigners frequently are unaware of the *connotations* of the words they use.

**conscientious** ADJ. scrupulous; careful. A *conscientious* editor, she checked every definition for its accuracy.

**consecrate** v. dedicate; sanctify. We shall *consecrate* our lives to this noble purpose.

**consensus** N. general agreement. The *consensus* indicates that we are opposed to entering into this pact.

**consequential** ADJ. pompous; self-important. Convinced of his own importance, the actor strutted about the dressing room with a *consequential* air.

**consort** V. associate with. We frequently judge people by the company with whom they *consort*. also N.

■ **conspicuous** ADJ. easily seen; noticeable; striking. Janet was *conspicuous* both for her red hair and for her height.

**conspiracy** N. treacherous plot. Brutus and Cassius joined in the *conspiracy* to murder Julius Caesar.

**constraint** N. compulsion; repression of feelings. There was a feeling of *constraint* in the room because no one dared to criticize the speaker. constrain, V.

**construe** V. explain; interpret. If I *construe* your remarks correctly, you disagree with the theory already advanced.

**consummate** ADJ. complete. I have never seen anyone who makes as many stupid errors as you do; you must be a *consummate* idiot. also V.

**contaminate** V. pollute. The sewage system of the city so *contaminated* the water that swimming was forbidden.

■ **contempt** N. scorn; disdain. Brave but unimaginative, he had nothing but *contempt* for cowards. contemptuous, ADJ.

**contend** V. assert earnestly; struggle; compete. Sociologist Harry Edwards *contends* that young black athletes are exploited by some college recruiters.

**contentious** ADJ. quarrelsome. We heard loud and *contentious* noises in the next room.

**context** N. writings preceding and following the passage quoted. Because these lines are taken out of *context*, they do not convey the message the author intended.

**contiguous** ADJ. adjacent to; touching upon. The two countries are *contiguous* for a few miles; then they are separated by the gulf.

**continence** N. self-restraint; sexual chastity. He vowed to lead a life of *continence*. continent, ADJ.

**contingent** ADJ. conditional. The continuation of this contract is *contingent* on the quality of your first output. contingency, N.

**contortions** N. twistings; distortions. As the effects of the opiate wore away, the *contortions* of the patient became more violent and demonstrated how much pain he was enduring.

**contraband** N, ADJ. illegal trade; smuggling. The Coast Guard tries to prevent traffic in *contraband* goods.

**contravene** V. contradict; infringe on. I will not attempt to *contravene* your argument for it does not affect the situation.

■ **contrite** ADJ. penitent. Her *contrite* tears did not influence the judge when he imposed sentence. contrition, N.

**controvert** V. oppose with arguments; contradict. To *controvert* your theory will require much time but it is essential that we disprove it.

**convene** V. assemble. Because much needed legislation had to be enacted, the governor ordered the legislature to *convene* in special session by January 15.

**converge** V. approach; tend to meet; come together. Demonstrators from all over the United States *converged* on Washington to take part in Martin Luther King's historic march.

**conversant** ADJ. familiar with. The lawyer is *conversant* with all the evidence.

■ **conviction** N. strongly held belief. Nothing could shake his *conviction* that she was innocent.

**convivial** ADJ. festive; gay; characterized by joviality. The *convivial* celebrators of the victory sang their college songs.

**convoke** V. call together. Congress was *convoked* at the outbreak of the emergency. convocation, N.

**copious** ADJ. plentiful. He had *copious* reasons for rejecting the proposal.

**coquette** N. flirt. Because she refused to give him any answer to his proposal of marriage, he called her a *coquette*. also V.

**cordial** ADJ. gracious; warm. Our hosts greeted us at the airport with a *cordial* welcome.

**corollary** N. consequence; accompaniment. Brotherly love is a complex emotion, with sibling rivalry its natural *corollary*.

**corporeal** ADJ. bodily; material. He was not a churchgoer; he was interested only in *corporeal* matters.

**corpulent** ADJ. very fat. The *corpulent* man resolved to reduce. corpulence, N.

**corroborate** V. confirm. Unless we find a witness to *corroborate* your evidence, it will not stand up in court.

**corrosive** ADJ. eating away by chemicals or disease. Stainless steel is able to withstand the effects of *corrosive* chemicals.

**cosmic** ADJ. pertaining to the universe; vast. *Cosmic* rays derive their name from the fact that they bombard the earth's atmosphere from outer space. cosmos, N.

**countenance** V. approve; tolerate. He refused to *countenance* such rude behavior on their part.

**countermand** V. cancel; revoke. The general *countermanded* the orders issued in his absence.

**counterpart** N. a thing that completes another; things very much alike. Night and day are *counterparts*.

**coup** N. highly successful action or sudden attack. As the news of his *coup* spread throughout Wall Street, his fellow brokers dropped by to congratulate him.

**covenant** N. agreement. We must comply with the terms of the *covenant*.

**covert** ADJ. secret; hidden; implied. She could understand the *covert* threat in the letter.

**covetous** ADJ. avaricious; eagerly desirous of. The child was *covetous* by nature and wanted to take the toys belonging to his classmates. covet, V.

**cower** V. shrink quivering, as from fear. The frightened child *cowered* in the corner of the room.

**coy** ADJ. shy; modest; coquettish. She was *coy* in her answers to his offer.

■ **crass** ADJ. very unrefined; grossly insensible. The philosophers deplored the *crass* commercialism.

**credence** N. belief. Do not place any *credence* in his promises.

■ **credulity** N. belief on slight evidence. The witch doctor took advantage of the *credulity* of the superstitious natives. credulous, ADJ.

**creed** N. system of religious or ethical belief. In any loyal American's *creed*, love of democracy must be emphasized.

**crescendo** N. increase in the volume or intensity, as in a musical passage; climax. The overture suddenly changed from a quiet pastoral theme to a *crescendo* with blaring trumpets and clashing cymbals.

**crestfallen** ADJ. dejected; dispirited. We were surprised at his reaction to the failure of his project; instead of being *crestfallen*, he was busily engaged in planning new activities.

**crevice** N. crack; fissure. The mountain climbers found footholds in the tiny *crevices* in the mountainside.

**cringe** V. shrink back, as if in fear. The dog *cringed*, expecting a blow.

■ **criterion** N. standard used in judging. What *criterion* did you use when you selected this essay as the prizewinner? criteria, PL.

**crux** N. crucial point. This is the *crux* of the entire problem.

---

## ETYMOLOGY 7

CONTRA (against) prefix
        **contradict**   disagree
        **controversy**   dispute (turning against)
        **contrary**   opposed
CORPOR (body)
        **incorporate**   organize into a body
        **corporeal**   pertaining to the body or physical mass
        **corpse**   dead body
CRED (to believe)
        **incredulous**   not believing, skeptical
        **credulity**   gullibility
        **credence**   belief

## TEST — Word List 7 — Synonyms

Each of the questions below consists of a word printed in italics, followed by five words or phrases numbered 1 to 5. Choose the numbered word or phrase which is most nearly similar in meaning to the word in italics and write the number of your answer on your answer paper.

121. *condone*  1 stop  2 evaluate  3 pierce  4 infuriate  5 overlook
122. *conspiracy*  1 treacherous plot  2 friendship  3 bloodletting  4 relief  5 understanding
123. *continence*  1 humanity  2 research  3 embryology  4 bodies of land  5 self-restraint
124. *confiscate*  1 discuss  2 discover  3 seize  4 exist  5 convey
125. *consensus*  1 general agreement  2 project  3 insignificance  4 sheaf  5 crevice
126. *conformity*  1 agreement  2 ambition  3 confinement  4 pride  5 restraint
127. *construe*  1 explain  2 promote  3 reserve  4 erect  5 block
128. *contingent*  1 slight  2 obscure  3 thorough  4 conditional  5 classified
129. *contaminate*  1 arrest  2 prepare  3 pollute  4 beam  5 inform
130. *connoisseur*  1 gourmand  2 lover of art  3 humidor  4 delinquent  5 interpreter
131. *contentious*  1 squealing  2 surprising  3 quarrelsome  4 smug  5 creative
132. *contraband*  1 purpose  2 rogue  3 rascality  4 difficulty  5 smuggling
133. *copious*  1 plentiful  2 cheating  3 dishonorable  4 adventurous  5 inspired
134. *contrite*  1 smart  2 penitent  3 restful  4 recognized  5 perspiring
135. *corpulent*  1 regenerate  2 obese  3 different  4 hungry  5 bloody
136. *controvert*  1 turn over  2 contradict  3 mind  4 explain  5 swing
137. *contiguous*  1 desirous  2 direct  3 adjacent  4 civilized  5 controlled
138. *constraint*  1 sensation  2 noise  3 silence  4 repression  5 classic
139. *crux*  1 acne  2 spark  3 events  4 crucial point  5 belief
140. *conversant*  1 ignorant  2 speaking  3 incorporated  4 familiar  5 pedantic

---

### Word List 8   cryptic - despoil

**cryptic** ADJ. mysterious; hidden; secret. His *cryptic* remarks could not be interpreted.

**culinary** ADJ. relating to cooking. Many chefs attribute their *culinary* skill to the wise use of spices.

**cull** V. pick out; reject. Every month the farmer *culls* the nonlaying hens from his flock and sells them to the local butcher. also N.

**culmination** N. attainment of highest point. His inauguration as President of the United States marked the *culmination* of his political career. culminate, V.

**culpable** ADJ. deserving blame. Corrupt politicians who condone the activities of the gamblers are equally *culpable*.

**cupidity** N. greed. The defeated people could not satisfy the *cupidity* of the conquerors, who demanded excessive tribute.

**cursory** ADJ. casual; hastily done. A *cursory* examination of the ruins indicates the possibility of arson; a more extensive study should be undertaken.

**curtail** V. shorten; reduce. During the coal shortage, we must *curtail* our use of this vital commodity.

■ **cynical** ADJ. skeptical; distrustful of human motives. *Cynical* at all times, she was suspicious of the altruistic actions of others. cynic, N.

**dank** ADJ. damp. The walls of the dungeon were *dank* and slimy.

**daunt** V. intimidate. Your threats cannot *daunt* me.

**dauntless** ADJ. bold. Despite the dangerous nature of the undertaking, the *dauntless* soldier volunteered for the assignment.

**dawdle** V. loiter; waste time. Inasmuch as we must meet a deadline, do not *dawdle* over this work.

**dearth** N. scarcity. The *dearth* of skilled labor compelled the employers to open trade schools.

**debacle** N. breaking up; downfall. This *debacle* in the government can only result in anarchy.

**debase** V. reduce to lower state. Do not *debase* yourself by becoming maudlin.

**debilitate** V. weaken; enfeeble. Overindulgence *debilitates* character as well as physical stamina.

**debonair** ADJ. friendly; aiming to please. The *debonair* youth was liked by all who met him, because of his cheerful and obliging manner.

■ **decadence** N. decay. The moral *decadence* of the people was reflected in the lewd literature of the period. decadent, ADJ.

**decorous** ADJ. proper. Her *decorous* behavior was praised by her teachers. decorum, N.

**decoy** N. lure or bait. The wild ducks were not fooled by the *decoy*. also V.

**decrepit** ADJ. worn out by age. The *decrepit* car blocked traffic on the highway.

**decry** V. disparage. Do not attempt to increase your stature by *decrying* the efforts of your opponents.

**deducible** ADJ. derived by reasoning. If we accept your premise, your conclusions are easily *deducible*. deduce, V.

■ **defamation** N. harming a person's reputation. Such *defamation* of character may result in a slander suit. defame, V.

**default** N. failure to do. As a result of her husband's failure to appear in court, she was granted a divorce by *default*. also V.

**defeatist** ADJ. attitude of one who is ready to accept defeat as a natural outcome. If you maintain your *defeatist* attitude, you will never succeed. also N.

**defection.** N. desertion. The children, who had made him an idol, were hurt most by his *defection* from our cause.

■ **deference** N. courteous regard for another's wish. In *deference* to her desires, the employers granted her a holiday.

**defile** V. pollute; profane. The hoodlums *defiled* the church with their scurrilous writing.

**definitive** ADJ. final; complete. Carl Sandburg's *Abraham Lincoln* may be regarded as the *definitive* work on the life of the Great Emancipator.

**deflect** V. turn aside. His life was saved when his cigarette case *deflected* the bullet.

**defunct** ADJ. dead; no longer in use or existence. The lawyers sought to examine the books of the *defunct* corporation.

**degrade** V. lower in rank or dignity; debase. Some secretaries object to fetching the boss a cup of coffee because they feel it *degrades* them to do non-secretarial work.

**deign** V. condescend. He felt that he would debase himself if he *deigned* to answer his critics.

**delete** V. erase; strike out. If you *delete* this paragraph, the composition will have more appeal.

■ **deleterious** ADJ. harmful. Workers in nuclear research must avoid the *deleterious* effects of radioactive substances.

■ **deliberate** V. consider; ponder. Offered the new job, she asked for time to *deliberate* before giving them her decision.

■ **delineate** V. portray. He is a powerful storyteller, but he is weak in *delineating* his characters. delineation, N.

**delirium** N. mental disorder marked by confusion. The drunkard in his *delirium* saw strange animals.

**delude** V. deceive. Do not *delude* yourself into believing that he will relent.

**deluge** N. flood; rush. When we advertised the position, we received a *deluge* of applications.

**delusion** N. false belief; hallucination. This scheme is a snare and a *delusion*. delusive, ADJ.

**demagogue** N. person who appeals to people's prejudice; false leader of people. He was accused of being a *demagogue* because he made promises which aroused futile hopes in his listeners.

**demean** V. degrade; humiliate. He felt that he would *demean* himself if he replied to the scurrilous letter.

**demeanor** N. behavior; bearing. Her sober *demeanor* quieted the noisy revelers.

**demise** N. death. Upon the *demise* of the dictator, a bitter dispute about succession to power developed.

**demolition** N. destruction. One of the major aims of the air force was the complete *demolition* of all means of transportation by bombing of rail lines and terminals.

**demur** V. delay; object. To *demur* at this time will only worsen the already serious situation; now is the time for action.

**demure** ADJ. reserved, modest; coy. She was *demure* and reserved.

**denizen** N. inhabitant of. Ghosts are *denizens* of the land of the dead who return to earth.

■ **denounce** V. condemn; criticize. The reform candidate *denounced* the corrupt city officers for having betrayed the public's trust. denunciation, N.

■ **depict** V. portray. In this book, the author *depicts* the slave owners as kind and benevolent masters.

■ **deplete** V. reduce; exhaust. We must wait until we *deplete* our present inventory before we order replacements.

**deplore** V. regret strongly; consider unfortunate or deserving of disapproval. Although I *deplore* the vulgarity of your language, I defend your right to express yourself freely.

**deploy** V. move troops so that the battle line is extended at the expense of depth. The general ordered the battalion to *deploy* in order to meet the offensive of the enemy.

■ **depravity** N. corruption; wickedness. The *depravity* of his behavior shocked all. depraved, ADJ.

■ **deprecate** V. disapprove regretfully. I must *deprecate* your attitude and hope that you will change your mind. deprecatory, ADJ.

**depreciate** V. lessen in value. If you neglect this property, it will *depreciate*.

**deranged** ADJ. insane. He was mentally *deranged*.

**derelict** ADJ. abandoned. The *derelict* craft was a menace to navigation. also N.

**derision** N. ridicule. They greeted his proposal with *derision* and refused to consider it seriously. deride, V.

■ **derivative** ADJ. unoriginal; derived from another source. Although her early poetry was clearly *derivative* in nature, the critics felt she had promise and eventually would find her own voice.

**derogatory** ADJ. expressing a low opinion. I resent your *derogatory* remarks.

**descry** V. catch sight of. In the distance, we could barely *descry* the enemy vessels.

**desecrate** V. profane; violate the sanctity of. The soldiers *desecrated* the temple.

**desiccate** v. dry up. A tour of this smokehouse will give you an idea of how the pioneers used to *desiccate* food in order to preserve it.

**despicable** ADJ. contemptible. Your *despicable* remarks call for no reply.

**despise** v. scorn. I *despise* your attempts at a reconciliation at this time.

**despoil** v. plunder. If you do not yield, I am afraid the enemy will *despoil* the buildings.

---

## ETYMOLOGY 8

CUR (to care)

      **curator**   person in charge

      **sinecure**   position without responsibility

      **secure**   safe

CURR, CURS (to run)

      **excursion**   journey

      **cursory**   brief

      **precursor**   forerunner

DE (down, away) prefix

      **debase**   lower in value

      **decadence**   deterioration

      **decant**   pour off

DEB, DEBIT (to owe)

      **debt**   something owed

      **indebtedness**   debt

      **debenture**   bond

DEMOS (people)

      **democracy**   rule of the people

      **demagogue**   (false) leader of the people

      **epidemic**   widespread disease (among the people)

DERM (skin)

      **epidermis**   skin

      **pachyderm**   thick-skinned quadruped

      **dermatology**   study of the skin and its disorders

---

## TEST — Word List 8 — Antonyms

Each of the questions below consists of a word printed in italics, followed by five words or phrases numbered 1 to 5. Choose the numbered word or phrase which is most nearly opposite in meaning to the word in italics and write the number of your choice on your answer paper.

141. *cryptic*   1 tomblike 2 secret 3 famous 4 candid 5 coded
142. *dank*   1 dry 2 guiltless 3 warm 4 babbling 5 reserved
143. *cupidity*   1 anxiety 2 tragedy 3 generosity 4 entertainment 5 love
144. *defamation*   1 illegitimacy 2 commendation 3 presence 4 warmth 5 sanity
145. *curtail*   1 mutter 2 lengthen 3 express 4 burden 5 shore
146. *dauntless*   1 stolid 2 weak 3 irrelevant 4 peculiar 5 particular
147. *cynical*   1 trusting 2 effortless 3 conclusive 4 gallant 5 vertical
148. *debilitate*   1 bedevil 2 repress 3 strengthen 4 animate 5 deaden
149. *debonair*   1 awkward 2 windy 3 balmy 4 sporty 5 stormy
150. *dearth*   1 trap 2 quadrangle 3 quarter 4 activity 5 plentifulness
151. *derogatory*   1 roguish 2 immediate 3 opinionated 4 praising 5 conferred
152. *decrepit*   1 momentary 2 emotional 3 suppressed 4 youthful 5 unexpected
153. *depravity*   1 goodness 2 sadness 3 heaviness 4 tidiness 5 seriousness
154. *defection*   1 determination 2 joining 3 invitation 4 affection 5 cancellation
155. *deranged*   1 sane 2 announced 3 neighborly 4 alphabetical 5 arranged
156. *degrade*   1 abscond 2 elope 3 observe 4 panic 5 enhance
157. *desecrate*   1 desist 2 integrate 3 confuse 4 intensify 5 consecrate
158. *defile*   1 manicure 2 ride 3 purify 4 assemble 5 order
159. *despicable*   1 steering 2 worthy of esteem 3 inevitable 4 featureless 5 incapable
160. *deletrious*   1 delaying 2 experimental 3 harmless 4 graduating 5 glorious

---

## Word List 9   despondent - diverse

■ **despondent** ADJ. depressed; gloomy. To the dismay of his parents, he became more and more *despondent* every year. despondency, N.

**despotism** N. tyranny. The people rebelled against the *despotism* of the king.

**destitute** ADJ. extremely poor. The illness left the family *destitute*.

**desultory** ADJ. aimless; jumping around. The animals' *desultory* behavior indicated that they had no awareness of their predicament.

■ **detached** ADJ. emotionally removed; calm and objective; indifferent. A psychoanalyst must maintain a *detached* point of view and stay uninvolved with her patients' personal lives. detachment, N. (secondary meaning)

■ **deterrent** N. something that discourages; hindrance. Does the threat of capital punishment serve as a *deterrent* to potential killers? deter, V.

**detonation** N. explosion. The *detonation* could be heard miles away.

**detraction** N. slandering; aspersion. He is offended by your frequent *detractions* of his ability as a leader.

■ **detrimental** ADJ. harmful; damaging. Your acceptance of her support will ultimately prove *detrimental* rather than helpful to your cause. detriment, N.

■ **deviate** V. turn away from. Do not *deviate* from the truth.

**devious** ADJ. going astray; erratic. Your *devious* behavior in this matter puzzles me since you are usually direct and straightforward.

**devoid** ADJ. lacking. He was *devoid* of any personal desire for gain in his endeavor to secure improvement in the community.

**devout** ADJ. pious. The *devout* man prayed daily.

**dexterous** ADJ. skillful. The magician was so *dexterous* that we could not follow him as he performed his tricks.

**diabolical** ADJ. devilish. This scheme is so *diabolical* that I must reject it.

**dictum** N. authoritative and weighty statement. He repeated the statement as though it were the *dictum* of the most expert worker in the group.

■ **didactic** ADJ. teaching; instructional. The *didactic* qualities of his poetry overshadow its literary qualities; the lesson he teaches is more memorable than the lines he writes.

**diffidence** N. shyness. You must overcome your *diffidence* if you intend to become a salesperson.

**diffusion** N. wordiness; spreading in all directions like a gas. Your composition suffers from a *diffusion* of ideas; try to be more compact. diffuse, ADJ. and V.

**digression** N. act of wandering away from the subject. His book was marred by his many *digressions*. digress, V.

**dilapidated** ADJ. ruined because of neglect. The *dilapidated* building needed several coats of paint. dilapidation, N.

**dilate** V. expand. In the dark, the pupils of your eyes *dilate*.

**dilatory** ADJ. delaying. Your *dilatory* tactics may compel me to cancel the contract.

**dilemma** N. problem; choice of two unsatisfactory alternatives. In this *dilemma*, he knew no one to whom he could turn for advice.

**dilettante** N. aimless follower of the arts; amateur; dabbler. He was not serious in his painting; he was rather a *dilettante*.

■ **diligence** N. steadiness of effort; persistent hard work. Her employers were greatly impressed by her *diligence* and offered her a partnership in the firm. diligent, ADJ.

**dilute** V. make less concentrated; reduce in strength. She preferred her coffee *diluted* with milk.

■ **diminution** N. lessening; reduction in size. The blockaders hoped to achieve victory as soon as the *diminution* of the enemy's supplies became serious.

**dire** ADJ. disastrous. People ignored her *dire* predictions of an approaching depression.

**dirge** N. lament with music. The funeral *dirge* stirred us to tears.

**disapprobation** N. disapproval; condemnation. The conservative father viewed his daughter's radical boyfriend with *disapprobation*.

**disarray** N. a disorderly or untidy state. After the New Year's party, the once orderly house was in total *disarray*.

**disavowal** N. denial; disclaiming. Her *disavowal* of her part in the conspiracy was not believed by the jury.

**discernible** ADJ. distinguishable; perceivable. The ships in the harbor were not *discernible* in the fog.

■ **discerning** ADJ. mentally quick and observant; having insight. Because he was considered the most *discerning* member of the firm, he was assigned the most difficult cases.

**disclaim** V. disown; renounce claim to. If I grant you this privilege, will you *disclaim* all other rights?

**disclose** V. reveal. Although competitors offered him bribes, he refused to *disclose* any information about his company's forthcoming product. disclosure, N.

**disconcert** V. confuse; upset; embarrass. The lawyer was *disconcerted* by the evidence produced by her adversary.

**disconsolate** ADJ. sad. The death of his wife left him *disconsolate*.

■ **discordant** ADJ. inharmonious; conflicting. She tried to unite the *discordant* factions.

**discredit** V. defame; destroy confidence in; disbelieve. The campaign was highly negative in tone; each candidate tried to *discredit* the other.

**discrete** ADJ. separate; unconnected. The universe is composed of *discrete* bodies.

■ **discretion** N. prudence; ability to adjust actions to circumstances. Use your *discretion* in this matter. discreet, ADJ.

■ **discriminating** ADJ. able to see differences; prejudiced. They feared he was not sufficiently *discriminating* to judge complex works of modern art. (secondary meaning) discrimination, N.

■ **discursive** ADJ. digressing; rambling. They were annoyed and bored by his *discursive* remarks.

■ **disdain** V. treat with scorn or contempt. You make enemies of all you *disdain*. also N.

**disgruntle** V. make discontented. The passengers were *disgruntled* by the numerous delays.

**disheartened** ADJ. lacking courage and hope. His failure to pass the bar exam *disheartened* him.

**disheveled** ADJ. untidy. Your *disheveled* appearance will hurt your chances in this interview.

■ **disinclination** N. preference for avoiding something; slight aversion. Some mornings I feel a great *disinclination* to get out of bed. disinclined. ADJ.

**disingenuous** ADJ. not naive; sophisticated. Although he was young, his remarks indicated that he was *disingenuous*.

**disinterested** ADJ. unprejudiced. The only *disinterested* person in the room was the judge.

**disjointed** ADJ. disconnected. Her remarks were so *disjointed* that we could not follow her reasoning.

**dismantle** V. take apart. When the show closed, they *dismantled* the scenery before storing it.

**dismiss** V. put away from consideration; reject. Believing in John's love for her, she *dismissed* the notion that he might be unfaithful. (secondary meaning)

■ **disparage** V. belittle. Do not *disparage* anyone's contribution; these little gifts add up to large sums.

**disparate** ADJ. basically different; unrelated. It is difficult, if not impossible, to organize these *disparate* elements into a coherent whole.

■ **disparity** N. difference; condition of inequality. The *disparity* in their ages made no difference at all.

■ **dispassionate** ADJ. calm; impartial. In a *dispassionate* analysis of the problem, he carefully examined the causes of the conflict and proceeded to suggest suitable remedies.

■ **dispel** V. scatter; drive away; cause to vanish. The bright sunlight eventually *dispelled* the morning mist.

■ **disperse** V. scatter. The police fired tear gas into the crowd to disperse the protesters. dispersion, N.

**dispirited** ADJ. lacking in spirit. The coach used all the tricks at her command to buoy up the enthusiasm of her team, which had become *dispirited* at the loss of the star player.

■ **disputatious** ADJ. argumentative; fond of argument. People avoided discussing contemporary problems with her because of her *disputatious* manner.

**dissection** N. analysis; cutting apart in order to examine. The *dissection* of frogs in the laboratory is particularly unpleasant to some students.

**dissemble** V. disguise; pretend. Even though you are trying to *dissemble* your motive in joining this group, we can see through your pretense.

■ **disseminate** V. scatter (like seeds). The invention of the radio has helped propagandists to *disseminate* their favorite doctrines very easily.

■ **dissent** V. disagree. In the recent Supreme Court decision, Justice Marshall *dissented* from the majority opinion. also N.

**dissertation** N. formal essay. In order to earn a graduate degree from many of our universities, a candidate is frequently required to prepare a *dissertation* on some scholarly subject.

**dissipate** V. squander. The young man quickly *dissipated* his inheritance.

**dissolute** ADJ. loose in morals. The *dissolute* life led by these people is indeed shocking.

■ **dissonance** N. discord. Some contemporary musicians deliberately use *dissonance* to achieve certain effects.

**dissuade** V. advise against. He could not *dissuade* his friend from joining the conspirators. dissuasion, N.

**distant** ADJ. reserved or aloof; cold in manner. His *distant* greeting made me feel unwelcome from the start. (secondary meaning)

**distend** V. expand; swell out. I can tell when he is under stress by the way the veins *distend* on his forehead.

**distortion** N. twisting out of shape. It is difficult to believe the newspaper accounts of this event because of the *distortions* and exaggerations written by the reporters.

**distraught** ADJ. upset; distracted by anxiety. The *distraught* parents searched the ravine for their lost child.

**diva** N. operatic singer; prima donna. Although world famous as a *diva*, she did not indulge in fits of temperament.

■ **diverge** V. vary; go in different directions from the same point. The spokes of the wheel *diverge* from the hub. divergent, ADJ.

■ **diverse** ADJ. differing in some characteristics; various. There are *diverse* ways of approaching this problem.

---

# ETYMOLOGY 9

**DIA (across) prefix**

| | | |
|---|---|---|
| **diagonal** | across a figure | |
| **diameter** | across a circle | |
| **diagram** | outline drawing (writing across) | |

**DIC, DICT (to say)**

| | | |
|---|---|---|
| **abdicate** | renounce | |
| **diction** | speech | |
| **verdict** | statement of jury | |

**DIS, DIF (not) prefix**

| | | |
|---|---|---|
| **discord** | lack of harmony | |
| **differ** | disagree (carry apart) | |
| **distrust** | lack of trust | |

## TEST — Word List 9 — Synonyms and Antonyms

Each of the questions below consists of a word printed in italics, followed by five words or phrases numbered 1 to 5. Choose the numbered word or phrase which is most nearly the same as or the opposite of the word in italics and write the number of your choice on your answer paper.

161. *disingenuous* 1 uncomfortable 2 eventual 3 naïve 4 complex 5 enthusiastic
162. *destitute* 1 reckless 2 dazzling 3 wealthy 4 characteristic 5 explanatory
163. *dilate* 1 procrastinate 2 expand 3 conclude 4 participate 5 divert
164. *devout* 1 quiet 2 dual 3 impious 4 loyal 5 faithless
165. *diminution* 1 expectation 2 context 3 validity 4 appreciation 4 difficulty
166. *devoid* 1 latent 2 eschewed 3 full of 4 suspecting 5 evident
167. *disconsolate* 1 examining 2 thankful 3 theatrical 4 joyous 5 prominent
168. *diabolical* 1 mischievous 2 lavish 3 seraphic 4 azure 5 red
169. *disheveled* 1 recognized 2 unkempt 3 short 4 written 5 witty
170. *diffidence* 1 sharpness 2 boldness 3 malcontent 4 dialogue 5 catalog
171. *dissonance* 1 admonition 2 splendor 3 discord 4 reflection 5 consonance
172. *dispassionate* 1 clever 2 industrial 3 calm 4 narrow 5 crooked
173. *disinterested* 1 prejudiced 2 horrendous 3 affected 4 arbitrary 5 bored
174. *dissipate* 1 economize 2 clean 3 accept 4 anticipate 5 withdraw
175. *disjointed* 1 satisfied 2 carved 3 understood 4 connected 5 evicted
176. *distend* 1 bloat 2 adjust 3 exist 4 materialize 5 finish
177. *dispirited* 1 current 2 dented 3 drooping 4 removed 5 dallying
178. *distant* 1 wavering 2 aloof 3 forgetful 4 prominent 5 tardy
179. *disparity* 1 resonance 2 elocution 3 relief 4 difference 5 symbolism
180. *dilatory* 1 narrowing 2 procrastinating 3 enlarging 4 portentous 5 sour

## Word List 10  diversion - enigma

■ **diversion** N. act of turning aside; pasttime. After studying for several hours, he needed a *diversion* from work. divert, V.

**diversity** N. variety; dissimilitude. The *diversity* of colleges in this country indicates that many levels of ability are being cared for.

**divest** V. strip; deprive. He was *divested* of his power to act.

**divulge** V. reveal. I will not tell you this news because I am sure you will *divulge* it prematurely.

**docile** ADJ. obedient; easily managed. As *docile* as he seems today, that old lion was once a ferocious, snarling beast.

**document** V. provide written evidence. She kept all the receipts from her business trip in order to *document* her expenses for the firm. (secondary meaning) also N.

**dogmatic** ADJ. positive; arbitrary. Do not be so *dogmatic* about that statement; it can be easily refuted.

**dolorous** ADJ. sorrowful. He found the *dolorous* lamentations of the bereaved family emotionally disturbing and he left as quickly as he could.

**dolt** N. stupid person. I thought I was talking to a mature audience; instead, I find myself addressing a pack of *dolts* and idiots.

**domineer** V. rule over tyrannically. Students prefer teachers who guide, not ones who *domineer*.

**dormant** ADJ. sleeping; lethargic; torpid. Sometimes *dormant* talents in our friends surprise those of us who never realized how gifted our acquaintances really are. dormancy, N.

**dour** ADJ. sullen; stubborn. The man was *dour* and taciturn.

**dowdy** ADJ. slovenly; untidy. She tried to change her *dowdy* image by buying a new fashionable wardrobe.

**dregs** N. sediment; worthless residue. The *dregs* of society may be observed in this slum area of the city.

**droll** ADJ. queer and amusing. He was a popular guest because his *droll* anecdotes were always amusing.

**drudgery** N. menial work. Cinderella's fairy godmother rescued her from a life of *drudgery*.

**dubious** ADJ. doubtful. He has the *dubious* distinction of being the lowest man in his class.

**duplicity** N. double-dealing; hypocrisy. People were shocked and dismayed when they learned of his *duplicity* in this affair for he had always seemed honest and straightforward.

**dutiful** ADJ. respectful; obedient. The *dutiful* child grew up to be a conscientious adult, aware of his civic obligations.

**ebullient** ADJ. showing excitement; overflowing with enthusiasm. Her *ebullient* nature could not be repressed; she was always laughing and gay. ebullience, N.

**eccentric** ADJ. odd; whimsical; irregular. The comet passed close by the earth in its *eccentric* orbit. eccentricity, N.

**ecstasy** N. rapture; joy; any overpowering emotion. The announcment that the war had ended brought on an *ecstasy* of joy that resulted in many uncontrolled celebrations. ecstatic, ADJ.

**edify** V. instruct; correct morally. Although his purpose was to *edify* and not to entertain his audience, many of his listeners were amused and not enlightened.

**eerie** ADJ. weird. In that *eerie* setting, it was easy to believe in ghosts and other supernatural beings.

**efface** V. rub out. The coin had been handled so many times that its date had been *effaced*.

**effectual** ADJ. efficient. If we are to succeed in this endeavor, we must seek *effectual* means of securing our goals.

■ **effervescence** N. inner excitement; exuberance. Nothing depressed her for long; her natural *effervescence* soon reasserted itself. effervescent, ADJ.

**efficacy** N. power to produce desired effect. The *efficacy* of this drug depends on the regularity of the dosage.

**effigy** N. dummy. The mob showed its irritation by hanging the judge in *effigy*.

**effrontery** N. shameless boldness. He had the *effrontery* to insult the guest.

**effusive** ADJ. pouring forth; gushing. Her *effusive* manner of greeting her friends finally began to irritate them. effusion, N.

**egoism** N. excessive interest in one's self; belief that one should be interested in one's self rather than in others. His *egoism* prevented him from seeing the needs of his colleagues.

**egotism** N. conceit; vanity. We found his *egotism* unwarranted and irritating.

**egregious** ADJ. gross; shocking. She was an *egregious* liar.

**egress** N. exit. Barnum's sign "To the *Egress*" fooled many people who thought they were going to see an animal and instead found themselves in the street.

■ **elaboration** N. addition of details; intricacy. Tell what happened simply, without any *elaboration*. elaborate, V.

■ **elated** ADJ. overjoyed; in high spirits. Grinning from ear to ear, Janet Evans was clearly *elated* by her Olympic victory. elation, N.

**elegiacal** ADJ. like an elegy; mournful. The essay on the lost crew was *elegiacal* in mood. elegy, N.

**elicit** V. draw out by discussion. The detectives tried to *elicit* where he had hidden his loot.

■ **eloquence** N. expressiveness; persuasive speech. The crowds were stirred by Martin Luther King's *eloquence*.

**elucidate** V. explain; enlighten. She was called upon to *elucidate* the disputed points in her article.

■ **elusive** ADJ. evasive; baffling; hard to grasp. His *elusive* dreams of wealth were costly to those of his friends who supported him financially.

**emaciated** ADJ. thin and wasted. Her long period of starvation had left her wan and *emaciated*.

**emancipate** V. set free. At first, the attempts of the Abolitionists to *emancipate* the slaves were unpopular in New England as well as in the South.

**embellish** V. adorn. His handwriting was *embellished* with flourishes.

**embezzlement** N. stealing. The bank teller confessed his *embezzlement* of the funds.

**embroil** V. throw into confusion; involve in strife; entangle. He became *embroiled* in the heated discussion when he tried to arbitrate the dispute.

**emend** V. correct; correct by a critic. The critic *emended* the book by selecting the passages which she thought most appropriate to the text.

**eminent** ADJ. high; lofty. After her appointment to this *eminent* position, she seldom had time for her former friends.

**emulate** V. rival; imitate. As long as our political leaders *emulate* the virtues of the great leaders of this country, we shall flourish.

**enamored** ADJ. in love. Narcissus became *enamored* of his own beauty.

**encompass** V. surround. Although we were *encompassed* by enemy forces, we were cheerful for we were well stocked and could withstand a siege until our allies joined us.

**encumber** V. burden. Some people *encumber* themselves with too much luggage when they take short trips.

**endearment** N. fond statement. Your gifts and *endearments* cannot make me forget your earlier insolence.

■ **endorse** V. approve; support. Everyone waited to see which one of the rival candidates the mayor would *endorse*. endorsement, N. (secondary meaning)

**energize** V. invigorate; make forceful and active. We shall have to re-*energize* our activities by getting new members to carry on.

**enervate** V. weaken. The hot days of August are *enervating*.

■ **engender** V. cause; produce. To receive praise for accomplishments *engenders* self-confidence in a child.

**engross** V. occupy fully. John was so *engrossed* in his studies that he did not hear his mother call.

■ **enhance** V. advance; improve. Your chances for promotion in this department will be *enhanced* if you take some more courses in evening school.

■ **enigma** N. puzzle. Despite all attempts to decipher the code, it remained an *enigma*. enigmatic, ADJ.

## ETYMOLOGY 10

DOC, DOCT (to teach)

**docile**    meek (teachable)

**document**    something that provides evidence

**doctor**    learned man (originally, teacher)

DOM, DOMIN (to rule)
> **dominate**   having power over
> **domain**   land under rule
> **dominant**   prevailing

DYNAM (power, strength)
> **dynamic**   powerful
> **dynamite**   powerful explosive
> **dynamo**   engine to make electrical power

EGO (I, self)
> **egoist**   person who is self-interested
> **egotist**   self-centered person
> **egocentric**   revolving about self

---

## TEST — Word List 10 — Synonyms

Each of the questions below consists of a word printed in italics, followed by five words or phrases numbered 1 to 5. Choose the numbered word or phrase which is most nearly similar in meaning to the word in italics and write the number of your choice on your answer paper.

181. *dutiful*   1 deadly 2 eloping 3 obedient 4 simple 5 petrified
182. *edify*   1 mystify 2 suffice 3 improve 4 erect 5 entertain
183. *dormant*   1 active 2 absurd 3 hibernating 4 unfortunate 5 permanent
184. *egress*   1 entrance 2 bird 3 exit 4 double 5 progress
185. *dubious*   1 external 2 straight 3 sincere 4 doubtful 5 filling in
186. *dogmatic*   1 benign 2 canine 3 impatient 4 petulant 5 arbitrary
187. *elated*   1 debased 2 respectful 3 drooping 4 gay 5 charitable
188. *droll*   1 rotund 2 amusing 3 fearsome 4 tiny 5 strange
189. *document*   1 withdraw 2 provide written evidence 3 make confusing 4 control 5 start
190. *effigy*   1 requisition 2 organ 3 charge 4 accordion 5 dummy
191. *dour*   1 sullen 2 ornamental 3 grizzled 4 lacking speech 5 international
192. *divulge*   1 look 2 refuse 3 deride 4 reveal 5 harm
193. *efface*   1 countenance 2 encourage 3 recognize 4 blackball 5 rub out
194. *effervescence*   1 exuberance 2 loyalty 3 sensitivity 4 interest 5 generosity
195. *emaciated*   1 garrulous 2 primeval 3 vigorous 4 disparate 5 thin
196. *enhance*   1 improve 2 doubt 3 scuff 4 gasp 5 agree
197. *embellish*   1 doff 2 don 3 balance 4 adorn 5 equalize
198. *enervate*   1 weaken 2 sputter 3 arrange 4 scrutinize 5 agree
199. *emend*   1 cherish 2 repose 3 correct 4 assure 5 worry
200. *eminent*   1 purposeful 2 high 3 delectable 4 curious 5 urgent

## Word List 11    ennui - extrovert

**ennui** N. boredom. The monotonous routine of hospital life induced a feeling of *ennui* which made him moody and irritable.

**enormity** N. hugeness (in a bad sense). He did not realize the *enormity* of his crime until he saw what suffering he had caused.

**ensconce** V. settle comfortably. The parents thought that their children were *ensconced* safely in the private school and decided to leave for Europe.

**enthrall** V. capture; enslave. From the moment he saw her picture, he was *enthralled* by her beauty.

**entree** N. entrance. Because of his wealth and social position, he had *entree* into the most exclusive circles.

**entrepreneur** N. businessman; contractor. Opponents of our present tax program argue that it discourages *entrepreneurs* from trying new fields of business activity.

■ **ephemeral** ADJ. short-lived; fleeting. The mayfly is an *ephemeral* creature.

**epic** N. long heroic poem, novel, or similar work of art. Kurosawa's film *Seven Samurai* is an *epic* portraying the struggle of seven warriors to destroy a band of robbers. also ADJ.

**epigram** N. witty thought or saying, usually short. Poor Richard's *epigrams* made Benjamin Franklin famous.

**epilogue** N. short speech at conclusion of dramatic work. The audience was so disappointed in the play that many did not remain to hear the *epilogue*.

**epitaph** N. inscription in memory of a dead person. In his will, he dictated the *epitaph* he wanted placed on his tombstone.

**epithet** N. descriptive word or phrase. Homer's writings featured the use of such *epithets* as ''rosy-fingered dawn.''

**epitome** N. summary; concise abstract. This final book is the *epitome* of all her previous books. epitomize, V.

**equanimity** N. calmness of temperament. In his later years, he could look upon the foolishness of the world with *equanimity* and humor.

**equity** N. fairness; justice. Our courts guarantee *equity* to all. equitable, ADJ.

■ **equivocal** ADJ. ambiguous; misleading. The audience saw through his *equivocal* comments and insisted that he come right out and say where he stood on the issue. equivocate, V.

**erode** V. eat away. The limestone was *eroded* by the dripping water. erosion, N.

■ **erratic** ADJ. odd; unpredictable. Investors become anxious when the stock market appears *erratic*.

■ **erroneous** ADJ. mistaken; wrong. I thought my answer was correct, but it was *erroneous*.

**erudite** ADJ. learned; scholarly. His *erudite* writing was difficult to read because of the many allusions which were unfamiliar to most readers. erudition, N.

**escapade** N. prank; flighty conduct. The headmaster could not regard this latest *escapade* as a boyish joke and expelled the young man.

**esoteric** ADJ. known only to the chosen few. Those students who had access to her *esoteric* discussions were impressed by the scope of her thinking.

**espouse** V. adopt; support. She was always ready to *espouse* a worthy cause.

■ **esteem** V. respect; value; judge. I *esteem* Ezra Pound's poetic insights, but I reject his fascist politics.

**estranged** ADJ. separated. The *estranged* wife sought a divorce.

**ethnic** ADJ. relating to races. Intolerance between *ethnic* groups is deplorable and usually is based on lack of information. ethnology, N.

**eulogy** N. praise. All the *eulogies* of his friends could not remove the sting of the calumny heaped upon him by his enemies. eulogistic, ADJ.

**euphemism** N. mild expression in place of an unpleasant one. The expression "He passed away" is a *euphemism* for "He died."

**euphonious** ADJ. pleasing in sound. Italian and Spanish are *euphonious* languages and therefore easily sung.

**evanescent** ADJ. fleeting; vanishing. For a brief moment, the entire skyline was bathed in an orange-red hue in the *evanescent* rays of the sunset.

■ **evasive** ADJ. not frank; eluding. Your *evasive* answers convinced the judge that you were withholding important evidence. evade, V.

**evoke** V. call forth. He *evoked* much criticism by his hostile manner.

■ **exacerbate** V. worsen; embitter. This latest arrest will *exacerbate* the existing discontent of the people.

**exaction** N. exorbitant demand; extortion. The colonies rebelled against the *exactions* of the mother country. exacting, ADJ.

■ **exalt** V. raise in rank or dignity; praise. The actor Alec Guiness was *exalted* to the rank of knighthood by the queen.

**exasperate** V. vex. Johnny often *exasperates* his mother with his pranks.

**exculpate** V. clear from blame. He was *exculpated* of the crime when the real criminal confessed.

■ **execute** V. put into effect; carry out. The choreographer wanted to see how well Margaret could *execute* a pirouette. (secondary meaning) execution, N.

**exemplary** ADJ. serving as a model; outstanding. Her *exemplary* behavior was praised at Commencement. exemplify, V.

**exertion** N. effort; expenditure of much physical work. The *exertion* spent in unscrewing the rusty bolt left her exhausted.

- **exhaustive** ADJ. thorough; comprehensive. We have made an *exhaustive* study of all published SAT tests and are happy to share our research with you.

**exhort** V. urge. The evangelist will *exhort* all sinners in his audience to reform.

**exigency** N. urgent situation. In this *exigency*, we must look for aid from our allies.

**exonerate** V. acquit; exculpate. I am sure this letter will *exonerate* you.

**exorbitant** ADJ. excessive. The people grumbled at his *exorbitant* prices but paid them because he had a monopoly.

**exotic** ADJ. not native; strange. Because of his *exotic* headdress, he was followed in the streets by small children who laughed at his strange appearance.

**expatiate** V. talk at length. At this time, please give us a brief resumé of your work; we shall permit you to *expatiate* later.

**expatriate** N. exile; someone who has withdrawn from his native land. Henry James was an American *expatriate* who settled in England.

- **expedient** ADJ. advantageous; suitable to achieve a particular end. It is often *expedient* for us to maintain diplomatic relations with foreign governments whose stands on human rights we unofficially deplore. also N.

- **expedite** V. hasten. We hope you will be able to *expedite* the delivery of our order.

**expertise** N. specialized knowledge; expert skill. Although she is knowledgeable in a number of fields, she was hired for her *expertise* in computer programming.

- **explicit** ADJ. clear; direct. In seeing her boyfriend secretly, she was defying her father's *explicit* orders.

- **exploit** N. deed or action, particularly a brave deed. Raoul Wallenberg was noted for his *exploits* in rescuing Jews from Hitler's forces.

- **exploit** V. make use of, sometimes unjustly. Cesar Chavez fought attempts to *exploit* migrant farm workers in California. exploitation, N.

**expunge** V. cancel; remove. If you behave, I will *expunge* this notation from your record.

**expurgate** V. clean; remove offensive parts of a book. The editors felt that certain passages in the book had to be *expurgated* before it could be used in the classroom.

**extant** ADJ. still in existence. Although the authorities suppressed the book, many copies are *extant* and may be purchased at exorbitant prices.

**extemporaneous** ADJ. not planned; impromptu. Because her *extemporaneous* remarks were misinterpreted, she decided to write all her speeches in advance.

**extenuate** V. weaken; mitigate. It is easier for us to *extenuate* our own shortcomings than those of others.

■ **extol** V. praise; glorify. The astronauts were *extolled* as the pioneers of the Space Age.

**extradition** N. surrender of prisoner by one state to another. The lawyers opposed the *extradition* of their client on the grounds that for more than five years he had been a model citizen.

■ **extraneous** ADJ. not essential; external. Do not pad your paper with *extraneous* matters; stick to essential items only.

■ **extricate** V. free; disentangle. He found that he could not *extricate* himself from the trap.

**extrinsic** ADJ. external; not inherent; foreign. Do not be fooled by *extrinsic* causes. We must look for the intrinsic reason.

**extrovert** N. person interested mostly in external objects and actions. A good salesman is usually an *extrovert,* who likes to mingle with people.

---

## ETYMOLOGY 11

ERR (to wander)
> **error**   mistake
> **erratic**   not reliable, not constant
> **knight-errant**   wandering knight

EU (good, well, beautiful) prefix
> **eulogize**   praise
> **euphemism**   substitution of pleasant way of saying something blunt or unpleasant
> **eupeptic**   having good digestion

EX (out) prefix
> **expel**   drive out
> **exit**   way out
> **extirpate**   root out

EXTRA (beyond, outside) prefix
> **extraordinary**   exceptional
> **extracurricular**   beyond the items in the curriculum
> **extraterritorial**   beyond the territory of a nation

---

## TEST — Word List 11 — Antonyms

Each of the following questions consists of a word printed in italics, followed by five words or phrases numbered 1 to 5. Choose the numbered word or phrase which is most nearly opposite in meaning to the word in italics and write the number of your choice on your answer paper.

201. *enormity*   1 neglect 2 consent 3 unimportance 4 gain 5 retreat
202. *exasperate*   1 confide 2 formalize 3 placate 4 betray 5 bargain
203. *equivocal*   1 mistaken 2 quaint 3 azure 4 clear 5 universal
204. *esteem*   1 decipher 2 dig 3 integrate 4 admit 5 scorn
205. *evasive*   1 frank 2 correct 3 empty 4 fertile 5 watchful
206. *equanimity*   1 agitation 2 stirring 3 volume 4 identity 5 luster
207. *ephemeral*   1 sensuous 2 passing 3 popular 4 distasteful 5 eternal
208. *euphonious*   1 strident 2 lethargic 3 literary 4 significant 5 musical
209. *expedient*   1 flat 2 decisive 3 disadvantageous 4 rough 5 scanty
210. *exhaustive*   1 innumerable 2 philosophic 3 physical 4 incomplete 5 meditative
211. *eulogistic*   1 pretty 2 critical 3 brief 4 stern 5 free
212. *ennui*   1 hate 2 excitement 3 seriousness 4 humility 5 kindness
213. *exculpate*   1 accuse 2 prevail 3 acquit 4 ravish 5 accumulate
214. *erudite*   1 professorial 2 stately 3 short 4 unknown 5 ignorant
215. *exonerate*   1 forge 2 accuse 3 record 4 doctor 5 reimburse
216. *extrovert*   1 clown 2 hero 3 ectomorph 4 neurotic 5 introvert
217. *exorbitant*   1 moderate 2 partisan 3 military 4 barbaric 5 expensive
218. *extrinsic*   1 reputable 2 inherent 3 swift 4 ambitious 5 cursory
219. *extraneous*   1 needless 2 decisive 3 essential 4 effective 5 expressive
220. *extemporaneous*   1 rehearsed 2 hybrid 3 humiliating 4 statesmanlike 5 picturesque

---

## Word List 12   exuberance - fluster

■ **exuberance** N. abundance; effusiveness; lavishness. His speeches were famous for the *exuberance* of his language and the vividness of his imagery. exuberant, ADJ.

**exude** V. discharge; give forth. The maple syrup is obtained from the sap that *exudes* from the trees in early spring. exudation, N.

**fabricate** V. build; lie. If we pre*fabricate* the buildings in this project, we can reduce the cost considerably. fabrication, N.

**facetious** ADJ. humorous; jocular. Your *facetious* remarks are not appropriate at this serious moment.

**facile** ADJ. easy; expert. Because he was a *facile* speaker, he never refused a request to address an organization.

■ **facilitate** V. make less difficult. He tried to *facilitate* matters at home by getting a part-time job.

**faction** N. party; clique; dissension. The quarrels and bickering of the two small *factions* within the club disturbed the majority of the members.

■ **fallacious** ADJ. misleading. Your reasoning must be *fallacious* because it leads to a ridiculous answer.

**fallible** ADJ. liable to err. I know I am *fallible*, but I feel confident that I am right this time.

**fallow** ADJ. plowed but not sowed; uncultivated. Farmers have learned that it is advisable to permit land to lie *fallow* every few years.

■ **fanaticism** N. excessive zeal. The leader of the group was held responsible even though he could not control the *fanaticism* of his followers.

**fancied** ADJ. imagined; unreal. You are resenting *fancied* insults. No one has ever said such things about you.

**fanciful** ADJ. whimsical; visionary. This is a *fanciful* scheme because it does not consider the facts.

**fantastic** ADJ. unreal; grotesque; whimsical. Your fears are *fantastic* because no such animal as you have described exists.

■ **fastidious** ADJ. difficult to please; squeamish. The waitresses disliked serving him dinner because of his very *fastidious* taste.

**fatalism** N. belief that events are determined by forces beyond one's control. With fatalism, he accepted the hardships which beset him. fatalistic, ADJ.

**fawning** ADJ. courting favor by cringing and flattering. She was constantly surrounded by a group of *fawning* admirers who hoped to win some favor.

**feasible** ADJ. practical. This is an entirely *feasible* proposal. I suggest we adopt it.

**feign** V. pretend. Lady Macbeth *feigned* illness in the courtyard.

**feint** N. trick; shift; sham blow. The boxer was fooled by his opponent's *feint* and dropped his guard. also V.

**felicitous** ADJ. apt; suitably expressed; well chosen. He was famous for his *felicitous* remarks and was called upon to serve as master-of-ceremonies at many a banquet. felicity, N.

**ferment** N. agitation; commotion. The entire country was in a state of *ferment*.

**fervent** ADJ. ardent; hot. He felt that the *fervent* praise was excessive and somewhat undeserved.

■ **fervor** N. glowing ardor. Their kiss was full of the *fervor* of first love. fervid, ADJ.

**fester** V. generate pus. When her finger began to *fester*, the doctor lanced it and removed the splinter which had caused the pus to form.

**fetid** ADJ. malodorous. The neglected wound became *fetid*.

**fetter** V. shackle. The prisoner was *fettered* to the wall.

**fiasco** N. total failure. Our ambitious venture ended in a *fiasco*.

■ **fickle** ADJ. changeable; faithless. He discovered she was *fickle*.

**fictitious** ADJ. imaginary. Although this book purports to be a biography of George Washington, many of the incidents are *fictitious*.

**finesse** N. delicate skill. The *finesse* and adroitness of the surgeon impressed the observers in the operating room.

**finicky** ADJ. too particular; fussy. The old lady was *finicky* about her food.

**finite** ADJ. limited. It is difficult for humanity with its *finite* existence to grasp the infinite.

**fitful** ADJ. spasmodic; intermittent. After several *fitful* attempts, he decided to postpone the start of the project until he felt more energetic.

**flagging** ADJ. weak; drooping. The encouraging cheers of the crowd lifted the team's *flagging* spirits. flag, V.

■ **flagrant** ADJ. conspicuously wicked. We cannot condone such *flagrant* violations of the rules.

**flair** N. talent. He has an uncanny *flair* for discovering new artists before the public has become aware of their existence.

**flamboyant** ADJ. ornate. Modern architecture has discarded the *flamboyant* trimming on buildings and emphasizes simplicity of line.

**flaunt** V. display ostentatiously. She is not one of those actresses who *flaunt* their physical charms; she can act.

**fleck** V. spot. Her cheeks, *flecked* with tears, were testimony to the hours of weeping.

■ **fledgling** ADJ. inexperienced. While it is necessary to provide these *fledgling* poets with an opportunity to present their work, it is not essential that we admire everything they write. also N.

**flick** N. light stroke as with a whip. The horse needed no encouragement; only one *flick* of the whip was all the jockey had to apply to get the animal to run at top speed.

**flippancy** N. trifling gaiety. Your *flippancy* at this serious moment is offensive.

**flora** N. plants of a region or era. Because she was a botanist, she spent most of her time studying the *flora* of the desert.

**flout** V. reject; mock. The headstrong youth *flouted* all authority; he refused to be curbed.

■ **fluctuate** V. waver. Meteorologists watch the way the barometer *fluctuates* in order that they may predict the weather. fluctuation, N.

**fluency** N. smoothness of speech. She spoke French with *fluency* and ease.

**fluster** V. confuse. The teacher's sudden question *flustered* him and he stammered his reply.

## ETYMOLOGY 12

FAC, FIC, FEC, FECT (to make, to do)
**factory**  place where things are made
**fiction**  manufactured story
**affect**  cause to change
FALL, FALS (to deceive)
**fallacious**  faulty
**infallible**  not prone to error, perfect
**falsify**  lie
FIC (making, causing) adjective suffix
**terrific**  causing fear or awe
**soporific**  making sleepy

## TEST — Word List 12 — Synonyms and Antonyms

Each of the questions below consists of a word printed in italics, followed by five words or phrases numbered 1 to 5. Choose the numbered word or phrase which is most nearly the same as or the opposite of the word in italics and write the number of your choice on your answer paper.

221. *finite*  1 bounded  2 established  3 affirmative  4 massive  5 finicky
222. *fiasco*  1 cameo  2 mansion  3 pollution  4 success  5 gamble
223. *flair*  1 conflagration  2 inspiration  3 bent  4 egregiousness  5 magnitude
224. *flamboyant*  1 old-fashioned  2 restrained  3 impulsive  4 cognizant  5 eloquent
225. *fanciful*  1 imaginative  2 knowing  3 elaborate  4 quick  5 lusty
226. *fanaticism*  1 prophecy  2 futility  3 zeal  4 need  5 dormancy
227. *fallacious*  1 misleading  2 illiterate  3 catastrophic  4 futile  5 inherent
228. *faction*  1 truth  2 degree  3 lesion  4 suture  5 clique
229. *fledgling*  1 weaving  2 bobbing  3 beginning  4 studying  5 flaying
230. *fallow*  1 uncultivated  2 magnificent  3 polished  4 puny  5 ridiculous
231. *fidelity*  1 brotherhood  2 parentage  3 treachery  4 conscience  5 consistency
232. *facilitate*  1 succeed  2 harvest  3 industrialize  4 complicate  5 resent
233. *facetious*  1 serious  2 rusty  3 ruined  4 patient  5 poetic
234. *fastidious*  1 fatal  2 natal  3 terrible  4 squeamish  5 tolerable
235. *ferment*  1 stir up  2 fill  3 ferret  4 mutilate  5 banish
236. *fickle*  1 fallacious  2 tolerant  3 loyal  4 hungry  5 stupid
237. *exude*  1 prevent  2 ooze  3 manage  4 protrude  5 insure
238. *feasible*  1 theoretical  2 impatient  3 constant  4 present  5 impractical

239. *feign*   1 deserve 2 condemn 3 condone 4 attend 5 pretend
240. *fluster*   1 combine 2 discompose 3 itch 4 cancel 5 resent

---

### Word List 13   flux - gloat

**flux** N. flowing; series of changes. While conditions are in such a state of *flux*, I do not wish to commit myself too deeply in this affair.

**foible** N. weakness; slight fault. We can overlook the *foibles* of our friends.

**foment** V. stir up; instigate. This report will *foment* dissension in the club.

**foolhardy** ADJ. rash. Don't be *foolhardy.* Get the advice of experienced people before undertaking this venture.

**forbearance** N. patience. We must use *forbearance* in dealing with him because he is still weak from his illness. forbear, V.

**foreboding** N. premonition of evil. Caesar ridiculed his wife's *forebodings* about the Ides of March.

■ **foresight** N. ability to foresee future happenings; prudence. A wise investor, she had the *foresight* to buy land just before the current real estate boom.

**formality** N. adherence to established rules of procedures. Signing this petition is a mere *formality;* it does not obligate you in any way.

**formidable** ADJ. menacing; threatening. We must not treat the battle lightly for we are facing a *formidable* foe.

**fortitude** N. bravery; courage. He was awarded the medal for his *fortitude* in the battle.

**fortuitous** ADJ. accidental; by chance. There is no connection between these two events; their timing is extremely *fortuitous.*

**foster** V. rear; encourage. According to the legend, Romulus and Remus were *fostered* by a she-wolf. also ADJ.

**frailty** N. weakness. Hamlet says, *"Frailty,* thy name is woman."

**franchise** N. right granted by authority. The city issued a *franchise* to the company to operate surface transit lines on the streets for ninety-nine years. also V.

**frantic** ADJ. wild. At the time of the collision, many people became *frantic* with fear.

**fraudulent** ADJ. cheating; deceitful. The government seeks to prevent *fraudulent* and misleading advertising.

**frenzied** ADJ. madly excited. As soon as they smelled smoke, the *frenzied* animals milled about in their cages.

**fret** V. to be annoyed or vexed. To *fret* over your poor grades is foolish; instead, decide to work harder in the future.

**friction** N. clash in opinion; rubbing against. At this time when harmony is essential, we cannot afford to have any *friction* in our group.

**frigid** ADJ. intensely cold. Alaska is in the *frigid* zone.

**fritter** V. waste. He could not apply himself to any task and *frittered* away his time in idle conversation.

■ **frivolity** N. lack of seriousness. We were distressed by his *frivolity* during the recent crisis.

**frolicsome** ADJ. prankish; gay. The *frolicsome* puppy tried to lick the face of its master.

**frugality** N. thrift. In these difficult days, we must live with *frugality*.

**fruition** N. bearing of fruit; fulfillment; realization. This building marks the *fruition* of all our aspirations and years of hard work.

**frustrate** V. thwart; defeat. We must *frustrate* this dictator's plan to seize control of the government.

**funereal** ADJ. sad; solemn. I fail to understand why there is such a *funereal* atmosphere; we have lost a battle, not a war.

**furor** N. frenzy; great excitement. The story of his embezzlement of the funds created a *furor* on the Stock Exchange.

■ **furtive** ADJ. stealthy. The boy gave a *furtive* look at his classmate's test paper.

**fusion** N. union; coalition. The opponents of the political party in power organized a *fusion* of disgruntled groups and became an important element in the election.

**futile** ADJ. ineffective; fruitless. Why waste your time on *futile* pursuits?

**gadfly** N. animal-biting fly; an irritating person. Like a *gadfly*, he irritated all the guests at the hotel; within forty-eight hours, everyone regarded him as an annoying busybody.

**gainsay** V. deny. She could not *gainsay* the truth of the report.

**galvanize** V. stimulate by shock; stir up. The entire nation was *galvanized* into strong military activity by the news of the attack on Pearl Harbor.

**gape** V. open widely. The huge pit *gaped* before him; if he stumbled, he would fall in.

■ **garbled** ADJ. mixed up; based on false or unfair selection. The *garbled* report confused many readers who were not familiar with the facts. garble, V.

**garish** ADJ. gaudy. She wore a *garish* rhinestone necklace.

**garner** V. gather; store up. He hoped to *garner* the world's literature in one library.

**garnish** V. decorate. Parsley was used to *garnish* the boiled potato. also N.

**garrulity** N. talkativeness. The man who married a dumb wife asked the doctor to make him deaf because of his wife's *garrulity* after her cure. garrulous, ADJ.

**generality** N. vague statement. This report is filled with *generalities;* you must be more specific in your statements.

**geniality** N. cheerfulness; kindliness; sympathy. This restaurant is famous and popular because of the *geniality* of the proprietor who tries to make everyone happy.

**genre** N. style of art illustrating scenes of common life. His painting of fisher folk at their daily tasks is an excellent illustration of *genre* art.

**genteel** ADJ. well-bred; elegant. We are looking for a man with a *genteel* appearance who can inspire confidence by his cultivated manner.

**gentility** N. those of gentle birth; refinement. Her family was proud of its *gentility*.

**germane** ADJ. pertinent; bearing upon the case at hand. The lawyer objected that the testimony being offered was not *germane* to the case at hand.

**ghastly** ADJ. horrible. The murdered man was a *ghastly* sight.

**gibber** V. speak foolishly. The demented man *gibbered* incoherently. gibberish, N.

**gibe** V. mock. As you *gibe* at their superstitious beliefs, do you realize that you, too, are guilty of similarly foolish thoughts?

**gist** N. essence. She was asked to give the *gist* of the essay in two sentences.

**glaze** V. cover with a thin and shiny surface. The freezing rain *glazed* the streets and made driving hazardous. also N.

**glean** V. gather leavings. After the crops had been harvested by the machines, the peasants were permitted to *glean* the wheat left in the fields.

**glib** ADJ. fluent. He is a *glib* speaker.

**gloat** V. express evil satisfaction; view malevolently. As you *gloat* over your ill-gotten wealth, do you think of the many victims you have defrauded?

---

## ETYMOLOGY 13

FY (to make) verb suffix

> **magnify**  make greater
> **petrify**  make into stone
> **beautify**  make beautiful

GAM (marriage)

> **monogamy**  marriage to one person
> **bigamy**  marriage to two people at the same time
> **polygamy**  having many spouses at the same time

GEN, GENER (class, race)

> **genus**  group of biological species with similar characteristics
> **generic**  characteristic of a class
> **gender**  class organized according to sex

---

## TEST — Word List 13 — Synonyms

Each of the questions below consists of a word printed in italics, followed by five words or phrases numbered 1 to 5. Choose the numbered word or phrase which is most nearly similar in meaning to the word in italics and write the number of your choice on your answer paper.

241. *garnish*  1 paint  2 garner  3 adorn  4 abuse  5 banish
242. *frugality*  1 foolishness  2 extremity  3 indifference  4 enthusiasm  5 economy
243. *forbearance*  1 patience  2 contest  3 ranger  4 intuition  5 ancestry
244. *gadfly*  1 humorist  2 nuisance  3 scholar  4 bum  5 thief
245. *foolhardy*  1 strong  2 unwise  3 brave  4 futile  5 erudite
246. *glib*  1 slippery  2 fashionable  3 antiquated  4 articulate  5 anticlimactic
247. *franchise*  1 subway  2 kiosk  3 license  4 reason  5 fashion
248. *furtive*  1 underhanded  2 coy  3 blatant  4 quick  5 abortive
249. *garner*  1 prevent  2 assist  3 collect  4 compute  5 consult
250. *gist*  1 chaff  2 summary  3 expostulation  4 expiation  5 chore
251. *foster*  1 speed  2 fondle  3 become infected  4 raise  5 roll
252. *fortuitous*  1 scanty  2 radical  3 orthodox  4 accidental  5 magnificent
253. *furor*  1 excitement  2 worry  3 flux  4 anteroom  5 lover
254. *germane*  1 bacteriological  2 middle European  3 prominent  4 warlike  5 relevant
255. *fritter*  1 soar  2 chafe  3 dissipate  4 cancel  5 abuse
256. *garish*  1 sordid  2 flashy  3 prominent  4 lusty  5 thoughtful
257. *formidable*  1 dangerous  2 outlandish  3 grandiloquent  4 impenetrable  5 vulnerable
258. *garrulity*  1 credulity  2 senility  3 loquaciousness  4 speciousness  5 artistry
259. *foment*  1 spoil  2 instigate  3 interrogate  4 settle  5 maintain
260. *friction*  1 lie  2 clash  3 armada  4 company  5 printer's proof

---

### Word List 14    glossy – homily

**glossy** ADJ. smooth and shining. I want this photograph printed on *glossy* paper.

**glut** V. overstock; fill to excess. The manufacturers *glutted* the market and could not find purchasers for the many articles they had produced. also N.

■ **glutton** N. person who overeats; greedy person. Who is the *glutton* who ate up all the chocolate chip cookies I made for dessert? gluttonous, ADJ.

**gnarled** ADJ. twisted. The *gnarled* oak tree had been a landmark for years and was mentioned in several deeds.

**goad** V. urge on. He was *goaded* by his friends until he yielded to their wishes. also N.

**gorge** V. stuff oneself. The gluttonous guest *gorged* himself with food as though he had not eaten for days.

**gory** ADJ. bloody. The audience shuddered as they listened to the details of the *gory* massacre.

**gourmet** N. connoisseur of food and drink. The *gourmet* stated that this was the best onion soup he had ever tasted.

**grandiloquent** ADJ. pompous; bombastic; using high-sounding language. The politician could never speak simply; she was always *grandiloquent*.

■ **grandiose** ADJ. imposing; impressive. His *grandiose* manner impressed those who met him for the first time.

**graphic** ADJ. pertaining to the art of delineating; vividly described. I was particularly impressed by the *graphic* presentation of the storm.

**gratify** V. please. Her parents were *gratified* by her success.

**gratis** ADJ. free. The company offered to give one package *gratis* to every purchaser of one of their products. also ADJ.

**gratuitous** ADJ. given freely; unwarranted. I resent your *gratuitous* remarks because no one asked for them. gratuity, N.

■ **gravity** N. seriousness. We could tell we were in serious trouble from the *gravity* of her expression. (secondary meaning) grave, ADJ.

**gregarious** ADJ. sociable. He was not *gregarious* and preferred to be alone most of the time.

■ **grudging** ADJ. unwilling; reluctant; stingy. We received only *grudging* support from the mayor despite his earlier promises of aid.

**grueling** ADJ. exhausting. The marathon is a *grueling* race.

**gruesome** ADJ. grisly. People screamed when his *gruesome* appearance was flashed on the screen.

**gruff** ADJ. rough-mannered. Although he was blunt and *gruff* with most people, he was always gentle with children.

**guffaw** N. boisterous laughter. The loud *guffaws* that came from the closed room indicated that the members of the committee had not yet settled down to serious business. also V.

■ **guile** N. deceit; duplicity. She achieved her high position by *guile* and treachery.

**guise** N. appearance; costume. In the *guise* of a plumber, the detective investigated the murder case.

■ **gullible** ADJ. easily deceived. He preyed upon *gullible* people, who believed his stories of easy wealth.

**gusto** N. enjoyment; enthusiasm. He accepted the assignment with such *gusto* that I feel he would have been satisfied with a smaller salary.

**gusty** ADJ. windy. The *gusty* weather made sailing precarious.

**hackneyed** ADJ. commonplace; trite. The English teacher criticized his story because of its *hackneyed* plot.

**haggard** ADJ. wasted away; gaunt. After his long illness, he was pale and *haggard*.

**haggle** V. argue about prices. I prefer to shop in a store that has a one-price policy because, whenever I *haggle* with a shopkeeper, I am never certain that I paid a fair price for the articles I purchased.

**hallowed** ADJ. blessed; consecrated. She was laid to rest in *hallowed* ground.

**hallucination** N. delusion. I think you were frightened by a *hallucination* which you created in your own mind.

■ **hamper** V. obstruct. The minority party agreed not to *hamper* the efforts of the leaders to secure a lasting peace.

■ **haphazard** ADJ. random; by chance. His *haphazard* reading left him unacquainted with the authors of the books.

**hapless** ADJ. unfortunate. This *hapless* creature had never known a moment's pleasure.

**harass** V. to annoy by repeated attacks. When he could not pay his bills as quickly as he had promised, he was *harassed* by his creditors.

**harbinger** N. forerunner. The crocus is an early *harbinger* of spring.

**harping** N. tiresome dwelling on a subject. After he had reminded me several times about what he had done for me, I told him to stop *harping* on my indebtedness to him. harp, V.

■ **haughtiness** N. pride; arrogance. I resent his *haughtiness* because he is no better than we are.

**hazardous** ADJ. dangerous. Your occupation is too *hazardous* for insurance companies to consider your application.

**hazy** ADJ. slightly obscure. In *hazy* weather, you cannot see the top of this mountain.

**hedonism** N. belief that pleasure is the sole aim in life. *Hedonism* and asceticism are opposing philosophies of human behavior.

■ **heed** V. pay attention to; consider. We hope you shall *heed* our advice and get a good night's sleep before the test. also N.

**heedless** ADJ. not noticing; disregarding. She drove on, *heedless* of the warnings placed at the side of the road that it was dangerous.

**heinous** ADJ. atrocious; hatefully bad. Hitler's *heinous* crimes will never be forgotten.

**heresy** N. opinion contrary to popular belief; opinion contrary to accepted religion. He was threatened with excommunication because his remarks were considered to be pure *heresy*.

**heretic** N. person who maintains opinions contrary to the doctrines of the church. She was punished by the Spanish Inquisition because she was a *heretic*.

**hermitage** N. home of a hermit. Even in his remote *hermitage* he could not escape completely from the world.

**heterogeneous** ADJ. dissimilar. In *heterogeneous* groupings, we have an unassorted grouping, while in homogeneous groupings we have people or things which have common traits.

**hiatus** N. gap; pause. There was a *hiatus* of twenty years in the life of Rip van Winkle.

**hibernate** V. sleep throughout the winter. Bears are one of the many species of animals that *hibernate.*

**hierarchy** N. body divided into ranks. It was difficult to step out of one's place in this *hierarchy.*

**hilarity** N. boisterous mirth. This *hilarity* is improper on this solemn day of mourning.

■ **hindrance** N. block; obstacle. Stalled cars along the highway are a *hindrance* to traffic. hinder, V.

**histrionic** ADJ. theatrical. He was proud of his *histrionic* ability and wanted to play the role of Hamlet. histrionics, N.

**hoary** ADJ. white with age. The man was *hoary* and wrinkled.

**homily** N. sermon; serious warning. His speeches were always *homilies,* advising his listeners to repent and reform.

---

## ETYMOLOGY 14

GRAPH, GRAM (writing)
>**epigram**  a pithy statement
>**telegram**  an instantaneous message over great distances (*tele*—far off)
>**stenography**  shorthand (writing narrowly)

GREG (flock, herd)
>**gregarious**  tending to group together as in a herd
>**aggregate**  group, total
>**egregious**  out of the group; now used in a bad sense as *wicked*

---

## TEST — Word List 14 — Antonyms

Each of the questions below consists of a word printed in italics, followed by five words or phrases numbered 1 to 5. Choose the numbered word or phrase which is most nearly opposite in meaning to the word in italics and write the number of your choice on your answer paper.

261.  *grandiose*   1 false   2 ideal   3 proud   4 simple   5 functional
262.  *hazy*   1 wintry   2 clear   3 local   4 seasonal   5 springlike
263.  *gregarious*   1 antisocial   2 anticipatory   3 glorious   4 horrendous   5 similar
264.  *gratuitous*   1 warranted   2 frank   3 ingenuous   4 frugal   5 pithy
265.  *hapless*   1 cheerful   2 consistent   3 fortunate   4 considerate   5 shapely
266.  *heterogeneous*   1 orthodox   2 pagan   3 unlike   4 similar   5 banished
267.  *gusto*   1 noise   2 panic   3 fancy   4 gloom   5 distaste
268.  *gusty*   1 calm   2 noisy   3 fragrant   4 routine   5 gloomy
269.  *haphazard*   1 fortuitous   2 indifferent   3 deliberate   4 accidental   5 conspiring
270.  *grudging*   1 scaly   2 willing   3 erudite   4 quiet   5 long
271.  *gullible*   1 incredulous   2 fickle   3 tantamount   4 easy   5 stylish
272.  *gorge*   1 diet   2 store   3 crush   4 magnify   5 sweeten
273.  *gourmet*   1 cook   2 maître d'   3 glutton   4 epicure   5 author
274.  *grandiose*   1 pacific   2 prior   3 subsequent   4 puerile   5 unimpressive
275.  *gravity*   1 magnetism   2 frivolity   3 weariness   4 eloquence   5 incompetence
276.  *hilarity*   1 gloom   2 heartiness   3 weakness   4 casualty   5 paucity
277.  *hackneyed*   1 carried   2 original   3 banal   4 timely   5 oratorical
278.  *heretic*   1 sophist   2 believer   3 interpreter   4 pacifist   5 owner
279.  *glossy*   1 dull   2 doubtful   3 untidy   4 pleasant   5 bearish
280.  *haggard*   1 shrewish   2 inspired   3 plump   4 maidenly   5 vast

---

## Word List 15   homogeneous - incarnate

**homogeneous** ADJ. of the same kind. Educators try to put pupils of similar abilities into classes because they believe that this *homogeneous* grouping is advisable. homogeneity, N.

**hubbub** N. confused uproar. The marketplace was a scene of *hubbub* and excitement; in all the noise, we could not distinguish particular voices.

**humane** ADJ. kind. Her *humane* and considerate treatment of the unfortunate endeared her to all.

**humdrum** ADJ. dull; monotonous. After her years of adventure, she could not settle down to a *humdrum* existence.

**humid** ADJ. damp. He could not stand the *humid* climate and moved to a drier area.

■ **humility** N. humbleness of spirit. He spoke with a *humility* and lack of pride which impressed his listeners.

**hybrid** N. mongrel; mixed breed. Mendel's formula explains the appearance of *hybrids* and pure species in breeding. also ADJ.

**hyperbole** N. exaggeration; overstatement. This salesman is guilty of *hyperbole* in describing his product; it is wise to discount his claims. hyperbolic, ADJ.

**hypochondriac** N. person unduly worried about his health; worrier without cause about illness. The doctor prescribed chocolate pills for her patient who was a *hypochondriac.*

■ **hypocritical** ADJ. pretending to be virtuous; deceiving. I resent his *hypocritical* posing as a friend for I know he is interested only in his own advancement.

■ **hypothetical** ADJ. based on assumptions or hypotheses. Why do we have to consider *hypothetical* cases when we have actual case histories which we may examine? hypothesis, N.

**iconoclastic** ADJ. attacking cherished traditions. George Bernard Shaw's *iconoclastic* plays often startled people. iconoclast, N.

**ideology** N. ideas of a group of people. That *ideology* is dangerous to this country because it embraces undemocratic philosophies.

**idiom** N. special usage in language. I could not understand their *idiom* because literal translation made no sense.

**idiosyncrasy** N. peculiarity; eccentricity. One of his personal *idiosyncrasies* was his habit of rinsing all cutlery given him in a restaurant.

**idolatry** N. worship of idols; excessive admiration. Such *idolatry* of singers of popular ballads is typical of the excessive enthusiasm of youth.

**ignoble** ADJ. of lowly origin; unworthy. This plan is inspired by *ignoble* motives and I must, therefore, oppose it.

**ignominious** ADJ. disgraceful. The country smarted under the *ignominious* defeat and dreamed of the day when it would be victorious. ignominy, N.

**illusion** N. misleading vision. It is easy to create an optical *illusion* in which lines of equal length appear different.

■ **illusory** ADJ. deceptive; not real. Unfortunately, the costs of running the lemonade stand were so high that Tom's profits proved *illusory.*

**imbalance** N. lack of balance or symmetry; disproportion. Because of the great *imbalance* between the number of males and females invited, the dance was unsuccessful.

**imbecility** N. weakness of mind. I am amazed at the *imbecility* of the readers of these trashy magazines.

**imbibe** V. drink in. The dry soil *imbibed* the rain quickly.

**immaculate** ADJ. pure; spotless. The West Point cadets were *immaculate* as they lined up for inspection.

**imminent** ADJ. impending; near at hand. The *imminent* battle will determine our success or failure in this conflict.

**immobility** N. state of being immovable. Modern armies cannot afford the luxury of *immobility*, as they are vulnerable to attack while standing still.

**immune** ADJ. exempt. She was fortunately *immune* from the disease and could take care of the sick.

■ **immutable** ADJ. unchangeable. Scientists are constantly seeking to discover the *immutable* laws of nature.

**impair** V. worsen; diminish in value. This arrest will *impair* his reputation in the community.

■ **impartial** ADJ. not biased; fair. As members of the jury, you must be *impartial*, showing no favoritism to either party but judging the case on its merits.

**impasse** N. predicament from which there is no escape. In this *impasse,* all turned to prayer as their last hope.

**impassive** ADJ. without feeling; not affected by pain. The American Indian has been incorrectly depicted as an *impassive* individual, undemonstrative and stoical.

**impeccable** ADJ. faultless. He was proud of his *impeccable* manners.

**impecunious** ADJ. without money. Now that he was wealthy, he gladly contributed to funds to assist the *impecunious* and the disabled.

**impediment** N. hindrance; stumbling-block. She had a speech *impediment* that prevented her speaking clearly. impede, V.

**impending** ADJ. nearing; approaching. The entire country was saddened by the news of his *impending* death.

**imperious** ADJ. domineering. Her *imperious* manner indicated that she had long been accustomed to assuming command.

**impermeable** ADJ. impervious; not permitting passage through its substance. This new material is *impermeable* to liquids.

**impertinent** ADJ. insolent. I regard your remarks as *impertinent* and resent them.

**imperturbability** N. calmness. We are impressed by her *imperturbability* in this critical moment and are calmed by it. imperturbable, ADJ.

**impervious** ADJ. not penetrable; not permitting passage through. You cannot change their habits for their minds are *impervious* to reasoning.

**impetuous** ADJ. violent; hasty; rash. We tried to curb his *impetuous* behavior because we felt that in his haste he might offend some people.

**impetus** N. moving force. It is a miracle that there were any survivors since the two automobiles that collided were traveling with great *impetus.*

**impious** ADJ. irreverent. The congregation was offended by his *impious* remarks. impiety, N.

**implacable** ADJ. incapable of being pacified. Madame Defarge was the *implacable* enemy of the Evremonde family.

■ **implication** N. that which is hinted at or suggested. If I understand the *implications* of your remark, you do not trust our captain.

**implicit** ADJ. understood but not stated. It is *implicit* that you will come to our aid if we are attacked.

**impolitic** ADJ. not wise. I think it is *impolitic* to raise this issue at the present time because the public is too angry.

**import** N. significance. I feel that you have not grasped the full *import* of the message sent to us by the enemy.

■ **impoverished** ADJ. poor. The loss of their ancestral farm left the family *impoverished* and without hope.

**impregnable** ADJ. invulnerable. Until the development of the airplane as a military weapon, the fort was considered *impregnable*.

**impromptu** ADJ. without previous preparation. His listeners were amazed that such a thorough presentation could be made in an *impromptu* speech.

**impropriety** N. state of being inappropriate. Because of the *impropriety* of her costume, she was denied entrance into the dining room.

**improvise** V. compose on the spur of the moment. He would sit at the piano and *improvise* for hours on themes from Bach and Handel.

**imputation** N. charge; reproach. You cannot ignore the *imputations* in his speech that you are the guilty party. impute, V.

■ **inadvertently** ADV. by oversight; carelessly or unintentionally. He *inadvertently* omitted two questions on the examination.

**inalienable** ADJ. not to be taken away; nontransferable. The Declaration of Independence mentions the *inalienable* rights that all of us possess.

■ **inane** ADJ. silly; senseless. Such comments are *inane* because they do not help us solve our problem. inanity, N.

**inanimate** ADJ. lifeless. She was asked to identify the still and *inanimate* body.

**inarticulate** ADJ. speechless; producing indistinct speech. He became *inarticulate* with rage and uttered sounds without meaning.

**incapacitate** V. disable. During the winter, many people were *incapacitated* by respiratory ailments.

**incarcerate** V. imprison. The warden will *incarcerate* the felon.

**incarnate** ADJ. endowed with flesh; personified. Your attitude is so fiendish that you must be a devil *incarnate*.

---

## ETYMOLOGY 15

IL, ILE (pertaining to, capable of) adjective suffix

      **puerile**    pertaining to a child

      **ductile**    capable of being led

      **civil**    pertaining to a citizen

## TEST — Word List 15 — Synonyms and Antonyms

Each of the questions below consists of a word printed in italics, followed by five words or phrases numbered 1 to 5. Choose the numbered word or phrase which is most nearly the same as or the opposite of the word in italics and write the number of your choice on your answer paper.

281. *immutable*  1 silent 2 changeable 3 articulate 4 loyal 5 varied
282. *incarcerate*  1 inhibit 2 acquit 3 account 4 imprison 5 force
283. *imbibe*  1 export 2 drink 3 exhibit 4 account 5 visit
284. *inalienable*  1 inherent 2 repugnant 3 closed to immigration 4 full 5 accountable
285. *impetuous*  1 rash 2 inane 3 just 4 flagrant 5 redolent
286. *impromptu*  1 prompted 2 appropriate 3 rehearsed 4 foolish 5 vast
287. *incapacitate*  1 debate 2 scour 3 rehabilitate 4 sanctify 5 ratify
288. *impervious*  1 impenetrable 2 vulnerable 3 chaotic 4 cool 5 perfect
289. *impeccable*  1 unmentionable 2 quotable 3 blinding 4 faulty 5 hampering
290. *impartial*  1 unbiased 2 false 3 extreme 4 inarticulate 5 cautious
291. *impassive*  1 active 2 demonstrative 3 perfect 4 anxious 5 irritated
292. *impair*  1 separate 2 make amends 3 make worse 4 falsify 5 cancel
293. *immaculate*  1 chastened 2 chewed 3 sullied 4 angered 5 beaten
294. *impolitic*  1 campaigning 2 advisable 3 appropriate 4 legal 5 fortunate
295. *hubbub*  1 bedlam 2 fury 3 cap 4 axle 5 wax
296. *impecunious*  1 affluent 2 afflicted 3 affectionate 4 affable 5 afraid
297. *hypothetical*  1 logical 2 fantastic 3 wizened 4 assumed 5 axiomatic
298. *hybrid*  1 product 2 species 3 mixture 4 fish 5 genus
299. *imbalance*  1 violation 2 symmetry 3 joke 4 play on words 5 canard
300. *inane*  1 passive 2 wise 3 intoxicated 4 mellow 5 silent

## Word List 16    incentive - intellect

**incentive** N. spur; motive. Students who dislike school must be given an *incentive* to learn.

**incessant** ADJ. uninterrupted. The crickets kept up an *incessant* chirping which disturbed our attempts to fall asleep.

■ **incidental** ADJ. not essential; minor. The scholarship covered his major expenses at college and some of his *incidental* expenses as well.

**incipient** ADJ. beginning; in an early stage. I will go to sleep early for I want to break an *incipient* cold.

**incisive** ADJ. cutting; sharp. Her *incisive* remarks made us see the fallacy in our plans.

■ **incite** V. arouse to action. The demagogue *incited* the mob to take action into its own hands.

**inclement** ADJ. stormy; unkind. I like to read a good book in *inclement* weather.

**inclusive** ADJ. tending to include all. This meeting will run from January 10 to February 15 *inclusive*.

**incognito** ADV. with identity concealed; using an assumed name. The monarch enjoyed traveling through the town *incognito* and mingling with the populace. also ADJ.

**incoherence** N. lack of relevance; lack of intelligibility. The bereaved father sobbed and stammered, caught up in the *incoherence* of his grief.

■ **incompatible** ADJ. inharmonious. The married couple argued incessantly and finally decided to separate because they were *incompatible*.

■ **incongruity** N. lack of harmony; absurdity. The *incongruity* of his wearing sneakers with formal attire amused the observers. incongruous, ADJ.

■ **inconsequential** ADJ. of trifling significance. Your objections are *inconsequential* and may be disregarded.

**incontrovertible** ADJ. indisputable. We must yield to the *incontrovertible* evidence which you have presented and free your client.

■ **incorrigible** ADJ. uncorrectable. Because he was an *incorrigible* criminal, he was sentenced to life imprisonment.

**incredulity** N. a tendency to disbelief. Your *incredulity* in the face of all the evidence is hard to understand.

**incriminate** V. accuse. The evidence gathered against the racketeers *incriminates* some high public officials as well.

**incumbent** N. officeholder. The newly elected public official received valuable advice from the present *incumbent*. also ADJ.

**indefatigable** ADJ. tireless. He was *indefatigable* in his constant efforts to raise funds for the Red Cross.

■ **indict** V. charge. If the grand jury *indicts* the suspect, he will go to trial.

■ **indifferent** ADJ. unmoved; lacking concern. Because she felt no desire to marry, she was *indifferent* to his constant proposals. indifference, N.

**indigenous** ADJ. native. Tobacco is one of the *indigenous* plants which the early explorers found in this country.

**indigent** ADJ. poor. Because he was *indigent,* he was sent to the welfare office.

**indignity** N. offensive or insulting treatment. Although he seemed to accept cheerfully the *indignities* heaped upon him, he was inwardly very angry.

■ **indiscriminate** ADJ. choosing at random; confused. She disapproved of her son's *indiscriminate* television viewing and decided to restrict him to educational programs.

**indisputable** ADJ. too certain to be disputed. In the face of these *indisputable* statements, I withdraw my complaint.

■ **indolence** N. laziness. The sultry weather in the tropics encourages a life of *indolence*. indolent, ADJ.

■ **indulgent** ADJ. humoring; yielding; lenient. An *indulgent* parent may spoil a child by creating an artificial atmosphere of leniency.

**ineffable** ADJ. unutterable; cannot be expressed in speech. Such *ineffable* joy must be experienced; it cannot be described.

**inept** ADJ. unsuited; absurd; incompetent. The constant turmoil in the office proved that he was an *inept* administrator.

**inert** ADJ. inactive; lacking power to move. Faced with the growing corruption scandal, the bureaucracy was *inert* and did nothing.

■ **inevitable** ADJ. unavoidable. Death and taxes are both *inevitable*.

**inexorable** ADJ. relentless; unyielding; implacable. After listening to the pleas for clemency, the judge was *inexorable* and gave the convicted man the maximum punishment allowed by law.

■ **infallible** ADJ. unerring. We must remember that none of us is *infallible*.

■ **infamous** ADJ. notoriously bad. Jesse James was an *infamous* outlaw.

■ **infer** V. deduce; conclude. We must be particularly cautious when we *infer* that a person is guilty on the basis of circumstantial evidence. inference, N.

**infinitesimal** ADJ. very small. In the twentieth century, physicists have made their greatest discoveries about the characteristics of *infinitesimal* objects like the atom and its parts.

**infirmity** N. weakness. His greatest *infirmity* was lack of willpower.

**inflated** ADJ. exaggerated; pompous; enlarged (with air or gas). His claims about the new product were *inflated;* it did not work as well as he had promised.

**ingenuous** ADJ. naive; young; unsophisticated. These remarks indicate that you are *ingenuous* and unaware of life's harsher realities.

**ingrate** N. ungrateful person. You are an *ingrate* since you have treated my gifts with scorn.

**ingratiate** V. become popular with. He tried to *ingratiate* himself into her parents' good graces.

**inherent** ADJ. firmly established by nature or habit. Her *inherent* love of justice compelled her to come to their aid.

■ **inhibit** V. prohibit; restrain. The child was not *inhibited* in his responses. inhibition, N.

**inimical** ADJ. unfriendly; hostile. She felt that they were *inimical* and were hoping for her downfall.

- **initiate** V. begin; originate; receive into a group. The college is about to *initiate* a program in reducing math anxiety among students.

- **injurious** ADJ. harmful. Smoking cigarettes can be *injurious* to your health.

  **inkling** N. hint. This came as a complete surprise to me as I did not have the slightest *inkling* of your plans.

- **innate** ADJ. inborn. His *innate* talent for music was soon recognized by his parents.

- **innocuous** ADJ. harmless. Let her drink it; it is *innocuous*.

- **innovation** N. change; introduction of something new. She loved *innovations* just because they were new. innovative, ADJ.

  **innuendo** N. hint; insinuation. I resent the *innuendos* in your statement more than the statement itself.

  **inopportune** ADJ. untimely; poorly chosen. A rock concert is an *inopportune* setting for quiet conversation.

  **insatiable** ADJ. not easily satisfied; greedy. His thirst for knowledge was *insatiable;* he was always in the library.

  **inscrutable** ADJ. incomprehensible; not to be discovered. I fail to understand the reasons for your outlandish behavior; your motives are *inscrutable*.

  **insinuate** V. hint; imply. What are you trying to *insinuate* by that remark?

- **insipid** ADJ. tasteless; dull. I am bored by your *insipid* talk.

  **insolent** ADJ. haughty and contemptuous. I resent your *insolent* manner.

- **insolvent** ADJ. bankrupt; unable to repay one's debts. When rumors that he was *insolvent* reached his creditors, they began to press him for payment of the money due them. insolvency, N.

  **insomnia** N. wakefulness; inability to sleep. He refused to join us in a midnight cup of coffee because he claimed it gave him *insomnia*.

- **instigate** V. urge; start; provoke. I am afraid that this statement will *instigate* a revolt.

  **insular** ADJ. like an island; narrow-minded. In an age of such rapid means of communication, we cannot afford to be hemmed in by such *insular* ideas.

  **insuperable** ADJ. insurmountable; invincible. In the face of *insuperable* difficulties they maintained their courage and will to resist.

- **insurgent** ADJ. rebellious. We will not discuss reforms until the *insurgent* troops have returned to their homes. also N.

  **integrate** V. make whole; combine; make into one unit. He tried to *integrate* all their activities into one program.

  **integrity** N. wholeness; purity; uprightness. He was a man of great *integrity*.

  **intellect** N. higher mental powers. He thought college would develop his *intellect*.

## ETYMOLOGY 16

IN (in, into, upon, toward) prefix
        **incursion**  invasion
        **insidious**  treacherous
IN (not, without) prefix
        **inconsequential**  not significant
        **inimical**  hostile, not friendly
        **insipid**  tasteless

## TEST — Word List 16 — Synonyms

Each of the questions below consists of a word printed in italics, followed by five words or phrases numbered 1 to 5. Choose the numbered word or phrase which is most nearly similar in meaning to the word in italics and write the number of your choice on your answer paper.

301. *incentive*   1 objective 2 goad 3 stimulation 4 beginning 5 simulation
302. *indiscriminate*   1 flagrant 2 optimistic 3 careful 4 secretive 5 unselective
303. *inconsequential*   1 disorderly 2 insignificant 3 subsequent 4 insufficient 5 preceding
304. *insinuate*   1 resist 2 suggest 3 report 4 rectify 5 lecture
305. *incorrigible*   1 narrow 2 straight 3 inconceivable 4 unreliable 5 unreformable
306. *ingenuous*   1 clever 2 stimulating 3 naive 4 wily 5 cautious
307. *indolence*   1 sloth 2 poverty 3 latitude 4 aptitude 5 anger
308. *innocuous*   1 not capable 2 not dangerous 3 not eager 4 not frank 5 not peaceful
309. *insipid*   1 witty 2 flat 3 wily 4 talkative 5 lucid
310. *incompatible*   1 capable 2 reasonable 3 faulty 4 indifferent 5 alienated
311. *incriminate*   1 exacerbate 2 involve 3 intimidate 4 lacerate 5 prevaricate
312. *infirmity*   1 disability 2 age 3 inoculation 4 hospital 5 unity
313. *infallible*   1 final 2 unbelievable 3 perfect 4 inaccurate 5 inquisitive
314. *indigent*   1 lazy 2 pusillanimous 3 penurious 4 affluent 5 contrary
315. *inclement*   1 unfavorable 2 abandoned 3 kindly 4 selfish 5 active
316. *integrate*   1 tolerate 2 unite 3 flow 4 copy 5 assume
317. *inimical*   1 antagonistic 2 anonymous 3 fanciful 4 accurate 5 seldom
318. *infer*   1 exculpate 2 deduce 3 exonerate 4 prepare 5 embarrass
319. *indignity*   1 pomposity 2 bombast 3 obeisance 4 insult 5 message
320. *incessant*   1 aggrieved 2 uninterrupted 3 angered 4 patent 5 prehensile

## Word List 17    interminable - levity

■ **interminable** ADJ. endless. Although his speech lasted for only twenty minutes, it seemed *interminable* to his bored audience.

**intermittent** ADJ. periodic; on and off. Our picnic was marred by *intermittent* rains.

**intimate** V. hint. She *intimated* rather than stated her preferences.

**intimidation** N. fear. A ruler who maintains his power by *intimidation* is bound to develop clandestine resistance.

**intractable** ADJ. stubborn; hard to manage. How do you deal with such an *intractable* child?

**intransigent** ADJ. refusing any compromise. The strike settlement has collapsed because both sides are *intransigent*.

**intrepid** ADJ. fearless. For his *intrepid* conduct in battle, he was promoted.

■ **intricate** ADJ. complex; knotty; tangled. Philip spent many hours designing mazes so *intricate* that none of his classmates could solve them. intricacy, N.

**intrinsic** ADJ. belonging to a thing in itself; inherent. Although the *intrinsic* value of this award is small, I shall always cherish it.

**introvert** N. one who is introspective; inclined to think more about oneself. In his poetry, he reveals that he is an *introvert* by his intense interest in his own problems. also V.

**intrude** V. trespass; enter as an uninvited person. He hesitated to *intrude* on their conversation.

**intuition** N. power of knowing without reasoning. She claimed to know the truth by *intuition*. intuitive, ADJ.

**inundate** V. overflow; flood. The tremendous waves *inundated* the town.

**invective** N. abuse. He had expected criticism but not the *invective* which greeted his proposal.

**inverse** ADJ. opposite. There is an *inverse* ratio between the strength of light and its distance.

**invidious** ADJ. designed to create ill will or envy. We disregarded her *invidious* remarks because we realized how jealous she was.

**invulnerable** ADJ. incapable of injury. Achilles was *invulnerable* except in his heel.

**iota** N. very small quantity. He hadn't an *iota* of common sense.

**irascible** ADJ. irritable; easily angered. His *irascible* temper frightened me.

■ **ironic** ADJ. resulting in an unexpected and contrary manner. It is *ironic* that her success came when she least wanted it. irony, N.

**irreconcilable** ADJ. incompatible; not able to be resolved. Because the separated couple were *irreconcilable*, the marriage counselor recommended a divorce.

**irrelevant** ADJ. not applicable; unrelated. This statement is *irrelevant* and should be disregarded by the jury.

**irreparable** ADJ. not able to be corrected or repaired. Your apology cannot atone for the *irreparable* damage you have done to his reputation.

■ **irresolute** ADJ. uncertain how to act; weak. She had no respect for him because he seemed weak-willed and *irresolute*.

**irreverent** ADJ. lacking proper respect. The worshippers resented his *irreverent* remarks about their faith.

**irrevocable** ADJ. unalterable. Let us not brood over past mistakes since they are *irrevocable*.

**itinerary** N. plan of a trip. Before leaving for his first visit to France and England, he discussed his *itinerary* with people who had been there and with his travel agent.

**jaded** ADJ. fatigued; surfeited. He looked for exotic foods to stimulate his *jaded* appetite.

**jargon** N. language used by special group; gibberish. We tried to understand the *jargon* of the peddlers in the market-place but could not find any basis for comprehension.

**jeopardy** *(jĕp-)* N. exposure to death or danger. He cannot be placed in double *jeopardy*.

**jettison** V. throw overboard. In order to enable the ship to ride safely through the storm, the captain had to *jettison* much of his cargo.

**jocular** ADJ. said or done in jest. Do not take my *jocular* remarks seriously.

**jollity** N. gaiety; cheerfulness. The festive Christmas dinner was a merry one, and old and young alike joined in the general *jollity*.

**jovial** ADJ. good-natured; merry. A frown seemed out of place on his invariably *jovial* face.

**jubilation** N. rejoicing. There was great *jubilation* when the armistice was announced.

**judicious** ADJ. wise; determined by sound judgment. I believe that this plan is not *judicious;* it is too risky.

**juxtapose** V. place side by side. Comparison will be easier if you *juxtapose* the two objects.

**ken** N. range of knowledge. I cannot answer your question since this matter is beyond my *ken*.

■ **kindle** V. start a fire; inspire. Her teacher's praise *kindled* a spark of hope inside her.

**kismet** N. fate. *Kismet* is the Arabic word for "fate."

**knavery** N. rascality. We cannot condone such *knavery* in public officials.

**knell** N. tolling of a bell at a funeral; sound of the funeral bell. "The curfew tolls the *knell* of parting day."

**knoll** N. little round hill. Robert Louis Stevenson's grave is on a *knoll* in Samoa.

**labyrinth** N. maze. Tom and Becky were lost in the *labyrinth* of secret caves.

**lacerate** V. mangle; tear. Her body was *lacerated* in the automobile crash.

**lackadaisical** ADJ. affectedly languid. He was *lackadaisical* and indifferent about his part in the affair.

**laconic** ADJ. brief and to the point. Will Rogers' *laconic* comments on the news made him world famous.

**laggard** ADJ. slow; sluggish. The sailor had been taught not to be *laggard* in carrying out orders.

**lagoon** N. shallow body of water near a sea; lake. They enjoyed their swim in the calm *lagoon*.

**laity** N. laymen; persons not connected with the clergy. The *laity* does not always understand the clergy's problems.

**laminated** ADJ. made of thin plates or scales. Banded gneiss is a *laminated* rock.

**lampoon** V. ridicule. This article *lampoons* the pretensions of some movie moguls. also N.

■ **languish** V. lose animation; lose strength. In stories, lovelorn damsels used to *languish* and pine away. languid, ADJ.

**largess** N. generous gift. Lady Bountiful distributed *largess* to the poor.

**lascivious** ADJ. lustful. The *lascivious* books were confiscated and destroyed.

**lassitude** N. languor; weariness. The hot, tropical weather created a feeling of *lassitude* and encouraged drowsiness.

**latent** ADJ. dormant; hidden. His *latent* talent was discovered by accident.

**lateral** ADJ. coming from the side. In order to get good plant growth, the gardener must pinch off all *lateral* shoots.

**latitude** N. freedom from narrow limitations. I think you have permitted your son too much *latitude* in this matter.

■ **laudatory** ADJ. expressing praise. The critics' *laudatory* comments helped to make her a star.

**lavish** ADJ. liberal; wasteful. The actor's *lavish* gifts pleased her. also V.

**lecherous** ADJ. impure in thought and act; lustful; unchaste. He is a *lecherous* and wicked old man.

■ **legacy** N. a gift made by a will. Part of my *legacy* from my parents is an album of family photographs.

**leniency** N. mildness; permissiveness. Considering the gravity of the offense, we were surprised by the *leniency* of the sentence. **lenient,** ADJ.

**lethal** ADJ. deadly. It is unwise to leave *lethal* weapons where children may find them.

■ **lethargic** ADJ. drowsy; dull. The stuffy room made him *lethargic*. lethargy, N.

■ **levity** N. lightness; unseemly frivolity. Such *levity* is improper on this serious occasion.

---

## ETYMOLOGY 17

INTER (between, among) prefix
> **intervene**   come between
> **international**   between nations
> **interjection**   a statement thrown in

IST (one who practices) noun suffix
> **humorist**   one who provides humor
> **optimist**   one who is hopeful

ITY (state of being) noun suffix
> **credulity**   state of being gullible
> **sagacity**   wisdom

IZE, ISE (to make) verb suffix
> **victimize**   make a victim
> **harmonize**   make peaceful

JAC, JACT, JEC (to throw)
> **projectile**   missile; something thrown forward
> **trajectory**   path taken by thrown object
> **reject**   throw back

JUR, JURAT (to swear)
> **abjure**   renounce
> **perjure**   testify falsely
> **jury**   group of men sworn to seek the truth

LABOR, LABORAT (to work)
> **laboratory**   place where work is done
> **collaborate**   work together with others
> **laborious**   difficult

LEG (law)
> **legislature**   law-making body
> **legitimate**   lawful
> **legal**   lawful

---

## TEST — Word List 17 — Antonyms

Each of the questions below consists of a word printed in italics, followed by five words or phrases numbered 1 to 5. Choose the numbered word or phrase which is most nearly opposite in meaning to the word in italics and write the number of your choice on your answer paper.

321. *intermittent*   1 heavy   2 fleeting   3 constant   4 fearless   5 responding
322. *irreverent*   1 related   2 mischievous   3 respecting   4 pious   5 violent

323. *inundate* 1 abuse 2 deny 3 swallow 4 treat 5 drain
324. *laconic* 1 milky 2 verbose 3 wicked 4 flagrant 5 derelict
325. *kindle* 1 quench 2 amuse 3 relate 4 frequent 5 abandon
326. *latent* 1 hidden 2 forbidding 3 execrable 4 early 5 obvious
327. *intransigent* 1 stationary 2 yielding 3 incorruptible 4 magnificent 5 grandiose
328. *jaded* 1 upright 2 stimulated 3 aspiring 4 applied 5 void
329. *levity* 1 bridge 2 dam 3 praise 4 blame 5 solemnity
330. *intricate* 1 simple 2 sophisticated 3 professional 4 wicked 5 ascetic
331. *lampoon* 1 darken 2 praise 3 abandon 4 sail 5 fly
332. *irrelevant* 1 lacking piety 2 fragile 3 congruent 4 pertinent 5 varied
333. *intrepid* 1 cold 2 hot 3 understood 4 callow 5 craven
334. *intrinsic* 1 extrinsic 2 abnormal 3 above 4 abandoned 5 basic
335. *lackadaisical* 1 monthly 2 possessing time 3 ambitious 4 pusillanimous 5 intelligent
336. *lethargic* 1 convalescent 2 beautiful 3 enervating 4 invigorating 5 interrogating
337. *irresolute* 1 accustomed 2 fitted 3 intestate 4 futile 5 decisive
338. *interminable* 1 whitened 2 inflamed 3 uninterrupted 4 aged 5 brief
339. *jubilation* 1 speed 2 mourning 3 fascination 4 pacifism 5 rebellion
340. *laudatory* 1 dirtying 2 disclaiming 3 defamatory 4 inflammatory 5 debased

---

## Word List 18    lewd - mendicant

**lewd** ADJ. lustful. They found his *lewd* stories objectionable.

**lexicon** N. dictionary. I cannot find this word in any *lexicon* in the library. lexicographer, N.

**libelous** ADJ. defamatory; injurious to the good name of a person. He sued the newspaper because of its *libelous* story.

**libretto** N. text of an opera. The composer of an opera's music is remembered more frequently than the author of its *libretto*.

**licentious** ADJ. wanton; lewd; dissolute. The *licentious* monarch helped bring about his country's downfall.

**limpid** ADJ. clear. A *limpid* stream ran through his property.

**linguistic** ADJ. pertaining to language. The modern tourist will encounter very little *linguistic* difficulty as English has become an almost universal language.

**liquidate** V. settle accounts; clear up. She was able to *liquidate* all her debts in a short period of time.

■ **listless** ADJ. lacking in spirit or energy. We had expected him to be full of enthusiasm and were surprised by his *listless* attitude.

**lithe** ADJ. flexible; supple. Her figure was *lithe* and willowy.

**loath** ADJ. averse; reluctant. They were both *loath* for him to go.

**loathe** V. detest. We *loathed* the wicked villain.

■ **lofty** ADJ. very high. They used to tease him about his *lofty* ambitions.

**longevity** N. long life. The old man was proud of his *longevity.*

**loquacious** ADJ. talkative. She is very *loquacious* and can speak on the telephone for hours.

**lout** N. clumsy person. The delivery boy is an awkward *lout.*

■ **lucid** ADJ. bright; easily understood. Her explanation was *lucid* and to the point.

**lucrative** ADJ. profitable. He turned his hobby into a *lucrative* profession.

**lugubrious** ADJ. mournful. The *lugubrious* howling of the dogs added to our sadness.

**luminous** ADJ. shining; issuing light. The sun is a *luminous* body.

**lunar** ADJ. pertaining to the moon. *Lunar* craters can be plainly seen with the aid of a small telescope.

**lurid** ADJ. wild; sensational. The *lurid* stories he told shocked his listeners.

**luscious** ADJ. pleasing to taste or smell. The ripe peach was *luscious.*

**luster** N. shine; gloss. The soft *luster* of the silk in the dim light was pleasing. lustrous, ADJ.

**luxuriant** ADJ. fertile; abundant; ornate. Farming was easy in this *luxuriant* soil.

**macabre** ADJ. gruesome; grisly. The city morgue is a *macabre* spot for the uninitiated.

**Machiavellian** ADJ. crafty; double-dealing. I do not think he will be a good ambassador because he is not accustomed to the *Machiavellian* maneuverings of foreign diplomats.

**machinations** N. schemes. I can see through your wily *machinations.*

**maelstrom** N. whirlpool. The canoe was tossed about in the *maelstrom.*

■ **magnanimous** ADJ. generous. The philanthropist was most *magnanimous.*

**magnate** N. person of prominence or influence. The steel *magnate* decided to devote more time to city politics.

**magnitude** N. greatness; extent. It is difficult to comprehend the *magnitude* of his crime.

**maim** V. mutilate; injure. The hospital could not take care of all who had been wounded or *maimed* in the railroad accident.

**malediction** N. curse. The witch uttered *maledictions* against her captors.

**malefactor** N. criminal. We must try to bring these *malefactors* to justice.

**malevolent** ADJ. wishing evil. We must thwart his *malevolent* schemes.

■ **malicious** ADJ. dictated by hatred or spite. The *malicious* neighbor spread the gossip.

**malign** V. speak evil of; defame. Because of her hatred of the family, she *maligns* all who are friendly to them.

**malignant** ADJ. having an evil influence; virulent. This is a *malignant* disease; we may have to use drastic measures to stop its spread.

**malingerer** N. one who feigns illness to escape duty. The captain ordered the sergeant to punish all *malingerers*.

**malleable** ADJ. capable of being shaped by pounding. Gold is a *malleable* metal.

**mammoth** ADJ. gigantic. The *mammoth* corporations of the twentieth century are a mixed blessing.

**mandatory** ADJ. obligatory. These instructions are *mandatory;* any violation will be severely punished.

**maniacal** ADJ. raving mad. His *maniacal* laughter frightened us.

**manifest** ADJ. understandable; clear. His evil intentions were *manifest* and yet we could not stop him. also V.

**manifesto** N. declaration; statement of policy. This statement may be regarded as the *manifesto* of the party's policy.

**manipulate** V. operate with the hands. How do you *manipulate* these puppets?

**marauder** N. raider; intruder. The sounding of the alarm frightened the *marauders*.

**marital** ADJ. pertaining to marriage. After the publication of his book on *marital* affairs, he was often consulted by married people on the verge of divorce.

**maritime** ADJ. bordering on the sea; nautical. The *Maritime* Provinces depend on the sea for their wealth.

■ **marred** ADJ. damaged. She had to refinish the *marred* surface of the table.

**martial** ADJ. warlike. The sound of *martial* music is always inspiring.

**martinet** N. strict disciplinarian. The commanding officer was a *martinet* who observed each regulation to the letter.

**maternal** ADJ. motherly. Many animals display *maternal* instincts only while their offspring are young and helpless.

**matricide** N. murder of a mother by a child. A crime such as *matricide* is inconceivable.

**maudlin** ADJ. effusively sentimental. I do not like such *maudlin* pictures. I call them tearjerkers.

**maverick** N. rebel. How can you keep such a *maverick* in line?

**maxim** N. proverb; a truth pithily stated. Aesop's fables illustrate moral *maxims*.

■ **meager** ADJ. scanty; inadequate. His salary was far too *meager* for him to afford to buy a new car.

■ **meander** V. to wind or turn in its course. It is difficult to sail up this stream because of the way it *meanders* through the countryside.

**meddlesome** ADJ. interfering. He felt his marriage was suffering because of his *meddlesome* mother-in-law.

**mediate** V. settle a dispute through the services of an outsider. Let us *mediate* our differences rather than engage in a costly strike.

**mediocre** ADJ. ordinary; commonplace. We were disappointed because he gave a rather *mediocre* performance in this role.

**meditation** N. reflection; thought. She reached her decision only after much *meditation*.

**medley** N. mixture. The band played a *medley* of Gershwin tunes.

**mellifluous** ADJ. flowing smoothly; smooth. Italian is a *mellifluous* language.

**memento** N. token; reminder. Take this book as a *memento* of your visit.

**mendacious** ADJ. lying; false. He was a pathological liar, and his friends learned to discount his *mendacious* stories.

**mendicant** N. beggar. From the moment we left the ship, we were surrounded by *mendicants* and peddlers.

---

## ETYMOLOGY 18

LOQU, LOCUT (to talk)
        **soliloquy**   speech by one individual
        **loquacious**   talkative
        **elocution**   speech

LUC (light)
        **elucidate**   enlighten
        **lucid**   clear
        **translucent**   allowing some light to pass through

MAL (bad) prefix
        **malevolent**   evil (wishing bad)
        **malediction**   curse (state of saying evil)
        **malefactor**   evildoer

MAR (sea)
        **maritime**   connected with seafaring
        **submarine**   undersea craft
        **mariner**   seaman

---

## TEST — Word List 18 — Synonyms and Antonyms

Each of the questions below consists of a word printed in italics, followed by five words or phrases numbered 1 to 5. Choose the numbered word or phrase which is most nearly the same as or the opposite of the word in italics and write the number of your choice on your answer paper.

341. *magnitude*  1 realization 2 fascination 3 enormity 4 gratitude 5 interference
342. *maniacal*  1 demoniac 2 saturated 3 sane 4 sanitary 5 handcuffed
343. *loquacious*  1 taciturn 2 sentimental 3 soporific 4 soothing 5 sedate
344. *malefactor*  1 quail 2 lawbreaker 3 beneficiary 4 banker 5 female agent
345. *mellifluous*  1 porous 2 honeycombed 3 strong 4 strident 5 viscous
346. *limpid*  1 erect 2 turbid 3 tangential 4 timid 5 weary
347. *mediocre*  1 average 2 bitter 3 medieval 4 industrial 5 agricultural
348. *macabre*  1 musical 2 frightening 3 chewed 4 wicked 5 exceptional
349. *malign*  1 intersperse 2 vary 3 emphasize 4 frighten 5 eulogize
350. *lithe*  1 stiff 2 limpid 3 facetious 4 insipid 5 vast
351. *lurid*  1 dull 2 duplicate 3 heavy 4 grotesque 5 intelligent
352. *malevolent*  1 kindly 2 vacuous 3 ambivalent 4 volatile 5 primitive
353. *manifest*  1 limited 2 obscure 3 faulty 4 varied 5 vital
354. *loath*  1 loose 2 evident 3 deliberate 4 eager 5 tiny
355. *malediction*  1 misfortune 2 hap 3 fruition 4 correct pronunciation 5 benediction
356. *malignant*  1 loquacious 2 virulent 3 rudimentary 4 qualitative 5 minimizing
357. *lugubrious*  1 frantic 2 cheerful 3 burdensome 4 oily 5 militant
358. *malleable*  1 brittle 2 blatant 3 brilliant 4 brownish 5 basking
359. *martial*  1 bellicose 2 celibate 3 divorced 4 quiescent 5 planetary
360. *meager*  1 alive 2 mundane 3 positive 4 scanty 5 friendly

---

## Word List 19    menial - nadir

**menial** ADJ. suitable for servants; low. I cannot understand why a person of your ability and talent should engage in such *menial* activities. also N.

**mentor** N. teacher. During this very trying period, he could not have had a better *mentor,* for the teacher was sympathetic and understanding.

**mercantile** ADJ. concerning trade. I am more interested in the opportunities available in the *mercantile* field than I am in those in the legal profession.

**mercenary** ADJ. interested in money or gain. I am certain that your action was prompted by *mercenary* motives. also N.

**mercurial** ADJ. fickle; changing. He was of a *mercurial* temperament and therefore unpredictable.

**metamorphosis** N. change of form. The *metamorphosis* of caterpillar to butterfly is typical of many such changes in animal life.

**metaphysical** ADJ. pertaining to speculative philosophy. The modern poets have gone back to the fanciful poems of the *metaphysical* poets of the seventeenth century for many of their images. metaphysics, N.

**mete** V. measure; distribute. She tried to be impartial in her efforts to *mete* out justice.

■ **methodical** ADJ. systematic. An accountant must be *methodical* and maintain order among his financial records.

■ **meticulous** ADJ. excessively careful. He was *meticulous* in checking his accounts.

**metropolis** N. large city. Every evening this terminal is filled with the thousands of commuters who are going from this *metropolis* to their homes in the suburbs.

**mettle** N. courage; spirit. When challenged by the other horses in the race, the thoroughbred proved its *mettle* by its determination to hold the lead.

**migrant** ADJ. changing its habitat; wandering. These *migrant* birds return every spring. also N.

**migratory** ADJ. wandering. The return of the *migratory* birds to the northern sections of this country is a harbinger of spring.

**mincing** ADJ. affectedly dainty. Yum-Yum walked across the stage with *mincing* steps.

■ **minute** ADJ. extremely small. The twins resembled one another closely; only *minute* differences set them apart.

**mirage** N. unreal reflection; optical illusion. The lost prospector was fooled by a *mirage* in the desert.

**misadventure** N. mischance; ill luck. The young explorer met death by *misadventure*.

**misanthrope** N. one who hates mankind. We thought the hermit was a *misanthrope* because he shunned our society.

**misapprehension** N. error; misunderstanding. To avoid *misapprehension*, I am going to ask all of you to repeat the instructions I have given.

**miscellany** N. mixture of writings on various subjects. This is an interesting *miscellany* of nineteenth-century prose.

**mischance** N. ill luck. By *mischance*, he lost his week's salary.

**misdemeanor** N. minor crime. The culprit pleaded guilty to a *misdemeanor* rather than face trial for a felony.

■ **miserly** ADJ. stingy; mean. The *miserly* man hoarded his coins not out of prudence but out of greed.

**misgivings** N. doubts. Hamlet described his *misgivings* to Horatio but decided to fence with Laertes despite his foreboding of evil.

**mishap** N. accident. With a little care you could have avoided this *mishap*.

**misnomer** N. wrong name; incorrect designation. His tyrannical conduct proved to all that his nickname, King Eric the Just, was a *misnomer*.

**missile** N. object to be thrown or projected. Scientists are experimenting with guided *missiles*.

**mite** N. very small object or creature; small coin. The criminal was so heartless that he even stole the widow's *mite*.

■ **mitigate** V. appease. Nothing he did could *mitigate* her wrath; she was unforgiving.

**mobile** ADJ. movable; not fixed. The *mobile* blood bank operated by the Red Cross visited our neighborhood today. mobility, N.

**modicum** N. limited quantity. Although his story is based on a *modicum* of truth, most of the events he describes are fictitious.

**modish** ADJ. fashionable. She always discarded all garments which were no longer *modish*.

**modulation** N. toning down; changing from one key to another. When she spoke, it was with quiet *modulation* of voice.

**mollify** V. soothe. We tried to *mollify* the hysterical child by promising her many gifts.

**molt** V. shed or cast off hair or feathers. The male robin *molted* in the spring.

**molten** ADJ. melted. The city of Pompeii was destroyed by volcanic ash rather than by *molten* lava flowing from Mount Vesuvius.

**momentous** ADJ. very important. On this *momentous* occasion, we must be very solemn.

**monotony** N. sameness leading to boredom. He took a clerical job, but soon grew to hate the *monotony* of his daily routine.

**moodiness** N. fits of depression or gloom. We could not discover the cause of his recurrent *moodiness*.

**moot** ADJ. debatable. Our tariff policy is a *moot* subject.

**morbid** ADJ. given to unwholesome thought; gloomy. These *morbid* speculations are dangerous; we must lighten our thinking by emphasis on more pleasant matters.

**mores** N. customs. The *mores* of Mexico are those of Spain with some modifications.

**moribund** ADJ. at the point of death. The doctors called the family to the bedside of the *moribund* patient.

■ **morose** ADJ. ill-humored; sullen. When we first meet Hamlet, we find him *morose* and depressed.

**mortician** N. undertaker. The *mortician* prepared the corpse for burial.

**mortify** V. humiliate; punish the flesh. She was so *mortified* by her blunder that she ran to her room in tears.

**motif** N. theme. This simple *motif* runs throughout the entire score.

**motley** ADJ. parti-colored; mixed. The captain had gathered a *motley* crew to sail the vessel.

**muddle** V. confuse; mix up. His thoughts were *muddled* and chaotic. also N.

**mundane** ADJ. worldly as opposed to spiritual. He was concerned only with *mundane* matters, especially the daily stock market quotations.

**munificent** ADJ. very generous. The *munificent* gift was presented to the bride.

**murkiness** N. darkness; gloom. The *murkiness* and fog of the waterfront that evening depressed me.

**muse** V. ponder. For a moment he *mused* about the beauty of the scene, but his thoughts soon changed as he recalled his own personal problems. also N.

**musty** ADJ. stale; spoiled by age. The attic was dark and *musty*.

**mutable** ADJ. changing in form; fickle. His opinions were *mutable* and easily influenced by anyone who had any powers of persuasion.

■ **muted** ADJ. silent; muffled; toned down. In the funeral parlor, the mourners' voices had a *muted* quality. mute, V.

**mutilate** V. maim. The torturer threatened to *mutilate* his victim.

**mutinous** ADJ. unruly; rebellious. The captain had to use force to quiet his *mutinous* crew.

**myriad** N. very large number. *Myriads* of mosquitoes from the swamps invaded our village every twilight. also ADJ.

**nadir** N. lowest point. Although few people realized it, the Dow-Jones averages had reached their *nadir* and would soon begin an upward surge.

## ETYMOLOGY 19

MITT, MISS (to send)

| | |
|---|---|
| **missile** | projectile |
| **admit** | allow in |
| **dismiss** | send away |
| **transmit** | send across |

MORI, MORT (to die)

| | |
|---|---|
| **mortuary** | funeral parlor |
| **moribund** | dying |
| **immortal** | not dying |

## TEST — Word List 19 — Synonyms

Each of the questions below consists of a word printed in italics, followed by five words or phrases numbered 1 to 5. Choose the numbered word or phrase which is most nearly similar in meaning to the word in italics and write the number of your choice on your answer paper.

361. *modish* 1 sentimental 2 stylish 3 vacillating 4 contrary 5 adorned
362. *methodical* 1 dying 2 systematic 3 fabricating 4 controlling 5 avenging
363. *mollify* 1 avenge 2 attenuate 3 attribute 4 mortify 5 appease
364. *menial* 1 intellectual 2 clairvoyant 3 servile 4 arrogant 5 laudatory
365. *minute* 1 extremely small 2 appropriate 3 leather bound 4 answering 5 hasty
366. *mirage* 1 dessert 2 illusion 3 water 4 mirror 5 statement
367. *mischance* 1 opportunity 2 ordinance 3 aperture 4 anecdote 5 adversity
368. *mundane* 1 global 2 futile 3 spiritual 4 heretic 5 worldly
369. *methodical* 1 variegated 2 systematic 3 multilateral 4 monotonous 5 multiplied
370. *moot* 1 visual 2 invisible 3 controversial 4 anticipatory 5 obsequious
371. *motley* 1 active 2 disguised 3 variegated 4 somber 5 sick
372. *mitigate* 1 appease 2 hold 3 record 4 print 5 fertilize
373. *munificent* 1 grandiose 2 puny 3 philanthropic 4 poor 5 gracious
374. *muted* 1 boring 2 fascinating 3 toned down 4 stationary 5 changed completely
375. *misanthrope* 1 benefactor 2 philanderer 3 hermit 4 aesthete 5 epicure
376. *mentor* 1 guide 2 genius 3 talker 4 philosopher 5 stylist
377. *meticulous* 1 steadfast 2 remiss 3 quaint 4 painstaking 5 overt
378. *muggy* 1 attacking 2 fascinating 3 humid 4 characteristic 5 gelid
379. *musty* 1 flat 2 necessary 3 indifferent 4 nonchalant 5 vivid
380. *misdemeanor* 1 felony 2 peccadillo 3 indignity 4 fiat 5 illiteracy

---

## Word List 20    naiveté - optional

**naiveté** N. quality of being unsophisticated. I cannot believe that such *naiveté* is unassumed in a person of her age and experience.

**natal** ADJ. pertaining to birth. He refused to celebrate his *natal* day because it reminded him of the few years he could look forward to.

**nauseate** V. cause to become sick; fill with disgust. The foul smells began to *nauseate* her.

**nebulous** ADJ. cloudy; hazy. Your theories are too *nebulous;* please clarify them.

**nefarious** ADJ. very wicked. He was universally feared because of his many *nefarious* deeds.

**negation** N. denial. I must accept his argument since you have been unable to present any *negation* of his evidence.

**nemesis** N. revenging agent. Captain Bligh vowed to be Christian's *nemesis.*

**neologism** N. new or newly coined word or phrase. As we invent new techniques and professions, we must also invent *neologisms* such as "microcomputer" and "astronaut" to describe them.

**neophyte** N. recent convert; beginner. This mountain slope contains slides that will challenge experts as well as *neophytes*.

**nettle** V. annoy; vex. Do not let him *nettle* you with his sarcastic remarks.

**nexus** N. connection. I fail to see the *nexus* which binds these two widely separated events.

**nicety** N. precision; minute distinction. I cannot distinguish between such *niceties* of reasoning.

**nocturnal** ADJ. done at night. Mr. Jones obtained a watchdog to prevent the *nocturnal* raids on his chicken coops.

**noisome** ADJ. foul smelling; unwholesome. I never could stand the *noisome* atmosphere surrounding the slaughter houses.

**nomadic** ADJ. wandering. Several *nomadic* tribes of Indians would hunt in this area each year.

**nominal** ADJ. in name only; trifling, insignificant. He offered to drive her to the airport for only a *nominal* fee.

**nonchalance** N. indifference; lack of interest. Few people could understand how he could listen to the news of the tragedy with such *nonchalance;* the majority regarded him as callous and unsympathetic.

**noncommittal** ADJ. neutral; unpledged; undecided. We were annoyed by his *noncommittal* reply for we had been led to expect definite assurances of his approval.

**nonentity** N. nonexistence; person of no importance. Of course you are a *nonentity;* you will continue to be one until you prove your value to the community.

**nostalgia** N. homesickness; longing for the past. The first settlers found so much work to do that they had little time for *nostalgia*.

**notorious** ADJ. outstandingly bad; unfavorably known. Captain Kidd was a *notorious* pirate. notoriety, N.

■ **novelty** N. something new; newness. The computer is no longer a *novelty* around the office. novel, ADJ.

**novice** N. beginner. Even a *novice* can do good work if he follows these simple directions.

**noxious** ADJ. harmful. We must trace the source of these *noxious* gases before they asphyxiate us.

**nullify** V. to make invalid. Once the contract was *nullified,* it no longer had any legal force.

**numismatist** N. person who collects coins. The *numismatist* had a splendid collection of antique coins.

**nurture** V. bring up; feed; educate. We must *nurture* the young so that they will develop into good citizens.

**nutrient** ADJ. providing nourishment. During the convalescent period, the patient must be provided with *nutrient* foods. also N.

**oaf** N. stupid, awkward person. He called the unfortunate waiter a clumsy *oaf*.

**obdurate** ADJ. stubborn. He was *obdurate* in his refusal to listen to our complaints.

**obese** ADJ. fat. It is advisable that *obese* people try to lose weight.

**obituary** ADJ. death notice. I first learned of his death when I read the *obituary* column in the newspaper. also N.

■ **objective** ADJ. not influenced by emotions; fair. Even though he was her son, she tried to be *objective* about his behavior. objectivity, N.

■ **objective** N. goal; aim. A degree in medicine was her ultimate *objective*.

**oblique** ADJ. slanting; deviating from the perpendicular or from a straight line. The sergeant ordered the men to march "*Oblique* Right."

■ **obliterate** V. destroy completely. The tidal wave *obliterated* several island villages.

■ **oblivion** N. forgetfulness. Her works had fallen into a state of *oblivion;* no one bothered to read them.

**obnoxious** ADJ. offensive. I find your behavior *obnoxious;* please amend your ways.

■ **obscure** ADJ. dark; vague; unclear. Even after I read the poem a fourth time, its meaning was still *obscure*. obscurity, N.

■ **obscure** V. darken; make unclear. At times he seemed purposely to *obscure* his meaning, preferring mystery to clarity.

**obsequious** ADJ. slavishly attentive; servile; sycophantic. Nothing is more disgusting to me than the *obsequious* demeanor of the people who wait upon you.

**obsession** N. fixed idea; continued brooding. This *obsession* with the supernatural has made him unpopular with his neighbors.

■ **obsolete** ADJ. outmoded. That word is *obsolete;* do not use it.

■ **obstinate** ADJ. stubborn. We tried to persuade him to give up smoking, but he was *obstinate* and refused to change.

**obtrusive** ADJ. pushing forward. I found him a very *obtrusive* person, constantly seeking the center of the stage.

**obtuse** ADJ. blunt; stupid. Because he was so *obtuse,* he could not follow the teacher's reasoning and asked foolish questions.

**obviate** V. make unnecessary; get rid of. I hope this contribution will *obviate* any need for further collections of funds.

**occult** ADJ. mysterious; secret; supernatural. The *occult* rites of the organization were revealed only to members. also N.

**odious** ADJ. hateful. I find the task of punishing you most *odious*. odium, N.

**odorous** ADJ. having an odor. This variety of hybrid tea rose is more *odorous* than the one you have in your garden.

**officious** ADJ. meddlesome; excessively trying to please. Browning informs us that the Duke resented the bough of cherries some *officious* fool brought to the Duchess.

**ogle** V. glance coquettishly at; make eyes at. Sitting for hours at the sidewalk cafe, the old gentleman would *ogle* the young girls and recall his youthful romances.

**olfactory** ADJ. concerning the sense of smell. The *olfactory* organ is the nose.

■ **ominous** ADJ. threatening. These clouds are *ominous;* they portend a severe storm.

**omnipotent** ADJ. all-powerful. The monarch regarded himself as *omnipotent* and responsible to no one for his acts.

**omniscient** ADJ. all-knowing. I do not pretend to be *omniscient,* but I am positive about this item.

**omnivorous** ADJ. eating both plant and animal food; devouring everything. Some animals, including man, are *omnivorous* and eat both meat and vegetables; others are either carnivorous or herbivorous.

**onslaught** N. vicious assault. We suffered many casualties during the unexpected *onslaught* of the enemy troops.

■ **opaque** ADJ. dark; not transparent. The *opaque* shade in the window kept the sunlight out of the room. opacity, N.

**opportune** ADJ. timely; well chosen. You have come at an *opportune* moment for I need a new secretary.

■ **opportunist** N. individual who sacrifices principles for expediency by taking advantage of situations. As an *opportunist,* he'll vote in favor of any bill that is personally advantageous to him.

■ **optimist** N. person who looks on the good side. The pessimist says the glass is half-empty; the *optimist* says it is half-full.

**optional** ADJ. not compulsory; left to one's choice. I was impressed by the range of *optional* accessories available for my microcomputer. option, N.

---

## ETYMOLOGY 20

NAV (ship)

    **navigate**   sail a ship
    **circumnavigate**   sail around the world
    **naval**   pertaining to ships

OMNI (all)

    **omniscient**   all knowing
    **omnipotent**   all powerful
    **omnivorous**   eating everything

OPER (to work)

    **operate**   work
    **cooperation**   working together
    **opera**   musical drama (specialized kind of work)

## TEST — Word List 20 — Antonyms

Each of the questions below consists of a word printed in italics, followed by five words or phrases numbered 1 to 5. Choose the numbered word or phrase which is most nearly opposite in meaning to the word in italics and write the number of your choice on your answer paper.

381. *obsession* 1 whim 2 loss 3 phobia 4 delusion 5 feud
382. *nefarious* 1 wanton 2 lacking 3 benign 4 impious 5 futile
383. *obdurate* 1 yielding 2 fleeting 3 finite 4 fascinating 5 permanent
384. *obtuse* 1 sheer 2 transparent 3 tranquil 4 timid 5 shrewd
385. *nocturnal* 1 harsh 2 marauding 3 patrolling 4 daily 5 fallow
386. *novelty* 1 old hat 2 rectangle 3 circle 4 dialogue 5 cure
387. *neophyte* 1 veteran 2 satellite 3 aspirant 4 handwriting 5 violence
388. *opportune* 1 occasional 2 fragrant 3 fragile 4 awkward 5 neglected
389. *obese* 1 skillful 2 cadaverous 3 clever 4 unpredictable 5 lucid
390. *oblivion* 1 distress 2 sleep 3 fame 4 laziness 5 despair
391. *notorious* 1 fashionable 2 renowned 3 infamous 4 intrepid 5 invincible
392. *odious* 1 fragrant 2 redolent 3 fetid 4 delightful 5 puny
393. *nebulous* 1 starry 2 clear 3 cold 4 fundamental 5 porous
394. *omniscient* 1 sophisticated 2 ignorant 3 essential 4 trivial 5 isolated
395. *obsolete* 1 heated 2 desolate 3 renovated 4 frightful 5 automatic
396. *obscure* 1 protected 2 biased 3 clear 4 bankrupt 5 placated
397. *omnipotent* 1 weak 2 democratic 3 despotic 4 passionate 5 late
398. *negation* 1 postulation 2 hypothecation 3 affirmation 4 violation 5 anticipation
399. *noisome* 1 quiet 2 dismayed 3 fragrant 4 sleepy 5 inquisitive
400. *obsequious* 1 successful 2 democratic 3 supercilious 4 ambitious 5 lamentable

## Word List 21   opulence - perfunctory

**opulence** N. wealth. Visitors from Europe are amazed at the *opulence* of this country.

**ordinance** N. decree. Passing a red light is a violation of a city *ordinance*.

**ornate** ADJ. excessively decorated; highly decorated. Furniture of the Baroque period can be recognized by its *ornate* carvings.

**oscillate** V. vibrate pendulumlike; waver. It is interesting to note how public opinion *oscillates* between the extremes of optimism and pessimism.

**ostensible** ADJ. apparent; professed; pretended. Although the *ostensible* purpose of this expedition is to discover new lands, we are really interested in finding new markets for our products.

**ostentatious** ADJ. showy; pretentious. The real hero is never *ostentatious*.

**ostracize** V. exclude from public favor; ban. As soon as the newspapers carried the story of his connection with the criminals, his friends began to *ostracize* him. ostracism, N.

**overt** ADJ. open to view. According to the United States Constitution, a person must commit an *overt* act before he may be tried for treason.

**pacifist** N. one opposed to force; antimilitarist. The *pacifists* urged that we reduce our military budget and recall our troops stationed overseas.

■ **painstaking** ADJ. showing hard work; taking great care. The new high frequency word list is the result of *painstaking* efforts on the part of our research staff.

**palatable** ADJ. agreeable; pleasing to the taste. Paying taxes can never be made *palatable*.

**palatial** ADJ. magnificent. She proudly showed us through her *palatial* home.

**palette** N. board on which painter mixes pigments. At the present time, art supply stores are selling a paper *palette* which may be discarded after use.

**palliate** V. ease pain; make less guilty or offensive. Doctors must *palliate* that which they cannot cure.

**pallid** ADJ. pale; wan. Because his occupation required that he work at night and sleep during the day, he had an exceptionally *pallid* complexion.

**palpable** ADJ. tangible; easily perceptible. I cannot understand how you could overlook such a *palpable* blunder.

**palpitate** V. throb; flutter. As he became excited, his heart began to *palpitate* more and more erratically.

**paltry** ADJ. insignificant; petty. This is a *paltry* sum to pay for such a masterpiece.

**panacea** N. cure-all; remedy for all diseases. There is no easy *panacea* that will solve our complicated international situation.

**pandemonium** N. wild tumult. When the ships collided in the harbor, *pandemonium* broke out among the passengers.

**panegyric** N. formal praise. The modest hero blushed as he listened to the *panegyrics* uttered by the speakers about his valorous act.

**panorama** N. comprehensive view; unobstructed view in all directions. Tourists never forget the impact of their first *panorama* of the Grand Canyon.

**pantomime** N. acting without dialogue. Because he worked in *pantomime*, the clown could be understood wherever he appeared. also V.

**papyrus** N. ancient paper made from stem of papyrus plant. The ancient Egyptians were among the first to write on *papyrus*.

**parable** N. short, simple story teaching a moral. Let us apply to our own conduct the lesson that this *parable* teaches.

**paradox** N. statement that looks false but is actually correct; a contradictory statement. Wordsworth's ''The child is father to the man'' is an example of *paradox*.

**paragon** N. model of perfection. The class disliked him because the teacher was always pointing to him as a *paragon* of virtue.

**parallelism** N. state of being parallel; similarity. There is a striking *parallelism* between the two ages.

**paranoia** N. chronic form of insanity marked by delusions of grandeur or persecution. The psychiatrists analyzed his ailment as *paranoia*.

**paraphernalia** N. equipment; odds and ends. His desk was cluttered with paper, pen, ink, dictionary and other *paraphernalia* of the writing craft.

**paraphrase** V. restate a passage in one's own words while retaining thought of author. In 250 words or less, *paraphrase* this article. also N.

**parasite** N. animal or plant living on another; toady; sycophant. The tapeworm is an example of the kind of *parasite* that may infest the human body.

**pariah** N. social outcast. I am not a *pariah* to be shunned and ostracized.

■ **parochial** ADJ. narrow in outlook; provincial; related to parishes. Although Jane Austen writes novels set in small rural communities, her concerns are universal, not *parochial*.

**parody** N. humorous imitation; travesty. We enjoyed the clever *parodies* of popular songs which the chorus sang.

**paroxysm** N. fit or attack of pain, laughter, rage. When he heard of his son's misdeeds, he was seized by a *paroxysm* of rage.

**parry** V. ward off a blow. He was content to wage a defensive battle and tried to *parry* his opponent's thrusts.

**parsimonious** ADJ. stingy; excessively frugal. His *parsimonious* nature did not permit him to enjoy any luxuries.

■ **partial** ADJ. incomplete. In this issue we have published only a *partial* list of contributors because we lack space to acknowledge everyone.

■ **partial** ADJ. biased; having a liking for something. I am extremely *partial* to chocolate eclairs. partiality, N.

■ **partisan** ADJ. one-sided; prejudiced; committed to a party. On certain issues of conscience, she refused to take a *partisan* stand. also N.

**passive** ADJ. not active; acted upon. Mahatma Gandhi urged his followers to pursue a program of *passive* resistance as he felt that it was more effective than violence and acts of terrorism.

**pastoral** ADJ. rural. In these stories of *pastoral* life, we find an understanding of the daily tasks of country folk.

**patent** ADJ. open for the public to read; obvious. It was *patent* to everyone that the witness spoke the truth. also N.

**pathetic** ADJ. causing sadness, compassion, pity; touching. Everyone in the auditorium was weeping by the time he finished his *pathetic* tale about the orphaned boy.

**pathos** N. tender sorrow; pity; quality in art or literature that produces these feelings. The quiet tone of *pathos* that ran through the novel never degenerated into the maudlin or the overly sentimental.

**patriarch** N. father and ruler of a family or tribe. In many primitive tribes, the leader and lawmaker was the *patriarch*.

**patronize** V. act superior toward. Experts in a field sometimes appear to *patronize* people who are less knowledgeable of the subject.

■ **paucity** N. scarcity. The poor test papers indicate that the members of this class have a *paucity* of intelligence.

■ **pedantic** ADJ. showing off learning; bookish. What you say is *pedantic* and reveals an unfamiliarity with the realities of life. pedant, N.

**pell-mell** ADV. in confusion; disorderly. The excited students dashed *pell-mell* into the stadium to celebrate the victory.

**penance** N. self-imposed punishment for sin. The Ancient Mariner said, "I have *penance* done and *penance* more will do," to atone for the sin of killing the albatross.

**penchant** N. strong inclination; liking. He had a strong *penchant* for sculpture.

**penitent** ADJ. repentant. When he realized the enormity of his crime, he became remorseful and *penitent*. also N.

**pensive** ADJ. dreamily thoughtful; thoughtful with a hint of sadness. The *pensive* youth gazed at the painting for a long time and then sighed.

**penurious** ADJ. stingy; parsimonious. He was a *penurious* man, averse to spending money even for the necessities of life.

**penury** N. extreme poverty. We find much *penury* and suffering in this slum area.

**perdition** N. damnation; complete ruin. She was damned to eternal *perdition*.

**peremptory** ADJ. demanding and leaving no choice. I resent your *peremptory* attitude.

**perennial** N. lasting. These plants are hardy *perennials* and will bloom for many years. also ADJ.

**perfidy** N. violation of a trust. When we learned of his *perfidy*, we were shocked and dismayed. perfidious, ADJ.

**perfunctory** ADJ. superficial; listless; not thorough. He overlooked many weaknesses when he inspected the factory in his *perfunctory* manner.

## ETYMOLOGY 21

PAC (peace)
>**pacify**  make peaceful
>**pacific**  peaceful
>**pacifist**  person opposed to war

PEL, PULS (to drive)
>**compulsion**  a forcing to do
>**repel**  drive back
>**expel**  drive out, banish

---

## TEST — Word List 21 — Synonyms and Antonyms

Each of the following questions consists of a word printed in italics, followed by five words or phrases numbered 1 to 5. Choose the numbered word or phrase which is most nearly the same as or the opposite of the word in italics and write the number of your choice on your answer paper.

401. *ostentatious*  1 occasional 2 flashy 3 intermittent 4 authentic 5 hospitable
402. *palliate*  1 smoke 2 quicken 3 substitute 4 alleviate 5 sadden
403. *pandemonium*  1 calm 2 frustration 3 efficiency 4 impishness 5 sophistication
404. *pariah*  1 village 2 suburb 3 outcast 4 disease 5 benefactor
405. *parochial*  1 proud 2 inconsequential 3 provincial 4 devious 5 unwarranted
406. *penchant*  1 distance 2 imminence 3 dislike 4 attitude 5 void
407. *perennial*  1 flowering 2 recurring 3 centennial 4 partial 5 deciduous
408. *partial*  1 logistical 2 philandering 3 biased 4 vagrant 5 warranted
409. *paucity*  1 pouch 2 peace 3 quickness 4 abundance 5 nuisance
410. *panegyric*  1 medication 2 panacea 3 rotation 4 vacillation 5 praise
411. *penitent*  1 dilatory 2 suspended 3 imprisoned 4 unremorseful 5 calculating
412. *opulence*  1 pessimism 2 patriotism 3 potency 4 passion 5 poverty
413. *painstaking*  1 careless 2 harmless 3 powerless 4 wounding 5 unemployed
414. *parable*  1 equality 2 allegory 3 frenzy 4 folly 5 cuticle
415. *paranoia*  1 fracture 2 statement 3 quantity 4 benefaction 5 sanity
416. *parsimonious*  1 grammatical 2 syntactical 3 effective 4 extravagant 5 esoteric

417. *penurious* 1 imprisoned 2 captivated 3 parsimonious 4 vacant 5 abolished
418. *perfunctory* 1 official 2 thorough 3 insipid 4 vicarious 5 distinctive
419. *perfidy* 1 perfection 2 hesitation 3 affluence 4 normality 5 loyalty
420. *paradox* 1 exaggeration 2 contradiction 3 hyperbole 4 invective 5 poetic device

---

### Word List 22    perimeter - precedent (n)

**perimeter** N. outer boundary. To find the *perimeter* of any quadrilateral, we add the four sides.

■ **peripheral** ADJ. marginal; outer. We lived, not in central London, but in one of those *peripheral* suburbs that spring up on the outskirts of a great city. periphery, N.

**perjury** N. false testimony while under oath. When several witnesses appeared to challenge his story, he was indicted for *perjury*.

**permeable** ADJ. porous; allowing passage through. Glass is *permeable* to light.

**permeate** V. pass through; spread. The odor of frying onions *permeated* the air.

**pernicious** ADJ. very destructive. He argued that these books had a *pernicious* effect on young and susceptible minds.

**perpetrate** V. commit an offense. Only an insane person could *perpetrate* such a horrible crime.

**perpetual** ADJ. everlasting. Ponce de Leon hoped to find *perpetual* youth.

**perspicacious** ADJ. having insight; penetrating; astute. We admired his *perspicacious* wisdom and sagacity.

**pert** ADJ. impertinent; forward. I think your *pert* and impudent remarks call for an apology.

**pertinent** ADJ. suitable; to the point. The lawyer wanted to know all the *pertinent* details.

**perturb** V. disturb greatly. I am afraid this news will *perturb* him. perturbation, N.

**perusal** N. reading. I am certain that you have missed important details in your rapid *perusal* of this document. peruse, V.

**pervade** V. spread throughout. As the news of the defeat *pervaded* the country, a feeling of anger directed at the rulers who had been the cause of the disaster grew.

**perverse** ADJ. stubborn; intractable. Because of your *perverse* attitude, I must rate you as deficient in cooperation.

**perversion** N. corruption; turning from right to wrong. Inasmuch as he had no motive for his crimes, we could not understand his *perversion*.

**perversity** N. stubborn maintenance of a wrong cause. I cannot forgive your *perversity* in repeating such an impossible story.

■ **pessimism** N. belief that life is basically bad or evil; gloominess. The good news we have been receiving lately indicates that there is little reason for your *pessimism*.

**petrify** V. turn to stone. His sudden and unexpected appearance seemed to *petrify* her.

■ **petty** ADJ. trivial; unimportant; very small. She had no major complaints about his work, only a few *petty* quibbles that were almost too minor to state.

**petulant** ADJ. touchy; peevish. The feverish patient was *petulant* and restless.

■ **phenomena** N. observable facts; subjects of scientific investigation. We kept careful records of the *phenomena* we noted in the course of these experiments.

**philanthropist** N. lover of mankind; doer of good. As he grew older, he became famous as a *philanthropist* and benefactor of the needy.

**philistine** N. narrow-minded person, uncultured and exclusively interested in material gain. We need more men of culture and enlightenment; we have too many *philistines* among us.

**phlegmatic** ADJ. calm; not easily disturbed. The nurse was a cheerful but *phlegmatic* person.

**physiognomy** N. face. He prided himself on his ability to analyze a person's character by studying his *physiognomy*.

**pied** ADJ. variegated; multicolored. The *Pied* Piper of Hamelin got his name from the multicolored clothing he wore.

**pillage** V. plunder. The enemy *pillaged* the quiet village and left it in ruins.

**pinnacle** N. peak. We could see the morning sunlight illuminate the *pinnacle* while the rest of the mountain lay in shadow.

■ **pious** ADJ. devout. The *pious* parents gave their children a religious up-bringing.

**piquant** ADJ. pleasantly tart-tasting; stimulating. The *piquant* sauce added to our enjoyment of the meal. piquancy, N.

**pique** N. irritation; resentment. She showed her *pique* by her refusal to appear with the other contestants at the end of the contest.

**pithy** ADJ. concise; meaty. I enjoy reading his essays because they are always compact and *pithy*.

■ **placate** V. pacify; conciliate. The teacher tried to *placate* the angry mother.

**placid** ADJ. peaceful; calm. After his vacation in this *placid* section, he felt soothed and rested.

**plagiarism** N. theft of another's ideas or writings passed off as original. The editor recognized the *plagiarism* and rebuked the culprit who had presented the manuscript as original.

**plaintive** ADJ. mournful. The dove has a *plaintive* and melancholy call.

**platitude** N. trite remark; commonplace statement. The *platitudes* in his speech were applauded by the vast majority in his audience; only a few people perceived how trite his remarks were.

■ **plausible** ADJ. having a show of truth but open to doubt; specious. Even though your argument is *plausible*, I still would like to have more proof.

**plebeian** ADJ. common; pertaining to the common people. His speeches were aimed at the *plebeian* minds and emotions; they disgusted the more refined.

**plethora** N. excess; overabundance. She offered a *plethora* of reasons for her shortcomings.

**podium** N. pedestal; raised platform. The audience applauded as the conductor made his way to the *podium*.

**poignant** ADJ. keen; piercing; severe. Her *poignant* grief left her pale and weak.

**politic** ADJ. expedient; prudent; well devised. Even though he was disappointed, he did not think it *politic* to refuse this offer.

**polyglot** ADJ. speaking several languages. New York City is a *polyglot* community because of the thousands of immigrants who settle there.

■ **pomposity** N. self-important behavior; acting like a stuffed shirt. Although the commencement speaker had some good things to say, we had to laugh at his *pomposity* and general air of parading his own dignity. pompous, ADJ.

**ponderous** ADJ. weighty; unwieldly. His humor lacked the light touch; his jokes were always *ponderous*.

**portend** V. foretell; presage. The king did not know what these omens might *portend* and asked his soothsayers to interpret them.

**portent** N. sign; omen; forewarning. She regarded the black cloud as a *portent* of evil. portentous, ADJ.

**portly** ADJ. stately; stout. The overweight gentleman was shown a size 44 *portly* suit.

**posterity** N. descendants; future generations. We hope to leave a better world to *posterity*.

**posthumous** ADJ. after death (as of child born after father's death or book published after author's death). The critics ignored his works during his lifetime; it was only after the *posthumous* publication of his last novel that they recognized his great talent.

**postulate** N. self-evident truth. We must accept these statements as *postulates* before pursuing our discussions any further. also V.

■ **potent** ADJ. powerful; persuasive; greatly influential. The jury was swayed by the highly *potent* testimony of the crime's sole eyewitness. potency, N.

**potentate** N. monarch; sovereign. The *potentate* spent more time at Monte Carlo than he did at home with his people.

**potential** ADJ. expressing possibility; latent. This juvenile delinquent is a *potential* murderer. also N.

**practical** ADJ. based on experience; useful. He was a *practical* man, opposed to theory.

**pragmatic** ADJ. practical; concerned with practical values. This test should provide us with a *pragmatic* analysis of the value of this course.

**prate** V. speak foolishly; boast idly. Let us not *prate* about our qualities; rather, let our virtues speak for themselves.

**prattle** V. babble. The children *prattled* endlessly about their new toys. also N.

**preamble** N. introductory statement. In the *Preamble* to the Constitution, the purpose of the document is set forth.

**precarious** ADJ. uncertain; risky. I think this stock is a *precarious* investment and advise against its purchase.

**precedent** N. something preceding in time which may be used as an authority or guide for future action. This decision sets a *precedent* for future cases of a similar nature.

---

# ETYMOLOGY 22

PON, POSIT (to place)
        **postpone**   place after
        **preposition**   that which goes before
        **positive**   definite, unquestioned (definitely placed)
PORT, PORTAT (to carry)
        **portable**   able to be carried
        **transport**   carry across
        **export**   carry out (of country)

---

# TEST — Word List 22 — Synonyms

Each of the questions below consists of a word printed in italics, followed by five words or phrases numbered 1 to 5. Choose the numbered word or phrase which is most nearly similar in meaning to the word in italics and write the number of your choice on your answer paper.

421. *pillage* 1 hoard 2 plunder 3 versify 4 denigrate 5 confide
422. *petrify* 1 turn to water 2 refine 3 turn to stone 4 turn to gas 5 repeat
423. *pernicious* 1 practical 2 comparative 3 destructive 4 tangible 5 detailed
424. *physiognomy* 1 posture 2 head 3 physique 4 face 5 size
425. *pertinent* 1 understood 2 living 3 discontented 4 puzzling 5 relevant
426. *permeate* 1 enlarge 2 produce 3 prod 4 disfigure 5 spread
427. *phlegmatic* 1 calm 2 cryptic 3 practical 4 salivary 5 dishonest
428. *pithy* 1 concise 2 consumptive 3 superficial 4 skilled 5 advertised
429. *permeable* 1 perishable 2 effective 3 plodding 4 porous 5 lasting
430. *perturb* 1 disturb 2 quiz 3 decline 4 profit 5 quarrel
431. *pert* 1 impertinent 2 perishable 3 moral 4 deliberate 5 stubborn
432. *potent* 1 worldly 2 powerful 3 disarming 4 seeking 5 inherent
433. *petulant* 1 angry 2 moral 3 declining 4 underhanded 5 touchy
434. *perpetual* 1 eternal 2 standard 3 serious 4 industrial 5 interpretive
435. *plaintive* 1 mournful 2 senseless 3 persistent 4 rural 5 evasive
436. *prattle* 1 express 2 report 3 reveal 4 submit 5 babble
437. *placate* 1 determine 2 transmit 3 pacify 4 allow 5 define
438. *pinnacle* 1 foothills 2 card game 3 pass 4 taunt 5 peak
439. *pique* 1 pyramid 2 revolt 3 resentment 4 struggle 5 inventory
440. *pious* 1 historic 2 devout 3 multiple 4 fortunate 5 authoritative

---

### Word List 23    precedent (adj.) - purport

**precedent** ADJ. preceding in time, rank, etc. Our discussions, *precedent* to this event, certainly did not give you any reason to believe that we would adopt your proposal.

**precept** N. practical rule guiding conduct. "Love thy neighbor as thyself" is a worthwhile *precept*.

**precipitate** ADJ. headlong; rash. Do not be *precipitate* in this matter; investigate further.

**precipitate** V. throw headlong; hasten. We must be patient as we cannot *precipitate* these results.

**precipitous** ADJ. steep. This hill is difficult to climb because it is so *precipitous*.

**precise** ADJ. exact. If you don't give me *precise* directions and a map, I'll never find your place.

■ **preclude** V. make impossible; eliminate. This contract does not *preclude* my being employed by others at the same time that I am working for you.

**precocious** ADJ. advanced in development. By her rather adult manner of discussing serious topics, the child demonstrated that she was *precocious.*

**predatory** ADJ. plundering. The hawk is a *predatory* bird.

■ **predecessor** N. former occupant of a post. I hope I can live up to the fine example set by my late *predecessor* in this office.

**predilection** N. partiality; preference. Although the artist used various media from time to time, he had a *predilection* for watercolor.

**preeminent** ADJ. outstanding; superior. The king traveled to Boston because he wanted the *preeminent* surgeon in the field to perform the operation.

**prelude** N. introduction; forerunner. I am afraid that this border raid is the *prelude* to more serious attacks.

**premeditate** V. plan in advance. He had *premeditated* the murder for months, reading about common poisons and buying weed-killer that contained arsenic.

**premonition** N. forewarning. We ignored these *premonitions* of disaster because they appeared to be based on childish fears.

**preposterous** ADJ. absurd; ridiculous. The excuse he gave for his lateness was so *preposterous* that everyone laughed.

**presentiment** N. premonition; foreboding. Hamlet felt a *presentiment* about his meeting with Laertes.

**prestige** N. impression produced by achievements or reputation. The wealthy man sought to obtain social *prestige* by contributing to popular charities.

**presumption** N. arrogance; effrontery. She had the *presumption* to disregard our advice.

■ **pretentious** ADJ. ostentatious; ambitious. I do not feel that your limited resources will permit you to carry out such a *pretentious* program.

**prevaricate** V. lie. Some people believe that to *prevaricate* in a good cause is justifiable and regard the statement as a "white lie."

**prim** ADJ. very precise and formal; exceedingly proper. Many people commented on the contrast between the *prim* attire of the young lady and the inappropriate clothing worn by her escort.

**primordial** ADJ. existing at the beginning (of time); rudimentary. The Neanderthal Man is one of our *primordial* ancestors.

**pristine** ADJ. characteristic of earlier times; primitive; unspoiled. This area has been preserved in all its *pristine* wilderness.

**probity** N. uprightness; incorruptibility. Everyone took his *probity* for granted; his defalcations, therefore, shocked us all.

**proclivity** N. inclination; natural tendency. He has a *proclivity* to grumble.

**procrastinate** V. postpone; delay. It is wise not to *procrastinate;* otherwise, we find ourselves bogged down in a mass of work which should have been finished long ago.

■ **prodigal** ADJ. wasteful; reckless with money. The *prodigal* son squandered his inheritance. also N.

■ **prodigious** ADJ. marvelous; enormous. He marveled at her *prodigious* appetite.

**profane** V. violate; desecrate. Tourists are urged not to *profane* the sanctity of holy places by wearing improper garb. also ADJ.

**profligate** ADJ. dissipated; wasteful; licentious. In this *profligate* company, he lost all sense of decency. also N.

■ **profound** ADJ. deep; not superficial; complete. Freud's remarkable insights into human behavior caused his fellow scientists to honor him as a *profound* thinker. profundity, N.

■ **profusion** N. lavish expenditure; overabundant condition. Seldom have I seen food and drink served in such *profusion.* profuse, ADJ.

**progenitor** N. ancestor. We must not forget the teachings of our *progenitors* in our desire to appear modern.

**progeny** N. children; offspring. He was proud of his *progeny* but regarded George as the most promising of all his children.

**prognosis** N. forecasted course of a disease; prediction. If the doctor's *prognosis* is correct, the patient will be in a coma for at least twenty-four hours. prognosticate, V.

■ **prolific** ADJ. abundantly fruitful. He was a *prolific* writer and wrote as many as three books a year.

**prolix** ADJ. verbose; drawn out. His *prolix* arguments irritated the jury.

**promiscuous** ADJ. mixed indiscriminately; haphazard; irregular. In the opera *La Boheme,* we get a picture of the *promiscuous* life led by the young artists of Paris.

**promulgate** V. make known by official proclamation or publication. As soon as the Civil Service Commission *promulgates* the names of the successful candidates, we shall begin to hire members of our staff.

**prone** ADJ. inclined to; prostrate. She was *prone* to sudden fits of anger.

**propagate** V. multiply; spread. I am sure disease must *propagate* in such unsanitary and crowded areas.

**propensity** N. natural inclination. I dislike your *propensity* to belittle every contribution he makes to our organization.

**propitiate** V. appease. The natives offered sacrifices to *propitiate* the gods.

**propitious** ADJ. favorable; kindly. I think it is advisable that we wait for a more *propitious* occasion to announce our plans.

**propound** V. put forth for analysis. In your discussion, you have *propounded* several questions; let us consider each one separately.

**propriety** N. fitness; correct conduct. I want you to behave at this dinner with *propriety;* don't embarrass me.

**prosaic** ADJ. commonplace; dull. I do not like this author because he is so unimaginative and *prosaic*.

**prostrate** V. stretch out full on ground. He *prostrated* himself before the idol. also ADJ.

**protégé** N. person under the protection and support of a patron. Cyrano de Bergerac refused to be a *protégé* of Cardinal Richelieu.

**protocol** N. diplomatic etiquette. We must run this state dinner according to *protocol* if we are to avoid offending any of our guests.

**protract** V. prolong. Do not *protract* this phone conversation as I expect an important business call within the next few minutes.

**protrude** V. stick out. Her fingers *protruded* from the holes in her gloves.

**provident** ADJ. displaying foresight; thrifty; preparing for emergencies. In his usual *provident* manner, he had insured himself against this type of loss.

■ **provincial** ADJ. pertaining to a province; limited. We have to overcome their *provincial* attitude and get them to become more aware of world problems.

**provocation** N. cause for anger or retaliation. In order to prevent a sudden outbreak of hostilities, we must give our foe no *provocation*.

■ **provoke** V. annoy; anger; incite to action; produce a reaction. The bully kicked sand in the little boy's face to *provoke* him into fighting. provocation, N.

**proximity** N. nearness. The deer sensed the hunter's *proximity* and bounded away.

**proxy** N. authorized agent. Please act as my *proxy* and vote for this slate of candidates.

■ **prudent** ADJ. cautious; careful. A miser hoards money not because he is *prudent* but because he is greedy. prudence, N.

**pseudonym** N. pen name. Samuel Clemens' *pseudonym* was Mark Twain.

**psyche** N. soul; mind. It is difficult to delve into the *psyche* of a human being.

**pugnacious** ADJ. combative; disposed to fight. As a child he was *pugnacious* and fought with everyone.

**pulchritude** N. beauty; comeliness. I do not envy the judges who have to select this year's Miss America from this collection of female *pulchitrude*.

**punctilious** ADJ. laying stress on niceties of conduct, form; precise. We must be *punctilious* in our planning of this affair; for any error may be regarded as a personal affront.

**pungent** ADJ. stinging; caustic. The *pungent* aroma of the smoke made me cough.

**punitive** ADJ. punishing. He asked for *punitive* measures against the offender.

**puny** ADJ. insignificant; tiny; weak. Our *puny* efforts to stop the flood were futile.

**purgatory** N. place of spiritual expiation. In this *purgatory*, he could expect no help from his comrades.

**purge** V. clean by removing impurities; to clear of charges. If you are to be *purged* of the charge of contempt of Congress, you must be willing to answer the questions previously asked. also N.

**purport** N. intention; meaning. If the *purport* of your speech was to arouse the rabble, you succeeded admirably. also V.

---

## ETYMOLOGY 23

PRE (before) prefix
> **precocious**  ahead of time
> **precursor**  forerunner

PRO (before, toward) prefix
> **prognosticate**  foretell
> **propulsive**  driving forward

---

## TEST — Word List 23 — Antonyms

Each of the questions below consists of a word printed in italics, followed by five words or phrases numbered 1 to 5. Choose the numbered word or phrase which is most nearly opposite in meaning to the word in italics and write the number of your choice on your answer paper.

441. *precipitate*  1 fast  2 anticipatory  3 cautious  4 considerate  5 dry
442. *prim*  1 informal  2 prior  3 exterior  4 private  5 cautious
443. *protract*  1 make circular  2 shorten  3 further  4 retrace  5 involve
444. *prelude*  1 intermezzo  2 overture  3 aria  4 aftermath  5 duplication
445. *probity*  1 regret  2 assumption  3 corruptibility  4 extent  5 upswing
446. *pretentious*  1 ominous  2 calm  3 unassuming  4 futile  5 volatile
447. *prodigal*  1 wandering  2 thrifty  3 consistent  4 compatible  5 errant
448. *prosaic*  1 pacified  2 reprieved  3 pensive  4 imaginative  5 rhetorical
449. *propitious*  1 rich  2 induced  3 promoted  4 indicative  5 unfavorable
450. *profound*  1 fragrant  2 superficial  3 lonely  4 lost  5 masterly
451. *pulchritude*  1 ugliness  2 notoriety  3 bestiality  4 masculinity  5 servitude
452. *prefatory*  1 outstanding  2 magnificent  3 conclusive  4 intelligent  5 predatory
453. *punctilious*  1 happy  2 active  3 vivid  4 careless  5 futile

454. *prudent*   1 uncomfortable 2 fashionable 3 articulate 4 healthy 5 rash
455. *prolix*   1 stupid 2 indifferent 3 redundant 4 livid 5 pithy
456. *profane*   1 sanctify 2 avenge 3 define 4 manifest 5 urge
457. *presumption*   1 assertion 2 activation 3 motivation 4 proposition 5 humility
458. *pristine*   1 cultivated 2 condemned 3 crude 4 cautious 5 critical
459. *prodigious*   1 infinitesimal 2 indignant 3 indifferent 4 indisposed 5 insufficient
460. *punitive*   1 large 2 vindictive 3 rewarding 4 restive 5 languishing

---

### Word List 24   pusillanimous - reiterate

**pusillanimous** ADJ. cowardly; fainthearted. You should be ashamed of your *pusillanimous* conduct during this dispute.

**putrid** ADJ. foul; rotten; decayed. The gangrenous condition of the wound was indicated by the *putrid* smell when the bandages were removed. putrescence, N.

**pyromaniac** N. person with an insane desire to set things on fire. The detectives searched the area for the *pyromaniac* who had set these costly fires.

**quack** N. charlatan; impostor. Do not be misled by the exorbitant claims of this *quack*.

**quail** V. cower; lose heart. He was afraid that he would *quail* in the face of danger.

■ **qualified** ADJ. limited; restricted. Unable to give the candidate full support, the mayor gave him only a *qualified* endorsement. (secondary meaning)

**qualms** N. misgivings. Her *qualms* of conscience had become so great that she decided to abandon her plans.

■ **quandary** N. dilemma. When the two colleges to which he had applied accepted him, he was in a *quandary* as to which one he should attend.

**quell** V. put down; quiet. The police used fire hoses and tear gas to *quell* the rioters.

**querulous** ADJ. fretful; whining. His classmates were repelled by his *querulous* and complaining statements.

**quibble** V. equivocate; play on words. Do not *quibble*; I want a straightforward and definite answer. also N.

**quiescent** ADJ. at rest; dormant. After this geyser erupts, it will remain *quiescent* for twenty-four hours.

**quietude** N. tranquility. He was impressed by the air of *quietude* and peace that pervaded the valley.

**quintessence** N. purest and highest embodiment. These books display the *quintessence* of wit.

**quip** N. taunt. You are unpopular because you are too free with your *quips* and sarcastic comments. also V.

**quirk** N. startling twist; caprice. By a *quirk* of fate, he found himself working for the man whom he had discharged years before.

**quixotic** ADJ. idealistic but impractical. He is constantly presenting these *quixotic* schemes.

**rabid** ADJ. like a fanatic; furious. She was a *rabid* follower of the Dodgers and watched them play whenever she could go to the ball park.

**ramification** N. branching out; subdivision. We must examine all the *ramifications* of this problem.

**rampant** ADJ. rearing up on hind legs; unrestrained. The *rampant* weeds in the garden killed all the flowers which had been planted in the spring.

**rancid** ADJ. having the odor of stale fat. A *rancid* odor filled the ship's galley.

**rancor** N. bitterness; hatred. Let us forget our *rancor* and cooperate in this new endeavor.

**rant** V. rave; speak bombastically. As we heard him *rant* on the platform, we could not understand his strange popularity with many people.

**rapacious** ADJ. excessively grasping; plundering. Hawks and other *rapacious* birds may be killed at any time.

■ **ratify** V. approve formally; verify. Before the treaty could go into effect, it had to be *ratified* by the President.

**rationalize** V. reason; justify an improper act. Do not try to *rationalize* your behavior by blaming your companions.

**raucous** ADJ. harsh and shrill. His *raucous* laughter irritated me.

**ravage** V. plunder; despoil. The marauding army *ravaged* the countryside.

**ravenous** ADJ. extremely hungry. The *ravenous* dog upset several garbage pails in its search for food.

**raze** V. destroy completely. The owners intend to *raze* the hotel and erect an office building on the site.

**realm** N. kingdom; sphere. The *realm* of possibilities for the new invention was endless.

■ **rebuttal** N. refutation; response with contrary evidence. The defense lawyer confidently listened to the prosecutor sum up his case, sure that she could answer his arguments in her *rebuttal*.

**recalcitrant** ADJ. obstinately stubborn. Donkeys are reputed to be the most *recalcitrant* of animals.

**recant** V. repudiate; withdraw previous statement. Unless you *recant* your confession, you will be punished severely.

**recapitulate** V. summarize. Let us *recapitulate* what has been said thus far before going ahead.

**recession** N. withdrawal; retreat. The *recession* of the troops from the combat area was completed in an orderly manner.

**recipient** N. receiver. Although he had been the *recipient* of many favors, he was not grateful to his benefactor.

**reciprocal** ADJ. mutual; exchangeable; interacting. The two nations signed a *reciprocal* trade agreement.

**reciprocate** V. repay in kind. If they attack us, we shall be compelled to *reciprocate* and bomb their territory.

**recluse** N. hermit. The *recluse* lived in a hut in the forest. reclusive, ADJ.

**reconcile** V. make friendly after quarrel; correct inconsistencies. Each month we *reconcile* our checkbook with the bank statement.

**recourse** N. resorting to help when in trouble. The boy's only *recourse* was to appeal to his father for aid.

**recrimination** N. countercharges. Loud and angry *recriminations* were her answer to his accusations.

■ **rectify** V. correct. I want to *rectify* my error before it is too late.

**recuperate** V. recover. The doctors were worried because the patient did not *recuperate* as rapidly as they had expected.

**recurrent** ADJ. occurring again and again. These *recurrent* attacks disturbed us and we consulted a physician.

**redoubtable** ADJ. formidable; causing fear. The neighboring countries tried not to offend the Russians because they could be *redoubtable* foes.

**redress** N. remedy; compensation. Do you mean to tell me that I can get no *redress* for my injuries? also V.

■ **redundant** ADJ. superfluous; excessively wordy; repetitious. Your composition is *redundant;* you can easily reduce its length.

**reek** V. emit (odor). The room *reeked* with stale tobacco smoke. also N.

**refraction** N. bending of a ray of light. When you look at a stick inserted in water, it looks bent because of the *refraction* of the light by the water.

■ **refute** V. disprove. The defense called several respectable witnesses who were able to *refute* the false testimony of the prosecution's only witness.

**regal** ADJ. royal. He has a *regal* manner.

**regale** V. entertain. John *regaled* us with tales of his adventures in Africa.

**regeneration** N. spiritual rebirth. Modern penologists strive for the *regeneration* of the prisoners.

**regime** N. method or system of government. When a Frenchman mentions the Old *Regime,* he refers to the government existing before the revolution.

**regimen** N. prescribed diet and habits. I doubt whether the results warrant our living under such a strict and inflexible *regimen.*

**rehabilitate** V. restore to proper condition. We must *rehabilitate* those whom we send to prison.

**reimburse** v. repay. Let me know what you have spent and I will *reimburse* you.

**reiterate** v. repeat. I shall *reiterate* this message until all have understood it.

---

## ETYMOLOGY 24

PUT, PUTAT (to trim, to calculate)
        **computation** a reckoning
        **amputate** cut off
        **putative** supposed (calculated)
QUAER, QUAESIT (to ask)
        **inquiry** investigation
        **inquisitive** questioning
        **query** question

---

## TEST — Word List 24 — Synonyms and Antonyms

Each of the questions below consists of a word printed in italics, followed by five words or phrases numbered 1 to 5. Choose the numbered word or phrase which is most nearly the same as or the opposite of the word in italics and write the number of your choice on your answer paper.

461. *rancid* 1 oppressive 2 fresh 3 major 4 basic 5 entertaining
462. *refute* 1 relinquish 2 settle 3 disprove 4 cancel 5 elicit
463. *quandary* 1 quagmire 2 dilemma 3 epigram 4 enemy 5 finish
464. *qualified* 1 articulate 2 sinkable 3 vaunted 4 useless 5 unrestricted
465. *raze* 1 shave 2 heckle 3 finish 4 tear down 5 write
466. *putrid* 1 sick 2 lovely 3 aromatic 4 arrogant 5 humid
467. *recuperate* 1 reenact 2 engage 3 recapitulate 4 recover 5 encounter
468. *ravage* 1 rank 2 revive 3 plunder 4 pillory 5 age
469. *quell* 1 return 2 incite 3 seal 4 scale 5 joke
470. *rectify* 1 remedy 2 avenge 3 create 4 assemble 5 attribute
471. *raucous* 1 mellifluous 2 uncooked 3 realistic 4 veracious 5 anticipating
472. *pusillanimous* 1 poverty-stricken 2 chained 3 posthumous 4 cowardly 5 strident
473. *querulous* 1 vacationing 2 fretful 3 indifferent 4 obliged 5 reviving
474. *quixotic* 1 rapid 2 exotic 3 longing 4 timid 5 idealistic
475. *rehabilitate* 1 clothe 2 destroy 3 avenge 4 vanish 5 embarrass
476. *redundant* 1 abstruse 2 distant 3 calm 4 impartial 5 repetitious

477. *reimburse*  1 remunerate 2 constitute 3 dip 4 demolish 5 patronize
478. *rebuttal*  1 impertinence 2 refutation 3 satisfaction 4 saturation 5 quiz
479. *reiterate*  1 gainsay 2 revive 3 revenge 4 repeat 5 return
480. *regal*  1 overflowing 2 effortless 3 royal 4 noisy 5 snoring

---

## Word List 25    rejuvenate - rococo

**rejuvenate** V. make young again. The charlatan claimed that his elixir would *rejuvenate* the aged and weary.

■ **relegate** V. banish; consign to inferior position. If we *relegate* these experienced people to positions of unimportance because of their political persuasions, we shall lose the services of valuably trained personnel.

**relevancy** N. pertinence; reference to the case in hand. I was impressed by the *relevancy* of your remarks. relevant, ADJ.

**relinquish** V. abandon. I will *relinquish* my claims to this property if you promise to retain my employees.

**relish** V. savor; enjoy. I *relish* a good joke as much as anyone else. also N.

**remedial** ADJ. curative; corrective. Because he was a slow reader, he decided to take a course in *remedial* reading.

**reminiscence** N. recollection. Her *reminiscences* of her experiences are so fascinating that she ought to write a book. reminiscent, ADJ.

**remiss** ADJ. negligent. He was accused of being *remiss* in his duty.

**remnant** N. remainder. I suggest that you wait until the store places the *remnants* of these goods on sale.

■ **remorse** N. guilt; self-reproach. The murderer felt no *remorse* for his crime.

**remunerative** ADJ. compensating; rewarding. I find my new work so *remunerative* that I may not return to my previous employment. remuneration, N.

**rend** V. split; tear apart. In his grief, he tried to *rend* his garments.

**render** V. deliver; provide; represent. She *rendered* aid to the needy and indigent.

**renegade** N. deserter; apostate. Because he refused to support his fellow members in their drive, he was shunned as a *renegade*.

■ **renounce** V. abandon; discontinue; disown; repudiate. Joan of Arc refused to *renounce* her statements even though she knew she would be burned at the stake as a witch.

**renovate** V. restore to good condition; renew. They claim that they can *renovate* worn shoes so that they look like new ones.

**renunciation** N. giving up; renouncing. Do not sign this *renunciation* of your right to sue until you have consulted a lawyer.

**reparable** ADJ. capable of being repaired. Fortunately, the damages we suffered in the accident were *reparable*.

**repartee** N. clever reply. He was famous for his witty *repartee* and his sarcasm.

**repellent** ADJ. driving away; unattractive. Mosquitoes find the odor so *repellent* that they leave any spot where this liquid has been sprayed. also N.

**repertoire** N. list of works of music, drama, etc., a performer is prepared to present. The opera company decided to include *Madame Butterfly* in its *repertoire* for the following season.

**replenish** V. fill up again. The end of rationing enabled us to *replenish* our supply of canned food.

**replica** N. copy. Are you going to hang this *replica* of the Declaration of Independence in the classroom or in the auditorium?

■ **reprehensible** ADJ. deserving blame. Your vicious conduct in this situation is *reprehensible*.

**reprieve** N. temporary stay. During the twenty-four-hour *reprieve*, the lawyers sought to make the stay of execution permanent. also V.

**reprimand** V. reprove severely. I am afraid that my parents will *reprimand* me when I show them my report card. also N.

■ **reproach** V. express disapproval. He never could do anything wrong without reflecting how his parents would *reproach* him for his misbehavior. also N.

■ **reprove** V. censure; rebuke. The principal *reproved* the students when they became unruly in the auditorium.

■ **repudiate** V. disown; disavow. She announced that she would *repudiate* all debts incurred by her husband.

**repugnance** N. loathing. She looked at the snake with *repugnance*.

**repulsion** N. act of driving back; distaste. The *repulsion* of the enemy forces was not accomplished bloodlessly; many of the defenders were wounded. repel, V.

**requiem** N. mass for the dead; dirge. They played Mozart's *Requiem* at the funeral.

**requisite** N. necessary requirement. Many colleges state that a student must offer three years of a language as a *requisite* for admission.

■ **rescind** V. cancel. Because of public resentment, the king had to *rescind* his order. rescission, N.

■ **reserved** ADJ. self-controlled; careful in expressing oneself. She was outspoken and uninhibited; he was cautious and *reserved*. reserved. N.

■ **resigned** ADJ. unresisting; patiently submissive. Bob Cratchit was too *resigned* to his downtrodden existence to protest when Scrooge bullied him. (secondary meaning)

■ **resolution** N. determination. Nothing could shake his *resolution* to succeed despite all difficulties. resolute, ADJ. (secondary meaning)

**resonant** ADJ. echoing; resounding; possessing resonance. His *resonant* voice was particularly pleasing.

■ **respite** N. delay in punishment; interval of relief; rest. The judge granted the condemned man a *respite* to enable his attorneys to file an appeal.

**resplendent** ADJ. brilliant; lustrous. The toreador wore a *resplendent* costume.

**responsiveness** N. state of reacting readily to appeals, orders, etc. The audience cheered and applauded, delighting the performers by its *responsiveness*.

**restitution** N. reparation; indemnification. He offered to make *restitution* for the window broken by his son.

**restive** ADJ. unmanageable; fretting under control. We must quiet the *restive* animals.

■ **restraint** N. controlling force. She dreamt of living an independent life, free of all *restraints*.

■ **retaliate** V. repay in kind (usually for bad treatment). Fear that we will *retaliate* immediately deters our foe from attacking us.

**retentive** ADJ. holding; having a good memory. The pupil did not need to spend much time in study as he had a *retentive* mind.

■ **reticence** N. reserve; uncommunicativeness; inclination to be silent. Because of the *reticence* of the key witness, the case against the defendant collapsed.

**retraction** N. withdrawal. He dropped his libel suit after the newspaper published a *retraction* of its statement.

**retribution** N. vengeance; compensation; punishment for offenses. The evangelist maintained that an angry Deity would exact *retribution* from the sinners.

**retroactive** ADJ. of a law which dates back to a period before its enactment. Because the law was *retroactive* to the first of the year, we found he was eligible for the pension.

**retrospective** ADJ. looking back on the past. It is only when we become *retrospective* that we can appreciate the tremendous advances made during this century.

■ **revere** V. respect; honor. In Asian societies, people *revere* their elders. reverent, ADJ.

**reverie** N. daydream; musing. He was awakened from his *reverie* by the teacher's question.

**revile** V. slander; vilify. He was avoided by all who feared that he would *revile* and abuse them if they displeased him.

**revulsion** N. sudden violent change of feeling; reaction. Many people in this country who admired dictatorships underwent a *revulsion* when they realized what Hitler and Mussolini were trying to do.

**rhapsodize** V. to speak or write in an exaggeratedly enthusiastic manner. She greatly enjoyed her Hawaiian vacation and *rhapsodized* about it for weeks.

■ **rhetorical** ADJ. pertaining to effective communication; insincere in language. To win his audience, the speaker used every *rhetorical* trick in the book.

**rife** ADJ. abundant; current. In the face of the many rumors of scandal, which are *rife* at the moment, it is best to remain silent.

**rift** N. opening; break. The plane was lost in the stormy sky until the pilot saw the city through a *rift* in the clouds.

**rigor** N. severity. Many settlers could not stand the *rigors* of the New England winters.

**risqué** ADJ. verging upon the improper; offcolor. Please do not tell your *risqué* anecdotes at this party.

**robust** ADJ. vigorous; strong. The candidate for the football team had a *robust* physique.

**rococo** ADJ. ornate; highly decorated. The *rococo* style in furniture and architecture, marked by scrollwork and excessive decoration, flourished during the middle of the eighteenth century.

---

## ETYMOLOGY 25

RID, RIS (to laugh)

> **derision** scorn
> **risibility** inclination to laughter
> **ridiculous** deserving to be laughed at

---

## TEST — Word List 25 — Synonyms

Each of the questions below consists of a word printed in italics, followed by five words or phrases numbered 1 to 5. Choose the numbered word or phrase which is most nearly similar in meaning to the word in italics and write the number of your choice on your answer paper.

481. *restive* 1 buoyant 2 restless 3 remorseful 4 resistant 5 retiring
482. *replenish* 1 polish 2 repeat 3 reinstate 4 refill 5 refuse
483. *remonstrate* 1 display 2 restate 3 protest 4 resign 5 reiterate
484. *repugnance* 1 belligerence 2 tenacity 3 renewal 4 pity 5 loathing

485. *repulsion*  1 distaste  2 restitution  3 resistance  4 magnificence  5 acceptance
486. *remiss*  1 lax  2 lost  3 foolish  4 violating  5 ambitious
487. *repudiate*  1 besmirch  2 appropriate  3 annoy  4 reject  5 avow
488. *repellent*  1 propulsive  2 unattractive  3 porous  4 stiff  5 elastic
489. *remedial*  1 therapeutic  2 corrective  3 traumatic  4 philandering  5 psychotic
490. *remorse*  1 reevaluation  2 assessment  3 loss  4 guilt  5 nonsense
491. *repartee*  1 witty retort  2 willful departure  3 spectator  4 monologue  5 sacrifice
492. *relish*  1 desire  2 nibble  3 savor  4 vindicate  5 avail
493. *replica*  1 museum piece  2 famous site  3 battle emblem  4 facsimile  5 replacement
494. *resolution*  1 result  2 determination  3 alteration  4 retaliation  5 resistance
495. *robust*  1 vigorous  2 violent  3 vicious  4 villainous  5 voracious
496. *restraint*  1 continuation  2 curb  3 application  4 slumber  5 assessment
497. *rife*  1 direct  2 scant  3 abundant  4 grim  5 mature
498. *reticence*  1 reserve  2 fashion  3 treachery  4 loquaciousness  5 magnanimity
499. *retribution*  1 vengeance  2 procrastination  3 elevation  4 discrepancy  5 reassurance
500. *retentive*  1 grasping  2 accepting  3 repetitive  4 avoiding  5 fascinating

---

## Word List 26   rote - silt

**rote** N. repetition. He recited the passage by *rote* and gave no indication he understood what he was saying.

**rotundity** N. roundness; sonorousness of speech. Washington Irving emphasized the *rotundity* of the governor by describing his height and circumference.

**rubble** N. fragments. Ten years after World War II, some of the *rubble* left by enemy bombings could still be seen.

**ruddy** ADJ. reddish; healthy-looking. His *ruddy* features indicated that he had spent much time in the open.

**rudimentary** ADJ. not developed; elementary. His dancing was limited to a few *rudimentary* steps.

**rueful** ADJ. regretful; sorrowful; dejected. The artist has captured the sadness of childhood in his portrait of the boy with the *rueful* countenance. rue, V.

**rummage** V. ransack; thoroughly search. When we *rummaged* through the trunks in the attic, we found many souvenirs of our childhood days. also N.

**ruse** N. trick; stratagem. You will not be able to fool your friends with such an obvious *ruse*.

**ruthless** ADJ. pitiless. The escaped convict was a dangerous and *ruthless* murderer.

**saccharine** ADJ. cloyingly sweet. She tried to ingratiate herself, speaking sweetly and smiling a *saccharine* smile.

**sacrilegious** ADJ. desecrating; profane. His stealing of the altar cloth was a very *sacrilegious* act.

**saga** N. Scandinavian myth; any legend. This is a *saga* of the sea and the men who risk their lives on it.

**sagacious** ADJ. keen; shrewd; having insight. He is much too *sagacious* to be fooled by a trick like that.

**salient** ADJ. prominent. One of the *salient* features of that newspaper is its excellent editorial page.

**sallow** ADJ. yellowish; sickly in color. We were disturbed by his *sallow* complexion.

**salubrious** ADJ. healthful. Many people with hay fever move to more *salubrious* sections of the country during the months of August and September.

**salutary** ADJ. tending to improve; beneficial; wholesome. The punishment had a *salutary* effect on the boy, as he became a model student.

**salvage** V. rescue from loss. All attempts to *salvage* the wrecked ship failed. also N.

■ **sanction** V. approve; ratify. Nothing will convince me to *sanction* the engagement of my daughter to such a worthless young man.

**sanguinary** ADJ. bloody. The battle of Iwo Jima was unexpectedly *sanguinary*.

**sanguine** ADJ. cheerful; hopeful. Let us not be too *sanguine* about the outcome.

**sapient** ADJ. wise; shrewd. The students enjoyed the professor's *sapient* digressions more than his formal lectures.

**sardonic** ADJ. disdainful; sarcastic; cynical. The *sardonic* humor of nightclub comedians who satirize or ridicule patrons in the audience strikes some people as amusing and others as rude.

**sate** V. satisfy to the full; cloy. Its hunger *sated*, the lion dozed.

**satiate** V. surfeit; satisfy fully. The guests, having eaten until they were *satiated*, now listened inattentively to the speakers. satiety, N.

■ **satirical** ADJ. mocking. The humor of cartoonist Gary Trudeau often is *satirical*; through the comments of the Doonesbury characters, Trudeau ridicules political corruption and folly.

■ **saturate** V. soak. Their clothes were *saturated* by the rain.

**saunter** V. stroll slowly. As we *sauntered* through the park, we stopped frequently to admire the spring flowers.

**savant** N. scholar. Our faculty includes many world-famous *savants*.

**savor** V. have a distinctive flavor, smell, or quality. I think your choice of a successor *savors* of favoritism.

■ **scanty** ADJ. meager; insufficient. Thinking his helping of food was *scanty*, Oliver Twist asked for more.

**scavenger** N. collector and disposer of refuse; animal that devours refuse and carrion. The Oakland *Scavenger* Company is responsible for the collection and disposal of the community's garbage.

**schism** N. division; split. Let us not widen the *schism* by further bickering.

**scintilla** N. shred; least bit. You have not produced a *scintilla* of evidence to support your argument.

**scintillate** V. sparkle; flash. I enjoy her dinner parties because the food is excellent and the conversation *scintillates*.

**scourge** N. lash; whip; severe punishment. They feared the plague and regarded it as a deadly *scourge*. also V.

■ **scrupulous** ADJ. conscientious; extremely thorough. I can recommend him for a position of responsibility for I have found him a very *scrupulous* young man.

■ **scrutinize** V. examine closely and critically. Searching for flaws, the sergeant *scrutinized* every detail of the private's uniform.

**scurrilous** ADJ. obscene; indecent. Your *scurrilous* remarks are especially offensive because they are untrue.

**secession** N. withdrawal. The *secession* of the Southern states provided Lincoln with his first major problem after his inauguration.

■ **seclusion** N. isolation; solitude. One moment she loved crowds; the next, she sought *seclusion*. secluded, ADJ.

**secular** ADJ. worldly; not pertaining to church matters; temporal. The church leaders decided not to interfere in *secular* matters.

**sedate** ADJ. composed; grave. The parents were worried because they felt their son was too quiet and *sedate*.

**sedentary** ADJ. requiring sitting. Because he had a *sedentary* occupation, he decided to visit a gymnasium weekly.

**sedulous** ADJ. diligent. Stevenson said that he played the "*sedulous* ape" and diligently imitated the great writers of the past.

**seethe** V. be disturbed; boil. The nation was *seething* with discontent as the noblemen continued their arrogant ways.

**sensual** ADJ. devoted to the pleasures of the senses; carnal; voluptuous. I cannot understand what caused him to drop his *sensual* way of life and become so ascetic.

**sententious** ADJ. terse; concise; aphoristic. After reading so many redundant speeches, I find his *sententious* style particularly pleasing.

**sequester** V. retire from public life; segregate; seclude. Although he had hoped for a long time to *sequester* himself in a small community, he never was able to drop his busy round of activities in the city.

**serenity** N. calmness; placidity. The *serenity* of the sleepy town was shattered by a tremendous explosion.

■ **servile** ADJ. slavish; cringing. Uriah Heep was a very *servile* individual.

**severance** N. division; partition; separation. The *severance* of church and state is a basic principle of our government.

**severity** N. harshness; plainness. The newspaper editorials disapproved of the *severity* of the sentence.

**shambles** N. slaughterhouse; scene of carnage. By the time the police arrived, the room was a *shambles*.

**sheaf** N. bundle of stalks of grain; any bundle of things tied together. The lawyer picked up a *sheaf* of papers as he rose to question the witness.

**sheathe** V. place into a case. As soon as he recognized the approaching men, he *sheathed* his dagger and hailed them as friends.

**shimmer** V. glimmer intermittently. The moonlight *shimmered* on the water as the moon broke through the clouds for a moment. also N.

**shoal** N. shallow place. The ship was stranded on a *shoal* and had to be pulled off by tugs.

**shoddy** ADJ. sham; not genuine; inferior. You will never get the public to buy such *shoddy* material.

■ **shrewd** ADJ. clever; astute. A *shrewd* investor, he took clever advantage of the fluctuations of the stock market.

**sibling** N. brother or sister. We may not enjoy being *siblings*, but we cannot forget that we still belong to the same family.

**silt** N. sediment deposited by running water. The harbor channel must be dredged annually to remove the *silt*.

---

## ETYMOLOGY 26

RUPT (to break)
        **interrupt**   break into
        **bankrupt**   insolvent
        **rupture**   a break

SCI (to know)
        **science**   knowledge
        **omniscient**   knowing all
        **conscious**   aware

SCRIB, SCRIPT (to write)
        **transcribe**   copy
        **script**   writing

**circumscribe**   enclose, limit (write around)

SEQUE, SECUT (to follow)

**consecutive**   following in order

**sequence**   arrangement

**sequel**   that which follows

---

## TEST — Word List 26 — Antonyms

Each of the questions below consists of a word printed in italics, followed by five words or phrases numbered 1 to 5. Choose the numbered word or phrase which is most nearly opposite in meaning to the word in italics and write the number of your choice on your answer paper.

501. *scurrilous*   1 savage 2 scabby 3 decent 4 volatile 5 major
502. *sagacious*   1 foolish 2 bitter 3 voracious 4 veracious 5 fallacious
503. *rudimentary*   1 pale 2 fundamental 3 asinine 4 developed 5 quiescent
504. *sanguine*   1 choleric 2 sickening 3 warranted 4 irritated 5 pessimistic
505. *saccharine*   1 happy 2 quaint 3 bitter 4 vacant 5 fortunate
506. *ruddy*   1 robust 2 witty 3 wan 4 exotic 5 creative
507. *salvage*   1 remove 2 outfit 3 burn 4 lose 5 confuse
508. *scanty*   1 religious 2 frank 3 authoritative 4 violent 5 plentiful
509. *rueful*   1 dangerous 2 cheerful 3 remote 4 indicative 5 nonsensical
510. *salubrious*   1 salty 2 bloody 3 miasmic 4 maudlin 5 wanted
511. *ruthless*   1 merciful 2 majestic 3 mighty 4 militant 5 maximum
512. *rotundity*   1 promenade 2 nave 3 grotesqueness 4 slimness 5 impropriety
513. *sallow*   1 salacious 2 ruddy 3 colorless 4 permitted 5 minimum
514. *rueful*   1 sad 2 content 3 capable 4 capital 5 zealous
515. *secular*   1 vivid 2 clerical 3 punitive 4 positive 5 varying
516. *shoddy*   1 superior 2 incomplete 3 inadequate 4 querulous 5 garrulous
517. *sedentary*   1 vicarious 2 loyal 3 accidental 4 active 5 afraid
518. *servile*   1 menial 2 puerile 3 futile 4 lowly 5 haughty
519. *sententious*   1 paragraphed 2 positive 3 posthumous 4 pacific 5 wordy
520. *severity*   1 virility 2 loquaciousness 3 forgetfulness 4 leniency 5 unity

---

### Word List 27   simile - sundry

**simile** N. comparison of one thing with another, using the word *like* or *as*. We are constantly using *similes* and metaphors to convey our thoughts to others.

**simulate** V. feign. He *simulated* insanity in order to avoid punishment for his crime.

**sinister** ADJ. evil. We must defeat the *sinister* forces that seek our downfall.

**sinuous** ADJ. winding; bending in and out; not morally honest. The snake moved in a *sinuous* manner.

■ **skeptic** N. doubter; one who suspends judgment until having examined the evidence supporting a point of view. I am a *skeptic* about this project; I want some proof that it can work. skepticism, N.

**skimp** V. provide scantily; live very economically. They were forced to *skimp* on necessities in order to make their limited supplies last the winter.

**skulk** V. move furtively and secretly. He *skulked* through the less fashionable sections of the city in order to avoid meeting any of his former friends.

■ **slander** N. defamation; utterance of false and malicious statements. Unless you can prove your allegations, your remarks constitute *slander*. also V.

**sleeper** N. something originally of little value or importance which in time becomes very valuable. Unnoticed by the critics at its publication, the eventual Pulitzer Prize winner was a classic *sleeper*.

**sloth** N. laziness. Such *sloth* in a young person is deplorable.

**sluggard** N. lazy person. "You are a *sluggard*, a drone, a parasite," the angry father shouted at his lazy son.

**sluggish** ADJ. slow; lazy; lethargic. After two nights without sleep, she felt *sluggish* and incapable of exertion.

**sobriety** N. soberness. The solemnity of the occasion filled us with *sobriety*.

■ **solemnity** N. seriousness; gravity. The minister was concerned that nothing should disturb the *solemnity* of the marriage service.

**solicitous** ADJ. worried; concerned. The employer was very *solicitous* about [the health of her employees as replacements were difficult to get.

**soliloquy** N. talking to oneself. The *soliloquy* is a device used by the dramatist to reveal a character's innermost thoughts and emotions.

**solvent** ADJ. able to pay all debts. By dint of very frugal living, he was finally able to become *solvent* and avoid bankruptcy proceedings.

**somnambulist** N. sleepwalker. The most famous *somnambulist* in literature is Lady Macbeth; her monologue in the sleepwalking scene is one of the highlights of Shakespeare's play.

**sonorous** ADJ. resonant. His *sonorous* voice resounded through the hall.

**soporific** ADJ. sleep producer. I do not need a sedative when I listen to one of his *soporific* speeches. also N.

**spasmodic** ADJ. fitful; periodic. The *spasmodic* coughing in the auditorium annoyed the performers.

**spatial** ADJ. relating to space. It is difficult to visualize the *spatial* extent of our universe.

**specious** ADJ. seemingly reasonable but incorrect. Let us not be misled by such *specious* arguments.

**spectral** ADJ. ghostly. We were frightened by the *spectral* glow that filled the room.

■ **sporadic** ADJ. occurring irregularly. Although there are *sporadic* outbursts of shooting, we may report that the major rebellion has been defeated.

**spurious** ADJ. false; counterfeit. He tried to pay the check with a *spurious* ten-dollar bill.

**squalid** ADJ. dirty; neglected; poor. It is easy to see how crime can breed in such a *squalid* neighborhood.

■ **squander** V. waste. The prodigal son *squandered* the family estate.

■ **stagnant** ADJ. motionless; stale; dull. The *stagnant* water was a breeding ground for disease. stagnate, V.

**staid** ADJ. sober; sedate. Her conduct during the funeral ceremony was *staid* and solemn.

**stamina** N. strength; staying power. I doubt that he has the *stamina* to run the full distance of the marathon race.

**stanch** V. check flow of blood. It is imperative that we *stanch* the gushing wound before we attend to the other injuries.

■ **stanza** N. division of a poem. Do you know the last *stanza* of "The Star-Spangled Banner"?

■ **static** ADJ. unchanging; lacking development. Nothing had changed at home; things were *static* there. stasis, N.

**statute** N. law. We have many *statutes* in our law books which should be repealed.

■ **steadfast** ADJ. loyal. I am sure you will remain *steadfast* in your support of the cause.

**stellar** ADJ. pertaining to the stars. He was the *stellar* attraction of the entire performance.

**stigmatize** V. brand; mark as wicked. I do not want to *stigmatize* this young offender for life by sending her to prison.

**stint** N. supply; allotted amount; assigned portion of work. He performed his daily *stint* cheerfully and willingly. also, V.

**stipend** N. pay for services. There is a nominal *stipend* attached to this position.

■ **stoic** N. person who is indifferent to pleasure or pain. The doctor called her patient a *stoic* because he had borne the pain of the examination without whimpering. also ADJ.

**stoke** V. to feed plentifully. They swiftly *stoked* themselves, knowing they would not have another meal until they reached camp.

**stolid** ADJ. dull; impassive. I am afraid that this imaginative poetry will not appeal to such a *stolid* person.

**strident** ADJ. loud and harsh. She scolded him in a *strident* voice.

**stringent** ADJ. binding; rigid. I think these regulations are too *stringent*.

**stupor** N. state of apathy; daze; lack of awareness. In his *stupor*, the addict was unaware of the events taking place around him.

**stymie** V. present an obstacle; stump. The detective was *stymied* by the contradictory evidence in the robbery investigation. also N.

**suavity** N. urbanity; polish. He is particularly good in roles that require *suavity* and sophistication.

**subjugate** V. conquer; bring under control. It is not our aim to *subjugate* our foe; we are interested only in establishing peaceful relations.

**sublimate** V. refine; purify. We must strive to *sublimate* these desires and emotions into worthwhile activities.

**sublime** ADJ. exalted; noble; uplifting. We must learn to recognize *sublime* truths.

**subsequent** ADJ. following; later. In *subsequent* lessons, we shall take up more difficult problems.

**subservient** ADJ. behaving like a slave; servile; obsequious. He was proud and dignified; he refused to be *subservient* to anyone.

**subsidiary** ADJ. subordinate; secondary. This information may be used as *subsidiary* evidence but is not sufficient by itself to prove your argument. also N.

**subsistence** N. existence; means of support; livelihood. In these days of inflated prices, my salary provides a mere *subsistence*.

**substantiate** V. verify; support. I intend to *substantiate* my statement by producing witnesses.

**subterfuge** N. pretense; evasion. As soon as we realized that you had won our support by a *subterfuge*, we withdrew our endorsement of your candidacy.

■ **subtlety** N. nicety; cunning; guile; delicacy. The *subtlety* of her remarks was unnoticed by most of her audience.

**subversive** ADJ. tending to overthrow or ruin. We must destroy such *subversive* publications.

**succinct** ADJ. brief; terse; compact. Her remarks are always *succinct*.

**succor** N. aid; assistance; relief. We shall be ever grateful for the *succor* your country gave us when we were in need. also V.

**succulent** ADJ. juicy; full of richness. The citrus foods from Florida are more *succulent* to some people than those from California. also N.

**sultry** ADJ. sweltering. He could not adjust himself to the *sultry* climate of the tropics.

**summation** N. act of finding the total; summary. In his *summation*, the lawyer emphasized the testimony given by the two witnesses.

**sumptuous** ADJ. lavish; rich. I cannot recall when I have had such a *sumptuous* feast.

**sundry** ADJ. various; several. My suspicions were aroused when I read *sundry* items in the newspapers about your behavior.

---

## ETYMOLOGY 27

SPEC, SPECT (to look at)
        **spectator** observer
        **aspect** appearance
        **circumspect** cautious (looking around)

---

## TEST — Word List 27 — Synonyms and Antonyms

Each of the following questions consists of a word printed in italics, followed by five words or phrases numbered 1 to 5. Choose the numbered word or phrase which is most nearly the same as or the opposite of the word in italics and write the number of your choice on your answer paper.

521. *squander* 1 fortify 2 depart 3 roam 4 preserve 5 forfeit
522. *sluggish* 1 halcyon 2 settled 3 energetic 4 soothed 5 ambulatory
523. *steadfast* 1 tractable 2 inquiring 3 dramatic 4 vain 5 loyal
524. *skeptic* 1 actor 2 doubter 3 friend 4 egoist 5 sluggard
525. *solvent* 1 enigmatic 2 bankrupt 3 fiducial 4 puzzling 5 gilded
526. *sloth* 1 penitence 2 filth 3 futility 4 poverty 5 industry
527. *spasmodic* 1 intermittent 2 fit 3 inaccurate 4 violent 5 physical
528. *sobriety* 1 inebriety 2 aptitude 3 scholasticism 4 monotony 5 aversion
529. *static* 1 fanciful 2 primitive 3 unchanging 4 uneasy 5 warranted
530. *stanza* 1 division of a poem 2 sunrise 3 pigsty 4 patriotic emblem 5 iniquity
531. *stagnant* 1 half-baked 2 loved 3 inappropriate 4 flowing 5 perilous
532. *sinister* 1 unwed 2 ministerial 3 good 4 returned 5 splintered
533. *sonorous* 1 resonant 2 reassuring 3 repetitive 4 resinous 5 sisterly
534. *substantiate* 1 toughen 2 trap 3 violate 4 refute 5 depart
535. *spurious* 1 genuine 2 angry 3 mitigated 4 interrogated 5 glorious
536. *stringent* 1 binding 2 reserved 3 utilized 4 lambent 5 indigent
537. *sublime* 1 unconscious 2 respected 3 exalted 4 sneaky 5 replaced
538. *stamina* 1 patience 2 pistils 3 weakness 4 fascination 5 patina
539. *sporadic* 1 seedy 2 latent 3 vivid 4 inconsequential 5 often
540. *suavity* 1 ingeniousness 2 indifference 3 urbanity 4 constancy 5 paucity

### Word List 28 supercilious - transcribe

**supercilious** ADJ. contemptuous; haughty. I resent your *supercilious* and arrogant attitude.

■ **superficial** ADJ. trivial; shallow. Since your report gave only a *superficial* analysis of the problem, I cannot give you more than a passing grade.

■ **superfluous** ADJ. excessive; overabundant; unnecessary. Please try not to include so many *superfluous* details in your report; just give me the bare facts. superfluity, N.

**supersede** V. cause to be set aside; replace. This regulation will *supersede* all previous rules.

**supplicate** V. petition humbly; pray to grant a favor. We *supplicate* your majesty to grant him amnesty.

■ **suppress** V. crush; subdue; inhibit. After the armed troops had *suppressed* the rebellion, the city was placed under martial law. suppression, N.

**surfeit** V. cloy; overfeed. I am *surfeited* with the sentimentality of the average motion picture film.

**surly** ADJ. rude; cross. Because of his *surly* attitude, many people avoided his company.

**surmise** V. guess. I *surmise* that he will be late for this meeting also. N.

■ **surpass** V. exceed. Her PSAT scores *surpassed* our expectations.

■ **surreptitious** ADJ. secret. News of their *surreptitious* meeting gradually leaked out.

**surveillance** N. watching; guarding. The FBI kept the house under constant *surveillance* in the hope of capturing all the criminals at one time.

**sustenance** N. means of support, food, nourishment. In the tropics, the natives find *sustenance* easy to obtain. sustain, V.

**swelter** V. be oppressed by heat. I am going to buy an air conditioning unit for my apartment as I do not intend to *swelter* through another hot and humid summer.

■ **swindler** N. cheat. She was gullible and trusting, an easy victim for the first *swindler* who came along.

■ **sycophant** N. servile flatterer. The king enjoyed the attention the *sycophant* paid him.

■ **symmetry** N. arrangement of parts so that balance is obtained; congruity. The addition of a second tower will give this edifice the *symmetry* it now lacks.

**synchronous** ADJ. similarly timed; simultaneous with. We have many examples of scientists in different parts of the world who have made *synchronous* discoveries. synchronize, V.

**synthesis** N. combining parts into a whole. Now that we have succeeded in isolating this drug, our next problem is to plan its *synthesis* in the laboratory.

**synthetic** ADJ. artificial; resulting from synthesis. During the twentieth century, many *synthetic* products have replaced the natural products. also N.

**tacit** ADJ. understood; not put into words. We have a *tacit* agreement.

■ **taciturn** ADJ. habitually silent; talking little. New Englanders are reputedly *taciturn* people.

**tactile** ADJ. pertaining to the organs or sense of touch. His calloused hands had lost their *tactile* sensitivity.

**tainted** ADJ. contaminated; corrupt. Health authorities are always trying to prevent the sale and use of *tainted* food.

**tantalize** V. tease; torture with disappointment. Tom loved to *tantalize* his younger brother.

**tantrum** N. fit of petulance; caprice. The child learned that he could have almost anything if he went into *tantrums*.

**tautological** ADJ. needlessly repetitious. In the sentence "It was visible to the eye," the phrase "to the eye" is *tautological*.

**tawdry** ADJ. cheap and gaudy. He won a few *tawdry* trinkets in Coney Island.

■ **tedious** ADJ. boring; tiring. The repetitious nature of assembly line work made Martin's job very *tedious*. tedium, N.

**temerity** N. boldness; rashness. Do you have the *temerity* to argue with me?

**temperate** ADJ. restrained; self-controlled. Noted for his *temperate* appetite, he seldom gained weight.

**tempo** N. speed of music. I find the conductor's *tempo* too slow for such a brilliant piece of music.

**temporal** ADJ. not lasting forever; limited by time; secular. At one time in our history, *temporal* rulers assumed that they had been given their thrones by divine right.

**tenacious** ADJ. holding fast. I had to struggle to break his *tenacious* hold on my arm. tenacity, N.

**tenet** N. doctrine; dogma. I cannot accept the *tenets* of your faith.

■ **tentative** ADJ. provisional; experimental. Your *tentative* plans sound plausible.

**tenuous** ADJ. thin; rare; slim. The allegiance of our allies is held by rather *tenuous* ties.

**tenure** N. holding of an office; time during which such an office is held. He has permanent *tenure* in this position.

**tepid** ADJ. lukewarm. During the summer, I like to take a *tepid* bath.

**terminate** V. to bring to an end. When his contract was *terminated* unexpectedly, he desperately needed a new job.

**terrestrial** ADJ. on the earth. We have been able to explore the *terrestrial* regions much more thoroughly than the aquatic or celestial regions.

■ **terse** ADJ. concise; abrupt; pithy. I admire his *terse* style of writing.

**testy** ADJ. irritable; short-tempered. My advice is to avoid discussing this problem with her today as she is rather *testy*.

**therapeutic** ADJ. curative. These springs are famous for their *therapeutic* qualities.

**thermal** ADJ. pertaining to heat. The natives discovered that the hot springs gave excellent *thermal* baths and began to develop their community as a health resort. also N.

■ **thrifty** ADJ. careful about money; economical. A *thrifty* shopper compares prices before making major purchases.

**thwart** V. baffle; frustrate. He felt that everyone was trying to *thwart* his plans.

**timidity** N. lack of self-confidence or courage. If you are to succeed as a salesman, you must first lose your *timidity*.

■ **tirade** N. extended scolding; denunciation. Long before he had finished his *tirade*, we were sufficiently aware of the seriousness of our misconduct.

**titanic** ADJ. gigantic. *Titanic* waves beat against the shore during the hurricane.

**torpid** ADJ. dormant; dull; lethargic. The *torpid* bear had just come out of his cave after his long hibernation. torpor, N.

**tortuous** ADJ. winding; full of curves. Because this road is so *tortuous*, it is unwise to go faster than twenty miles an hour on it.

**touchy** ADJ. sensitive; irascible. Do not discuss this phase of the problem as he is very *touchy* about it.

**toxic** ADJ. poisonous. We must seek an antidote for whatever *toxic* substance he has eaten.

**tract** N. pamphlet; a region of indefinite size. The King granted William Penn a *tract* of land in the New World.

**tractable** ADJ. docile. You will find the children in this school very *tractable* and willing to learn.

**traduce** V. expose to slander. His opponents tried to *traduce* the candidate's reputation by spreading rumors about his past.

**tranquility** N. calmness; peace. After the commotion and excitement of the city, I appreciate the *tranquility* of these fields and forests.

**transcend** V. exceed; surpass. This accomplishment *transcends* all our previous efforts, transcendental, ADJ.

**transcribe** V. copy. When you *transcribe* your notes, please send a copy to Mr. Smith and keep the original for our files. transcription, N.

## ETYMOLOGY 28

TEMPOR (time)
>**contemporary**    at the same time
>**extemporaneous**    impromptu
>**temporize**    to delay

TEN, TENT (to hold)
>**tenable**    able to be held
>**tenacity**    retention
>**tenure**    holding of office

TERR (land)
>**terrestrial**    pertaining to earth
>**subterranean**    underground

---

## TEST — Word List 28 — Synonyms

Each of the following questions consists of a word printed in italics, followed by five words or phrases numbered 1 to 5. Choose the numbered word or phrase which is most nearly similar in meaning to the word in italics and write the number of your choice on your answer paper.

541. *temperate*   1 irate 2 experienced 3 self-controlled 4 attentive 5 accepted
542. *surfeit*   1 belittle 2 cloy 3 drop 4 estimate 5 claim
543. *tacit*   1 spoken 2 allowed 3 neural 4 understood 5 unwanted
544. *supercilious*   1 haughty 2 highbrow 3 angry 4 subservient 5 philosophic
545. *surreptitious*   1 secret 2 snakelike 3 nightly 4 abstract 5 furnished
546. *tirade*   1 dictator 2 pride 3 fatigue 4 scolding 5 fidelity
547. *superficial*   1 abnormal 2 portentous 3 shallow 4 angry 5 tiny
548. *tedious*   1 monotonous 2 vain 3 foolish 4 rapt 5 mystified
549. *tawdry*   1 orderly 2 meretricious 3 reclaimed 4 filtered 5 proper
550. *torpid*   1 intolerant 2 swallowing 3 dormant 4 finishing 5 flexible
551. *sycophantic*   1 quiet 2 recording 3 servilely flattering 4 frolicsome 5 eagerly awaiting
552. *tenacious*   1 fast running 2 intentional 3 obnoxious 4 holding fast 5 collecting
553. *superfluous*   1 irreligious 2 experimental 3 subjunctive 4 necessary 5 grammatical
554. *synthetic*   1 simplified 2 doubled 3 tuneful 4 artificial 5 fiscal
555. *tepid*   1 boiling 2 lukewarm 3 freezing 4 gaseous 5 cold
556. *tantalize*   1 tease 2 wax 3 warrant 4 authorize 5 total
557. *tenuous*   1 vital 2 thin 3 careful 4 dangerous 5 necessary

558. *temerity*  1 timidity  2 resourcefulness  3 boldness  4 tremulousness
     5 caution
559. *tentative*  1 prevalent  2 certain  3 mocking  4 wry  5 experimental
560. *temporal*  1 priestly  2 scholarly  3 secular  4 sleepy  5 sporadic

---

### Word List 29    transgression - veer

**transgression** N. violation of a law; sin. Forgive us our *transgressions*.

**transient** ADJ. fleeting; quickly passing away; staying for a short time. This hotel caters to a *transient* trade.

**translucent** ADJ. partly transparent. We could not recognize the people in the next room because of the *translucent* curtains which separated us.

**transparent** ADJ. permitting light to pass through freely; easily detected. Your scheme is so *transparent* that it will fool no one.

**transpire** V. exhale; become known; happen. In spite of all our efforts to keep the meeting a secret, news of our conclusions *transpired*.

**traverse** V. go through or across. When you *traverse* this field, be careful of the bull.

**treatise** N. article treating a subject systematically and thoroughly. He is preparing a *treatise* on the Elizabethan playwrights for his graduate degree.

**trek** V. travel; migrate. The tribe *trekked* further north that summer in search of available game. also N.

**tremor** N. trembling; slight quiver. She had a nervous *tremor* in her right hand.

**tremulous** ADJ. trembling; wavering. She was *tremulous* more from excitement than from fear.

**trenchant** ADJ. cutting; keen. I am afraid of his *trenchant* wit for it is so often sarcastic.

■ **trepidation** N. fear; trembling agitation. We must face the enemy without *trepidation* if we are to win this battle.

**tribulation** N. distress; suffering. After all the trials and *tribulations* we have gone through, we need this rest.

**tribute** N. tax levied by a ruler; mark of respect. The colonists refused to pay *tribute* to a foreign despot.

**trite** ADJ. hackneyed; commonplace. The *trite* and predictable situations in many television programs alienate many viewers.

■ **trivia** N. trifles; unimportant matters. Too many magazines ignore newsworthy subjects and feature *trivia*. trivial, ADJ.

**truculent** ADJ. aggressive; savage. They are a *truculent* race, ready to fight at any moment.

■ **turbulence** N. state of violent agitation. We were frightened by the *turbulence* of the ocean during the storm.

**tutelage** N. guardianship; training. Under the *tutelage* of such masters of the instrument, he made rapid progress as a virtuoso.

■ **tyranny** N. oppression; cruel government. Frederick Douglass fought against the *tyranny* of slavery throughout his entire life.

**tyro** N. beginner; novice. For a mere *tyro*, you have produced some marvelous results.

**ubiquitous** ADJ. being everywhere; omnipresent. You must be *ubiquitous* for I meet you wherever I go.

**ulterior** ADJ. situated beyond; unstated. You must have an *ulterior* motive for your behavior.

**ultimate** ADJ. final; not susceptible to further analysis. Scientists are searching for the *ultimate* truths.

**ultimatum** N. last demand; warning. Since they have ignored our *ultimatum*, our only recourse is to declare war.

**unanimity** N. complete agreement. We were surprised by the *unanimity* with which our proposals were accepted by the different groups.

**unassuming** ADJ. modest. He is so *unassuming* that some people fail to realize how great a man he really is.

**uncanny** ADJ. strange; mysterious. You have the *uncanny* knack of reading my innermost thoughts.

**unconscionable** ADJ. unscrupulous; excessive. He found the loan shark's demands *unconscionable* and impossible to meet.

**uncouth** ADJ. outlandish; clumsy; boorish. Most biographers portray Lincoln as an *uncouth* and ungainly young man.

**unctuous** ADJ. oily; bland; insincerely suave. Uriah Heep disguised his nefarious actions by *unctuous* protestations of his "'umility."

■ **undermine** V. weaken; sap. The recent corruption scandals have *undermined* many people's faith in the city government.

**undulate** V. move with a wavelike motion. The waters *undulated* in the breeze.

**unequivocal** ADJ. plain; obvious. My answer to your proposal is an *unequivocal* and absolute "No."

**unerringly** ADV. infallibly. My teacher *unerringly* pounced on the one typographical error in my essay.

**unfaltering** ADJ. steadfast. She approached the guillotine with *unfaltering* steps.

**ungainly** ADJ. awkward. He is an *ungainly* young man.

■ **uniformity** N. sameness; monotony. After a while, the *uniformity* of TV situation comedies becomes boring. uniform, ADJ.

**unimpeachable** ADJ. blameless and exemplary. His conduct in office was *unimpeachable*.

**uninhibited** ADJ. unrepressed. The congregation was shocked by her *uninhibited* laughter during the sermon.

**unique** ADJ. without an equal; single in kind. You have the *unique* distinction of being the first student whom I have had to fail in this course.

**unison** N. unity of pitch; complete accord. The choir sang in *unison*.

**unkempt** ADJ. disheveled; with uncared-for appearance. The beggar was dirty and *unkempt*.

**unmitigated** ADJ. harsh; severe; not lightened. I sympathize with you in your *unmitigated* sorrow.

■ **unobtrusive** ADJ. inconspicuous; not blatant. The secret service agents in charge of protecting the President tried to be as *unobtrusive* as possible.

**unpretentious** ADJ. not showy; modest; plain. Although she was a wealthy woman, she lived in an *unpretentious* house in a modest neighborhood.

**unruly** ADJ. disobedient; lawless. The only way to curb this *unruly* mob is to use tear gas.

**unseemly** ADJ. unbecoming; indecent. Your levity is *unseemly* at this time.

**untenable** ADJ. unsupportable. I find your theory *untenable* and must reject it.

**unwitting** ADJ. unintentional; not knowing. He was the *unwitting* tool of the swindlers.

**upshot** N. outcome. The *upshot* of the rematch was that the former champion proved that he still possessed all the skills of his youth.

**urbane** ADJ. suave; refined; elegant. The courtier was *urbane* and sophisticated. urbanity, N.

■ **vacillation** N. fluctuation; wavering. His *vacillation* when confronted with a problem annoyed all of us who had to wait until he made his decision. vacillate, V.

**vacuous** ADJ. empty; inane. The *vacuous* remarks of the politician annoyed the audience, who had hoped to hear more than empty platitudes.

**vagary** N. caprice; whim. She followed every *vagary* of fashion.

**vainglorious** ADJ. boastful; excessively conceited. He was a *vainglorious* and arrogant individual.

**validate** V. confirm; ratify. I will not publish my findings until I *validate* my results.

**vanguard** N. forerunners; advance forces. We are the *vanguard* of a tremendous army that is following us.

**vapid** ADJ. insipid; inane. She delivered an uninspired and *vapid* address.

**variegated** ADJ. many-colored. He will not like this blue necktie as he is addicted to *variegated* clothing.

**vaunted** ADJ. boasted; bragged; highly publicized. This much *vaunted* project proved a disappointment when it collapsed.

**veer** v. change in direction. After what seemed an eternity, the wind *veered* to the east and the storm abated.

---

## ETYMOLOGY 29

URB (city)

    **urban**    pertaining to the city
    **urbane**    polished, sophisticated (pertaining to a city dweller)
    **suburban**    outside of the city

---

## TEST — Word List 29 — Antonyms

Each of the following questions consists of a word printed in italics, followed by five words or phrases numbered 1 to 5. Choose the numbered word or phrase which is most nearly opposite in meaning to the word in italics and write the number of your choice on your answer paper.

561. *unimpeachable*   1 fruitful 2 rampaging 3 faulty 4 pensive 5 thorough
562. *ulterior*   1 tipped 2 stated 3 sparking 4 uncompromising 5 corrugated
563. *transient*   1 carried 2 close 3 permanent 4 removed 5 certain
564. *ungainly*   1 ignorant 2 graceful 3 detailed 4 dancing 5 pedantic
565. *tyro*   1 infant 2 rubber 3 personnel 4 idiot 5 expert
566. *unfeigned*   1 pretended 2 fashionable 3 wary 4 switched 5 colonial
567. *turbulence*   1 reaction 2 approach 3 impropriety 4 calm 5 hostility
568. *undermine*   1 prop up 2 gnaw 3 clean 4 fling 5 reach out
569. *unpretentious*   1 showy 2 improbable 3 invariable 4 honest 5 turgid
570. *ultimate*   1 competing 2 throbbing 3 poisonous 4 incipient 5 powerful
571. *trite*   1 correct 2 original 3 distinguished 4 premature 5 certain
572. *vaunted*   1 unvanquished 2 fell 3 belittled 4 exacting 5 believed
573. *unkempt*   1 bombed 2 washed 3 neat 4 shabby 5 tawdry
574. *unobtrusive*   1 conspicuous 2 countless 3 soggy 4 papered 5 homicidal
575. *vacillation*   1 remorse 2 relief 3 respect 4 steadfastness 5 inoculation
576. *unruly*   1 chatting 2 obedient 3 definite 4 lined 5 curious
577. *untenable*   1 supportable 2 tender 3 sheepish 4 tremulous 5 adequate
578. *vanguard*   1 regiment 2 rear 3 echelon 4 protection 5 loyalty
579. *unseemly*   1 effortless 2 proper 3 conducive 4 pointed 5 informative
580. *unwitting*   1 clever 2 intense 3 sensitive 4 freezing 5 intentional

---

### Word List 30    vehement - zephyr

**vehement** ADJ. impetuous; with marked vigor. He spoke with *vehement* eloquence in defense of his client.

**venal** ADJ. capable of being bribed. The *venal* policeman accepted the bribe offered him by the speeding motorist whom he had stopped.

**veneer** N. thin layer; cover. Casual acquaintances were deceived by his *veneer* of sophistication and failed to recognize his fundamental shallowness.

**venerable** ADJ. deserving high respect. We do not mean to be disrespectful when we refuse to follow the advice of our *venerable* leader.

■ **venerate** V. revere. In China, the people *venerate* their ancestors.

**vent** N. a small opening; outlet. The wine did not flow because the air *vent* in the barrel was clogged.

**vent** V. express; utter. He *vented* his wrath on his class.

**venturous** ADJ. daring. The five *venturous* young men decided to look for a new approach to the mountain top.

**veracious** ADJ. truthful. I can recommend him for this position because I have always found him *veracious* and reliable.

■ **verbose** ADJ. wordy. This article is too *verbose;* we must edit it.

**verity** N. truth; reality. The four *verities* were revealed to Buddha during his long meditation.

**versatile** ADJ. having many talents; capable of working in many fields. He was a *versatile* athlete; at college he had earned varsity letters in baseball, football, and track.

**vertex** N. summit. Let us drop a perpendicular line from the *vertex* of the triangle to the base.

**vertigo** N. dizziness. We test potential plane pilots for susceptibility to spells of *vertigo*.

**vestige** N. trace; remains. We discovered *vestiges* of early Indian life in the cave.

■ **viable** ADJ. capable of maintaining life; capable of working, functioning, or developing adequately. The infant, though prematurely born, is *viable* and has a good chance to survive.

**vicarious** ADJ. acting as a substitute; done by a deputy. Many people get a *vicarious* thrill at the movies by imagining they are the characters on the screen.

**vicissitude** N. change of fortune. I am accustomed to life's *vicissitudes,* having experienced poverty and wealth, sickness and health, and failure and success.

**vie** V. contend; compete. When we *vie* with each other for her approval, we are merely weakening ourselves and strengthening her. vying, ADJ.

**vigilance** N. watchfulness. Eternal *vigilance* is the price of liberty.

■ **vigor** N. active strength. Although he was over seventy years old, Jack had the *vigor* of a man in his prime. vigorous, ADJ.

■ **vilify** V. slander. Why is he always trying to *vilify* my reputation?

**vindicate** V. clear of charges. I hope to *vindicate* my client and return him to society as a free man.

**vindictive** ADJ. revengeful. She was very *vindictive* and never forgave an injury.

**virile** ADJ. manly. I do not accept the premise that a man is *virile* only when he is belligerent.

■ **virtuoso** N. highly skilled artist. Heifetz is a violin *virtuoso*.

■ **virulent** ADJ. extremely poisonous. The virus is highly *virulent* and has made many of us ill for days.

**visage** N. face; appearance. The stern *visage* of the judge indicated that he had decided to impose a severe penalty.

**visionary** ADJ. produced by imagination; fanciful; mystical. He was given to *visionary* schemes which never materialized. also N.

**vitriolic** ADJ. corrosive; sarcastic. Such *vitriolic* criticism is uncalled for.

**vituperative** ADJ. abusive; scolding. He became more *vituperative* as he realized that we were not going to grant him his wish.

**vivacious** ADJ. animated; gay. She had always been *vivacious* and sparkling.

**vociferous** ADJ. clamorous; noisy. The crowd grew *vociferous* in its anger and threatened to take the law into its own hands.

**vogue** N. popular fashion. Slacks became the *vogue* on many college campuses.

■ **volatile** ADJ. evaporating rapidly; lighthearted; mercurial. Ethyl chloride is a very *volatile* liquid.

**volition** N. act of making a conscious choice. She selected this dress of her own *volition*.

**voluble** ADJ. fluent; glib. He was a *voluble* speaker, always ready to talk.

**voluptuous** ADJ. gratifying the senses. The nobility during the Renaissance led *voluptuous* lives.

**voracious** ADJ. ravenous. The wolf is a *voracious* animal.

**vouchsafe** V. grant condescendingly; guarantee. I can safely *vouchsafe* you a fair return on your investment.

■ **vulnerable** ADJ. susceptible to wounds. Achilles was *vulnerable* only in his heel.

**waive** V. give up temporarily; yield. I will *waive* my rights in this matter in order to expedite our reaching a proper decision.

**wan** ADJ. having a pale or sickly color; pallid. Suckling asked, "Why so pale and *wan*, fond lover?"

**wane** V. grow gradually smaller. From now until December 21, the winter equinox, the hours of daylight will *wane*.

**wanton** ADJ. unruly; unchaste; excessive. His *wanton* pride cost him many friends.

**wary** ADJ. very cautious. The spies grew *wary* as they approached the sentry.

**wheedle** V. cajole; coax; deceive by flattery. She knows she can *wheedle* almost anything she wants from her father.

**whet** V. sharpen; stimulate. The odors from the kitchen are *whetting* my appetite; I will be ravenous by the time the meal is served.

■ **whimsical** ADJ. capricious; fanciful; quaint. *Peter Pan* is a *whimsical* play.

**whit** N. smallest speck. There is not a *whit* of intelligence or understanding in your observations.

**wily** ADJ. cunning; artful. He is as *wily* as a fox in avoiding trouble.

■ **wither** V. shrivel; decay. Cut flowers are beautiful for a day, but all too soon they *wither*.

**witless** ADJ. foolish; idiotic. Such *witless* and fatuous statements will create the impression that you are an ignorant individual.

**witticism** N. witty saying; facetious remark. What you regard as *witticisms* are often offensive to sensitive people.

**wizened** ADJ. withered; shriveled. The *wizened* old man in the home for the aged was still active and energetic.

**wreak** V. inflict. I am afraid he will *wreak* his wrath on the innocent as well as the guilty.

**wrest** V. pull away; take by violence. With only ten seconds left to play, our team *wrested* victory from their grasp.

■ **zealot** N. fanatic; person who shows excessive zeal. It is good to have a few *zealots* in our group for their enthusiasm is contagious. zealous, ADJ.

**zenith** N. point directly overhead in the sky; summit. When the sun was at its *zenith*, the glare was not as strong as at sunrise and sunset.

**zephyr** N. gentle breeze; west wind. When these *zephyrs* blow, it is good to be in an open boat under a full sail.

---

## ETYMOLOGY 30

VID, VIS (to see)
  **vision** sight
  **evidence** things seen
  **vista** view
VINC, VICT, VANQU (to conquer)
  **invincible** unconquerable
  **victory** winning
  **vanquish** defeat
VOC, VOCAT (to call)
  **avocation** calling, minor occupation

**provocation**   calling or rousing the anger of
**invocation**   calling in prayer
VOLV, VOLUT (to roll)
**revolve**   roll around
**evolve**   roll out, develop
**convolution**   coiled state

---

## TEST — Word List 30 — Synonyms and Antonyms

Each of the questions below consists of a word printed in italics,
followed by five words or phrases numbered 1 to 5. Choose the
numbered word or phrase which is most nearly the same as or the
opposite of the word in italics and write the number of your choice
on your answer paper.

581. *vestige*   1 trek 2 trail 3 trace 4 trial 5 tract
582. *venturous*   1 timorous 2 confiscatory 3 lethal 4 tubercular 5 dorsal
583. *vehement*   1 substantial 2 regular 3 calm 4 cautious 5 sad
584. *whimsical*   1 poetic 2 capricious 3 argumentative 4 autumnal 5 frequent
585. *venerate*   1 revere 2 age 3 reject 4 reverberate 5 degenerate
586. *verity*   1 sanctity 2 reverence 3 falsehood 4 rarity 5 household
587. *viable*   1 functionable 2 unforgettable 3 unmistaken 4 fearful 5 fragrant
588. *vicarious*   1 substitutional 2 aggressive 3 sporadic 4 reverent 5 internal
589. *vulnerable*   1 springlike 2 susceptible 3 angry 4 indifferent 5 going
590. *veracious*   1 worried 2 slight 3 alert 4 truthful 5 instrumental
591. *zealot*   1 miser 2 beginner 3 fanatic 4 convict 5 victim
592. *visage*   1 doubt 2 personality 3 hermitage 4 face 5 armor
593. *vertex*   1 whirlpool 2 drift 3 vehicle 4 base 5 context
594. *virulent*   1 sensuous 2 malignant 3 masculine 4 conforming 5 approaching
595. *vigor*   1 wand 2 cruelty 3 strength 4 diffidence 5 anxiety
596. *verbose*   1 nasty 2 affluent 3 wordy 4 sweet 5 embarrassed
597. *vigilance*   1 bivouac 2 guide 3 watchfulness 4 mob rule 5 posse
598. *vindictive*   1 revengeful 2 fearful 3 divided 4 literal 5 convincing
599. *vilify*   1 erect 2 eulogize 3 better 4 magnify 5 horrify
600. *vindicate*   1 point out 2 blame 3 declare 4 evict 5 menace

## Answer Key

### Word List 1

| | | |
|---|---|---|
| 1. 5 | 8. 1 | 15. 1 |
| 2. 4 | 9. 3 | 16. 2 |
| 3. 2 | 10. 2 | 17. 3 |
| 4. 5 | 11. 1 | 18. 4 |
| 5. 1 | 12. 3 | 19. 1 |
| 6. 5 | 13. 5 | 20. 1 |
| 7. 3 | 14. 4 | |

### Word List 2

| | | |
|---|---|---|
| 21. 2 | 28. 2 | 35. 4 |
| 22. 2 | 29. 2 | 36. 5 |
| 23. 4 | 30. 3 | 37. 5 |
| 24. 5 | 31. 4 | 38. 4 |
| 25. 5 | 32. 4 | 39. 3 |
| 26. 1 | 33. 3 | 40. 2 |
| 27. 1 | 34. 4 | |

### Word List 3

| | | |
|---|---|---|
| 41. 2 | 48. 4 | 55. 3 |
| 42. 3 | 49. 4 | 56. 4 |
| 43. 1 | 50. 5 | 57. 2 |
| 44. 4 | 51. 4 | 58. 3 |
| 45. 5 | 52. 3 | 59. 3 |
| 46. 3 | 53. 1 | 60. 4 |
| 47. 3 | 54. 2 | |

### Word List 4

| | | |
|---|---|---|
| 61. 4 | 68. 3 | 75. 2 |
| 62. 5 | 69. 4 | 76. 2 |
| 63. 2 | 70. 5 | 77. 1 |
| 64. 1 | 71. 4 | 78. 3 |
| 65. 3 | 72. 4 | 79. 2 |
| 66. 2 | 73. 2 | 80. 1 |
| 67. 2 | 74. 1 | |

### Word List 5

| | | |
|---|---|---|
| 81. 2 | 88. 3 | 95. 4 |
| 82. 5 | 89. 5 | 96. 2 |
| 83. 2 | 90. 3 | 97. 3 |
| 84. 5 | 91. 3 | 98. 1 |
| 85. 4 | 92. 3 | 99. 5 |
| 86. 2 | 93. 1 | 100. 1 |
| 87. 4 | 94. 4 | |

### Word List 6

| | | |
|---|---|---|
| 101. 2 | 108. 2 | 115. 3 |
| 102. 1 | 109. 1 | 116. 2 |
| 103. 1 | 110. 4 | 117. 4 |
| 104. 4 | 111. 1 | 118. 4 |
| 105. 5 | 112. 5 | 119. 5 |
| 106. 1 | 113. 5 | 120. 4 |
| 107. 1 | 114. 4 | |

### Word List 7

| | | |
|---|---|---|
| 121. 5 | 128. 4 | 135. 2 |
| 122. 1 | 129. 3 | 136. 2 |
| 123. 5 | 130. 2 | 137. 3 |
| 124. 3 | 131. 3 | 138. 4 |
| 125. 1 | 132. 5 | 139. 4 |
| 126. 1 | 133. 1 | 140. 4 |
| 127. 1 | 134. 2 | |

### Word List 8

| | | |
|---|---|---|
| 141. 4 | 148. 3 | 155. 1 |
| 142. 1 | 149. 1 | 156. 5 |
| 143. 3 | 150. 5 | 157. 5 |
| 144. 2 | 151. 4 | 158. 3 |
| 145. 2 | 152. 4 | 159. 2 |
| 146. 2 | 153. 1 | 160. 3 |
| 147. 1 | 154. 2 | |

## Word List 9

| | | |
|---|---|---|
| 161. 3 | 168. 3 | 175. 4 |
| 162. 3 | 169. 2 | 176. 1 |
| 163. 2 | 170. 2 | 177. 3 |
| 164. 3 | 171. 3 | 178. 2 |
| 165. 4 | 172. 3 | 179. 4 |
| 166. 3 | 173. 1 | 180. 2 |
| 167. 4 | 174. 1 | |

## Word List 10

| | | |
|---|---|---|
| 181. 3 | 188. 2 | 195. 5 |
| 182. 3 | 189. 2 | 196. 1 |
| 183. 3 | 190. 5 | 197. 4 |
| 184. 3 | 191. 1 | 198. 1 |
| 185. 4 | 192. 4 | 199. 3 |
| 186. 5 | 193. 5 | 200. 2 |
| 187. 4 | 194. 1 | |

## Word List 11

| | | |
|---|---|---|
| 201. 3 | 208. 1 | 215. 2 |
| 202. 3 | 209. 3 | 216. 5 |
| 203. 4 | 210. 4 | 217. 1 |
| 204. 5 | 211. 2 | 218. 2 |
| 205. 1 | 212. 2 | 219. 3 |
| 206. 1 | 213. 1 | 220. 1 |
| 207. 5 | 214. 5 | |

## Word List 12

| | | |
|---|---|---|
| 221. 1 | 228. 5 | 235. 1 |
| 222. 4 | 229. 3 | 236. 3 |
| 223. 3 | 230. 1 | 237. 2 |
| 224. 2 | 231. 3 | 238. 5 |
| 225. 1 | 232. 4 | 239. 5 |
| 226. 3 | 233. 1 | 240. 2 |
| 227. 1 | 234. 4 | |

## Word List 13

| | | |
|---|---|---|
| 241. 3 | 248. 1 | 255. 3 |
| 242. 5 | 249. 3 | 256. 2 |
| 243. 1 | 250. 2 | 257. 1 |
| 244. 2 | 251. 4 | 258. 3 |
| 245. 2 | 252. 4 | 259. 2 |
| 246. 4 | 253. 1 | 260. 2 |
| 247. 3 | 254. 5 | |

## Word List 14

| | | |
|---|---|---|
| 261. 4 | 268. 1 | 275. 2 |
| 262. 2 | 269. 3 | 276. 1 |
| 263. 1 | 270. 2 | 277. 2 |
| 264. 1 | 271. 1 | 278. 2 |
| 265. 3 | 272. 1 | 279. 4 |
| 266. 4 | 273. 3 | 280. 3 |
| 267. 5 | 274. 5 | |

## Word List 15

| | | |
|---|---|---|
| 281. 2 | 288. 1 | 295. 1 |
| 282. 4 | 289. 4 | 296. 1 |
| 283. 2 | 290. 1 | 297. 4 |
| 284. 1 | 291. 2 | 298. 3 |
| 285. 1 | 292. 3 | 299. 2 |
| 286. 3 | 293. 3 | 300. 2 |
| 287. 3 | 294. 2 | |

## Word List 16

| | | |
|---|---|---|
| 301. 2 | 308. 2 | 315. 1 |
| 302. 5 | 309. 2 | 316. 2 |
| 303. 2 | 310. 5 | 317. 1 |
| 304. 2 | 311. 2 | 318. 2 |
| 305. 5 | 312. 1 | 319. 4 |
| 306. 3 | 313. 3 | 320. 2 |
| 307. 1 | 314. 3 | |

## Word List 17

| | | |
|---|---|---|
| 321. 3 | 328. 2 | 335. 3 |
| 322. 4 | 329. 5 | 336. 4 |
| 323. 5 | 330. 1 | 337. 5 |
| 324. 2 | 331. 2 | 338. 5 |
| 325. 1 | 332. 4 | 339. 2 |
| 326. 5 | 333. 5 | 340. 3 |
| 327. 2 | 334. 1 | |

## Word List 18

| | | |
|---|---|---|
| 341. 3 | 348. 2 | 355. 5 |
| 342. 3 | 349. 5 | 356. 2 |
| 343. 1 | 350. 1 | 357. 2 |
| 344. 2 | 351. 1 | 358. 1 |
| 345. 4 | 352. 1 | 359. 1 |
| 346. 2 | 353. 2 | 360. 4 |
| 347. 1 | 354. 4 | |

## Word List 19

| | | |
|---|---|---|
| 361. 2 | 368. 5 | 375. 3 |
| 362. 2 | 369. 2 | 376. 1 |
| 363. 5 | 370. 3 | 377. 4 |
| 364. 3 | 371. 3 | 378. 3 |
| 365. 1 | 372. 1 | 379. 1 |
| 366. 2 | 373. 3 | 380. 2 |
| 367. 5 | 374. 3 | |

## Word List 20

| | | |
|---|---|---|
| 381. 1 | 388. 4 | 395. 3 |
| 382. 3 | 389. 2 | 396. 3 |
| 383. 1 | 390. 3 | 397. 1 |
| 384. 5 | 391. 2 | 398. 3 |
| 385. 4 | 392. 4 | 399. 3 |
| 386. 1 | 393. 2 | 400. 3 |
| 387. 1 | 394. 2 | |

## Word List 21

| | | |
|---|---|---|
| 401. 2 | 408. 3 | 415. 5 |
| 402. 4 | 409. 4 | 416. 4 |
| 403. 1 | 410. 5 | 417. 3 |
| 404. 3 | 411. 4 | 418. 2 |
| 405. 3 | 412. 5 | 419. 5 |
| 406. 3 | 413. 1 | 420. 2 |
| 407. 2 | 414. 2 | |

## Word List 22

| | | |
|---|---|---|
| 421. 2 | 428. 1 | 435. 1 |
| 422. 3 | 429. 4 | 436. 5 |
| 423. 3 | 430. 1 | 437. 3 |
| 424. 4 | 431. 1 | 438. 5 |
| 425. 5 | 432. 2 | 439. 3 |
| 426. 5 | 433. 5 | 440. 2 |
| 427. 1 | 434. 1 | |

## Word List 23

| | | |
|---|---|---|
| 441. 3 | 448. 4 | 455. 5 |
| 442. 1 | 449. 5 | 456. 1 |
| 443. 2 | 450. 2 | 457. 5 |
| 444. 4 | 451. 1 | 458. 1 |
| 445. 3 | 452. 3 | 459. 1 |
| 446. 3 | 453. 4 | 460. 3 |
| 447. 2 | 454. 5 | |

## Word List 24

| | | |
|---|---|---|
| 461. 2 | 468. 3 | 475. 2 |
| 462. 3 | 469. 2 | 476. 5 |
| 463. 2 | 470. 1 | 477. 1 |
| 464. 5 | 471. 1 | 478. 2 |
| 465. 4 | 472. 4 | 479. 4 |
| 466. 3 | 473. 2 | 480. 3 |
| 467. 4 | 474. 5 | |

**Word List 25**

| | | |
|---|---|---|
| 481. 2 | 488. 2 | 495. 1 |
| 482. 4 | 489. 2 | 496. 2 |
| 483. 3 | 490. 4 | 497. 3 |
| 484. 5 | 491. 1 | 498. 1 |
| 485. 1 | 492. 3 | 499. 1 |
| 486. 1 | 493. 4 | 500. 1 |
| 487. 4 | 494. 2 | |

**Word List 26**

| | | |
|---|---|---|
| 501. 3 | 508. 5 | 515. 2 |
| 502. 1 | 509. 2 | 516. 1 |
| 503. 4 | 510. 3 | 517. 4 |
| 504. 5 | 511. 1 | 518. 5 |
| 505. 3 | 512. 4 | 519. 5 |
| 506. 3 | 513. 2 | 520. 4 |
| 507. 4 | 514. 2 | |

**Word List 27**

| | | |
|---|---|---|
| 521. 4 | 528. 1 | 535. 1 |
| 522. 3 | 529. 3 | 536. 1 |
| 523. 5 | 530. 1 | 537. 3 |
| 524. 2 | 531. 4 | 538. 3 |
| 525. 2 | 532. 3 | 539. 5 |
| 526. 5 | 533. 1 | 540. 3 |
| 527. 1 | 534. 4 | |

**Word List 28**

| | | |
|---|---|---|
| 541. 3 | 548. 1 | 555. 2 |
| 542. 2 | 549. 2 | 556. 1 |
| 543. 4 | 550. 3 | 557. 2 |
| 544. 1 | 551. 3 | 558. 3 |
| 545. 1 | 552. 4 | 559. 5 |
| 546. 4 | 553. 4 | 560. 3 |
| 547. 3 | 554. 4 | |

**Word List 29**

| | | |
|---|---|---|
| 561. 3 | 568. 1 | 575. 4 |
| 562. 2 | 569. 1 | 576. 2 |
| 563. 3 | 570. 4 | 577. 1 |
| 564. 2 | 571. 2 | 578. 2 |
| 565. 5 | 572. 3 | 579. 2 |
| 566. 1 | 573. 3 | 580. 5 |
| 567. 4 | 574. 1 | |

**Word List 30**

| | | |
|---|---|---|
| 581. 3 | 588. 1 | 595. 3 |
| 582. 1 | 589. 2 | 596. 3 |
| 583. 3 | 590. 4 | 597. 3 |
| 584. 2 | 591. 3 | 598. 1 |
| 585. 1 | 592. 4 | 599. 2 |
| 586. 3 | 593. 4 | 600. 2 |
| 587. 1 | 594. 2 | |

# 4 The Verbal Sections: Strategies, Tips, and Practice

In Chapter 2 you learned about the four types of verbal questions that appear on the SAT. In this chapter you'll learn how best to handle each type of verbal question, using strategies and tips that have helped thousands of SAT-takers before you. You'll also find practice exercises for each question type. And, as you well know, "practice makes perfect," so be sure to do the exercises. You'll feel confident taking the exam because you'll be familiar with the types of questions on it; your mind will switch easily into SAT gear.

**Long-Range Strategy:** The best way to have prepared for the verbal sections of the SAT is to have read a great deal of good writing over the past five or ten years. Through reading, you not only increase your vocabulary, but you also grow accustomed to the way words are used in context. Unfortunately, there is not enough time between now and the SAT for you to fit in five years' worth of reading. However, you can make a conscious effort to pay attention to the vocabulary in anything you do read. If you are not sure of the meaning of a word, look it up.

### General Tips for Answering Verbal Questions

1. An important point to remember when you are answering the verbal questions is that the test is looking for the best answer, the most likely answer. This is not the time to try to show how clever you can be by imagining exotic situations that would justify different answers. If you can imagine a weird situation that would make one of the sentence completions correct—Forget it! This

test is scored by a machine, and a machine has absolutely no imagination or sense of humor. To a machine, an imaginative answer is a wrong answer. Stick to the most likely answer.

2. Remember also that except for the reading comprehension part each section of the verbal tests begins with easy questions and gets harder as it goes along. That means there will be easy analogy, antonym, and sentence completion questions. If you get bogged down in the first part of the test and forget about the time, you may never get to the easy questions up ahead.

3. The reading comprehension questions take by far the most time. To make sure you get to all the others, save the reading comprehension for last. You don't get any more credit for a reading comprehension question than you do for an antonym, but the reading passage may take you five minutes to read and the antonym question may take you ten seconds.

4. Glance quickly through the entire test section before you begin. There may be a short section of sentence completion questions or analogies after the reading comprehension section. Do that before you start the reading. There is no rule about the order in which you should do the questions. Just make sure you put your answers in the right places on the answer sheet.

## THE ANTONYM QUESTION

In the antonym question, you are looking for a word or phrase most nearly <u>opposite</u> in meaning to the capitalized word. You have five possible choices. Look at each one of them.

**Long-Range Strategy:**   The key strategy for learning antonyms is (once again): READ. However, there are some helpful things you can do using the Basic Word List in the previous chapter.

Use the Basic Word List as a guide in making flash cards. Scan a list looking for words you don't quite know—not words you are totally unfamiliar with, but words you are on the brink of knowing. Look for words you have heard or seen before but can't use in a sentence or define. Effort you put into mastering such "borderline" words will pay off—soon!

Be brief—but include all the information you need. On one side write the word. On the other side write <u>concise</u> definitions—two or three words at most—for each major meaning of the word you want to learn. Include an antonym, too: the synonym-antonym associations can help you remember both words. To fix the word in your mind, use it in a short phrase. Then write that phrase down.

Carry a few of your flash cards with you every day. Look them over whenever you have a spare moment or two. Work in short bursts. Try going through five flash cards at a time, shuffling through them rapidly so that you can build up your rapid sight recognition of the words for the test. You want these words and their antonyms to spring to your mind instantaneously, so that you can speed through the antonym section of the SAT.

## Tips to Help You Cope

1. Think of a context for the capitalized word. Take a quick look at the word in capital letters. If you don't recollect its meaning right away, try to think of a phrase or sentence in which you have heard it used. The context may help you come up with the word's meaning.

2. Before you look at the choices, think of antonyms for the capitalized word. If the question word is a word you know, try quickly to think of opposites for it before you look at the answer choices. Even if you don't find those very words in the answers, you may find it easier to look for similar words.

3. Read all the choices before you decide which is best. A possible answer is not always the *best* answer.

4. Choose an answer as extreme as the capitalized word. Words have shades of meaning. In matching a word with its opposite, you must pay attention to these shades of meaning. Check to see whether the capitalized word and your answer have the same degree of intensity. Suppose that the question word is "adore"

and the answer choices include both "dislike" and "loathe." The second would be a much better answer, since "dislike" is a much milder term. But if the question word were "approve," then "dislike" would be the better answer. "Loathe" would be too strong.

5. Look at the answer choices to determine the main word's part of speech. Words may have more than one part of speech. If you don't know whether you're dealing with the common noun "contract" or the less common verb "contract" (make smaller), look at the answer choices. They'll all have the same part of speech.

6. Consider secondary meanings of the capitalized word as well as its primary meaning. If none of the answer choices seems right to you, take another look at the capitalized word. It may have more than one meaning. The SAT often constructs questions that make use of secondary, less well-known meanings of deceptively familiar words.

7. Break down unfamiliar words into recognizable parts. When you come upon a totally unfamiliar word, don't give up. Break it down and see if you recognize any of its parts. Pay particular attention to prefixes—word parts added to the beginning of a word—and to roots, the building blocks of the language. For example, if you know the root "ver," truth, in the word "verify," you can figure out that "veracity," "veracious," and "verisimilitude" must all have something to do with truth.

8. Watch out for eye-catchers, answer choices that are designed to tempt the unwary into guessing wrong. Eye-catchers are words that somehow remind you of the capitalized word. They're related in a way; they feel as if they belong together. Remember, though, that you're looking for opposites.

9. In eliminating answer choices, test words for their positive or negative connotations. In other words, even if you are dealing with a word that you cannot define or use in a sentence, try to remember the word's general

tone. If you are sure the capitalized word has a positive feeling to it, then, since you are looking for an antonym, you *know* the correct answer must have a negative feeling. Thus, you can toss out any positive answer choices and guess among the negative ones that are left.

**Examples to Get You Started**

EXAMPLE 1

CONFISCATE:   (A) correct   (B) distribute   (C) hasten   (D) organize   (E) shatter

Think of the sentence "The police confiscated the gang's weapons." From the context you realize that to *confiscate* weapons is to seize or commandeer them. The opposite of seizing weapons is giving them out or *distributing* them. *Distribute* (B) is correct.

EXAMPLE 2

DEBASE:   (A) recall   (B) import   (C) found   (D) participate   (E) enhance

To *debase* something is to lower or lessen it in value. In thinking of possible antonyms for *debase*, you may have come up with words like *elevate, augment,* or *exalt*, words signifying raising something or increasing it in value. *Elevate, augment,* and *exalt* are all synonyms for *enhance*. The correct answer is (E) *enhance*.

EXAMPLE 3

MINUTE:   (A) large   (B) unpatriotic   (C) gigantic   (D) whole   (E) average

If you are in a hurry, you may choose (A) *large* as your answer. After all, the adjective *minute* (pronounced mī-ʹnüt) means small, right? And the opposite of small is large.

Wrong. *Minute* is an adjective meaning *extremely* small. *Gigantic* (C) is a better answer because it means *extremely* large.

## EXAMPLE 4

IMPORT:   (A) definition   (B) insignificance   (C) cost
(D) lack of direction   (E) product

> Are you dealing with *import* the verb or *import* the noun?
> A look at the answer choices reveals that they are all nouns. (The *-tion* and *-ance* word endings are common noun endings.) One definition of the noun *import* is significance, or meaning. Its opposite is *insignificance*, choice (B).

## EXAMPLE 5

CONVICTION:   (A) crime   (B) veto   (C) dearth
(D) argument   (E) uncertainty

> The most familiar context for the word *conviction* is a legal one. The District Attorney is out to get a *conviction*, to prove someone guilty of a crime. However, a *conviction* is also a strong persuasion or belief. Its antonyms are *doubt, lack of belief*—in other words, *uncertainty*. Choice (E) is the best answer.

## EXAMPLE 6

BENEFACTOR:   (A) mysterious stranger   (B) committed rebel
(C) evildoer   (D) young child   (E) intruder

> You may not know the word *benefactor,* but you know the word *benefit.* Benefit concerts to aid people starving in Ethiopia, bake sales and car washes to benefit the baseball team—these are attempts to do good. *Bene* basically means "good." A *benefactor* is someone who does good works to benefit others. So the antonym of *benefactor* is *evildoer.* Your answer is choice (C).

## EXAMPLE 7

UNDERMINE:   (A) entangle   (B) parch   (C) overwork
(D) enter   (E) support

> What's the opposite of *under?* *Over.* What's the opposite of *undermine?* No, it's not *overwork.* Be suspicious of answers that

come too easily. This actual SAT question is a classic eye-catcher. People associate *under* and *over* and think of mining as a particular kind of work. That's why *overwork* reminds you of *undermine.* To undermine, however, means to weaken something or cause it to collapse by removing its underlying supports. The opposite of to *undermine* is choice (E), to *support.*

## EXAMPLE 8

BANEFUL: (A) brilliant    (B) beneficial    (C) mysterious
(D) rough    (E) careful

See how positive and negative connotations can help you narrow down the possible answer choices for this question from an actual SAT. You're unsure of the meaning of *baneful.* However, you do feel sure the word is negative in tone. You therefore can toss out choices (C) and (D), *mysterious* and *rough,* neither of which are positive. You've eliminated two choices, and are in a great position to guess. As it turns out, *baneful* (ruinous; harmful) is the opposite of *beneficial* (helpful). The correct answer is choice (B).

**Practice Exercises**        **Answers given on page 176.**

---

Each question below consists of a word in capital letters, followed by five lettered words or phrases. Choose the word or phrase that is most nearly <u>opposite</u> in meaning to the word in capital letters. Since some of the questions require you to distinguish fine shades of meaning, consider all the choices before deciding which is best.

Example:

GOOD: (A) sour    (B) bad    (C) red    (D) hot
(E) ugly

Ⓐ ● Ⓒ Ⓓ Ⓔ

## Exercise A

1. CANDOR: (A) hypocrisy (B) inability (C) sweetmeat
   (D) pleasure (E) velocity
2. CHASTISE: (A) reward (B) pursue (C) abuse (D) stop
   (E) prolong
3. REBUKE: (A) assign (B) mature (C) matriculate
   (D) commend (E) falsify
4. DEARTH: (A) birth (B) brevity (C) abundance
   (D) brightness (E) morning
5. MAUDLIN: (A) outrageous (B) modish (C) unemotional
   (D) unimaginative (E) exaggerated
6. HOMOGENEOUS: (A) female (B) triangular (C) milky
   (D) stirred (E) motley
7. WANE: (A) enlarge (B) endorse (C) darken (D) enforce
   (E) anger
8. INFINITE: (A) wise (B) enduring (C) limited (D) gracious
   (E) placid
9. DEMISE: (A) repetition (B) residence (C) act (D) arrival
   (E) birth
10. FRUGALITY: (A) extravagance (B) ripening (C) timeliness
    (D) anxiety (E) ire
11. GARRULOUS: (A) laconic (B) strangling (C) ecstatic
    (D) frozen (E) tiny
12. ILLICIT: (A) literate (B) private (C) weary (D) angry
    (E) lawful
13. INDIGENCE: (A) nativity (B) tolerance (C) gossip
    (D) wealth (E) altruism
14. PERIPHERAL: (A) central (B) lasting (C) mandatory
    (D) glorious (E) picturesque
15. LOQUACIOUS: (A) situated (B) gregarious (C) tactical
    (D) antisocial (E) taciturn
16. DISCRETE: (A) wise (B) foolish (C) unkempt
    (D) organized (E) continuous
17. PERFUNCTORY: (A) thorough (B) individual (C) anxious
    (D) irate (E) sinister
18. COGENT: (A) docile (B) major (C) illiterate (D) irrelevant
    (E) aromatic
19. PRETENTIOUS: (A) real (B) excusing (C) modest
    (D) unpardonable (E) typical
20. EFFUSIVE: (A) vapid (B) assumed (C) desirous
    (D) reserved (E) eroded

21. ABSTEMIOUS: (A) fastidious (B) punctilious (C) pusillanimous (D) disappointed (E) intemperate
22. GERMANE: (A) feminine (B) healthful (C) irrelevant (D) massive (E) puny
23. EGREGIOUS: (A) nostalgic (B) splendid (C) abortive (D) maturing (E) birdlike
24. AUTONOMOUS: (A) magnanimous (B) ambiguous (C) exiguous (D) dependent (E) operated by hand
25. CONTENTIOUS: (A) pacific (B) masterful (C) satisfied (D) dissatisfied (E) hungry
26. ASSUAGE: (A) meet (B) delay (C) separate (D) irritate (E) demonstrate
27. INDIGENOUS: (A) alien (B) digestible (C) comestible (D) pleased (E) irate
28. RESPITE: (A) reason (B) interment (C) exertion (D) friendship (E) anger
29. DISCORD: (A) noise (B) amity (C) irritation (D) scrap (E) use
30. ABOMINATE: (A) love (B) despair (C) abate (D) deplore (E) attach

## Exercise B

1. CURIOUS: (A) impulsive (B) reliable (C) silent (D) ordinary (E) permanent
2. COMMENCE: (A) graduate (B) terminate (C) send away (D) hold back (E) exaggerate
3. COMPLY: (A) disobey (B) hint (C) supply (D) endure (E) disorganize
4. SERENITY: (A) ignorance (B) formality (C) commotion (D) simplicity (E) incompetence
5. IMPAIR: (A) duplicate (B) despair (C) improve (D) continue (E) expose
6. LAVISH: (A) sparing (B) unwashed (C) vexed (D) nervous (E) hostile
7. DEFERENCE: (A) support (B) vanity (C) postponement (D) value (E) disrespect
8. PROVOKE: (A) shout (B) regret (C) mollify (D) deny (E) intensify
9. PROFOUND: (A) lost (B) greatly admired (C) unwilling to move (D) lacking in depth (E) supercilious
10. TACITURNITY: (A) wordiness (B) tactlessness (C) irony (D) escalation (E) futility

11. ALIENATE: (A) renovate (B) conciliate (C) deviate
(D) rectify (E) eliminate

12. CRYPTIC: (A) ghastly (B) lawful (C) perceptive
(D) identical (E) unconcealed

13. LOATH: (A) despicable (B) adoring (C) fragrant
(D) choleric (E) avid

14. AMENABLE: (A) inactive (B) discursive (C) irreparable
(D) contentious (E) embarrassed

15. RAUCOUS: (A) impartial (B) bloody (C) gentle
(D) vacuous (E) innocuous

16. CALLOUS: (A) concerned (B) blameless (C) irritated
(D) noxious (E) careless

17. DEMURE: (A) objective (B) complete (C) bold
(D) illiterate (E) intolerant

18. URBANITY: (A) openness (B) rural area (C) cautious outlook
(D) naive manner (E) restlessness

19. DISSUADE: (A) urge strongly (B) extract (C) diminish in
strength (D) divide equally (E) antagonize

20. ORTHODOX: (A) matchless (B) communal (C) massive
(D) plain (E) heretical

21. FERVOR: (A) candor (B) futility (C) freedom
(D) responsibility (E) indifference

22. LAUDATORY: (A) imposing (B) unjust (C) defamatory
(D) clandestine (E) scanty

23. LACKADAISICAL: (A) copious (B) enthusiastic
(C) harmonious (D) livid (E) fortunate

24. SALUTARY: (A) harmful (B) respectful (C) flavorful
(D) valedictory (E) anxious

25. BANE: (A) ignorance (B) sensitivity (C) source of bliss
(D) lack of permission (E) proclivity

26. SCHISM: (A) union (B) spasm (C) failure (D) conspiracy
(E) doctrine

27. ANOMALOUS: (A) essential (B) regular (C) outstanding
(D) protected (E) prolific

28. QUELL: (A) withhold (B) extol (C) heed (D) incur
(E) incite

29. SYCOPHANT: (A) lunatic (B) profiteer (C) renegade
(D) faith healer (E) dignified leader

30. EXPATIATE: (A) alienate (B) approve (C) demonstrate
(D) summarize (E) return

## Answer Key

### Exercise A

| | | | | |
|---|---|---|---|---|
| 1. **A** | 7. **A** | 13. **D** | 19. **C** | 25. **A** |
| 2. **A** | 8. **C** | 14. **A** | 20. **D** | 26. **D** |
| 3. **D** | 9. **E** | 15. **E** | 21. **E** | 27. **A** |
| 4. **C** | 10. **A** | 16. **E** | 22. **C** | 28. **C** |
| 5. **C** | 11. **A** | 17. **A** | 23. **B** | 29. **B** |
| 6. **E** | 12. **E** | 18. **D** | 24. **D** | 30. **A** |

### Exercise B

| | | | | |
|---|---|---|---|---|
| 1. **D** | 7. **E** | 13. **E** | 19. **A** | 25. **C** |
| 2. **B** | 8. **C** | 14. **D** | 20. **E** | 26. **A** |
| 3. **A** | 9. **D** | 15. **C** | 21. **E** | 27. **B** |
| 4. **C** | 10. **A** | 16. **A** | 22. **C** | 28. **E** |
| 5. **C** | 11. **B** | 17. **C** | 23. **B** | 29. **E** |
| 6. **A** | 12. **E** | 18. **D** | 24. **A** | 30. **D** |

---

# THE ANALOGY QUESTION

Analogy questions challenge your ability to analyze relationships which may be similar or parallel. In some questions you are asked to carry an analogy from a concrete example to a more abstract or less tangible one.

SURGEON : SCALPEL :: satirist : words

A *surgeon* literally uses a *scalpel* to make an incision, to cut. A *satirist* uses *words* to cut and ridicule the pride and folly of his subjects. As you can see, answering such questions correctly involves more than knowing single meanings of words.

---

**Long-Range Strategy:** Continue to build up your vocabulary and to study the connotations as well as the literal meanings of words. Also, learn the common types of relationships that may exist between words.

1. **Definition**
REFUGE : SHELTER
A refuge (place of asylum) by definition shelters.

2. **Defining Characteristic**
TIGER : CARNIVOROUS
A tiger is defined as a carnivorous or meat-eating animal.

3. **Class and Member**
REPTILE : SALAMANDER
A salamander is a kind of reptile.

4. **Group and Member**
HOUND : PACK
A hound is a member of a pack.

5. **Antonyms**
WAX : WANE
Wax, to grow larger, and wane, to dwindle, are opposites.

6. **Antonym Variants**
NERVOUS : POISE
Nervous means lacking in poise.

7. **Synonyms**
MAGNIFICENT : GRANDIOSE
Magnificent and grandiose are synonyms; they have the same meaning.

8. **Synonym Variants**
VERBOSE : WORDINESS
Someone verbose is wordy; he or she exhibits wordiness.

9. **Degree of Intensity**
FLURRY : BLIZZARD
A flurry or shower of snow is less extreme than a blizzard.

10. **Part to Whole**
ISLAND : ARCHIPELAGO
Many islands make up an archipelago.

11. Function
    BALLAST : STABILITY
    Ballast provides stability.

12. Manner
    STRUT : WALK
    To strut is to walk in a proud manner.

13. Action and Its Significance
    WINCE : PAIN
    A wince is a sign that one feels pain.

14. Worker and Article Created
    POET : SONNET
    A poet creates a sonnet.

15. Worker and Tool
    PAINTER : BRUSH
    A painter uses a brush.

16. Worker and Action
    ACROBAT : CARTWHEEL
    An acrobat performs a cartwheel.

17. Worker and Workplace
    MINER : QUARRY
    A miner works in a quarry or pit.

18. Tool and Its Action
    CROWBAR : PRY
    A crowbar is a tool used to pry things apart.

19. Cause and Effect
    SEDATIVE : SLEEPINESS
    A sedative causes sleepiness.

20. Sex
    DOE : STAG
    A doe is a female deer; a stag, a male deer.

**21.** Age
COLT : STALLION
A colt is a young stallion.

**22.** Time Sequence
CORONATION : REIGN
The coronation precedes the reign.

**23.** Spatial Sequence
ROOF : FOUNDATION
The roof is the highest point of a house; the foundation, the lowest point.

**24.** Symbol and Quality It Represents
DOVE : PEACE
A dove is the symbol of peace.

**Tips to Help You Cope**

1. Before you look at the choices, try to state the relationship between the capitalized words in a good sentence. Then use the word pairs from the answer choices in the same sentence. Frequently, only one will make sense, and you will have the correct answer.

2. Do not be misled if the choices are from different fields or areas, or seem to deal with different items, from the given pair. Study the capitalized words until you see the connection between them; then search for the same relationship among the choices. BOTANIST : MICROSCOPE :: CARPENTER : HAMMER, even though the two workers may have little else in common besides their use of tools.

3. If more than one answer fits the relationship in your sentence, look for a narrower approach. For example:

    MITTEN : HAND :: (A) bracelet : wrist

    (B) belt : waist    (C) muffler : neck

    (D) ring : finger    (E) sandal : foot

    You make up the sentence, "You wear a

mitten on your hand." Unfortunately, *all* the answer choices will fit that sentence. So you say to yourself, "Why do you wear a mitten? You wear a mitten to keep your hand warm." Now when you try to substitute, only choice (C) works, so you have your answer.

4. Watch out for errors stemming from grammatical reversals. Ask yourself who is doing what to whom. BEGGAR : PLEAD is not the same as LAUGHINGSTOCK : MOCK. A beggar is the person who pleads; a laughingstock is the person who *is* mocked.

5. Again, don't confuse "contract" the verb with "contract" the noun. Use the answer choices as a source of information about the original pair of words. If your answer choices are a noun and a verb, your original pair are a noun and a verb also. If they are an adjective and a noun, your original pair are an adjective and a noun.

6. Watch out for eye-catchers among your answer choices. Remember, these distracting answer choices are set up to remind you in some way of the original capitalized pair. Try spotting the eye-catcher in the following SAT analogy.

> GIBE : SCORN :: (A) confess : punishment
> (B) smile : awe    (C) rebuff : friendship
> (D) twitch : fury    (E) chortle : exultation

The eye-catcher here is choice (D), *twitch : fury*. It's there to tempt readers who mentally associate the words *fury* and *scorn*.

7. Eliminate answer choices whose terms are only casually linked. One of your basic SAT strategies is to eliminate as many wrong answer choices as you can. In the case of analogy questions, look for answer pairs whose terms lack a clear, defined relationship. In your capitalized pairs, the words are always clearly linked:

> An island *is part of* an archipelago.
> Something perfunctory *is lacking in* enthusiasm.
> To gibe or sneer *is to exhibit* scorn.

In the answer pairs, the relationship between the words

may sometimes seem casual at best. Take, for example, choice (D) in the previous analogy. There's no clear, defined relationship between *twitch* and *fury*. There's no relationship whatsoever between *smile* and *awe*. Discard such choices.

### Examples to Get You Started

**EXAMPLE 1**

CONSTELLATION : STARS :: (A) prison : bars
(B) assembly : speaker    (C) troupe : actors
 (D) mountain : peak    (E) flock : shepherds

A *constellation* is made up of *stars*. A *troupe* (not *troop* but *troupe*) is made up of *actors* (and actresses, of course). Choice (C) is correct.

**EXAMPLE 2**

ELEVATOR : SHAFT :: (A) magnet : electricity
(B) soda : bottle    (C) bridge : tunnel    (D) water : conduit
 (E) rifle : shell

Suppose you phrase your sentence as follows: "You find an *elevator* in a *shaft.*" You can immediately eliminate choices (A), (C), and (E). However, you still have to choose between choices (B) and (D).

Rephrase your sentence: "An *elevator* moves up and down a *shaft.*" *Water* flows through a *conduit* (a pipe or channel). Choice (D) is correct.

**EXAMPLE 3**

SUCCESS : ASSIDUITY :: (A) irritation : perseverance
(B) incompetence : diligence    (C) stupidity : failure
 (D) sweetness : light    (E) proficiency : practice

In this analogy you are dealing with a cause and effect relationship in which the visual order is reversed. The effect (*success*) is presented before the cause (*assiduity,* or hard work). A good model sentence is *"Success comes from assiduity."* In the same way that success comes from assiduity, *proficiency* comes from *practice.* Choice (E) is correct.

## EXAMPLE 4

PURSE : MOUTH :: (A) pierce : ear    (B) lift : chin
(C) collapse : lung    (D) squint : eye    (E) flair : nostril

At first glance, *purse* and *mouth* seem unrelated. After all, a purse is a handbag or a pocketbook. However, if you take a look at the answer pairs, you'll see that *pierce* and *lift* are verbs, not nouns. *Purse* must be a verb as well. When you purse your mouth, you draw it closed; your lips become puckered. That most resembles what happens when you squint your eye. The correct answer is choice (D).

**Practice Exercises**      **Answers given on page 187.**

---

Each question below consists of a related pair of words or phrases, followed by five lettered pairs of words or phrases. Select the lettered pair that <u>best</u> expresses a relationship similar to that expressed in the original pair.

Example:

  YAWN : BOREDOM :: (A) dream : sleep
  (B) anger : madness    (C) smile : amusement
    (D) face : expression    (E) impatience : rebellion

                         Ⓐ Ⓑ ● Ⓓ Ⓔ

---

## Exercise A

1. CUB : LION :: (A) kit : fox    (B) dam : beaver
  (C) tigress : tiger    (D) pack : wolf    (E) beak : eagle

2. DIET : WEIGHT :: (A) alter : shape    (B) measure : length
  (C) copy : pattern    (D) bleach : color    (E) calculate : odds

**3.** SIGNATURE : ILLUSTRATION :: (A) byline : column
(B) alias : charge  (C) credit : purchase  (D) note : scale
(E) reference : recommendation

**4.** CHAINS : CLANK :: (A) glasses : shatter  (B) flowers : sway
(C) bells : chime  (D) birds : flutter  (E) boards : warp

**5.** ENROLL : STUDENT :: (A) interview : applicant
(B) dismiss : employee  (C) enact : lawyer  (D) enlist : soldier
(E) evaluate : counselor

**6.** MASTHEAD : NEWSPAPER :: (A) footnote : essay
(B) credits : film  (C) spine : book  (D) ream : paper
(E) advertisement : magazine

**7.** REPOSE : WEARY :: (A) clothing : meek  (B) shelter : thirsty
(C) protection : poor  (D) refreshment : spirited
(E) nourishment : hungry

**8.** PARCHED : MOISTURE :: (A) listless : energy
(B) feverish : warmth  (C) frail : delicacy  (D) unruffled : poise
(E) erect : posture

**9.** FRAYED : FABRIC :: (A) thawed : ice  (B) renovated : building
(C) frazzled : nerves  (D) watered : lawn
(E) cultivated : manner

**10.** INDOLENT : WORK :: (A) decisive : act  (B) gullible : cheat
(C) perceptive : observe  (D) theatrical : perform
(E) taciturn : speak

**11.** SURPRISE : EXCLAMATION :: (A) insolence : bow
(B) dismay : groan  (C) happiness : grimace
(D) deference : nod  (E) contentment : mutter

**12.** PERFORATE : HOLES :: (A) speckle : spots
(B) evaporate : perfume  (C) decorate : rooms
(D) filter : water  (E) repent : sins

**13.** MAP : CARTOGRAPHER :: (A) blueprint : draftsman
(B) building : inspector  (C) photograph : topographer
(D) scheme : surveyor  (E) chart : optician

**14.** EXCESSIVE : MODERATION :: (A) extensive : duration
(B) arbitrary : courage  (C) impulsive : reflection
(D) distinguished : reverence  (E) expensive : cost

**15.** IRREFUTABLE : DISPROVED :: (A) intolerable : biased
(B) insoluble : eradicated  (C) interminable : remembered
(D) incomparable : applauded  (E) irreparable : mended

**16.** DEADBEAT : PAY :: (A) killjoy : lament  (B) spoilsport : refrain
(C) daredevil : risk  (D) diehard : quit  (E) turncoat : betray

**17.** LACHRYMOSE : TEARS :: (A) effusive : requests
(B) ironic : jests  (C) morose : speeches  (D) profound : sighs
(E) verbose : words

18. DRUDGERY : IRKSOME :: (A) encumbrance : burdensome
    (B) journey : wearisome    (C) ambivalence : suspicious
    (D) compliance : forced    (E) dissonance : harmonious

19. CANONIZE : SAINT :: (A) train : athlete    (B) guard : dignitary
    (C) deify : sinner    (D) lionize : celebrity
    (E) humanize : scholar

20. TIRADE : ABUSIVE :: (A) monologue : lengthy
    (B) aphorism : boring    (C) prologue : conclusive
    (D) encomium : laudatory    (E) critique : insolent

## Exercise B

1. SNOW : DRIFT :: (A) mountain : boulder    (B) sand : dune
   (C) pane : glass    (D) desert : oasis    (E) mud : rain

2. HEART : PUMP :: (A) lungs : collapse    (B) appendix : burst
   (C) stomach : digest    (D) intestine : twist    (E) teeth : ache

3. STANZA : POEM :: (A) flag : anthem    (B) story : building
   (C) mural : painting    (D) program : recital    (E) rhyme : prose

4. SPARK : BLAZE :: (A) nick : gash    (B) ember : coal
   (C) flag : badge    (D) wind : banner    (E) flood : shower

5. MURAL : WALL :: (A) statue : courtyard    (B) painting : portrait
   (C) quarry : stone    (D) etching : paper
   (E) water color : tempera

6. FOLLOW : STALK :: (A) regret : rejoice    (B) look : spy
   (C) execute : condemn    (D) lurk : hide    (E) beckon : gesture

7. DAMPEN : DRENCH :: (A) glide : drift    (B) gambol : play
   (C) simmer : boil    (D) stagnate : flow    (E) ignite : quench

8. SHRUG : INDIFFERENCE :: (A) grin : deference
   (B) wave : fatigue    (C) nod : assent    (D) blink : scorn
   (E) scowl : desire

9. TETHER : HORSE :: (A) safari : tiger    (B) specimen : animal
   (C) brand : calf    (D) bone : dog    (E) handcuff : prisoner

10. FRIVOLOUS : SERIOUSNESS :: (A) acute : perception
    (B) meticulous : organization    (C) outspoken : reticence
    (D) lavish : money    (E) industrious : perseverance

11. ALLAY : PAIN :: (A) mollify : fright    (B) cancel : order
    (C) arbitrate : dispute    (D) mitigate : offense
    (E) testify : court

12. HECKLER : JEER :: (A) snob : flatter    (B) grumbler : complain
    (C) mentor : repent    (D) laughingstock : mock
    (E) miser : weep

13. SLINK : STEALTH :: (A) whine : querulousness
    (B) snarl : mockery    (C) disguise : alias
    (D) praise : friendship    (E) invest : capital

14. AMUSING : UPROARIOUS :: (A) puzzling : dumbfounding
    (B) quiet : noisy    (C) intractable : stubborn
    (D) petty : narrow-minded    (E) exhausted : weary

15. ANGER : CHOLERIC :: (A) wrath : ironic    (B) love : idyllic
    (C) island : volcanic    (D) greed : avaricious
    (E) pride : malicious

16. OLFACTORY : NOSE :: (A) peripheral : eyes
    (B) gustatory : tongue    (C) ambulatory : patient
    (D) tactile : ears    (E) perfunctory : skin

17. CARAPACE : TURTLE :: (A) speed : hare
    (B) chameleon : lizard    (C) amphibian : frog    (D) shell : snail
    (E) kennel : dog

18. BACTERIUM : COLONY :: (A) microbe : disease
    (B) fish : shoal    (C) stockade : settlement
    (D) virus : immunization    (E) sovereign : kingdom

19. TURNCOAT : TREACHEROUS :: (A) seamstress : generous
    (B) firebrand : mysterious    (C) mountebank : serious
    (D) spoilsport : notorious    (E) killjoy : lugubrious

20. SHUN : PARIAH :: (A) hunt : predator
    (B) transmute : alchemist    (C) beg : mendicant
    (D) flatter : sycophant    (E) ridicule : butt

## Exercise C

1. PEA : POD :: (A) orange : section    (B) bean : crock
   (C) pumpkin : stem    (D) nut : shell    (E) potato : stew

2. CANDLE : TALLOW :: (A) banana : peel    (B) temple : altar
   (C) statue : bronze    (D) fireplace : hearth
   (E) furniture : polish

3. THERMOMETER : HEAT :: (A) filament : light
   (B) chronometer : color    (C) odometer : waves
   (D) Geiger counter : radiation    (E) barometer : electricity

4. AIRPLANE : HANGAR :: (A) ship : channel    (B) jet : runway
   (C) helicopter : pad    (D) motorcycle : sidecar
   (E) automobile : garage

5. SIP : GULP :: (A) giggle : guffaw    (B) eat : dine
   (C) marry : divorce    (D) fret : worry    (E) hunt : fish

6. SPINE : CACTUS :: (A) backbone : man    (B) quill : porcupine
   (C) root : oak    (D) pit : olive    (E) binding : book

7. TRUNK : BOUGH :: (A) hook : eye (B) leaf : branch
   (C) detour : highway (D) torso : arm (E) keg : flask

8. COBBLER : SHOES :: (A) mechanic : automobile
   (B) carpenter : saw (C) painter : easel (D) spy : plans
   (E) interrogator : questions

9. FROWN : DISPLEASURE :: (A) blush : pallor
   (B) smile : commiseration (C) sneer : contempt
   (D) snore : relief (E) smirk : regret

10. PRIDE : LION :: (A) bevy : quail (B) lair : bear
    (C) fish : minnow (D) flag : banner (E) anger : symbol

11. MENTOR : COUNSEL :: (A) poet : criticism (B) plea : mercy
    (C) bodyguard : protection (D) sermon : conscience
    (E) judge : lawyer

12. CREST : WAVE :: (A) basin : water (B) crown : tree
    (C) sand : dune (D) mountain : range (E) dregs : wine

13. INVENTORY : MERCHANDISE :: (A) repertory : theater
    (B) roster : members (C) gadget : profits
    (D) bankruptcy : debts (E) dormitory : college

14. UNATTRACTIVE : HIDEOUS :: (A) complex : confused
    (B) dormant : sleeping (C) marred : spoiled
    (D) thrifty : parsimonious (E) profane : sacred

15. ENTREPRENEUR : PROFITS :: (A) philanthropist : charity
    (B) organizer : union (C) charlatan : converts
    (D) hermit : companionship (E) scholar : knowledge

16. INDIGENT : WEALTHY :: (A) irate : sober (B) taciturn : silent
    (C) meticulous : painstaking (D) frivolous : serious
    (E) scholarly : witty

17. POET : ECLOGUE :: (A) philosopher : nature
    (B) dramatist : scenery (C) sculptor : marble (D) seamstress
    : gown (E) astronomer : planet

18. VIRTUOSO : EXPERIENCED :: (A) rogue : knavish
    (B) democrat : dictatorial (C) saint : dissolute
    (D) leader : deferential (E) evildoer : repentant

19. ASCETIC : INTEMPERANCE :: (A) hypocrite : brevity
    (B) fanatic : zeal (C) bigot : idolatry (D) altruist : fidelity
    (E) miser : extravagance

20. DIATRIBE : INVECTIVE :: (A) elegy : mirth
    (B) encomium : praise (C) statute : limitation
    (D) circumlocution : clarity (E) parody : performance

**Answer Key**

**Exercise A**

| | | | | |
|---|---|---|---|---|
| 1. **A** | 5. **D** | 9. **C** | 13. **A** | 17. **E** |
| 2. **D** | 6. **B** | 10. **E** | 14. **C** | 18. **A** |
| 3. **A** | 7. **E** | 11. **B** | 15. **E** | 19. **D** |
| 4. **C** | 8. **A** | 12. **A** | 16. **D** | 20. **D** |

**Exercise B**

| | | | | |
|---|---|---|---|---|
| 1. **B** | 5. **D** | 9. **E** | 13. **A** | 17. **D** |
| 2. **C** | 6. **B** | 10. **C** | 14. **A** | 18. **B** |
| 3. **B** | 7. **C** | 11. **D** | 15. **D** | 19. **E** |
| 4. **A** | 8. **C** | 12. **B** | 16. **B** | 20. **E** |

**Exercise C**

| | | | | |
|---|---|---|---|---|
| 1. **D** | 5. **A** | 9. **C** | 13. **B** | 17. **D** |
| 2. **C** | 6. **B** | 10. **A** | 14. **D** | 18. **A** |
| 3. **D** | 7. **D** | 11. **C** | 15. **E** | 19. **E** |
| 4. **E** | 8. **A** | 12. **B** | 16. **D** | 20. **B** |

# THE SENTENCE COMPLETION QUESTION

The sentence completion questions ask you to choose the best way to complete a sentence from which one or two words have been omitted. You have five possible choices. One fits *best*.

**Long-Range Strategy:**   When you encounter a new word, don't just memorize its meaning in rote fashion. Study the way it is used, and then use it correctly yourself in three or more sentences. Try to work the word into conversations and discussions, even if it startles your friends. The way to make a word your own is to use it.

**Tips to Help You Cope**

1. Before you look at the choices, read the sentence and think of a word that makes sense. The word you think of may not be the exact word that appears in the answer choices, but it will probably be similar in meaning to the right answer.

2. Look at all the possible answers before you make your final choice. You are looking for the word that *best* fits the meaning of the sentence as a whole. In order to be sure you have not been hasty in making your decision, substitute all the answer choices for the missing word. That way you can satisfy yourself that you have come up with the answer that best fits.

3. In double-blank sentences, go through the answers, testing the *first* word in each choice (and eliminating those that don't fit). Read through the entire sentence. Then insert the first word of each answer pair in the sentence's first blank. Ask yourself whether this particular word makes sense in this blank. If the initial word of an answer pair makes no sense in the sentence, you can eliminate that answer pair.

4. Use your knowledge of word parts and context clues to get at the meanings of unfamiliar words. If a word used by the author is unfamiliar, or if an answer choice is unknown to you, look at its context in the sentence to see whether the context provides a clue to the meaning of the word. Often authors will use an unfamiliar word and then immediately define it within the same sentence. Similarly, look for familiar word parts—prefixes, suffixes, and roots—in unfamiliar words.

5. Watch out for negative words and words signaling frequency or duration. Only a small change makes these two sentences very different in meaning:

   They were not lovers.

   They were not often lovers.

6. Look for words or phrases that indicate a contrast between one idea and another—words like *although,*

*however, despite,* or *but.* In such cases an antonym or near-antonym for another word in the sentence should provide the correct answer.

7. Look for words or phrases that indicate similarities— words like *in the same way, in addition,* and *also.* In such cases, a synonym or near-synonym for another word in the sentence may provide the correct answer.

8. Look for words or phrases that indicate that one thing causes another—words like *because, since, therefore,* or *thus.*

9. In eliminating answer choices, check words for positive or negative connotations. Ask yourself whether the sentence calls for a positive or negative word.

### Examples to Get You Started

EXAMPLE 1

See how the first tip works with the following sentence.

The psychologist set up the experiment to test the rat's ----; he wished to see how well the rat adjusted to the changing conditions it had to face.

Even before you look at the answer choices, you can figure out what the answer *should* be.

A psychologist is trying to test some particular quality or characteristic of a rat. What quality? How do you get the answer?

Look at the sentence's second clause, the part following the semicolon. This clause is being used to define or clarify what the psychologist is trying to test. He is trying to see how well the rat *adjusts.* What words does this suggest to you? *Flexibility,* possibly, or *adaptability.* Either of these words could complete the sentence's thought.

Here are the five answer choices given.

(A) reflexes     (B) communicability     (C) stamina
(D) sociability     (E) adaptability

The best answer clearly is (E) adaptability.

## EXAMPLE 2

When you're racing the clock, you feel like marking down the first correct-sounding answer you come across. *Don't.* You may be going too fast.

Because the enemy had a reputation for engaging in sneak attacks, we were ---- on the alert.

(A) frequently  (B) furtively  (C) evidently  (D) constantly
(E) occasionally

A hasty reader might be content with choice (A), *frequently,* but *frequently* is not the best fit. The best answer is choice (D), *constantly,* because "frequent" periods of alertness would not be enough to provide the necessary protection against sneak attacks that could occur at any time. "Constant" vigilance is called for: the troops would have to be always on the alert.

## EXAMPLE 3

Dealing with double-blank sentences can be tricky. Testing the first word of each answer pair helps you narrow things down.

The opossum is ---- the venom of snakes in the rattlesnake subfamily and thus views the reptiles not as ---- enemies but as a food source.

(A) vulnerable to..natural  (B) indicative of..mortal
(C) impervious to..lethal   (C) impervious to..lethal
(D) injurious to..deadly  (E) defenseless against..potential

Your first job is to eliminate any answer choices you can on the basis of their first word. While opossums might be *vulnerable* or *impervious* to snake poison, and might even be *defenseless* against it, they're unlikely to be *indicative* or suggestive of it. They're even less likely to be *injurious* or harmful to the poison. The words make no sense; you can eliminate choices (B) and (D).

Now examine the second half of the sentence. Oppossums look on rattlesnakes as a food source. They can eat rattlers *because* they're *impervious* to the poison (that is, unharmed by it). That's the reason they can treat the rattlesnake as a potential source of food and not as a *lethal* or deadly enemy. The correct answer is choice (C).

Note the cause-and-effect signal *thus.* The nature of the opossum's response to the venom explains *why* it can look on a dangerous snake as a possible prey.

## EXAMPLE 4

After a tragedy, many people claim to have had a ---- of disaster.

(A) taste  (B) dislike  (C) presentiment  (D) context
(E) verdict

Take the unfamiliar word *presentiment.* Break it down into parts. A *sentiment* is a *feeling* (the root *sens* means *feel*). *Pre-* means *before.* A *presentiment* is something you *feel before* it happens, a foreboding. Your best answer is choice (C).

## EXAMPLE 5

Watch out for *not:* it's easy to overlook, but it's a key word.

Madison was not ---- person and thus made few public addresses; but those he made were memorable, filled with noble phrases.

(A) a reticent  (B) a stately  (C) an inspiring
(D) an introspective  (E) a communicative

What would happen if you overlooked *not* in this question? Probably you'd wind up choosing (A):

Madison was a *reticent* (quiet; reserved) man. *For this reason* he made few public addresses.

Unfortunately, you'd have gotten things backwards. The sentence isn't telling you what Madison was like. It's telling you what he was *not* like. And he was not a *communicative* person; he didn't express himself freely. However, when he did get around to expressing himself, he had valuable things to say.

## EXAMPLE 6

We expected him to be jubilant over his victory, but he was ---- instead.

(A) triumphant  (B) adult  (C) morose  (D) talkative
(E) culpable

*But* suggests that the winner's expected reaction contrasts with his actual one. Instead of being "jubilant" (extremely joyful), he is sad. The correct answer is choice (C), *morose*.

### EXAMPLE 7

The simplest animals are those whose bodies are simplest in structure and which do the things done by all animals, such as eating, breathing, moving, and feeling, in the most ---- way.

(A) haphazard    (B) bizarre    (C) advantageous
(D) primitive    (E) unique

The transition *and* signals you that the writer intends to develop the concept of simplicity introduced in the sentence. You should know from your knowledge of biology that *primitive* life forms were simple in structure and that the more complex forms evolved later. Choice (C) may seem possible. However, to secure the most *advantageous* way of conducting the activities of life, the animal would have to become specialized and complex. Thus, choice (D) *(primitive)* is best, because it is the only choice that develops the idea of simplicity.

### EXAMPLE 8

Because his delivery was ----, the effect of his speech on the voters was nonexistent.

(A) halting    (B) plausible    (C) moving    (D) respectable
(E) audible

What sort of delivery would cause a speech to have no effect? Obviously, you would not expect a moving or eloquent delivery to have such a sorry result. A *halting* or stumbling speech, however, would normally have little or no effect. Thus, choice (A) is best.

### EXAMPLE 9

He had a delightfully indulgent way of showing his ---- for his friends; these actions in themselves ---- a kind heart.

(A) respect . . . contradicted    (B) concern . . . deprecated
(C) disdain . . . established    (D) intolerance . . . denoted
(E) fondness . . . betokened

The phrase "delightfully indulgent" indicates that the person being described treats his friends in a friendly, loving manner. Therefore, you know that only positive words (such as love, respect, fondness, or concern) make sense in the first blank, and you can eliminate any answers with negative first words. Thus, you can immediately eliminate choices (C) and (D).

Go on to the second blank. The person's actions are positive, friendly. Such actions would signify or *betoken* a kind heart. The correct answer is choice (E).

**Practice Exercises**     **Answers given on page 200.**

---

Each sentence below has one or two blanks, each blank indicating that something has been omitted. Beneath the sentence are five lettered words or sets of words. Choose the word or set of words that <u>best</u> fits the meaning of the sentence as a whole.

Example:

Although its publicity has been ----, the film itself is intelligent, well-acted, handsomely produced, and altogether ----.

(A) tasteless..respectable     (B) extensive..moderate
  (C) sophisticated..amateur     (D) risqué..crude
    (E) perfect..spectacular

---

## Exercise A

1. Although the play was not praised by the critics, it did not ---- thanks to favorable word-of-mouth comments.

   (A) succeed     (B) translate     (C) function     (D) close
     (E) continue

2. Perhaps because something in us instinctively distrusts such displays of natural fluency, some readers approach John Updike's fiction with ----.

   (A) indifference     (B) suspicion     (C) veneration
     (D) recklessness     (E) bewilderment

3. We lost confidence in him because he never ---- the grandiose promises he had made.

   (A) forgot about  (B) reneged on  (C) tired of
   (D) delivered on  (E) retreated from

4. Because the hawk is ---- bird, farmers try to keep it away from their chickens.

   (A) a migratory  (B) an ugly  (C) a predatory  (D) a reclusive
   (E) a huge

5. We were amazed that a woman who had been heretofore the most ---- of public speakers could, in a single speech, electrify an audience and bring them cheering to their feet.

   (A) enthralling  (B) accomplished  (C) pedestrian
   (D) auspicious  (E) masterful

6. Despite the mixture's ---- nature, we found that by lowering its temperature in the laboratory we could dramatically reduce its tendency to vaporize.

   (A) resilient  (B) volatile  (C) homogeneous  (D) insipid
   (E) acerbic

7. New concerns about growing religious tension in northern India were ---- this week after at least fifty people were killed and hundreds were injured or arrested in rioting between Hindus and Moslems.

   (A) lessened  (B) invalidated  (C) restrained  (D) dispersed
   (E) fueled

8. In a revolutionary development in technology, several manufacturers now make biodegradable forms of plastic: some plastic six-pack rings, for example, gradually ---- when exposed to sunlight.

   (A) harden  (B) stagnate  (C) inflate  (D) propagate
   (E) decompose

9. To alleviate the problem of contaminated chicken, the study panel recommends that the federal government shift its inspection emphasis from cursory bird-by-bird visual checks to a more ---- random sampling for bacterial and chemical contamination.

   (A) rigorous  (B) perfunctory  (C) symbolic  (D) discreet
   (E) dubious

10. Shy and hypochondriacal, Madison was uncomfortable at public gatherings; his character made him a most ---- lawmaker and practicing politician.

   (A) conscientious  (B) unlikely  (C) fervent  (D) gregarious
   (E) effective

11. The tapeworm is an example of ---- organism, one that lives within or on another creature, deriving some or all of its nutriment from its host.

   (A) a hospitable  (B) an exemplary  (C) a parasitic
   (D) an autonomous  (E) a protozoan

12. Truculent in defending their rights of sovereignty under the Articles of Confederation, the newly-formed states ---- constantly.

   (A) apologized  (B) digressed  (C) conferred  (D) acquiesced
   (E) squabbled

13. Written in an amiable style, the book provides a comprehensive overview of European wines that should prove inviting to both the virtual ---- and the experienced connoisseur.

   (A) prodigal  (B) novice  (C) zealot  (D) miser  (E) glutton

14. Traffic speed limits are set at a level that achieves some balance between the danger of ---- speed and the desire of most people to travel as quickly as possible.

   (A) marginal  (B) normal  (C) prudent  (D) inadvertent
   (E) excessive

15. Although the economy suffers downturns, it also has strong ---- and self-correcting tendencies.

   (A) unstable  (B) recidivist  (C) inauspicious
   (D) recuperative  (E) self-destructive

## Exercise B

1. More than one friendly whale has nudged a boat with such ---- that passengers have been knocked overboard.

   (A) enthusiasm  (B) lethargy  (C) hostility  (D) serenity
   (E) animosity

2. Chaotic in conception but not in ----, Kelly's canvases are as neat as the proverbial pin.

   (A) conceit   (B) theory   (C) execution   (D) origin
   (E) intent

3. Some students are ---- and want to take only the courses for which they see immediate value.

   (A) theoretical   (B) impartial   (C) pragmatic   (D) idealistic
   (E) opinionated

4. Although Josephine Tey is arguably as good a mystery writer as Agatha Christie, she is clearly far less ---- than Christie, having written only six books in comparison to Christie's sixty.

   (A) coherent   (B) prolific   (C) equivocal   (D) pretentious
   (E) gripping

5. Fitness experts claim that jogging is ----; once you begin to jog regularly, you may be unable to stop, because you are sure to love it more and more all the time.

   (A) exhausting   (B) illusive   (C) addictive   (D) exotic
   (E) overrated

6. The ---- of such utopian notions is reflected by the quick disintegration of the idealistic community of Brooke Farm.

   (A) timeliness   (B) creativity   (C) impracticability
   (D) effervescence   (E) vindication

7. Although newscasters often use the terms Chicano and Latino ----, students of Hispanic-American culture are profoundly aware of the ---- the two.

   (A) interchangeably . . . dissimilarities between
   (B) indifferently . . . equivalence of
   (C) deprecatingly . . . controversies about
   (D) unerringly . . . significance of
   (E) confidently . . . origins of

8. I was so bored with the verbose and redundant style of Victorian novelists that I welcomed the change to the ---- style of Hemingway.

   (A) prolix   (B) consistent   (C) terse   (D) logistical
   (E) florid

9. His listeners enjoyed his ---- wit but his victims often ---- at its satire.

   (A) lugubrious . . . suffered     (B) caustic . . . laughed
   (C) kindly . . . smarted     (D) subtle . . . smiled
   (E) trenchant . . . winced

10. A code of ethics governing the behavior of physicians during epidemics did not exist until 1846, when it was ---- by the American Medical Association.

    (A) rescinded     (B) promulgated     (C) presupposed
    (D) depreciated     (E) implied

11. Breaking with established artistic and social conventions, Dali was ---- genius whose heterodox works infuriated the traditionalists of his day.

    (A) a derivative     (B) an iconoclastic     (C) an uncontroversial
    (D) a venerated     (E) a trite

12. Dr. Smith cautioned that the data so far are not sufficiently ---- to warrant dogmatic assertions by either side in the debate.

    (A) hypothetical     (B) tentative     (C) controversial
    (D) unequivocal     (E) imponderable

13. She is an interesting ----, an infinitely shy person who, in apparent contradiction, possesses an enormously intuitive ---- for understanding people.

    (A) aberration . . . disdain     (B) caricature . . . talent
    (C) specimen . . . loathing     (D) phenomenon . . . disinclination
    (E) paradox . . . gift

14. There is nothing ---- or provisional about Moore's early critical pronouncements; she deals ---- with what were then radical new developments in poetry.

    (A) tentative . . . confidently     (B) positive . . . expertly
    (C) dogmatic . . . arbitrarily     (D) shallow . . . superficially
    (E) imprecise . . . inconclusively

15. So intense was his ambition to attain the pinnacle of worldly success that not even the opulence and lavishness of his material possessions seemed ---- the ---- of that ambition.

    (A) necessary for . . . fulfillment     (B) adequate to . . . fervor
    (C) appropriate to . . . ebullience     (D) relevant to . . . languor
    (E) consonant with . . . insignificance

## Exercise C

1. John Gielgud crowns a distinguished career of playing Shakespearean roles by giving a performance that is ----.

   (A) mediocre    (B) outmoded    (C) superficial
      (D) unsurpassable    (E) insipid

2. Like many other reformers, Alice Paul, author of the Equal Rights Amendment introduced in Congress in 1923, received little honor in her lifetime but has gained considerable fame ----.

   (A) posthumously    (B) anonymously    (C) privately
      (D) prematurely    (E) previously

3. This well-documented history is of importance because it carefully ---- the ---- accomplishments of Indian artists who are all too little known to the public at large.

   (A) recognizes . . . negligible    (B) overlooks . . . purported
      (C) scrutinizes . . . illusory    (D) distorts . . . noteworthy
       (E) substantiates . . . considerable

4. Fossils may be set in stone, but their interpretation is not; a new find may necessitate the ---- of a traditional theory.

   (A) ambiguity    (B) revision    (C) formulation    (D) validation
      (E) assertion

5. The linguistic ---- of refugee children is reflected in their readiness to adopt the language of their new homeland.

   (A) conservatism    (B) inadequacy    (C) adaptability
      (D) philosophy    (E) structure

6. It is remarkable that a man so in the public eye, so highly praised and imitated, can retain his ----.

   (A) magniloquence    (B) dogmas    (C) bravado
      (D) idiosyncrasies    (E) humility

7. As a sportscaster, Cosell is apparently never ----; he makes ---- comments about every boxing match he covers.

   (A) excited . . . hysterical    (B) relevant . . . pertinent
      (C) satisfied . . . disparaging    (D) amazed . . . awe-struck
       (E) impressed . . . laudatory

8. Despite the growing ---- of Hispanic actors in the American theater, many Hispanic experts feel that the Spanish-speaking population is ---- on the stage.

   (A) decrease . . . inappropriate   (B) emergence . . . visible
   (C) prominence . . . underrepresented   (D) skill . . . alienated
   (E) number . . . misdirected

9. The incidence of smoking among women, formerly ----, has grown to such a degree that lung cancer, once a minor problem, has become the chief ---- of cancer-related deaths among women.

   (A) negligible . . . cause   (B) minor . . . antidote
   (C) pre-eminent . . . cure   (D) relevant . . . modifier
   (E) pervasive . . . opponent

10. Despite the numerous films he had to his credit and his reputation for technical ----, the moviemaker lacked originality; all his films were sadly ---- of the work of others.

    (A) skill . . . independent   (B) ability . . . unconscious
    (C) expertise . . . derivative   (D) competence . . . contradictory
    (E) blunders . . . enamored

11. He is much too ---- in his writings: he writes a page when a sentence should suffice.

    (A) devious   (B) lucid   (C) verbose   (D) efficient   (E) pleasant

12. An experienced politician who knew better than to launch a campaign in troubled political waters, she intended to wait for a more ---- occasion before she announced her plans.

    (A) propitious   (B) provocative   (C) unseemly
    (D) questionable   (E) theoretical

13. No real life hero of ancient or modern days can surpass James Bond with his nonchalant ---- of death and the ---- with which he bears torture.

    (A) contempt . . . distress   (B) disregard . . . fortitude
    (C) veneration . . . guile   (D) concept . . . terror
    (E) impatience . . . fickleness

14. Surrounded by sycophants who invariably ---- her singing,  Callas wearied of the constant adulation and longed for honest criticism.

    (A) orchestrated   (B) thwarted   (C) assailed   (D) extolled
    (E) reciprocated

15. Unlike the highly ---- Romantic poets of the previous century, Arnold and his fellow Victorian poets were ---- and interested in moralizing.

(A) rhapsodic . . . lyrical   (B) frenetic . . . distraught
(C) emotional . . . didactic   (D) sensitive . . . strange
(E) dramatic . . . warped

## Answer Key

### Exercise A

| | | | |
|---|---|---|---|
| 1. D | 5. C | 9. A | 13. B |
| 2. B | 6. B | 10. B | 14. E |
| 3. D | 7. E | 11. C | 15. D |
| 4. C | 8. E | 12. E | |

### Exercise B

| | | | |
|---|---|---|---|
| 1. A | 5. C | 9. E | 13. E |
| 2. C | 6. C | 10. B | 14. A |
| 3. C | 7. A | 11. B | 15. B |
| 4. B | 8. C | 12. D | |

### Exercise C

| | | | |
|---|---|---|---|
| 1. D | 5. C | 9. A | 13. B |
| 2. A | 6. E | 10. C | 14. D |
| 3. E | 7. C | 11. C | 15. C |
| 4. B | 8. C | 12. A | |

# THE READING COMPREHENSION QUESTION

The reading comprehension questions take more time than any other questions on the test because you have to read a passage before you can answer them. They test your ability to understand and interpret what you read, which is probably the most important ability you will need in college and afterward.

**Long-Range Strategy:**   Read, Read, Read! Just do it.

There is no substitute for extensive reading as a preparation for the SAT and for college work. The only way to obtain proficiency in reading is by reading books of all kinds. As you read, you will develop speed, stamina, and the ability to comprehend the printed page. If you want to turn yourself into the kind of reader the colleges are looking for, you must develop the habit of reading—every day.

**Tips to Help You Cope**

1. Save the reading comprehension questions for last. On the SAT, you get the same points for answering a "quick and easy" question correctly as you do for answering a time-consuming one. Reading questions take time. Answer the less time-consuming questions first.

2. Tackle passages with familiar subjects before passages with unfamiliar ones. It is hard to concentrate when you read about something wholly unfamiliar to you. Give yourself a break. First tackle the reading passages that interest you or that deal with topics you are well-grounded in. You'll do better on them.

3. First read the passage; then read the questions. Reading the questions before you read the passage will not save you time. It will cost you time. If you read the questions first, when you turn to the passage you will have a number of question words and phrases dancing around in your head. You will be so involved in trying to spot the places they occur in the passage that you'll be unable to concentrate on comprehending the passage as a whole.

4. Read as rapidly as you can with understanding, but do not force yourself. Do not worry about the time element. If you worry about not finishing the test, you will begin to take short cuts and miss the correct answer in your haste.

5. As you read the opening sentences, try to anticipate what the passage will be about. Ask yourself who or what the author is talking about.

6. As you continue reading, try to remember in which part of the passage the author makes major points. In that way, when you start looking for the phrase or sentence which will justify your choice of answer, you will be able to save time by going to that section of the passage immediately rather than having to reread the entire selection.

7. When you tackle the questions, <u>go back to the passage</u> to verify your choice of answer. Do not rely on memory, and, above all, do not rely on knowledge you've gained outside of the paragraph.

8. Watch out for words or phrases in the question that can alert you to the kind of question being asked.

   Questions asking for information stated in the passage:

   *the author asserts*
   *the author mentions all of the following EXCEPT*
   *according to the passage*
   *according to the author*

   Questions asking you to draw a conclusion:

   *it can be inferred*
   *would most likely*
   *is best described*
   *it can be argued*
   *suggests that*
   *the author implies*
   *the author probably considers*
   *would probably*

   Questions asking about the main idea of the passage:

   *which of the following titles*
   *main/central/primary purpose*
   *main point of the passage*
   *chiefly concerned with*
   *passage as a whole*
   *primary emphasis*

Questions asking about contextual meaning:
*as used in the passage*
*what the author means in saying*
*in context, the word/phrase*
*in the context of the passage*

9. When asked to find the main idea, be sure to check the opening and summary sentences of each paragraph. Authors typically provide readers with a sentence that expresses a paragraph's main idea succinctly. Although such <u>topic sentences</u> may appear anywhere in the paragraph, readers customarily look for them in the opening or closing sentences.

10. When asked to choose a title, watch out for choices that are too specific or too broad. A paragraph is a group of sentences revolving around a central theme. An appropriate title for a paragraph, therefore, must include this central theme. It should be neither too broad nor too narrow in its scope; it should be specific and yet comprehensive enough to include all the essential ideas presented by the sentences. A good title for a passage of two or more paragraphs should include the thoughts of ALL the paragraphs.

11. When asked to make inferences, take as your answer what the passage logically suggests, not what it states directly. Look for clues in the passage; then choose as your answer a statement which is a logical development of the information the author has provided.

12. When asked to determine questions of attitude, mood, or tone, look for words that convey emotion, express values, or paint pictures. These images and descriptive phrases get the author's feelings across.

Remember, sentence completion and vocabulary techniques may also help you answer reading comprehension questions.

### Examples to Get You Started

EXAMPLE 1

Your mind, like your body, is a thing whereof the powers are developed by effort. That is a principal use, as I see it, of hard work in studies. Unless you train your body you cannot be an athlete, and unless you train your mind you cannot be much of a scholar. The four miles an oarsman covers at top speed is in itself nothing to the good, but the physical capacity to hold out over the course is thought to be of some worth. So a good part of what you learn by hard study may not be permanently retained, and may not seem to be of much final value, but your mind is a better and more powerful instrument because you have learned it. "Knowledge is power," but still more the faculty of acquiring and using knowledge is power. If you have a trained and powerful mind, you are bound to have stored it with something, but its value is more in what it can do, what it can grasp and use, than in what it contains; and if it were possible, as it is not, to come out of college with a trained and disciplined mind and nothing useful in it, you would still be ahead, and still, in a manner, educated.

The title that best expresses the ideas of this passage is
(A) "Knowledge is Power"    (B) How to Retain and Use Facts
(C) Why Acquire Knowledge    (D) Physical and Mental Effort
  (E) The Trained Mind

### Analysis of Passage

Look at the opening and summary sentences of the paragraph: "Your *mind,* like your body, is a thing whereof the powers are developed by effort. . . . if it were possible, as it is not, to come out of college with *a trained and disciplined mind* and nothing useful in it, you would still be ahead, and still, in a manner, educated." Note the italicized phrases.

In this passage, the author stresses the need for hard work in studies. He concedes that you may forget much that you learn, but he stresses the value of knowing how to get and use knowledge. This comes from training. It is not the knowledge that you get from college that is valuable, but the training of your mind.

Now go through the choices. You may eliminate choice (A) ("Knowledge Is Power"): the author states that the faculty of acquiring knowledge is more important than the knowledge itself. You may eliminate choice (B) (How to Retain and Use Facts): the passage is not a "how-to" guide. Choice (C) (Why Acquire Knowledge) may be supported by the quotation that "Knowledge is Power," but you can see that the author is undercutting this statement in the sentence in which he quotes it. You may argue in favor of choice (D) (Physical and Mental Effort) because you recognize that the author is making an analogy between the training of the athlete and the training of the scholar. However, choice (D) is not as good as choice (E) (The Trained Mind) because *throughout the passage* the author is stressing that the trained mind is something that must be developed and that is in itself a valuable and important faculty.

## EXAMPLE 2

We all know people who would welcome a new American car to their stables, but one cannot expect to find a sports-car man among them. He cannot be enticed into such a circus float without feeling soiled. He resents the wanton use of chromium as much as he shudders at the tail fins, the grotesquely convoluted bumpers, and other "dishonest" lines. He blanches at the enormous bustle that adds weight and useless space, drags on ramps and curbstones, and complicates the process of parking even in the car's own garage. The attitude of the owner of a Detroit product is reflected in the efforts of manufacturers to "take the drive out of driving." The sports-car addict regards this stand as outrageous. His interest in a car, he is forever telling himself and other captive listeners, lies in the fun of driving it, in "sensing its alertness on the road," and in "pampering it as a thoroughbred."

The passage implies that sport cars are very

(A) colorful    (B) showy    (C) maneuverable    (D) roomy
(E) grotesque

### Analysis of Passage

If the owner of the sports car takes delight in "sensing its alertness on the road" he is finding pleasure in its maneuverability, choice (C). The sports car addict would object to the color, the show, the excessive roominess and the grotesque appearance of the Detroit product.

**Practice Exercises**     **Answers given on page 225.**

---

Each passage below is followed by questions based on its content. Answer all questions following a passage on the basis of what is <u>stated</u>, or <u>implied</u> in that passage.

---

## Exercise A

Perhaps the first point to grasp about natural selection is that a complex creature, or even a complex part of a creature, such as the eye, did not arise in one evolutionary step. Rather it evolved through a series of small steps. Exactly what is meant by small is not necessarily obvious since the growth of an organism is controlled by an elaborate program written in its genes. A small change in a key part of the program can make a large difference. For example, an alteration in one gene in *Drosophila* can produce a fruit fly with legs in place of its antennae.

Each small step is caused by a random alteration in the genetic instructions. Many of these random alterations may do the organism no good (some may even kill it before it is born), but occasionally a particular chance alteration may give that particular organism a selective advantage. This means that in the last analysis the organism will, on average, leave more offspring than it would otherwise. If this advantage persists in its descendants then this beneficial mutant will gradually, over many generations, spread through the population. In favorable cases, every individual will come to possess the improved version of the gene. The older version will have been eliminated. Natural selection is thus a beautiful mechanism for turning rare events (strictly, favorable rare events) into common ones.

1. The author's attitude towards the process of natural selection can best be described as one of

   (A) mild skepticism
   (B) puzzled fascination
   (C) controlled apprehension
   (D) appreciative admiration
   (E) lofty detachment

2. The author's primary purpose in introducing the reference to *Drosophila* is to

   (A) indicate his familiarity with laboratory experiments on fruit flies
   (B) describe the process by which a genetic alteration changes the body
   (C) provide a vivid illustration of extreme effects of a slight genetic change
   (D) give an example of a favorable genetic mutation
   (E) demonstrate that it took several evolutionary steps for the fruit fly to reach its present form

3. In explaining what he means by a selective advantage, the author emphasizes that it is

   (A) immutable
   (B) reproductive
   (C) limited
   (D) mental
   (E) inequitable

        Tapestries are made on looms. Their distinctive weave is basically simple: the colored weft threads interface regularly with the monochrome warps, as in darning or plain cloth, but as they do so, they form a design by reversing their direction when a change of color is needed. The wefts are beaten down to cover the warps completely. The result is a design or picture that is the fabric itself, not one laid upon a ground like an embroidery, a print, or brocading. The back and front of a tapestry show the same design. The weaver always follows a preexisting model, generally a drawing or painting, known as the cartoon, which in most cases he reproduces as exactly as he can. Long training is needed to become a professional tapestry weaver. It can take as much as a year to produce a yard of very finely woven tapestry.

Tapestry-woven fabrics have been made from China to Peru and from very early times to the present day, but large wall hangings in this technique, mainly of wool, are typically Northern European. Few examples predating the late fourteenth century have survived, but from about 1400 tapestries were an essential part of aristocratic life. The prince or great nobleman sent his plate and his tapestries ahead of him to furnish his castles before his arrival as he traveled through his domains; both had the same function, to display his wealth and social position. It has frequently been suggested that tapestries helped to heat stone-walled rooms, but this is a modern idea; comfort was of minor importance in the Middle Ages. Tapestries were portable grandeur, instant splendor, taking the place, north of the Alps, of painted frescoes further south. They were hung without gaps between them, covering entire walls and often doors as well. Only very occasionally were they made as individual works of art such as altar frontals. They were usually commissioned or bought as sets, or "chambers," and constituted the most important furnishings of any grand room, except for the display of plate, throughout the Middle Ages and the sixteenth century. Later, woven silks, ornamental wood carving, stucco decoration, and painted leather gradually replaced tapestry as expensive wall coverings, until at last wallpaper was introduced in the late eighteenth century and eventually swept away almost everything else.

4. Tapestry weaving may be characterized as which of the following?

   I. Time-consuming
   II. Spontaneous in concept
   III. Faithful to an original
   (A) I only
   (B) III only
   (C) I and I only
   (D) I and III only
   (E) II and III only

5. Renaissance nobles carried tapestries with them to demonstrate their

   (A) piety
   (B) consequence
   (C) aesthetic judgment
   (D) need for privacy
   (E) dislike for cold

6. The primary purpose of the passage is to

(A) explain the process of tapestry-making
(B) contrast Eastern and Western schools of tapestry
(C) analyze the reasons for the decline in popularity of tapestries
(D) introduce the history and technique of tapestry-woven fabrics
(E) advocate a return to a more colorful way of life

An oft-used, but valuable, analogy compares the immune system with an army. The defending troops are the white blood cells called lymphocytes, born in the bone marrow, billeted in the lymph nodes and spleen, and on exercise in the blood and lymph systems. A body can muster some 200m cells, making the immune system comparable in mass to the liver or brain.

The lymphocytes are called to action when the enemy makes itself known. They attack anything foreign. Their job is to recognize the enemy for what it is, and then destroy it. One of the key features of the immune system is its specificity. Inoculation with smallpox provokes an attack on any smallpox virus, but on nothing else. This specificity of response depends on the lymphocyte's ability to identify the enemy correctly by the molecules on its surface, called antigens.

An antigen is an enemy uniform. It can be a protein on the surface of a cold virus, or it can be a protein on the surface of a pollen grain, in which case the immune response takes the form of an allergy. An antigen can also be a protein on the surface of a transplanted organ, in which case the immune response "rejects" the transplant. Organs can therefore be transplanted only between closely related people—in whom the antigens are the same—or into people treated with a drug that suppresses the immune system, such as cyclosporin.

7. The author's primary purpose in the passage is to do which of the following?

(A) Demonstrate the inadequacy of an analogy.
(B) Propose a method to strengthen the immune system.
(C) Compare the immune system to the brain.
(D) Clarify the workings of the body's defense system.
(E) Merge two differing views of a bodily process.

8. The author provides information to answer which of the following questions?

   (A) What is the process by which antigens are produced?
   (B) What is the mechanism by which cyclosporin suppresses the immune system?
   (C) What is the process that prevents closely related persons from developing dissimilar antigens?
   (D) How does inoculation with smallpox wear off over a period of years?
   (E) Where do the body's lymphocytes originate?

9. It can be inferred from the passage that treatment with cyclosporin might result in which of the following?

   I. An increased susceptibility to invasion by disease
   II. The rejection of a transplanted organ
   III. An increased effectiveness of antigens

   (A) I only
   (B) II only
   (C) I and II only
   (D) I and III only
   (E) I, II and III

10. In describing the immune system, the author does all of the following EXCEPT

   (A) define a term
   (B) illustrate through a comparison
   (C) refer to an authority
   (D) give an approximation
   (E) develop an extended metaphor

   Sir Thomas was indeed the life of the party, who at his suggestion now seated themselves round the fire. He had the best right to be the talker; and the delight of his sensations in being again in his own house, in the center of his family, after such a separation, made him communicative and chatty in a very unusual degree; and he was ready to answer every question of his two sons almost before it was put. All the little particulars of his proceedings and events, his arrivals and departures, were most promptly delivered, as he sat by Lady Bertram and looked with heartfelt satisfaction at the faces around him—interrupting himself more than once, however, to remark on his good fortune in finding them all at home—coming unexpectedly as he did—all collected together exactly as he could have wished, but dared not depend on.

By not one of the circle was he listened to with such unbroken unalloyed enjoyment as by his wife, whose feelings were so warmed by his sudden arrival, as to place her nearer agitation than she had been for the last twenty years. She had been *almost* fluttered for a few minutes, and still remained so sensibly animated as to put away her work, move Pug from her side, and give all her attention and all the rest of her sofa to her husband. She had no anxieties for anybody to cloud *her* pleasure; her own time had been irreproachably spent during his absence; she had done a great deal of carpet work and made many yards of fringe; and she would have answered as freely for the good conduct and useful pursuits of all the young people as for her own. It was so agreeable to her to see him again, and hear him talk, to have her ear amused and her whole comprehension filled by his narratives, that she began particularly to feel how dreadfully she must have missed him, and how impossible it would have been for her to bear a lengthened absence.

Mrs. Norris was by no means to be compared in happiness to her sister. Not that *she* was incommoded by many fears of Sir Thomas's disapprobation when the present state of his house should be known, for her judgment had been so blinded, that she could hardly be said to show any sign of alarm; but she was vexed by the *manner* of his return. It had left her nothing to do. Instead of being sent for out of the room, and seeing him first, and having to spread the happy news through the house, Sir Thomas, with a very reasonable dependence perhaps on the nerves of his wife and children, had sought no confidant but the butler, and had been following him almost instantaneously into the drawing-room. Mrs. Norris felt herself defrauded of an office on which she had always depended, whether his arrival or his death were to be the thing unfolded; and was now trying to be in a bustle without having any thing to bustle about. Would Sir Thomas have consented to eat, she might have gone to the housekeeper with troublesome directions; but Sir Thomas resolutely declined all dinner; he would take nothing, nothing till tea came—he would rather wait for tea. Still Mrs. Norris was at intervals urging something different; and in the most interesting moment of his passage to England, when the alarm of a French privateer was at the height, she burst through his recital with the proposal of soup. "Sure, my dear Sir Thomas, a basin of soup would be a much better thing for you than tea. Do have a basin of soup."

Sir Thomas could not be provoked. "Still the same anxiety for everybody's comfort, my dear Mrs. Norris," was his answer. "But indeed I would rather have nothing but tea."

**11.** Which of the following titles best describes the passage?

(A) An Unexpected Return
(B) The Conversation of the Upper Class
(C) Mrs. Norris's Grievance
(D) A Romantic Reunion
(E) An Account of a Voyage Abroad

**12.** We can infer from the opening paragraph that Sir Thomas is customarily

(A) unwelcome at home
(B) tardy in business affairs
(C) dissatisfied with life
(D) more restrained in speech
(E) lacking in family feeling

**13.** The passage suggests that Sir Thomas's sudden arrival

(A) was motivated by concern for his wife
(B) came as no surprise to Lady Bertram
(C) was timed by him to coincide with a family reunion
(D) was expected by the servants
(E) was received with mixed emotions

**14.** Sir Thomas's attitude toward Mrs. Norris can best be described as one of

(A) sharp irritation
(B) patient forbearance
(C) solemn disapproval
(D) unreasoned alarm
(E) unmixed delight

**15.** The office of which Mrs. Norris feels herself defrauded is most likely that of

  (A) butler
  (B) housekeeper
  (C) wife
  (D) traveler
  (E) message-bearer

## Exercise B

Peyton Farquhar was a well-to-do planter, of an old and highly respected Alabama family. Being a slave-owner, and, like other slave-owners, a politician, he was naturally an original secessionist and ardently devoted to the Southern cause. Circumstances had prevented him from taking service with the gallant army which had fought the disastrous campaigns ending with the fall of Corinth, and he chafed under the inglorious restraint, longing for the release of his energies, the larger life of the soldier, the opportunity for distinction. That opportunity, he felt, would come, as it comes to all in war time. Meanwhile, he did what he could. No service was too humble for him to perform in aid of the South, no adventure too perilous for him to undertake if consistent with the character of a civilian who was at heart a soldier, and who in good faith and without too much qualification assented to at least a part of the frankly villainous dictum that all is fair in love and war.

One evening while Farquhar and his wife were sitting near the entrance to his grounds, a grey-clad soldier rode up to the gate and asked for a drink of water. Mrs. Farquhar was only too happy to serve him with her own white hands. While she was gone to fetch the water, her husband approached the dusty horseman and inquired eagerly for news from the front.

"The Yanks are repairing the railroads," said the man, "and are getting ready for another advance. They have reached the Owl Creek bridge, put it in order, and built a stockade on the other bank. The commandant has issued an order, which is posted everywhere, declaring that any civilian caught interfering with the railroad, its bridges, tunnels, or trains, will be summarily hanged. I saw the order."

"How far is it to the Owl Creek bridge?" Farquhar asked.

"About thirty miles."

"Is there no force on this side of the creek?"

"Only a picket post half a mile out, on the railroad, and a single sentinel at this end of the bridge."

"Suppose a man—a civilian and a student of hanging—should elude the picket post and perhaps get the better of the sentinel," said Farquhar, smiling, "what could he accomplish?"

The soldier reflected. "I was there a month ago," he replied. "I observed that the flood of last winter had lodged a great quantity of driftwood against the wooden pier at the end of the bridge. It is now dry and would burn like tow."

The lady had now brought the water, which the soldier drank. He thanked her ceremoniously, bowed to her husband, and rode away. An hour later, after nightfall, he repassed the plantation, going northward in the direction from which he had come. He was a Yankee scout.

1. Peyton Farquhar would most likely consider which of the following a good example of how a citizen should behave in wartime?

   (A) He should use even underhanded methods to support his cause.
   (B) He should enlist in the army without delay.
   (C) He should turn to politics as a means of enforcing his will.
   (D) He should avoid involving himself in disastrous campaigns.
   (E) He should concentrate on his duties as a planter.

2. It can be inferred from the second paragraph that Mrs. Farquhar is

   (A) sympathetic to the Confederate cause
   (B) uninterested in news of the war
   (C) too proud to perform menial tasks
   (D) reluctant to ask her slaves to fetch water
   (E) inhospitable by nature

3. As used in the next-to-last paragraph, <u>tow</u> is

   (A) an act of hauling something
   (B) a tugboat
   (C) a railroad bridge
   (D) a highly combustible substance
   (E) a picket post

4. This passage was most likely taken from

   (A) a history textbook
   (B) Peyton Farquhar's autobiography
   (C) a story set in Civil War times
   (D) a commentary on the effects of Federal orders on civilians
   (E) a treatise on military strategy

5. We may infer from the passage that

   (A) the soldier has deserted from the Southern army
   (B) the soldier has lost his sense of direction
   (C) the scout has been tempting Farquhar into an unwise action
   (D) Farquhar knew the soldier was a Yankee scout
   (E) the soldier returned to the plantation unwillingly

(This passage was written prior to 1950.)

We now know that what constitutes practically all of matter is empty space; relatively enormous voids in which revolve with lightning velocity infinitesimal particles so utterly small that they have never been seen or photographed. The existence of these particles has been demonstrated by mathematical physicists and their operations determined by ingenious laboratory experiments. It was not until 1911 that experiments by Sir Ernest Rutherford revealed the architecture of the mysterious atom. Moseley, Bohr, Fermi, Millikan, Compton, Urey, and others have also worked on the problem.

Matter is composed of molecules whose average diameter is about 1/125 millionth of an inch. Molecules are composed of atoms so small that about 5 million could be placed in a row on the period at the end of this sentence. Long thought to be the ultimate, indivisible constituent of matter, the atom has been found to consist roughly of a proton, the positive electrical element in the atomic nucleus, surrounded by electrons, the negative electric elements swirling about the proton.

6. The main purpose of this passage is to

   (A) honor the pioneering work of Sir Ernest Rutherford and his
        followers
   (B) refute the existence of submicroscopic particles
   (C) illustrate how scientists measure molecular diameter
   (D) summarize the then current findings on the composition of matter
   (E) analyze evidence against one theory of atomic structure

7. The style of the passage can best be described as

(A) expository
(B) persuasive
(C) contemplative
(D) oratorical
(E) deprecatory

8. According to the passage, all of the following were true of the center of the atom EXCEPT that it

(A) had not yet been seen by the naked eye
(B) contained both positive and negative elements
(C) was very little larger than a molecule
(D) followed experimentally determinable processes
(E) was smaller than 1/125 millionth of an inch

9. By referring to the period at the end of the sentence, the author intends to point up the atom's

(A) density
(B) mystery
(C) velocity
(D) consistency
(E) minuteness

10. Which of the following relationships most closely parallels the relationship between the proton and the electrons described in the passage?

(A) A hawk to its prey
(B) A blueprint to a framework
(C) A planet to its satellites
(D) A magnet to iron filings
(E) A compound to its elements

During the decade of 1880–1890 it was becoming increasingly evident that the factors which had brought about the existence of two separate suffrage institutions were steadily diminishing in importance.

The National Woman Suffrage Association had been launched by the intellectually irrepressible Elizabeth Cady Stanton and the ever catholic Susan B. Anthony. Both were ready to work with anyone, whatever their views on other matters, as long as they wholeheartedly espoused woman suffrage. Consequently in its earlier years the National was both aggressive and unorthodox. It damned both Republicans and Democrats who brushed the suffrage question aside. It was willing to take up the cudgels for distressed women whatever their circumstances, be they "fallen women," divorce cases, or underpaid seamstresses.

The American Woman Suffrage Association, by contrast, took its tone and outlook from a New England which had turned its back on those fiery days when abolitionists, men and women alike, had stood up to angry mobs. Its advocacy of worthy causes was highly selective. Lucy Stone was not interested in trade unionism and wished to keep the suffrage cause untarnished by concern with divorce or "the social evil." The very epitome of the American's attitude was its most distinguished convert and leader, Julia Ward Howe—erudite, honored lay preacher, the revered author of "The Battle Hymn of the Republic," who cast a highly desirable aura of prestige and propriety over the women's cause.

It was not that Mrs. Howe in herself made suffrage respectable; she was a symbol of the forces that were drawing the suffrage movement into the camp of decorum. American society was becoming rapidly polarized. The middle class was learning to identify organized labor with social turmoil. A succession of strikes during the depression of 1873–1878, in textiles, mining, and railroads, culminated in the Great Railroad Strike of 1877 involving nearly 100,000 workers from the Atlantic coast to the Mississippi valley; they did not help to reassure women taught by press and pulpit to identify any type of militancy with radicalism. Nor was this trend allayed by the hysteria whipped up over the Molly Maguire trials for secret conspiracy among Pennsylvania coal miners, or the alleged communistic influences at work in such growing organizations as the Knights of Labor and the A.F. of L. The existence of a small number of socialists was used to smear all organized labor with the taint of "anarchism." The crowning touch took place during the widespread agitation for an eight-hour day in 1886 when a bomb, thrown by a hand unknown to this day into a radical meeting in Chicago's Haymarket Square, touched off a nation-wide wave of panic.

The steady trend of the suffrage movement toward the conservative and the conventional during the last twenty years of the nineteenth century must be viewed in this setting, in order to avoid the misconception that a few conservative women took it over, through their own superior ability and the passivity of the former militants. Even the latter were changing their views, judging by their actions. It was one thing to challenge the proprieties at the Centennial of 1876; ten years later it would have been inconceivable even to the women who took part in the demonstration. Susan Anthony herself would have thought twice about flouting Federal election laws and going to jail in an era which witnessed the Haymarket hysteria.

11. The author's primary purpose in the passage is to

    (A) contrast Susan B. Anthony with Julia Ward Howe
    (B) recount the advances in the suffrage movement from 1880 to 1890
    (C) account for the changes occurring in the suffrage movement from 1880 to 1890
    (D) explain the growing divisions within the women's movement
    (E) point out aspects of the suffrage movement which exist in contemporary feminism

12. The passage singles out Julia Ward Howe as an example of

    (A) a venerated figurehead
    (B) an overzealous advocate
    (C) a heterodox thinker
    (D) an ordained cleric
    (E) a militant activist

13. The author's attitude toward the public reaction to the Molly Maguire trials is that the reaction was

    (A) appropriate
    (B) disorganized
    (C) overwrought
    (D) necessary
    (E) understated

14. The author stresses the growing antiradical bias of the American middle class during the decade 1880–1890 in order to

    (A) question a trend that proved destructive to the suffrage movement
    (B) explain the unexpected emergence of an able body of radical leaders
    (C) refute the contention that Anthony was unchanged by her experiences

(D)  correct a misapprehension about changes in the suffrage movement

(E)  excuse the growing lack of militancy on the part of the National

**15.** The passage suggests that, by 1890, attempts to effect woman suffrage by violating the proprieties and defying Federal laws would probably have been viewed even by movement members with

(A)  indifference
(B)  defiance
(C)  disapprobation
(D)  respect
(E)  optimism

## Exercise C

When I arrived at a few minutes before seven, I found the platoon assembled and ready to go. It was cold, and in the ranks the men were shivering and dancing up and down to keep warm. I was only the second-in-command of the platoon at that time, under instruction from a senior lieutenant, who was the platoon commander. Punctually at seven I said to Broadhurst, "March off, Sergeant. To the aerodrome, at the double."

Broadhurst asked doubtfully whether we hadn't better wait for the platoon commander, who had not turned up. Unversed in the ways of the army, I said, "No, march off. The men are cold." We doubled off.

Three or four minutes later the platoon commander, who had about fourteen years of service, appeared. He was in a towering rage. He rushed straight up to Broadhurst and asked him furiously what he meant by marching off without permission.

Broadhurst said, "I'm sorry, sir."

My feet wouldn't move. My mouth wouldn't open. I made a gigantic effort and said, "Sir—" But the lieutenant had given Broadhurst a final blast and taken command. I looked at Broadhurst, but he was busy. After parade I apologized to him, but I never explained to the lieutenant. Broadhurst told me the incident wasn't worth worrying about.

Does this seem a small crime to remember all one's life? I don't think so. It was the worst thing that I ever did in the army, because in it I showed cowardice and disloyalty. The only excuses I could find for myself were that it happened quickly and that I was very young. It had a result, though. I had been frightened of the lieutenant, frightened of being reprimanded, frightened of failure even in the smallest endeavor. I discovered now that being ashamed of yourself is worse than any fear. Duty, orders, loyalty, obedience—all things boiled down to one simple idea: whatever the consequences, a man must act so that he can live with himself.

1. It can be inferred from the passage that the narrator never explained the truth to the platoon commander because

   (A) army custom forbade his doing so
   (B) he felt that the incident was unimportant
   (C) he hoped that Broadhurst would do it for him
   (D) he feared the reaction of the platoon commander
   (E) the episode happened too quickly

2. Which statement can most safely be made about the platoon commander?

   (A) He refused to give the narrator any instructions.
   (B) He gave command of the troops to Broadhurst.
   (C) He lacked experience as a soldier.
   (D) He expected his subordinates to execute orders on their own.
   (E) He observed army customs to the letter.

3. From the passage the reader can most logically infer that Broadhurst was

   (A) familiar with army routine
   (B) proud of the platoon
   (C) friendly with the platoon commander
   (D) higher in rank than the platoon commander
   (E) inconsiderate of the narrator

4. It is most probable that *before* this episode took place

   (A) plans had been made for the troops to march
   (B) the narrator had not been told the time of departure
   (C) plans had been made for Broadhurst to stay behind
   (D) the narrator had given several incorrect orders
   (E) the platoon commander had relied greatly upon the narrator

In "Pseudoscience and Society in Nineteenth-Century America," Arthur Wrobel remarks that belief in phrenology, homeopathy, and hydropathy was not confined to the poor and the ignorant, but pervaded much of 19th-century literature. Such credulity is not as extensive in contemporary literature, but astrology is one pseudoscience that does seem to engage a big segment of the reading public. Literary allusions to it abound, appearing in everything from Shakespeare to Don DeLillo's "Libra." A 1986 Gallup poll showed that 52 percent of American teenagers subscribe to it, as does at least 50 percent of the nation's departing First Couple.

Given these figures, it may not be entirely inappropriate to note here that no mechanism through which the alleged zodiacal influences exert themselves has ever been specified by astrologers. Gravity certainly cannot account for these natal influences, since even the gravitational pull of the attending obstetrician is orders of magnitude greater than that of the relevant planet or planets. Nor is there any empirical evidence; top astrologers (as determined by their peers) have failed repeatedly to associate personality profiles with astrological data at a rate higher than that of chance. Neither of these fatal objections to astrology, of course, is likely to carry much weight with literate but innumerate people who don't estimate magnitudes or probabilities, or who are overimpressed by vague coincidences yet unmoved by overwhelming statistical evidence.

**5.** The author regards the lack of empirical evidence for astrology as

    (A) an oversight on the part of the astrologers
    (B) a strong argument against its validity
    (C) a flaw that will be corrected in time
    (D) the unfortunate result of too small a sampling
    (E) a major reason to keep searching for fresh data

**6.** The author's attitude toward astrology can best be described as one of

    (A) grudging respect
    (B) compassionate tolerance
    (C) open disdain
    (D) disguised hostility
    (E) puzzled fascination

7. The term "innumerate" (last sentence) is best interpreted to mean which of the following?

   (A) various in kind
   (B) too numerous to count
   (C) scientifically sophisticated
   (D) unable to use mathematics
   (E) indifferent to astrology

8. The author cites the abundance of literary allusions to astrology primarily in order to

   (A) argue for its acceptance
   (B) refute its scientific validity
   (C) establish its pervasiveness
   (D) contrast it with the pseudosciences
   (E) explain the mechanisms by which it works

I walk to the window to watch this extraordinary game that the jackdaws are playing with the wind. A game? Yes, indeed, it is a game, in the most literal sense of the word: practised movements, indulged in and enjoyed for their own sake and not for the achievement of a special object. And rest assured, these are not merely inborn, purely instinctive actions, but movements that have been carefully learned. All these feats that the birds are performing, their wonderful exploitation of the wind, their amazingly exact assessment of distances and, above all, their understanding of local wind conditions, their knowledge of all the up-currents, air pockets and eddies—all this proficiency is no inheritance, but, for each bird, an individually acquired accomplishment.

And look what they do with the wind! At first sight, you, poor human being, think that the storm is playing with the birds, like a cat with a mouse, but soon you see, with astonishment, that it is the fury of the elements that here plays the role of the mouse and that the jackdaws are treating the storm exactly as the cat its unfortunate victim. Nearly, but only nearly, do they give the storm its head, let it throw them high, high into the heavens, till they seem to fall upwards, then, with a casual flap of a wing, they turn themselves over, open their pinions for a fraction of a second from below against the wind, and dive—with an acceleration far greater than that of a falling stone—into the depths below. Another tiny jerk of the wing and they return to their normal position and, on close-reefed sails, shoot away with breathless speed into the teeth of the gale, hundreds of yards to the west: this all playfully and without effort, just to spite the stupid wind that tries to drive them towards the east. The sightless monster itself must perform the work of propelling the birds through the air at a rate of well over 80 miles an hour; the jackdaws do nothing to help beyond a few lazy adjustments of their black wings. Sovereign control over the power of the elements, intoxicating triumph of the living organism over the pitiless strength of the inorganic!

9. According to the passage, the bird's skill in adapting to wind conditions is

   (A) genetically determined
   (B) limited
   (C) undependable
   (D) dependent on the elements
   (E) gained through practice

10. It can be inferred that the "sightless monster" mentioned in the next-to-last sentence is

   (A) an unobservant watcher
   (B) a falling stone
   (C) an airplane
   (D) the powerful windstorm
   (E) a blind predator

11. The author does all of the following EXCEPT

   (A) use a metaphor
   (B) refer to a historical event
   (C) clarify a term
   (D) describe a behavior
   (E) dismiss a notion

Given the persistent and intransigent nature of the American race system, which proved quite impervious to black attacks, Du Bois in his speeches and writings moved from one proposed solution to another, and the salience of various parts of his philosophy changed as his perceptions of the needs and strategies of black America shifted over time. Aloof and autonomous in his personality, Du Bois did not hesitate to depart markedly from whatever was the current mainstream of black thinking when he perceived that the conventional wisdom being enunciated by black spokesmen was proving inadequate to the task of advancing the race. His willingness to seek different solutions often placed him well in advance of his contemporaries, and this, combined with a strong-willed, even arrogant personality made his career as a black leader essentially a series of stormy conflicts.

Thus Du Bois first achieved his role as a major black leader in the controversy that arose over the program of Booker T. Washington, the most prominent and influential black leader at the opening of the twentieth century. Amidst the wave of lynchings, disfranchisement, and segregation laws, Washington, seeking the good will of powerful whites, taught blacks not to protest against discrimination, but to elevate themselves through industrial education, hard work, and property accumulation; then, they would ultimately obtain recognition of their citizenship rights. At first Du Bois agreed with this gradualist strategy, but in 1903 with the publication of his most influential book, *Souls of Black Folk,* he became the chief leader of the onslaught against Washington that polarized the black community into two wings—the "conservative" supporters of Washington and his "radical" critics.

12. The author's primary purpose in the passage is to

   (A) explain how Du Bois was influenced by Washington
   (B) compare the personalities of Du Bois and Washington
   (C) explain why Du Bois gained power in the black community
   (D) describe Du Bois's role in early twentieth century black leadership
   (E) correct the misconception that Du Bois shunned polarization

13. Which of the following statements about Du Bois does the passage best support?

   (A) He sacrificed the proven strategies of earlier black leaders to his craving for political novelty.
   (B) Preferring conflict to harmony, he followed a disruptive course that alienated him from the bulk of his followers.
   (C) He proved unable to change with the times in mounting fresh attacks against white racism.
   (D) He relied on the fundamental benevolence of the white population for the eventual success of his movement.
   (E) Once an adherent of Washington's policies, he ultimately lost patience with them for their ineffectiveness.

**14.** It can be inferred that Booker T. Washington in comparison with Du Bois could be described as all of the following EXCEPT

(A) submissive to the majority
(B) concerned with financial success
(C) versatile in adopting strategies
(D) traditional in preaching industry
(E) respectful of authority

**15.** The author's attitude towards Du Bois's departure from conventional black policies can best be described as

(A) skeptical
(B) derisive
(C) shocked
(D) approving
(E) resigned

### Answer Key

#### Exercise A

| | | | |
|---|---|---|---|
| 1. D | 5. B | 9. A | 13. E |
| 2. C | 6. D | 10. C | 14. B |
| 3. B | 7. D | 11. A | 15. E |
| 4. D | 8. E | 12. D | |

#### Exercise B

| | | | |
|---|---|---|---|
| 1. A | 5. C | 9. E | 13. C |
| 2. A | 6. D | 10. D | 14. D |
| 3. D | 7. A | 11. C | 15. C |
| 4. C | 8. C | 12. A | |

#### Exercise C

| | | | |
|---|---|---|---|
| 1. D | 5. B | 9. E | 13. E |
| 2. E | 6. B | 10. D | 14. C |
| 3. A | 7. D | 11. B | 15. D |
| 4. A | 8. D | 12. D | |

# 5 The Test of Standard Written English

The Test of Standard Written English determines the candidate's ability to recognize the common errors that crop up in sentences.

---

**Long-Range Strategy:** Review the rules of grammar. In particular, be aware of the 10 common types of errors listed below.

---

| 1. **Incomplete sentences** | *Not:* | Our school is famous for its teams. Especially the football team. |
| | *But:* | Our school is famous for its teams, especially the football team. |

---

| 2. **Run-on sentences** | *Not:* | He hit the ball, it was a homerun. |
| | *But:* | He hit the ball. It was a homerun. |

---

| 3. **Lack of agreement between subject and verb** | *Not:* | Each of the blocks are numbered. |
| | *But:* | Each of the blocks is numbered. |

---

| 4. **Lack of agreement between pronoun and antecedent** | *Not:* | Not one of the girls returned their gifts. |
| | *But:* | Not one of the girls returned her gifts. |

---

| 5. **Wrong tense** | *Not:* | When I worked for a month, I asked for a day off. |
| | *But:* | When I had worked for a month, I asked for a day off. |

6. **Misuse of subjunctive mood**

   *Not:* If I was President, things would be different.

   *But:* If I were President, things would be different.

7. **Incorrect comparison of adjectives**

   *Not:* Joe is taller than any boy in his class.

   *But:* Joe is taller than any other boy in his class.

   *Not:* Ann is the oldest of the two girls.

   *But:* Ann is the older of the two girls.

8. **Misuse of adjectives and adverbs**

   *Not:* Bill dances good.

   *But:* Bill dances well.

   *Not:* I admire these kind of paintings.

   *But:* I admire this kind of paintings.

   *Not:* I feel badly about the accident.

   *But:* I feel bad about the accident.

9. **Dangling participles**

   *Not:* Driving along the highway, the mountain came into view.

   *But:* Driving along the highway, I saw the mountain.

10. **Lack of parallel structure**

   *Not:* I like fishing, hunting, and to play golf.

   *But:* I like to fish, to hunt, and to play golf.

**Tips to Help You Cope**

1. Bear in mind that the error, if there is one, occurs in the underlined portion of the sentence.
2. Look first for common errors, such as lack of agreement between subject and verb.
3. Remember that what is tested here is correct *written* English. The standards for spoken English are less rigorous.

## Ten Typical Questions, with Answers Explained, to Get You Started

In each of the sentences below, there are four underlined words or phrases. If you think there is an error in usage, grammar, or punctuation in the underlined part, write the appropriate letter on your answer paper. If there is no error in any of the underlined parts, write E.

1. For modern man, the acquisition of facts is <u>like</u> a habit-forming
   (A)

   <u>drug; the</u> more he takes, <u>the more</u> craving he has. <u>No error</u>
     (B)              (C)         (D)     (E)

2. <u>This play</u> is different <u>than</u> the <u>one</u> we <u>saw</u> last night. <u>No error</u>
     (A)              (B)   (C)   (D)          (E)

3. The house looked <u>it's</u> <u>age,</u> despite our efforts to <u>beautify</u> it. <u>No error</u>
                    (A) (B)   (C)            (D)     (E)

4. It <u>may be</u> difficult to find an acceptable definition <u>of style;</u> every critic
       (A)                                   (B)

   has <u>their</u> <u>own.</u> <u>No error</u>
      (C)  (D)   (E)

5. <u>Dozens</u> of phrases can be offered to describe <u>style, but</u> perhaps the
    (A)                                 (B)

   best one <u>is:</u> "Style—it is the <u>man."</u> <u>No error</u>
          (C)               (D)   (E)

6. The laborer <u>today</u> has greater leisure, is less <u>provincial,</u> <u>enjoying</u> the
           (A)                         (B)       (C)

   fruits of his labors to a <u>far greater degree</u> than was hitherto possible.
                             (D)

   <u>No error</u>
     (E)

7. This is <u>one</u> of the paintings <u>which</u> <u>is going</u> to be sold <u>at auction</u> this
    (A)                 (B)   (C)           (D)

   afternoon. <u>No error</u>
            (E)

> Each of the sentences below has an underlined portion that may be correct or have an error in grammar, diction, style, punctuation or capitalization. From the five choices listed, select the one which you believe is correct.

8. In the normal course of events, <u>John will graduate high school and enter</u> college in two years.

   (A) John will graduate high school and enter
   (B) John will graduate from High School and enter
   (C) John will be graduated from High School and enter
   (D) John will be graduated from high school and enter
   (E) John will have graduated from high school and enter

9. The teacher asked, <u>"Have you read 'What makes Sammy Run'?"</u>

   (A) "Have you read 'What makes Sammy Run'?"
   (B) "Have you read 'What makes Sammy Run?' "
   (C) "Have you read 'What Makes Sammy Run'?"
   (D) "Have you read 'What Makes Sammy Run?' "
   (E) "Have you read What Makes Sammy Run?"

10. With the exception of <u>Frank and I, everyone in the class finished</u> the assignment before the bell rang.

   (A) Frank and I, everyone in the class finished
   (B) Frank and me, everyone in the class finished
   (C) Frank and me, everyone in the class had finished
   (D) Frank and I, everyone in the class had finished
   (E) Frank and me everyone in the class finished

## Answers and Explanations

1. **D.** Lack of parallel structure. The sentence is better as: *The more he takes, the more he craves.*
2. **B.** *Different from* is the preferred form.
3. **A.** *It's* is the contraction for *it is.* The possessive pronoun is *its.*
4. **C.** Error in agreement. *Their* should be *his* (singular) to agree with *critic* (singular).

5. **E.** Sentence is correct.

6. **C.** Lack of parallel structure. Substitute a verb for the participle to parallel the preceding verbs. Sentence is better as: *The laborer today has greater leisure, is less provincial, and enjoys. . . .*

7. **C.** Error in agreement between pronoun and verb. The antecedent of *which* is paintings (plural). *Which* (plural) should be followed by *are going* (plural).

8. **D.** This corrects the two errors in the sentence—the idiom error (*to be graduated*) and the error in capitalization.

9. **C.** This corrects the error in the sentence—the capitalization of *Makes*—without introducing any new errors.

10. **C.** This corrects the two errors in the sentence—the error in case (*me* for *I*) and the error in tense (*had finished* for *finished*).

**Practice Exercises**     **Answers given on page 234.**

---

<u>Directions:</u> The following sentences contain problems in grammar, usage, diction (choice of words), and idiom.

Some sentences are correct.
No sentence contains more than one error.

You will find that the error, if there is one, is underlined and lettered. Assume that elements of the sentence that are not underlined are correct and cannot be changed. In choosing answers, follow the requirements of standard written English.

If there is an error, select the <u>one underlined part</u> that must be changed to make the sentence correct and blacken the corresponding space on your answer sheet.

If there is no error, blacken answer space E.

EXAMPLE:

The region has a climate <u>so severe that</u> plants <u>growing there</u>
                          A                           B

rarely <u>had been</u> more than twelve inches <u>high.</u> <u>No error</u>
       C                                      D        E

SAMPLE ANSWER
Ⓐ Ⓑ ● Ⓓ Ⓔ

1. The conditions governing the truce <u>which</u> <u>has been arranged</u> by the
$\qquad\qquad\qquad\qquad\qquad$ (A) $\qquad\qquad$ (B)

   <u>United Nations</u> <u>has</u> not been revealed. <u>No error</u>
   $\quad$ (C) $\qquad$ (D) $\qquad\qquad\qquad\qquad$ (E)

2. <u>Each</u> one of the dogs in the <u>show</u> <u>require</u> a special kind of <u>diet.</u>
   (A) $\qquad\qquad\qquad\qquad$ (B) $\quad$ (C) $\qquad\qquad\qquad\qquad$ (D)

   <u>No error</u>
   (E)

3. By order of the <u>Student Council,</u> the <u>wearing of</u> jeans by <u>we</u> girls in
   $\qquad\qquad\qquad$ (A) $\qquad\qquad\qquad$ (B) $\qquad\qquad$ (C)

   school <u>has been permitted.</u> <u>No error</u>
   $\qquad$ (D) $\qquad\qquad$ (E)

4. The major difficulty <u>confronting</u> the authorities was the <u>reluctance</u> of
   $\qquad\qquad\qquad$ (A) $\qquad\qquad\qquad\qquad\qquad$ (B)

   the people <u>to talk;</u> they had been warned not to say <u>nothing</u> to the
   $\qquad\qquad$ (C) $\qquad\qquad\qquad\qquad\qquad\qquad$ (D)

   police. <u>No error</u>
   $\qquad$ (E)

5. We were <u>already</u> to leave for the amusement park when <u>John's</u> car
   $\qquad\qquad$ (A) $\qquad\qquad\qquad\qquad\qquad\qquad\qquad$ (B)

   <u>broke down;</u> we <u>were forced</u> to postpone our outing. <u>No error</u>
   $\quad$ (C) $\qquad\qquad$ (D) $\qquad\qquad\qquad\qquad\qquad$ (E)

6. We have heard that the <u>principal</u> has decided <u>whom</u> the prize
   $\qquad\qquad\qquad\qquad$ (A) $\qquad\qquad\qquad$ (B)

   winners <u>will be</u> and <u>will announce</u> the names in the assembly today.
   $\qquad$ (C) $\qquad\qquad$ (D)

   <u>No error</u>
   (E)

7. She sang <u>like</u> she wished the <u>people</u> in the next <u>county</u> <u>to hear</u> her.
   $\qquad\qquad$ (A) $\qquad\qquad\qquad$ (B) $\qquad\qquad$ (C) $\quad$ (D)

   <u>No error</u>
   (E)

8. Although the news <u>had come</u> as a surprise to <u>all</u> in the room,
   $\qquad\qquad\qquad$ (A) $\qquad\qquad\qquad$ (B)

   everyone tried to do <u>their</u> work <u>as though</u> nothing had happened.
   $\qquad\qquad\qquad$ (C) $\qquad$ (D)

   <u>No error</u>
   (E)

9.  The committee <u>had intended</u> <u>both</u> you and <u>I</u> to speak at the
        (A)          (B)            (C)

    <u>assembly; however,</u> only one of us will be able to talk. <u>No error</u>
        (D)                                                          (E)

10. "At that moment<u>,"</u> John reported, "the teacher said<u>,</u> 'Speak
                  (A)                          (B)              (C)

    louder.'" <u>No error</u>
       (D)       (E)

---

Directions: In each of the following sentences, some part or all of
            the sentence is underlined. Below each sentence you
            will find five ways of phrasing the underlined part.
            Select the answer that produces the most effective
            sentence, one that is clear and exact, without awkward-
            ness or ambiguity, and blacken the corresponding
            space on your answer sheet. In choosing answers,
            follow the requirements of standard written English.
            Choose the answer that best expresses the meaning of
            the original sentence.

            Answer (A) is always the same as the underlined part.
            Choose answer (A) if you think the original sentence
            needs no revision.

EXAMPLE:

Laura Ingalls Wilder published her first book <u>and she was</u>
<u>sixty-five years old then</u>.

(A)  and she was sixty-five years old then
(B)  when she was sixty-five years old
(C)  at age sixty-five years old
(D)  upon reaching sixty-five years
(E)  at the time when she was sixty-five

SAMPLE ANSWER

**11.** The child is <u>neither encouraged to be critical or to examine</u> all the evidence for his opinion.

    (A) neither encouraged to be critical or to examine

    (B) neither encouraged to be critical nor to examine

    (C) either encouraged to be critical or to examine

    (D) encouraged either to be critical nor to examine

    (E) not encouraged either to be critical or to examine

**12.** The process by which the community <u>influence the actions of its members</u> is known as social control.

    (A) influence the actions of its members

    (B) influences the actions of its members

    (C) had influenced the actions of its members

    (D) influences the actions of their members

    (E) will influence the actions of its members

**13.** To be sure, there would be scarcely no time left over for other things if school children <u>would have been expected to have considered</u> all sides of every matter on which they hold opinions.

    (A) would have been expected to have considered

    (B) should have been expected to have considered

    (C) were expected to consider

    (D) will be expected to have been considered

    (E) were expected to be considered

**14.** <u>Examining the principal movements sweeping through the world, it can be seen</u> that they are being accelerated by the war.

    (A) Examining the principal movements sweeping through the world, it can be seen

    (B) Having examined the principal movements sweeping through the world

    (C) Examining the principal movements sweeping through the world can be seen

    (D) Examining the principal movements sweeping through the world, we can see

    (E) It can be seen examining the principal movements sweeping through the world

15. However many mistakes have been made in our past, the tradition of America, <u>not only the champion of freedom but also fair play,</u> still lives among millions who can see light and hope scarcely anywhere else.

(A) not only the champion of freedom but also fair play,
(B) the champion of not only freedom but also of fair play,
(C) the champion not only of freedom but also of fair play,
(D) not only the champion but also freedom and fair play,
(E) not the champion of freedom only, but also fair play,

### Answer Key

| | | | | |
|---|---|---|---|---|
| 1. **D** | 4. **D** | 7. **A** | 10. **E** | 13. **C** |
| 2. **C** | 5. **A** | 8. **C** | 11. **E** | 14. **D** |
| 3. **C** | 6. **B** | 9. **C** | 12. **B** | 15. **C** |

# 6

# The Mathematics Sections: Strategies, Tips, and Practice

The SAT assumes that you are familiar with arithmetic, elementary algebra, and plane geometry. The questions on the test are about equally divided among those three areas. You do not need to know any more advanced mathematics to do well on this part of the SAT.

As you learned in Chapter 2, there are two types of questions in the mathematics sections: quantitative comparison questions, which make up about one third of the test, and standard multiple-choice questions, which make up the other two thirds of the test. In this chapter, you'll find test-taking tips and strategies that will help you with both types of questions. You'll also find review and practice in basic mathematics.

A sound knowledge of basic mathematics together with good test-taking skills will assure you of doing your best on the mathematics sections of the SAT. So study the math review, learn the testing tips, and do the practice exercises in this chapter. You'll be more confident and relaxed when you take the test, because you'll know what to expect and you'll be familiar with the material covered.

## General Tips for Answering Mathematics Questions

1. Round off and estimate whenever possible. Simplify your calculations. $3,978 \times 289$ can be rounded off to $4,000 \times 300$. Then if only one of the answer choices is slightly less than 1,200,000 you have your answer.

2. Look for shortcuts. These are often built into problems. For example, you know that an odd number multiplied by an odd number will give you an odd number. If only one of the answer choices is an odd number, it has to be the right answer.

3. Do not panic if a question has an unusual symbol. Replace the symbol with the specially designed definition that accompanies the symbol.

4. Work in consistent units. If one side of a square measures 30 inches and the other measures 2 feet, don't try multiplying to find the area until you have both measurements in either feet or inches.

5. Have important rules and formulas at your fingertips. Use the information supplied at the top of the first page of each mathematics section. Or, better yet, memorize these and other important facts and formulas before the test date.

6. Read the question carefully. Do not assume anything that is not actually stated. Some questions are not similar to questions you usually encounter in regular math classes.

7. Beware of positive and negative numbers. If the problem does not specifically state that the value of an unknown is positive, then it could also be negative. The square root of a number can be positive or negative.

8. Use your time wisely. If you have absolutely no idea how to solve a particular problem, do not waste time on it. Circle it, and leave it. If you have time at the end of the test, you can go back and try again.

9. Avoid lengthy computation. None of the questions on the test will require terribly complicated computations. If you find yourself about to start on a long string of complicated computations to solve a problem, you are doing something wrong. Either you missed a shortcut, or you are solving the wrong problem. Read the question again.

10. Use the exam booklet wisely. Don't try to do all computations in your head. Write in the test booklet. Mark up any diagrams if it will help you.

11. Check the diagrams. The diagrams may be drawn accurately or they may be accompanied by a statement

saying that the figure is not drawn to scale. In the latter case you may want to redraw the diagram slightly to make it accurate.

12. Be on the lookout for irrelevant material in a word problem. There probably will be at least one question that gives you more information than you need. Don't assume that you have to use it all to solve the problem. If what you need to know is how many people were wearing red hats, it doesn't matter how many were wearing blue shoes.

13. Don't rush to get to the most challenging problems. Questions get harder as you go along in the math section.

14. Don't hesitate to work back from the answers. On this test you do not have to show how you arrived at the answer. First plug in the answer which is easiest to try. Usually, this is the correct choice.

15. Do not panic when you are faced with mathematical terminology. Try putting the problem into simpler words. "S is a set of integers on the number line 1-100 inclusive" just means "S is all the numbers from 1 through 100."

16. Substitute for unknowns, if necessary. If you are having trouble solving a problem with several unknowns, try substituting simple numbers for the unknowns.

**Long-Range Strategy:**    You are most likely to do well on the mathematics section of the SAT if you know your math. All the tactics in the world cannot substitute for knowledge. In the long run, the ability to solve problems quickly and accurately is going to be far more useful than the ability to psych out the testers.

However, not all students are gifted mathematicians, and even those who are may have forgotten some of the topics they covered a year or two ago in algebra and geometry. Almost all of you could benefit from some review. The facts and formulas that follow in this chapter provide a minimal review. Go over these points and, as far as possible, commit them to memory. And if you feel you need more review in some areas, go over those topics in your textbooks.

## MATHEMATICS REVIEW

### Symbols

| | | | |
|---|---|---|---|
| = | equals | ≃ | is congruent to |
| ≠ | is not equal to | ~ | is similar to |
| > | is more than | ⊥ | is perpendicular to |
| < | is less than | ‖ | is parallel to |
| ≧ | is greater than or equal to | ± | plus or minus |
| ≦ | is less than or equal to | | |

### Important Definitions

Sum is the result of addition.

Difference is the result of subtraction.

Product is the result of multiplication.

In division,

$$\frac{\text{Dividend}}{\text{Divisor}} = \text{Quotient} + \frac{\text{Remainder}}{\text{Divisor}}$$

A fraction is an indicated division.

A decimal is an implied fraction with a denominator of 10, 100, 1000, . . . .

A percent is a fraction with a denominator of 100.

A ratio compares two quantities by dividing one by the other.

A proportion is an equation, both sides of which are fractions.

A *positive* number is one that is greater than zero; a *negative* number is one that is less than zero. The meaning and the use of signed numbers are basic in the study of algebra. Positive numbers are preceded by a plus sign (+); negative numbers, by a minus sign (−).

### Arithmetic Concepts

Any quantity multiplied by zero is zero ($x \cdot 0 = 0$).

Any quantity except zero raised to the zero power is 1 ($x^0 = 1$ if $x \neq 0$).

If $x^2 = 4$, then $x = +2$ or $-2$.

Any fraction multiplied by its reciprocal equals 1:

$$\left(\frac{x}{y}\right)\left(\frac{y}{x}\right) = 1$$

### Odd and Even Numbers

even + even = even
odd + odd = even
even + odd = odd
even × even = even
even × odd = even
odd × odd = odd

### Helpful Tips on Divisibility

1. An integer is divisible by 2 if the last digit is evenly divisible by 2.
2. An integer is divisible by 3 if the sum of its digits is evenly divisible by 3.
3. An integer is evenly divisible by 5 if the last digit is either zero or 5.

### Important Formulas

Average $= \dfrac{\text{Sum of number}}{\text{Quantity of numbers}}$

Rate × Time = Distance

Time $= \dfrac{\text{Distance}}{\text{Rate}}$

Rate $= \dfrac{\text{Distance}}{\text{Time}}$

Percentage composition $= \dfrac{\text{Quantity dissolved}}{\text{Total quantity of mixture}} \times 100$

Part of task done $= \dfrac{\text{Time actually worked}}{\text{Time required to complete entire task}}$

### Algebra Concepts

In algebra, we use letters as well as numbers. When no sign appears between a combination of numbers and letters, it indicates that the items are to be multiplied. Thus $4abc$ means $4 \times a \times b \times c$.

Only *like* algebraic terms may be combined.

*Always check your answer in the original equation.*

In *algebraic expressions*, break problems down to their simplest form and try to eliminate any equivalent answer choices. In simplifying, remember to multiply and divide before adding and subtracting; simplify exponents and fractions; combine like terms.

If an expression has more than one set of parentheses, get rid of the inner parentheses first and work outward through the rest of the parentheses.

### Factoring

To **factor** an expression means to find two or more expressions whose product is the given expression. Every expression can be written as the product of itself and 1. Any expression that cannot be factored in any other way is called **prime.**

*Type 1.* To factor a polynomial that has a common monomial factor, find the greatest monomial that will divide into each term of the polynomial. This is one factor. Divide the polynomial by this factor to obtain the other factor.

Example

$$\text{Factor } 4x^3y^3 - 22xy^2.$$
$$4x^3y^3 - 22xy^2 = 2xy^2(2x^2y - 11)$$

*Type 2.* To factor an expression that is the difference of two perfect squares, find the square root of each term. The sum of the two square roots is one factor, and the difference of the two square roots is the other factor. This factoring rule can be easily visualized as follows:

$$a^2 - b^2 = (a + b)(a - b)$$

Example

$$\text{Factor } x^2 - 64.$$
$$x^2 - 64 = (x - 8)(x + 8)$$

*Type 3.* Trinomials of the form $ax^2 + bx + c$. When two binomials of the form $mx + n$ and $px + q$ are multiplied, the result is a trinomial with this rather complicated-looking form:

$$mpx^2 + (mq + np)x + nq$$

When the actual multiplication is carried out, of course, the result is not nearly so awesome, since the real numbers $m$, $n$, $p$, and $q$ all combine to produce the simplified form

$$ax^2 + bx + c$$

For example,

$$x^2 - 6x + 8 = (x - 4)(x - 2)$$
$$x^2 + 8x + 12 = (x + 6)(x + 2)$$
$$x^2 - 3x - 10 = (x - 5)(x + 2)$$

Any factor of a term is called the *coefficient* of the remaining factors. In usual practice, the numerical value that is multiplied by the remaining terms is regarded as the coefficient. In $6ab$, 6 is regarded as the coefficient of $ab$; in $abc$, 1 is the coefficient of $abc$.

### Exponents

An exponent is a smaller number or letter written above and to the right of another number or letter. It indicates how many times the number or letter is multiplied by itself. Thus:

$$2^5 = 2 \times 2 \times 2 \times 2 \times 2 = 32$$
$$y^4 = y \times y \times y \times y$$

### Rules for Handling Exponents

$$x^a \cdot x^b = x^{a+b} \qquad \left(\frac{x}{y}\right)^a = \frac{x^a}{y^a}$$
$$x^a \div x^b = x^{a-b} \qquad x^0 = 1 \text{ if } x \neq 0$$
$$(x^a)^b = x^{ab} \qquad$$
$$(xy)^a = x^a y^a \qquad x^{-a} = \frac{1}{x^a}$$
$$x^{1/a} = \sqrt[a]{x}$$

### Solving Equations

An equation is a mathematical sentence which states that two expressions name the same number. Thus $4x = 20$ is an equation that is true when $x$ is 5 and false when $x$ is anything else.

A root (or solution) of an equation is a number that makes the equation true when used in place of the variable. The root of the equation $4x = 20$ is 5. Some equations have more than one root. The roots of the equation $x^2 - 7x + 12 = 0$ are 4 and 3.

Addition, subtraction, multiplication, or division of each side of an equation by the same quantity results in a new equation that has the same roots. (Division by 0, of course, is excluded here as in every other place in mathematics.) These operations are used on equations whose roots are not immediately apparent in order to find new equations that are simpler.

Example

If 4 is subtracted from one-fourth of a number, the result is 20. Find the number.

Let $x =$ the number. Then the first sentence readily translates into the equation

$$\frac{1}{4}x - 4 = 20$$

This equation is solved by first multiplying both sides by 4 and then adding 16 to each side:

$$x = 96$$

To check, note that $\frac{1}{4}$ of 96 is 24, and when 4 is subtracted from 24 the result is 20.

### Axioms Involving Inequalities

The whole is greater than any of its parts.

If equal quantities are added to unequal quantities, the sums are unequal in the same order.

If equal quantities are subtracted from unequal quantities, the remainders are unequal in the same order.

If unequal quantities are added to unequal quantities in the same order, the sums are unequal in the same order.

If unequal quantities are subtracted from unequal quantities, the remainders are unequal in the opposite order.

Doubles of unequals are unequal in the same order.

Halves of unequals are unequal in the same order.

If the first of three quantities is greater than the second, and the second is greater than the third, then the first is greater than the third.

### Geometry Concepts

#### Right Triangles

In a right triangle, $(\text{leg})^2 + (\text{leg})^2 = (\text{hypotenuse})^2$, or $a^2 + b^2 = c^2$.

In a 30°–60°–90° triangle:

the leg opposite the 30° angle equals $\frac{1}{2}$ the hypotenuse;

the leg opposite the 60° angle equals $\frac{1}{2}$ the hypotenuse times $\sqrt{3}$;

the ratio of the shorter leg to the hypotenuse is 1:2.

In a 45°–45°–90° triangle:
the hypotenuse equals a leg times $\sqrt{2}$;

the leg equals $\frac{1}{2}$ the hypotenuse times $\sqrt{2}$.

#### Equilateral Triangles

In an equilateral triangle, an altitude equals $\frac{1}{2}$ the side times $\sqrt{3}$.

#### Areas of Polygons

Area of a rectangle = $bh$

Area of a square = $s^2$

Area of a parallelogram = $bh$

Area of a triangle = $\frac{1}{2} bh$

Area of a right triangle = $\frac{1}{2}$ leg × leg

## Circles

Circumference of a circle $= \pi d$ or $2\pi r$

Length of an arc $= \dfrac{n}{360} \times 2\pi r$

Area of a circle $= \pi r^2$

## Coordinate Geometry

Distance between two points =
$$\sqrt{(x_1 - x_2)^2 + (y_1 - y_2)^2}$$

Coordinates of midpoint of line =
$$\frac{1}{2}(x_1 + x_2), \frac{1}{2}(y_1 + y_2)$$

## Basic Quantities To Know ($\approx$ Represents "Approximately Equals")

$$\pi \approx 3.1416 \approx \frac{22}{7}$$

$$\sqrt{2} \approx 1.1414$$

$$\sqrt{3} \approx 1.732$$

## Important Solutions of the Pythagorean Theorem

3–4–5 triangle
5–12–13 triangle
1–1–$\sqrt{2}$ triangle (45°–45°–90°)
1–$\sqrt{3}$–2 triangle (30°–60°–90°)

## Important Theorems in Geometry

## Triangles

If two sides of a triangle are congruent, the angles opposite these sides are congruent. (Base angles of an isosceles triangle are congruent.)

The sum of the measure of the angles of a triangle is equal to a straight angle (180°).

If two angles of a triangle are congruent, the sides opposite these angles are congruent.

Two right triangles are congruent if the hypotenuse and leg of one triangle are congruent to the hypotenuse and corresponding leg of the other.

If two triangles have the three angles of one congruent respectively to the three angles of the other, the triangles are similar.

If, in a right triangle, the altitude is drawn upon the hypotenuse:
(a) the two triangles thus formed are similar to the given triangle and similar to each other;
(b) the length of each leg of the given triangle is the mean proportional between the hypotenuse and the projection of that leg on the hypotenuse.

If an angle of one triangle is equal to an angle of another triangle and the sides including these angles are proportional, the triangles are similar.

The areas of two similar triangles are to each other as the squares of any two corresponding sides.

If two sides of a triangle are unequal, the angles opposite these sides are unequal and the greater angle lies opposite the greater side.

If two angles of a triangle are unequal, the sides opposite these angles are unequal and the greater side lies opposite the greater angle.

## Circles

In a circle, a diameter perpendicular to a chord bisects the chord and its two arcs.

In a circle or in congruent circles, congruent chords of equal length are equally distant from the center.

Tangents drawn to a circle from an external point are equal in length.

An angle formed by a tangent and a chord drawn from the point of contact is measured by one-half its intercepted arc.

If two chords intersect within a circle, the product of the segments of one chord is equal to the product of the segments of the other.

If from a point outside a circle a tangent and a secant are drawn to the circle, the tangent is the mean proportional between the secant and its external segment.

An angle inscribed in a circle is measured by one-half its intercepted arc.

An angle formed by two chords intersecting within a circle is measured by one-half the sum of the intercepted arcs.

An angle formed by two secants meeting outside a circle is measured by one-half the difference of the intercepted arcs.

An angle formed by a tangent and a secant is measured by one-half the difference of the intercepted arcs.

An angle formed by the intersection of two tangents is measured by one-half the difference of the intercepted arcs.

### Parallelograms

If two lines are cut by a transversal and a pair of alternate interior angles are congruent, the two lines are parallel.

The opposite sides of a parallelogram are congruent and the opposite angles are congruent.

The diagonals of a parallelogram bisect each other.

If the opposite sides of a quadrilateral are congruent, the figure is a parallelogram.

If two sides of a quadrilateral are congruent and parallel, the figure is a parallelogram.

---

## THE STANDARD MULTIPLE-CHOICE QUESTION

The standard multiple-choice questions are like the questions you've had on your math tests in school. They may involve solving simple equations, finding the area of a triangle, or adding several fractions. You'll also find word problems that require knowledge of such topics as ratio and proportion, averages, and motion, to mention just a few. You've had these types of problems on your math tests, too, so you'll be familiar with them.

The general tips given at the beginning of this chapter will help you with the standard multiple-choice questions. In addition, study the following tips on solving specific types of problems.

---

**Tips on Solving Important Types of Problems**
**1. Fractions**

*Case 1.* To find a number that is a fractional part of a given number, multiply the number by the fraction.

**Example:** Find $\frac{7}{8}$ of 48.

$$\frac{7}{\cancel{8}} \times \frac{\cancel{48}^{6}}{1} = 42$$

**Example:** Mr. Brown, who owns $\frac{3}{7}$ of the interest in a company, sells $\frac{1}{2}$ of his share to Mr. Wein. What part of the business does Mr. Wein own after completing this transaction?

$$\frac{1}{2} \times \frac{3}{7} = \frac{3}{14}$$

*Case 2.* To find what fractional part one number is of another, divide the number representing the part by the number representing the whole:

$$\frac{\text{Part}}{\text{Whole}} = \text{Fractional part}$$

*Hint:* In most problems, the *part* follows the word "is" and the *whole* follows the word "of."

**Example:** In a class of 26, there are 16 girls. What part of the class is made up of girls?

$$\frac{16}{26} = \frac{8}{13}$$

**Example:** What part of a quarter is a nickel?

$$\frac{\text{Nickel}}{\text{Quarter}} = \frac{5 \text{ cents}}{25 \text{ cents}} = \frac{5}{25} = \frac{1}{5}$$

*Case 3.* To find a number when a fractional part of it is known, divide the given part by the fraction:

$$\frac{\text{Part}}{\text{Fractional part}} = \text{Whole}$$

*Note:* Most students prefer to solve problems of this type algebraically.

**Example:**  6 is $\frac{2}{3}$ of what number?

$$\frac{6}{\frac{2}{3}} = 6 \div \frac{2}{3} \text{ or } \overset{3}{\cancel{6}} \times \frac{3}{\cancel{2}} = 9$$

Or algebraically, let $x$ = the number:

$$\frac{2}{3}x = 6$$

$$x = 9$$

## 2. Percent

1. Substitute a letter ($x$, $y$, $z$, etc.) for the *unknown* quantity, such as "what," "what number," "what fraction," or "how many."

2. Substitute an equal sign for words such as "is equal to," "equals," or "is the equivalent of."

3. Apply the definition of "percent" as "hundredths." Thus $\frac{x}{100}$ is substituted for $x\%$, $\frac{3}{100}$ is substituted for 3%, etc.

4. Substitute parentheses (indicating multiplication) for such words as "of" or "part of." At this point you have set up the required equation.

5. Solve the equation.

**Example:**  A book sold for $4.80 after being discounted by 20%. What was the list price?

List price $\times$ Rate of discount = Discount          (1)
List price $-$ Discount = Net price          (2)

Let $x$ = List price
(Using formula 1)                     $x(.20)$ = discount
(Using formula 2)                     $x - .20x = 4.80$
                                            $.80x = 4.80$
                                               $x =$ **$6.00**

or, since a discount of 20% of the list price was allowed, $4.80 represents 80% of the list price. Thus $.60 represents 10% of the list price, and $6.00 represents 100% (the whole) of the list price.

## 3. Averages

*Case 1.*   To find the average of a group of numbers, add the numbers and divide the sum by the quantity of numbers added.

**Example:**   A boy in a chemistry class reports the following readings on a thermometer during an experiment: 5°, 0°, −2°, 9°. What is the average temperature?

$$
\begin{array}{r}
5° \\
0° \\
-2° \\
9° \\
\hline
12° \text{ (sum)}
\end{array}
\qquad
\frac{12°}{4} = 3° \text{ (average)}
$$

*Case 2.*   The sum is equal to the product of the average and the quantity of numbers.

**Example:**   A student has an average of 80% for six semesters in high school. What average must he earn in his next semester so that his average at the end of the seventh semester will be 82%?

His present average being 80%, the sum is 80% × 6 or 480%. His desired average is 82% so that the sum will need to be 82% × 7 or 574%.

In his seventh term his average will have to be 574% − 480% or 94%.

*Case 3. Weighted Averages.*   If two or more averages are combined into a single average, appropriate weight must be given each average.

**Example:** A student attended a certain high school for two semesters and earned an average of 90%. The same student earned an average of 85% in another school during a period of five terms. What is the scholastic average of this student for his high school work?

The sum in the first school is 90% × 2 or 180%.
The sum in the second school is 85% × 5 or 425%.
The sum for both schools is 180 + 425 or 605%.

Divide by the number of terms (7):
605% ÷ 7 = 86.4%

## 4. Motion

Problems involving motion can be solved by applying one of the following formulas:

$$\text{Distance} = \text{Rate} \times \text{Time} \tag{1}$$

$$\text{Rate} = \frac{\text{Distance}}{\text{Time}} \tag{2}$$

$$\text{Time} = \frac{\text{Distance}}{\text{Rate}} \tag{3}$$

**Example:** How many miles can be covered in 3 hours by a train traveling at 45 miles per hour?

Apply formula 1:

$$\text{Distance} = \frac{45 \text{ miles}}{\text{hour}} \times 3 \text{ hours}$$

$$\text{Distance} = 135 \text{ miles}$$

**Example:** A motorist covers 93 miles in 3 hours. What is the average rate during this trip?

Apply formula 2:

$$\text{Rate} = \frac{93 \text{ miles}}{3 \text{ hours}} = \frac{31 \text{ miles}}{\text{hour}}$$

**Example:** How long will it take a plane to cover a distance of 900 miles if it maintains an average rate of 90 miles per hour?

Apply formula 3:

$$\text{Time} = \frac{900 \text{ miles}}{\dfrac{90 \text{ miles}}{\text{hour}}}$$

or $\quad 900 \text{ miles} \div \dfrac{90 \text{ miles}}{\text{hour}}$

or $\quad 900 \text{ miles} \times \dfrac{\text{hour}}{90 \text{ miles}}$

$$= 10 \text{ hours}$$

## 5. Ratio and Proportion

A *ratio* is an expression that compares two quantities by dividing one by the other. In a class with 10 girls and 13 boys, it can be said that the ratio of girls to boys is 10:13 or $\dfrac{10}{13}$, or that the ratio of boys to girls is 13:10 or $\dfrac{13}{10}$.

A *maximum ratio* is the ratio that has the largest numerical value. Since a ratio may be written as a fraction, to find the maximum ratio among a given number of cases determine which fraction has the greatest numerical value.

In any ratio the unit must be the same. Thus, to express the ratio of the length of a room to the width, both units of measurement must be the same.

**Example:** The dimensions of a room are: length 120 inches, width 1.2 feet. What is the ratio of the width to the length?

$$\frac{\text{Width}}{\text{Length}} = \frac{1.2 \text{ feet}}{120 \text{ inches}} = \frac{1.2 \text{ feet}}{10 \text{ feet}} = \frac{12}{100} = \frac{3}{25}$$

The ratio is therefore 3:25.

**Example:** Two numbers are in the ratio of 7:3. Their difference is 20. Find the numbers.

Since 7:3 represents the reduced ratio, we can represent the original numbers by multiplying each number by $n$.

Let the smaller number = 3*n*.
Let the larger number = 7*n*.

$$7n - 3n = 20$$
$$4n = 20$$
$$n = 5$$
$$3n = 15; \ 7n = 35$$

A *proportion* is a statement of equality that exists between two ratios. For example, $\frac{1}{2} = \frac{5}{10}$ is a proportion. It consists of four terms. The first and last are called *extremes.* The second and third are called *means.* In the above example, 1 and 10 are the extremes; 2 and 5 are the means. In any proportion, the product of the means equals the product of the extremes:

$$\frac{1}{2} \searrow \nearrow \frac{5}{10}$$
$$(1)(10) = (2)(5)$$

The principles of ratio and proportion can help solve many problems. First decide whether a proportion exists. Then determine whether it is a direct proportion or an inverse proportion.

*Direct proportion.* Two variables are directly proportional if their corresponding values have a constant ratio. If one quantity is multiplied or divided by the same number, the ratio of the variables is unchanged.

*Inverse proportion.* Two variables are inversely proportional if an increase by multiplication in one variable results in a corresponding decrease in the other, and a decrease by division in one variable results in a corresponding increase in the other.

**Example:** One cup of crushed graham crackers can be obtained from 12 crackers. How many cups can be obtained from 36 such crackers?

This is obviously a direct proportion since the greater the number of crackers used, the greater will be the number of cups of crushed graham crackers.

$$\frac{1 \text{ cup}}{12 \text{ crackers}} = \frac{x \text{ cups}}{36 \text{ crackers}}$$

$$12x = 36$$

$$x = 3 \text{ cups}$$

Thus:

$$\frac{1 \text{ cup}}{12 \text{ crackers}} = \frac{3 \text{ cups}}{36 \text{ crackers}}$$

In this case, the ratio is $\frac{1}{12}$. Multiplying the quantities by 3 yields the ratio $\frac{3}{36}$, which is equal to $\frac{1}{12}$.

**Example:** If 4 boys can clear the snow around a house in 3 hours, how long will 8 boys working at the same rate take to perform this task?

Obviously, by increasing the number of boys, we will cut down on the time. This is an inverse proportion. Since the man power has been doubled, the time will be cut in half.

In an inverse proportion, it one quantity (4 boys) is the numerator of the first fraction, its related quantity (3 hours) is the denominator of the second fraction:

$$\frac{\text{Original number of boys}}{\text{New number of boys}} = \frac{\text{Time required by new number of boys}}{\text{Time required by original number of boys}}$$

$$\frac{4 \text{ boys}}{8 \text{ boys}} = \frac{x \text{ hours}}{3 \text{ hours}}$$

$$\frac{4}{8} = \frac{x}{3}$$

$$8x = 12$$

$$x = \frac{12}{8} \text{ or } 1\frac{1}{2} \text{ hours}$$

### 6. Mixtures and Solutions

Problems involving mixtures or solutions apply the principles of fractions. An important formula is:

$$\frac{\text{Quantity of substance dissolved}}{\text{Total quantity of solution}} = \text{Part of solution containing dissolved substance}$$

**Example:** A 10 galllon solution of disinfectant contains 1 gallon of disinfectant. What is the percent concentration of the solution?

$$\frac{1 \text{ gallon}}{10 \text{ gallons}} = \frac{1}{10} = 10\%$$

**Example:** How many pounds of pure salt must be added to 30 pounds of a 2% solution of salt and water to increase it to a 10% solution?

The given solution contains (2%) of 30 pounds of salt, or (.02)(30 pounds) or .06 pound of salt.

We must add a certain quantity of pure salt to the 30 pounds of solution so that:

$$\frac{\text{Quantity of salt}}{\text{Quantity of solution}} = 10\%$$

Let $x$ = number of pounds of salt to be added to the quantity of salt already in the solution. Therefore the solution will now contain 30 pounds of solution plus $x$ pounds of salt.

$$\frac{x + .6}{x + 30} = 10\%$$
$$\frac{x + .6}{x + 30} = \frac{1}{10}$$
$$10(x + .6) = x + 30$$
$$10x + 6 = x + 30$$
$$9x = 24$$
$$x = 2\frac{2}{3} \text{ pounds}$$

## 7. Work

Problems involving work are actually applications of the principles involving fractions. A student who has 4 hours of homework does $\frac{1}{4}$ of his task when he works 1 hour. A simple formula to remember is:

$$\frac{\text{Time actually spent working}}{\text{Time required to do the task}} = \text{Part of task done}$$

**Example:** A man can paint a room in 6 hours. His son can paint the same room in 8 hours alone. How long will it take the man and his son if they work together?

Let $x$ = number of hours it will take if they work togehter.

In 1 hour the man would perform $\frac{1}{6}$ of the task. In 1 hour the son would perform $\frac{1}{8}$ of the task. Likewise, in $x$ hours the man would perform $\frac{x}{6}$ part of the task. Since they will complete the *entire* task by each performing his part, we may say that the sum of the fractions equals 1 (the whole job):

$$\frac{x}{6} + \frac{x}{8} = 1$$
$$8x + 6x = 48$$
$$14x = 48$$
$$x = 3\frac{3}{7} \text{ hours}$$

**Example:** Mr. Jones can do a job in 10 days. After working 3 days he hires a helper and the two complete the task in 5 days. How long would it have taken the helper to complete the task alone?

Let $x$ = number of days required by helper working alone to complete the task.

Mr. Jones completed $\frac{3}{10}$ of the task before he was joined by the helper. During the 5 day period when he was assisted by a helper he completed $\frac{5}{10}$ or $\frac{1}{2}$ of the task. If we assume that the helper could do the task in $x$ days, then in 5 days he completed $\frac{5}{x}$ part of the entire task.

$$\frac{3}{10} + \frac{1}{2} + \frac{5}{x} = 1$$
$$3x + 5x + 50 = 10x$$
$$-2x = -50$$
$$x = 25 \text{ days}$$

**Practice Exercises    Answers given on pages 268–274.**

Directions: In this section solve each problem, using any available space on the page for scratchwork. Then decide which is the best of the choices given and blacken the corresponding space on the answer sheet.

The following information is for your reference in solving some of the problems.

Circle of radius $r$:
Area $= \pi r^2$;
Circumference $= 2\pi r$
The number of degrees of arc in a circle is 360.

Triangle: The sum of the measures in degrees of the angles of a triangle is 180.

The measure in degrees of a straight angle is 180.

If $\angle CDA$ is a right angle, then

(1) area of $\triangle ABC = \dfrac{AB \times CD}{2}$

(2) $AC^2 = AD^2 + DC^2$

**Definitions of symbols:**

| | |
|---|---|
| = is equal to | ≤ is less than or equal to |
| ≠ is unequal to | ≥ is greater than or equal to |
| < is less than | ‖ is parallel to |
| > is greater than | ⊥ is perpendicular to |

Note: Figures that accompany problems in this test are intended to provide information useful in solving the problems. They are drawn as accurately as possible EXCEPT when it is stated in a specific problem that its figure is not drawn to scale. All figures lie in a plane unless otherwise indicated. All numbers used are real numbers.

## Exercise A

1. What is the value of $\dfrac{x}{x-a} + \dfrac{a}{a-x}$ when $x$ is 50 and $a$ is 10?

   (A) 0    (B) 1    (C) 10    (D) 5    (E) 50

2. If $x$ is doubled and $y$ is tripled in the expression $z = \dfrac{3x}{y}$, then the value of $z$ is

   (A) doubled
   (B) tripled
   (C) halved
   (D) multiplied by 6
   (E) multiplied by a factor of $\dfrac{2}{3}$

3. If $x^2 + y^2 = 2$ and $x^2 - y^2 = 2$, then $x^4 - y^4 =$

   (A) 0    (B) 2    (C) 4    (D) 5    (E) 8

---

**4.** $\dfrac{8(11-2)-5(11-2)}{3} =$

(A) 1    (B) 11    (C) 9    (D) 3    (E) 5

---

**5.** If $27 \cdot 27 = 3 \cdot 3 \cdot x$, then $x =$

(A) 9    (B) 27    (C) 81    (D) 243    (E) 36

---

**6.** A certain type of bacteria triples in number every 20 minutes. At the end of 5 hours there are $x$ bacteria in the colony. In how many hours more will there be $27x$?

(A) 1    (B) $1\frac{1}{3}$    (C) $1\frac{2}{3}$    (D) 2    (E) $\frac{2}{3}$

---

**7.** If $\dfrac{x}{\sqrt{2}} = \sqrt{2}$, then $x =$

(A) 2    (B) $\sqrt{2}$    (C) $\frac{1}{2}$    (D) $\frac{1}{\sqrt{2}}$    (E) $\frac{\sqrt{2}}{2}$

---

**8.** If $\dfrac{1}{y} = \dfrac{1}{x-2}$, all of the following are true EXCEPT

(A) $y - x = 2$
(B) $y + 2 = x$
(C) $y - x = -2$
(D) $x - y = 2$
(E) $x - y - 2 = 0$

---

**9.** If $x = -1$, $ax^5 + bx^3 - 4 = 0$. What is the value of this equation when $x = 1$?

(A) 0    (B) 1    (C) 6    (D) $-8$    (E) $-4$

---

**10.** What is the area, in square inches, of a square if its diagonal is 6 inches?

(A) 9     (B) 6     (C) 36     (D) 12     (E) 18

**11.** Suppose $a * b = c$ is true only if $b^c = a$. When $64 * 4 = y$, then $y =$

(A) $\frac{1}{2}$     (B) 2     (C) 3     (D) 4     (E) $\frac{1}{4}$

**12.** The statement $3x - 1 \neq 2x$ is true for all values of $x$ EXCEPT

(A) $x \neq 1$
(B) $x = -1$
(C) $x = 1$
(D) $x > 1$
(E) $x < 1$

**13.** A bag contains 28 pounds of sugar which is to be separated into packages containing 14 ounces each. How many such packages can be made?

(A) 2     (B) 4     (C) 8     (D) 16     (E) 32

**14.** What is the value of $1^{3a} + 1^{2a}$?

(A) 0
(B) 1
(C) 2
(D) 5
(E) It cannot be determined from the informaton given

**15.** The approximate value of $\sqrt{15}$ is 3.87. Which of the following is the best approximation to $\sqrt{\dfrac{5}{3}}$?

(A) 0.2    (B) 0.4    (C) 1.29    (D) 6.10    (E) 3.66

---

**16.** Which of the following has the greatest value?

(A) $\dfrac{1 - \dfrac{1}{3}}{3}$    (B) $\dfrac{-3}{-\dfrac{1}{3}}$    (C) $\dfrac{-3}{\dfrac{1}{3}}$    (D) 0    (E) $\dfrac{3 - \dfrac{1}{3}}{3}$

---

**17.** When $x$ is 1, 2, 3, or 4, the expression $x^2 + x + 17$ has the values 19, 23, 29, and 37, respectively. All of these results are prime numbers. What is the least positive integer that will not yield a prime in the formula?

(A) 5    (B) 7    (C) 11    (D) 13    (E) 16

---

**18.** The area of $\triangle ABC =$

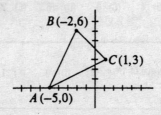

(A) $13\dfrac{1}{2}$    (B) 12    (C) 11    (D) 9    (E) $9\dfrac{1}{2}$

19. If $y = \dfrac{3x - 6}{x}$, for what values of $x$ will $y$ be positive?

    (A) $x > 2$ or $x < 0$
    (B) only when $x$ is positive
    (C) only when $x$ is negative
    (D) $-2 < x < 2$
    (E) $-2 < x < 2$ but not 0

20. In $ABCD$, $AD$ and $BC$ are parallel. The length of $BC =$

    (A) $x$
    (B) $x + y$
    (C) $x + 2y$
    (D) $2x + y$
    (E) $2x + 2y$

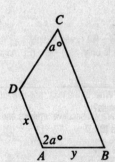

21. Suppose $a * b = c$ is true if and only if $c$ is the remainder after $a$ is divided by $b$. The value of $\dfrac{5 * 3}{10 * 6} =$

    (A) 2    (B) $\dfrac{1}{2}$    (C) 4    (D) 3    (E) 1

22. If $(0.4)(y) = 5$, then $(4.44)(y) =$

    (A) 5.055    (B) 0.555    (C) 555    (D) 55.5    (E) 5.55

23. If $\dfrac{1}{2 - \dfrac{x}{1-x}} = \dfrac{1}{2}$, what is the value of $x$?

    (A) 12    (B) $-2$    (C) 0    (D) 1    (E) $-1$

24. If $p > 1$, which of the following expressions decrease(s) as $p$ increases?

    I. $p + \dfrac{1}{p}$

    II. $p^2 - 10p$

    III. $\dfrac{1}{p+1}$

    (A) III only    (B) I and III only
    (C) II and III only    (D) all    (E) none

25. If $y$ and $z$ are consecutive integers and $z^2 = x^2 + y^2$, which of the following is true?

    (A) $z = x + y$
    (B) $x^2 = 1 + 2y$
    (C) $y^2 = 2x + 1$
    (D) $z = 1 + 2x$
    (E) $x = y + 2z$

## Exercise B

1. If the circumference of a circle increases from $\pi$ inches to $2\pi$ inches, what change occurs in the area?

    (A) It remains the same.
    (B) It doubles.
    (C) It triples.
    (D) It quadruples.
    (E) It is halved.

2. $31(m - n) - 32(m - n) + (m - n) =$

   (A) $-n$   (B) $-m$   (C) 0   (D) 1   (E) $m$

3. If $3x = 2y$ and $6y = 7z$, what is the ratio of $x$ to $z$?

   (A) 2:3   (B) 7:9   (C) 3:2   (D) 5:7   (E) 5:3

4. If $x$ must be greater than 4, which of the following must have the least value?

   (A) $\dfrac{4}{x + 1}$   (B) $\dfrac{4}{x - 1}$   (C) $\dfrac{4}{x}$   (D) $\dfrac{x}{4}$   (E) $\dfrac{x + 1}{1}$

5. $\dfrac{\dfrac{1}{5} + \dfrac{1}{10}}{\dfrac{1}{15} + \dfrac{1}{5}} =$

   (A) $\dfrac{7}{15}$   (B) $\dfrac{2}{3}$   (C) $\dfrac{9}{8}$   (D) 15   (E) 5

6. Six consecutive integers are given. The sum of the first three is 27. What is the sum of the last three?

   (A) 29   (B) 30   (C) 32   (D) 33   (E) 36

7. What are all values of $x$ for which $-x = \sqrt[3]{x}$?

   (A) 1
   (B) 0 and $-1$
   (C) 0 only
   (D) $-8$
   (E) No values are possible.

8. If the points given in A through E are the endpoints of segments that have their other ends at the origin, which segment has a midpoint that is farthest from the origin?

   (A) (3, 3)   (B) (2, 5)   (C) (1, 6)   (D) (0, 7)   (E) (4, 3)

9. An arithmetic progression is a sequence of numbers for which each new number is found by adding a given number $p$ to the previous number. In the arithmetic progression below, only two numbers are known.

   $$—, —, \frac{5}{—}, —, —, \frac{17}{—}, —$$

   What number comes after 17?

   (A) 19   (B) 20   (C) 21   (D) 18   (E) 23

10. Suppose $x > y$ and $xy < 0$. Which of the following must be negative?

    (A) $y$
    (B) $x$
    (C) $x - y$
    (D) $x^2 - y^2$
    (E) $(y - x)^2$

11. What will the result be if $\dfrac{x + 10}{2}$ is subtracted from $\dfrac{x}{2} + 10$?

    (A) 5
    (B) $x$
    (C) $\dfrac{x}{2}$
    (D) 0
    (E) $x + 10$

12. A mathematical law states that the sum of the first $n$ odd counting numbers is $n^2$. Which of the following is an example of this law?

   (A) $1 + 3 = 4$
   (B) $1 + 9 + 16 = 26$
   (C) $1 + 2 = 3$
   (D) $1 + 3 + 5 = 1 + 2(4)^2$
   (E) $1 + 4 = 5$

---

13. What is the area of triangle $ABC$ if, for each point $(x, y)$ of line $AB$, $y = 2x - 8$?

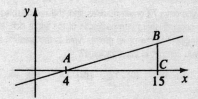

   (A) 100   (B) 121   (C) 144   (D) 169   (E) 132

---

14. $\dfrac{y^2 + 4y - 5}{y^2 - 1} =$

   (A) $\dfrac{y + 5}{y + 1}$   (B) $y + 4$   (C) $\dfrac{y + 1}{y + 5}$   (D) $\dfrac{5y}{4}$   (E) $5y$

---

15. $\dfrac{4^3 + 4^4}{4^3} =$

   (A) 1   (B) 2   (C) 4   (D) 5   (E) 8

16. Which of the following is the simplest form of $\dfrac{x - \frac{1}{y}}{y - \frac{1}{x}}$?

(A) $\dfrac{x}{y}$    (B) $\dfrac{y}{x}$    (C) $\dfrac{x - 1}{y - 1}$    (D) $\dfrac{y - 1}{x - 1}$    (E) $\dfrac{xy - 1}{xy}$

17. If $a = b + 3$, what is the value of $(a - b)^3$?

(A) 1    (B) 8    (C) 27    (D) 64    (E) 0

18. Suppose you have 72 green marbles and 108 red marbles to sell. You decide to separate them into packages of the same size, each containing either all red or all green. What is the greatest number of marbles you can put in each package?

(A) 3    (B) 18    (C) 12    (D) 24    (E) 36

19. If the length of a rectangle is increased by 20 percent and the width is decreased by 20 percent, what percent change occurs in the area?

(A) It remains the same.
(B) It increases 5%.
(C) It decreases 4%.
(D) It increases 2%.
(E) It decreases 2%.

20. What percent of $\dfrac{1}{2}$ is $\dfrac{3}{4}$?

(A) 100%    (B) 120%    (C) 125%    (D) 140%
(E) 150%

21. Which of the following is the square (second power) of $\sqrt{1 + \sqrt{1}}$?

   (A) 1
   (B) 2
   (C) 4
   (D) 3
   (E) $1 + \sqrt{2}$

22. If $x = 1 + 3^a$ and $y = 1 + 3^{-a}$ which of the following is a formula for $y$ in terms of $x$?

   (A) $x$
   (B) $x - 1$
   (C) $\dfrac{1}{x - 1}$
   (D) $\dfrac{x}{x - 1}$
   (E) $x + 1$

23. If $\dfrac{p \times p \times p}{p + p + p} = 3$, $p =$

   (A) $\dfrac{1}{3}$   (B) $\dfrac{1}{9}$   (C) 27   (D) $\pm 3$   (E) 9

24. $S(x)$ is defined as follows:
   $$S(x) = 1 \text{ when } x > 1,$$
   $$S(x) = x \text{ when } -1 \leq x \leq 1, \text{ and}$$
   $$S(x) = -1 \text{ when } x < -1.$$
   What is the value of $S(5) + S(4) + S(0)$?

   (A) 1   (B) 0   (C) 3   (D) 2   (E) −1

---

**25.** $5 - [7 - (9 - 11)] =$

    (A) $-4$    (B) 3    (C) $-2$    (D) 7    (E) 5

---

## Answer Key

### Exercise A

| | | | | |
|---|---|---|---|---|
| 1. **B** | 6. **A** | 11. **C** | 16. **B** | 21. **B** |
| 2. **E** | 7. **A** | 12. **C** | 17. **E** | 22. **D** |
| 3. **C** | 8. **A** | 13. **E** | 18. **A** | 23. **C** |
| 4. **C** | 9. **D** | 14. **C** | 19. **A** | 24. **A** |
| 5. **C** | 10. **E** | 15. **C** | 20. **B** | 25. **B** |

### Exercise B

| | | | | |
|---|---|---|---|---|
| 1. **D** | 6. **E** | 11. **A** | 16. **A** | 21. **B** |
| 2. **C** | 7. **B** | 12. **A** | 17. **C** | 22. **D** |
| 3. **B** | 8. **D** | 13. **B** | 18. **E** | 23. **D** |
| 4. **A** | 9. **B** | 14. **A** | 19. **C** | 24. **D** |
| 5. **C** | 10. **A** | 15. **D** | 20. **E** | 25. **A** |

## Answer Explanations

### Exercise A

1. **(B)** Instead of time-consuming substitution of values, note that $a - x = -(x - a)$. Therefore, the fractions can be combined to get $\dfrac{x - a}{x - a} = 1$ regardless of the values of $x$ and $a$ (as long as $x$ does not equal $a$, of course).

2. **(E)** The trap is to cancel the 3 in the numerator with the 3 that appears in the denominator when the denominator is tripled. If this is done, the result is $\dfrac{2x}{y}$. If cancellation is not performed, the result can be written as $\dfrac{2}{3}\left(\dfrac{3x}{y}\right)$ or $\dfrac{2}{3}z$. The obvious solution is the correct one.

3. **(C)** Factor the difference between two perfect squares:
$$x^4 - y^4 = (x^2 + y^2)(x^2 - y^2) = (2)(2)$$

4. **(C)** The calculation is not really lengthy, but note:
$$\frac{8(11 - 2) - 5(11 - 2)}{3} = \frac{3(11 - 2)}{3}$$
$$= 11 - 2 = 9$$

5. **(C)** $27 \cdot 27 = (3 \cdot 3)(9 \cdot 9)$. Thus $x = 9 \cdot 9 = 81$.

6. **(A)** Since the question asks "how many hours more?" you can ignore the first 5 hours. In 20 minutes $x$ will triple to $3x$; in 20 more minutes $3x$ will triple to $3(3x)$; and at end of 1 hour there will be $(3)(3)(3x)$ or $27x$ bacteria.

7. **(A)** Cross-multiply: $\sqrt{2} \cdot \sqrt{2} = 2$, $x = 2$.

8. **(A)** Since the numerators are equal, the denominators are equal. Therefore, $y = x - 2$. Choice (B) is true because, by adding 2 to each side of the equation, you get $y + 2 = x$. Choice (C) is true because, by subtracting $x$ from both sides of the equation, you get $y - x = -2$. Choice (D) is true because, by subtracting $y$ and adding 2, you get $x - y = 2$. Choice (E) is true because, by subtracting $y$, you get $x - y - 2 = 0$. Choice (A) is not true because it contradicts (C); therefore, (A) is the right answer.

9. **(D)** If $x$ is replaced by $-1$, $ax^5 + bx^3 - 4$ becomes $-a - b - 4$. Since you are told that $-a - b - 4 = 0$, $-4 = a + b$. If $x$ is now replaced by 1, $ax^5 + bx^3 - 4$ becomes $a + b - 4$; hence $a + b - 4$ is $-4 - 4$ or $-8$.

10. **(E)** The square has diagonals that bisect each other, are perpendicular, and separate the square into four triangles of the same area. Thus you have four right triangles with legs of length 3 and areas of $\frac{9}{2}$; and $4\left(\frac{9}{2}\right) = 18$.

11. **(C)** By direct substitution into the formula given you get $4^y = 64$. Since $64 = 4^3$, $y = 3$.

12. **(C)** Any value that makes $3x - 1 \neq 2x$ true makes $3x - 1 = 2x$ false. The latter is true for $x = 1$.

13. **(E)** Changing pounds to ounces gives $28 \times 16$, but do not multiply it out. Cancel: $\dfrac{\overset{2}{28}(16)}{\underset{}{(14)}} = 32$.

14. **(C)** No matter what $a$ is, $1^{3n} = 1$ and $1^{2n} = 1$.

**15. (C)** You must change $\sqrt{\dfrac{5}{3}}$ to a form that will use the given approximation of $\sqrt{15}$:

$$\sqrt{\frac{5}{3}} = \sqrt{\frac{5 \times 3}{3 \times 3}} = \frac{\sqrt{15}}{\sqrt{9}} = \frac{\sqrt{15}}{3} = \frac{3.87}{3} = 1.29$$

**16. (B)** (A), (B), and (E) are positive, so (C) and (D) can be eliminated since they are not positive. (E) is greater than (A) since $3 - \dfrac{1}{3}$ is greater than $1 - \dfrac{1}{3}$. (B) is 9. (E) is $\dfrac{2\frac{2}{3}}{3}$, which is $\dfrac{1}{3}$ of $2\dfrac{2}{3}$ and hence less than 1. A routine and lengthy approach is to simplify each of them.

**17. (E)** Rewrite $x^2 + x + 17$ as $x(x + 1) + 17$. In order for the entire expression to have a factor, 17 must divide into either $x$ or $x + 1$. Thus either $x$ or $x + 1$ must equal 17. If $x = 16$ (E), $x + 1 = 17$. For any value of $x$ less than 16, neither $x$ nor $x + 1$ will be divisible by 17 and the number will be prime.

**18. (A)** Draw perpendiculars to the $x$-axis from $B$ and $C$ and then add and subtract the necessary pieces.

(1) Area of triangle $ABB' = \dfrac{1}{2}(3)(6) = 9$.

(2) Area of trapezoid $BB'C'C = \dfrac{1}{2}(6 + 3)3 = 13\dfrac{1}{2}$.

(3) Area of triangle $ACC' = \dfrac{1}{2}(6)(3) = 9$.

Add (1) and (2), then subtract (3).

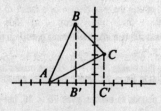

**19. (A)** $\dfrac{3x - 6}{x} = 3 - \dfrac{6}{x}$, which will be positive as long as $3 > \dfrac{6}{x}$. The value of $\dfrac{6}{x}$ will be less than 3 when (1) $x$ is negative, or (2) $x > 2$.

**20. (B)** Draw $AP$ bisecting $\angle DAB$. $PC = x$ since $PADC$ is a parallelogram. $\angle APB$ has measure $a°$ since $\angle APB$ and $\angle C$ are corresponding angles. $PB = y$ since $\angle PAB$ and $\angle BPA$ have the same measure.

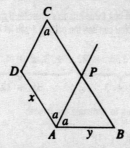

**21. (B)** By direct division $5 * 3 = 2$ and $10 * 6 = 4$. The fraction $\frac{2}{4} = \frac{1}{2}$.

**22. (D)**
$$0.4y = 5$$
$$0.04y = 0.5 \text{ (multiply by 0.1)}$$
$$+ \quad 4\,y = 50 \text{ (multiply original equation by 10)}$$
$$\overline{4.44y = 55.5}$$

**23. (C)** Do no lengthy computation; recognize that the fractions can be equal when $\frac{x}{1-x} = 0$, which means $x$ must equal zero.

**24. (A)** Only III. As the denominator $(p + 1)$ increases, the value of the fraction decreases.

**25. (B)** $z = y + 1$, so $z^2 = y^2 + 2y + 1 = x^2 + y^2$. Thus $2y + 1 = x^2$.

## Exercise B

**1. (D)** Since the circumference is doubled, the radius is doubled. The area is based on the square of the radius. Squaring the factor of 2 thus introduced makes the area change by a factor of 4.

**2. (C)** $31(m - n) + (m - n) = 32(m - n)$. Thus the value of the expression is $32(m - n) - 32(m - n) = 0$.

**3. (B)** Multiply both sides of $3x = 2y$ by 3 to get $9x = 6y$. Since $6y = 7z$, by substitution $9x = 7z$. Divide the latter equation by $9z$ to yield $\frac{x}{z} = \frac{7}{9}$.

**4. (A)** Choices (D) and (E) can be excluded because greater values of $x$ will increase the numerator and thereby the fraction. Choices (A), (B), and (C) all have the same numerator, so the fraction with the least value will be the one with the greatest denominator.

**5. (C)** Avoid lengthy computation. Multiply the original fraction by $\dfrac{30}{30}$ to get

$$\frac{6+3}{2+6} \text{ or } \frac{9}{8}.$$

**6. (E)** The sum of the last three integers must be 9 more than the sum of the first three. You can see the pattern if you let $x$ be the first of these integers:

$$\underbrace{x,\ x+1,\ x+2,}_{3x+3}\ \underbrace{x+3,\ x+4,\ x+5}_{3x+12}$$

**7. (B)** Cube both sides to eliminate the radical:
$-x^3 = x$.
$-(0)^3 = 0$ and $-(-1)^3 = -1$

**8. (D)** If the midpoint is farthest from the origin, then the endpoint will also be farthest from the origin. To save time, avoid computation; make a sketch and locate each given endpoint. Observe that $D$ is farthest from the origin.

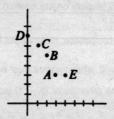

**9. (B)** Ignore the first two terms, and get the result strictly from the definition given. The terms, starting with 5, are as follows:
$$\_,\ \_,\ 5,\ 5+p,\ 5+2p,\ 5+3p,\ 5+4p$$
$5 + 4p = 17$, so $p$ is 3 and the next term is 20.

**10. (A)** Since $xy$ is negative, either $x$ or $y$ is negative, but not both. Since $x > y$, then $y$ must be negative.

**11. (A)** $\dfrac{x+10}{2} = \dfrac{x}{2} + 5$, which will leave 5 when subtracted from $\dfrac{x}{2} + 10$.

**12. (A)** Only two choices, (A) and (D), involve sums of consecutive odd counting numbers. In (D), the sum is incorrect and it is not a square.

**13. (B)** The length of the base can be computed: $15 - 4 = 11$. To find the height, note that the $y$-coordinate of B gives the height. Since $y = 2x - 8$ for each point of the line and $x = 15$ at B, $y = 22$.
$$\text{Area} = \frac{1}{2}(11)(22) = 121$$

**14. (A)** Factor and cancel:

$$\frac{y^2 + 4y - 5}{y^2 - 1} = \frac{(y + 5)(y - 1)}{(y + 1)(y - 1)}$$

**15. (D)** Divide:

$$4^3 \div 4^3 = 1 \text{ and}$$
$$4^4 \div 4^3 = 4 \text{ or}$$
$$\frac{4^3 + 4^4}{4^3} = 1 + 4 = 5$$

**16. (A)** Multiply by $\dfrac{xy}{xy}$ to get

$$\frac{x^2y - x}{xy^2 - y} = \frac{x(xy - 1)}{y(xy - 1)} = \frac{x}{y}$$

**17. (C)** If $a = b + 3$, then
$$a - b = 3 \text{ and } (a - b)^3 = 3^3 = 27$$

**18. (E)** $72 = 2 \times 2 \times 2 \times 3 \times 3$
$108 = 2 \times 2 \times 3 \times 3 \times 3$
By inspecting factors, you can see that the greatest number which will divide both is $2 \times 2 \times 3 \times 3$.

**19. (C)** $(1.20L)(.0.80W) = 0.96LW$ is the new area, or a decrease of $0.04LW$ or 4%.

**20. (E)** The fraction $\dfrac{3}{4}$ is $\dfrac{1}{2}$ plus half of $\dfrac{1}{2}$ or 100% plus 50%.

**21. (B)** $\sqrt{1} = 1$; therefore $\sqrt{1 + \sqrt{1}} = \sqrt{1 + 1} = \sqrt{2}$, which when squared gives 2.

**22. (D)** From the given information we can conclude that
$$x - 1 = 3^a$$
$$y = 1 + 3^{-a}$$
$$y = 1 + \frac{1}{3^a} = 1 + \frac{1}{x - 1}$$
$$y = \frac{x - 1}{x - 1} + \frac{1}{x - 1} = \frac{x}{x - 1}$$

**23. (D)** $\dfrac{p^3}{3p} = 3$
$\dfrac{p^2}{3} = 3$
$p^2 = 9$
$p = \pm 3$

**24. (D)** From the three-part formula we may conclude that
$$S(5) = 1, \ S(4) = 1, \ S(0) = 0$$
Therefore, $1 + 1 + 0 = 2$.

**25. (A)** Remove the innermost parentheses first:
$$5 - [7 - (9 - 11)] =$$
$$5 - [7 - (-2)] =$$
$$5 - [7 + 2] =$$
$$5 - 9 = -4$$

---

# THE QUANTITATIVE COMPARISON QUESTION

In this type of question you are given two quantities, with information regarding either or both, and are asked to decide which, if either, is the greater quantity. Actually, these questions apply various principles of mathematics already covered in this chapter and involve less reading and less computation than the other types of multiple-choice questions. The directions state that diagrams are not necessarily drawn to scale, and that facts pertaining to one or both quantities are centered above both columns. After comparing the two quantities, one in one column and the other in another column, you choose

A  if the quantity in Column A is greater,
B  if the quantity in Column B is greater,
C  if the two quantities are equal,
D  if the relationship cannot be determined from the information given.

Observe that in these questions there are four choices as compared with five for the other types of questions.

---

**Tips for Solving Quantitative Comparison Questions**

1. Quantitative comparison questions require less time than standard multiple-choice questions. Be prepared to answer some questions in a few seconds.
2. Eliminate from consideration any quantity that appears in both columns.
3. Do not choose (E) for these questions. There are only four possible answers.

4. Remember that straightforward computation problems have only three choices. Since there <u>must</u> be a solution for a problem involving straightforward computation do not choose (D).

5. Be on the alert when working with negative numbers. Be careful to note that if $x^2 = 25$, then $x = +5$ or $-5$.

6. Multiplication could be tricky. Bear in mind that multiplication usually makes a number larger, but when you multiply it by a fraction you make the number *smaller*. And don't forget the reverse: when you divide a number by a fraction, you make it *larger*.

7. Don't rush to get to the more challenging questions. Questions get harder as you go along.

### Examples to Get You Started

Directions: Each of the following questions consists of two quantities, one in Column A and one in Column B. You are to compare the two quantities and on the answer sheet blacken space

A if the quantity in Column A is greater;
B if the quantity in Column B is greater;
C if the two quantities are equal;
D if the relationship cannot be determined from the information given.

**AN E RESPONSE WILL NOT BE SCORED.**

Notes: 1. In certain questions, information concerning one or both of the quantities to be compared is centered above the two columns.

2. In a given question, a symbol that appears in both columns represents the same thing in Column A as it does in Column B.

3. Letters such as *x, n,* and *k* stand for real numbers.

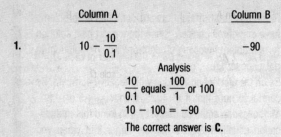

| Column A | Column B |
|---|---|
| | |

**1.** $10 - \dfrac{10}{0.1}$      $-90$

Analysis

$\dfrac{10}{0.1}$ equals $\dfrac{100}{1}$ or 100

$10 - 100 = -90$

The correct answer is **C.**

---

**2.**      50%      $\dfrac{1}{0.02}$

Analysis

The value of $\dfrac{1}{0.02} = 50$

50 is greater than 50%

The correct answer is **B.**

---

Both J.J. High School and K.K. High School have two chemistry classes. In J.J. High School, one chemistry class had an average of 70% on a citywide test; the other had an average of 75% on this test. In K.K. High School, the average mark in the two chemistry classes was 72.5% for this test.

**3.** School average for the citywide test at J.J. High School.      School average for the citywide test at K.K. High School.

Analysis

Since we do not have the number of students involved in these various classes we may not assign equal weight to the averages given.

The correct answer is **D.**

---

| Column A | Column B |
|----------|----------|

In rectangle *ABCD*, *AB* = $\pi$ and *BC* = the diameter of circle *O* = 4.

**4.** Area of *ABCD*                    Area of circle *O*

Analysis

Area of rectangle = length × width

Area of rectangle *ABCD* = $4\pi$

Radius of circle = 2

Area of circle *O* = $\pi r^2 = 4\pi$

The correct answer is **C**.

---

**Practice Exercises    Answers given on pages 286–292.**

---

<u>Directions:</u> Each of the following questions consists of two quantities, one in Column A and one in Column B. You are to compare the two quantities and on the answer sheet blacken space

A if the quantity in Column A is greater;

B if the quantity in Column B is greater;

C if the two quantities are equal;

D if the relationship cannot be determined from the information given.

**AN E RESPONSE WILL NOT BE SCORED.**

<u>Notes:</u>  1.  In certain questions, information concerning one or both of the quantities to be compared is centered above the two columns.

2.  In a given question, a symbol that appears in both columns represents the same thing in Column A as it does in Column B.

3.  Letters such as *x*, *n*, and *k* stand for real numbers.

**Exercise A**

| | Column A | Column B |
|---|---|---|

$x = 2, y = 3$

**1.** $\dfrac{xy}{\dfrac{1}{x} + \dfrac{1}{y}}$   7

---

$a > 0$

**2.** $\dfrac{5a - 3}{6a} + \dfrac{3a + 7}{10a}$   $\dfrac{17a + 3}{15a}$

---

$x + 13 = 4y$
$3x + 4y = 25$

**3.** $x$   $y$

---

$x^2 + 25 = 10x$
$y^2 + 36 = 12y$

**4.** $x$   $y$

---

$x = 2, y = 3, z = 4$

**5.** $\dfrac{x^2 + y^2}{z^2}$   $\dfrac{x + y}{z}$

---

$a - 2b = 11$
$5a + 4b = 27$

**6.** $5a$   $35$

---

|  | Column A | Column B |
|---|---|---|

$$(x - y)^2 = 16$$
$$x^2 + y^2 = 58$$

**7.**         $xy$                                $(x - y)^2$

---

$$x \sqrt{0.01} = 1$$

**8.**         $x$                                 10

---

**9.**    $\dfrac{x}{y} + \dfrac{a}{b}$               $\dfrac{xb + ya}{by}$

---

**10.**    $(a + b)(a - b)$               $a^2 - b^2$

---

$$x^2 = 4$$
$$y^2 = 9$$

**11.**        $x$                                 $y$

---

**12.**       0.3%                             $\dfrac{3}{1000}$

---

**13.**    0.04% of 600                      4% of 600

---

**14.**       102                           102% of 100

---

| Column A | Column B |
|---|---|
| | |

**15.** List price of $500 with discounts of 10% and 20%     List price of $490 less 20%

---

The average weight of Lori,
Michael, and Sara is 45 pounds.

**16.** The combined weight of Lori and Michael      The combined weight of Lori and Sara

---

**17.** Percent increase from 800 to 1400      Percent increase from 1400 to 2000

---

**18.** The distance covered in 3 hours at an average rate of 40 miles per hour      The distance covered traveling at 50 miles per hour for one hour and 30 miles per hour for the next 2 hours

---

**19.** The average rate of a motorcyclist who covers a mile in one minute and 20 seconds      The average rate of a motorist traveling for one hour and covering 45 miles

---

**20.** The work done by $m$ men in $h$ hours      The work done by $n$ men in $h$ hours

---

|   | Column A | Column B |
|---|----------|----------|

**21.** The record of a team that won $W$ games and lost $L$ games

The record of a team that won $W$ games of the $W + L$ games played

---

Perimeter of square $ABCD = 8a$

**22.**      Side of $ABCD$                     $2a$

---

$$x^n = 1$$
$$n > 0$$

**23.**           $x$                            1

---

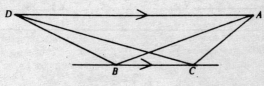

**24.**      Area of $\triangle ABC$          Area of $\triangle DBC$

---

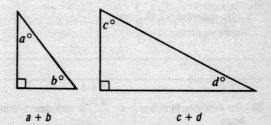

**25.**          $a + b$                          $c + d$

**Exercise B**

|  | Column A | Column B |
|---|---|---|
| **1.** | $3^2$ | $2^3$ |
| **2.** | $\dfrac{6 + \dfrac{3}{4}}{2 - \dfrac{5}{4}}$ | $(3)^2$ |
| **3.** | $\dfrac{1}{3}$ of 8 | $66\dfrac{2}{3}\%$ of 4 |
| **4.** | $\sqrt{\dfrac{1}{4}} + \sqrt{\dfrac{1}{25}}$ | $\sqrt{\dfrac{1}{4} + \dfrac{1}{25}}$ |

$$x = 3$$
$$y = \dfrac{1}{6}$$

|  | Column A | Column B |
|---|---|---|
| **5.** | $2x - 18y$ | $3x - 36y$ |
| **6.** | The average of $\sqrt{0.49}$, $\dfrac{3}{4}$, and 0.8 | 75% |

$$B = 0$$
$$A > 1$$
$$C > 1$$

|  | Column A | Column B |
|---|---|---|
| **7.** | $2B(A + C)$ | $A(B + C)$ |

|     | Column A | Column B |
|-----|----------|----------|

**8.**  $\dfrac{n + a}{a}$          $\dfrac{n}{a} + 1$

---

**9.**  $\sqrt{\dfrac{1}{0.25}}$          4

---

$$x < 0$$
$$y < 0$$

**10.**  $x + y$          $x - y$

---

In triangle *ABC*, the measure of $\angle ACB = 60$

**11.**  $\angle B$          $\angle A$

---

**12.** Michael has 5 green marbles and the same number of red marbles. The number of red marbles in his collection is $\dfrac{1}{2}$ the number of white marbles and $\dfrac{1}{3}$ the number of blue ones.

Philip has 35 marbles in his collection.

---

**13.** The number of posts needed by Mr. *A* to hold a wire fence 120 feet long if he places posts 12 feet apart in a straight line.

Mr. *B* uses 10 posts to support a similar wire fence.

---

|                    Column A                    |                    Column B                    |
| :--------------------------------------------: | :--------------------------------------------: |

$$0 < x < 10$$
$$0 < y < 12$$

14.                        $x$                                                    $y$

---

15. Mark received either an 80% or a 90% on each of four physics tests.

Sara's average for these four physics tests was 85%.

---

16. Ann earns $10 a day for clerical work in the dean's office.

Joan earns $50 a week for work in the dean's office during vacation periods.

---

17. Last week Martin received $10 in commission for selling 100 copies of a magazine.

Last week Miguel sold 100 copies of this magazine. He received his basic salary of $5 per week plus a commission of 2¢ for each of the first 25 copies sold, 3¢ for each of the next 25 copies sold, and 4¢ for each copy thereafter.

---

|       Column A       |       Column B       |
| :------------------: | :------------------: |

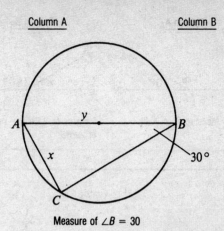

Measure of $\angle B = 30$

**18.**    $2x$    $y$

---

**19.**    $\sqrt{\dfrac{1}{9}+\dfrac{1}{16}}$    $\sqrt{\dfrac{1}{16}}+\sqrt{\dfrac{1}{9}}$

---

$$3 - 2x < 9$$

**20.**    $x$    $-3$

---

$$a < 0$$
$$b < 0$$

**21.**    $a - b$    $a + b$

---

$$x > 0, y > 0, \frac{x}{y} > 2$$

**22.**    $2y$    $x$

Column A        Column B

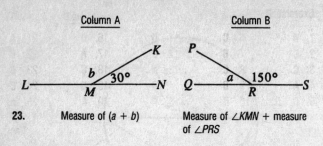

23.    Measure of $(a + b)$     Measure of $\angle KMN$ + measure of $\angle PRS$

---

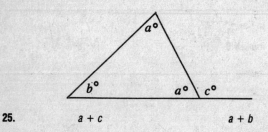

$$\frac{1}{x} = \sqrt{0.09}$$

24.        $x$                  $3\frac{1}{3}$

---

25.      $a + c$              $a + b$

---

### Answer Key

**Exercise A**

| | | | | |
|---|---|---|---|---|
| 1. **A** | 6. **C** | 11. **D** | 16. **D** | 21. **C** |
| 2. **C** | 7. **A** | 12. **C** | 17. **A** | 22. **C** |
| 3. **B** | 8. **C** | 13. **B** | 18. **A** | 23. **D** |
| 4. **B** | 9. **C** | 14. **C** | 19. **C** | 24. **C** |
| 5. **B** | 10. **C** | 15. **B** | 20. **D** | 25. **C** |

**Exercise B**

| | | | | |
|---|---|---|---|---|
| 1. **A** | 6. **C** | 11. **D** | 16. **D** | 21. **A** |
| 2. **C** | 7. **B** | 12. **C** | 17. **A** | 22. **B** |
| 3. **C** | 8. **C** | 13. **A** | 18. **C** | 23. **C** |
| 4. **A** | 9. **B** | 14. **D** | 19. **B** | 24. **C** |
| 5. **C** | 10. **B** | 15. **D** | 20. **A** | 25. **A** |

## Answer Explanations

**Exercise A**

1. **(A)** Substitute given values.

$$\frac{(2)(3)}{\frac{1}{2} + \frac{1}{3}} = \frac{6}{\frac{5}{6}} = (6)(\frac{6}{5}) = \frac{36}{5} = 7\frac{1}{5}$$

$$7\frac{1}{5} > 7$$

2. **(C)** In Column A

multiply by $\frac{5}{5}$: $\frac{25a - 15}{30a}$

multiply by $\frac{3}{3}$: $\frac{9a + 21}{30a}$

$$\frac{25a + 15}{30a} + \frac{9a + 21}{30a} = \frac{34a + 6}{30a}$$

In Column B

multiply by $\frac{2}{2}$: $\frac{17a + 3}{15a} = \frac{34a + 6}{30a}$

3. **(B)**
$$x + 13 = 4y$$
$$x - 4y = -13$$
$$3x + 4y = 25$$

By addition: $\quad 4x = 12$
$$x = 3$$

By subtraction: $\quad 3 + 13 = 4y$
$$16 = 4y$$
$$4 = y$$
$$y > x$$

4. **(B)** $\quad x^2 + 25 = 10x$
$$x^2 - 10x + 25 = 0$$
$$(x - 5)(x - 5) = 0$$
$$x = 5$$

$$y^2 + 36 = 12y$$
$$y^2 - 12y + 36 = 0$$
$$(y - 6)(y - 6) = 0$$
$$y = 6$$
$$y > x$$

5. **(B)** Substitute given values:

$$\frac{(2)^2 + (3)^2}{(4)^2} = \frac{13}{16} \text{ (Column A)}$$

$$\frac{2 + 3}{4} = \frac{5}{4} \text{ (Column B)}$$

$$\frac{5}{4} \text{ or } \frac{20}{16} > \frac{13}{16}$$

6. **(C)** Multiply the first equation by 2:
$$2a - 4b = 22$$
$$5a + 4b = 27$$
By addition: $7a = 49$
$$a = 7$$
$$5a = 35$$

7. **(A)**
$$(x - y)^2 = 16$$
$$x^2 - 2xy + y^2 = 16$$
Substitute value of $x^2 + y^2$: $58 - 2xy = 16$
$$-2xy = -42$$
$$2xy = 42$$
$$xy = 21$$
$$21 > 16$$

8. **(C)** $x\sqrt{0.01} = 1$
Square both sides: $.01x^2 = 1$
Multiply by 100: $x^2 = 100$
Extract square root: $x = 10$

9. **(C)** In Column A, obtain common denominators and add:
$$\frac{xb}{by} + \frac{ya}{by} = \frac{xb + ya}{by}$$

10. **(C)** In Column B, factor $a^2 - b^2$:
$$a^2 - b^2 = (a + b)(a - b)$$

11. **(D)** $x^2 = 4$ and $x = +4, -4$
$y^2 = 9$ and $y = +3, -3$

12. **(C)** $0.3\% = \frac{0.3}{100} = \frac{3}{1000}$

13. **(B)** 0.04% or 0.0004 of 600 = 0.24
4% or 0.04 of 600 = 24

**14. (C)** 100% of 100 = 100
    2% of 100 = 2
    102% of 100 = 102

**15. (B)** For Column A, deduct second discount after deducting first discount: $500 − $50 = $450 less $90 = $360. For Column B, deduct 20% of $490 (or $98) for the price $392.

**16. (D)** When we consider the information that the average weight is 45 pounds we may assume only that the combined weight of Lori, Michael, and Sara is 135 pounds.

**17. (A)** To find percent increase, recall that change divided by original yields a fraction which must be converted to percentage.

In Column A: $\dfrac{600}{800} = \dfrac{3}{4}$ or 75%

In Column B: $\dfrac{600}{1400} = \dfrac{3}{7}$ or 43%

Or, consider that $\dfrac{3}{4} > \dfrac{3}{7}$.

**18. (A)** Recall: Rate × Time = Distance
    In Column A: (40 MPH)(3 hrs.) = 120 miles
    In Column B:  (50 MPH)(1 hr.) = 50 miles and
                 (30 MPH)(2 hrs.) = 60 miles for a total of 110 miles

**19. (C)** Recall: Rate = $\dfrac{\text{Distance}}{\text{Time}}$

In Column A: $\dfrac{1 \text{ mile}}{1\,1/3 \text{ minutes}}$ or $\dfrac{1 \text{ mile}}{4/180 \text{ hr.}}$ or $\dfrac{1 \text{ mile}}{1/45 \text{ hr.}} =$

$1 \div 1/45$ or 45 miles per hour

In Column B: $\dfrac{45 \text{ miles}}{1 \text{ hr.}} = 45$ miles per hour

**20. (D)** This problem could be solved only if $m = n$.

**21. (C)** In Column A the team played $W + L$ games and obtained a record of $\dfrac{W}{W + L}$. The team described in Column B had the identical record.

**22. (C)** The side of a square is one-fourth of the perimeter.

$(\dfrac{1}{4})(8a) = 2a$

**23. (D)** If $n$ = an even whole number, then $x = 1$.
    If $n$ = an odd whole number, then $x = -1$.

**24. (C)** Both triangles share base $BC$. Since $DA \parallel BC$, the perpendicular distances from point $D$ to $CB$ extended and point $A$ to $BC$ extended are equal. This distance is equal to the altitudes of the triangles. Since the triangles share a base and have equal altitudes they have equal areas.

**25. (C)** Recall acute angles of a right triangle are complementary.

## Exercise B

**1. (A)** $3^2 = (3)(3) = 9$
$2^3 = (2)(2)(2) = 8$

**2. (C)** Multiply Column A by $\frac{4}{4}$.

$\frac{24 + 3}{8 - 5} = \frac{27}{3} = 9$

$3^2 = (3)(3) = 9$

**3. (C)** $66\frac{2}{3}\% = \frac{2}{3}$

$\frac{1}{3}$ of $8 = \frac{2}{3}$ of $4$

**4. (A)** $\sqrt{\frac{1}{4}} + \sqrt{\frac{1}{25}} = \frac{1}{2} + \frac{1}{5} = \frac{7}{10}$

$\sqrt{\frac{1}{4} + \frac{1}{25}} = \sqrt{\frac{25}{100} + \frac{4}{100}}$

$= \sqrt{\frac{29}{100}} = \frac{1}{10}\sqrt{29}$

Since $\sqrt{29} = 5.3+$, $\frac{1}{10}$ of $5.3+ = 0.53 + \frac{7}{10}$ or $0.7 > 0.53$

**5. (C)** $2x - 18y$
$6 - 3$ (Substitution) $= 3$
$3x - 36y$
$9 - 6$ (Substitution) $= 3$

**6. (C)** *Hint:* Change all to decimals before adding.
$\sqrt{0.49} = 0.7$

$\frac{3}{4} = 0.75$

$\underline{\phantom{2.25}0.8\phantom{2.25}}$
$2.25$   Sum

$\frac{\text{Sum}}{3} = $ Average $= 0.75$ or $75\%$

Alternatively, observe that 0.75 is the median—the middle between 0.7 and 0.8—and is therefore the average.

**7. (B)** In Column A, since $B = 0$, the value of the expression is zero. In Column B, the zero value ($B$) is added to a positive value ($C$) and is then multiplied by another positive value ($A$) to yield a positive value.

**8. (C)** $\dfrac{n+a}{a} = \dfrac{n}{a} + \dfrac{a}{a}$ or $\dfrac{n}{a} + 1$

**9. (B)** $\sqrt{\dfrac{1}{0.25}} = \dfrac{1}{0.5} = \dfrac{10}{5} = 2$

**10. (B)** Since $x$ and $y$ have negative values, Column A $= -|x| - |y|$ and Column B $= -|x| + |y|$.

**11. (D)** The only fact we may conclude is that the measure of $\angle B$ + the measure of $\angle C = 120°$.

**12. (C)** We must determine how many marbles Michael has. We know he has 5 green, 5 red, 10 white, and 15 blue for a total of 35.

**13. (A)** Mr. A has $120 \div 12$ spaces between his posts. There is one post at the beginning of the fence and one more at the end of each of the 10 spaces: $1 + 10 = 11$ posts in all.

**14. (D)** The value of $x$ may vary from just above 0 to just below 10, and the value of $y$ may vary from just above 0 to just below 12.

**15. (D)** We may conclude that the sum of Sara's four tests is 340. There are many possible combinations for Mark's performance. For example, if he had three tests with 90% and one worth 80%, his average would be 87.5%.

**16. (D)** We do not know how many days make up the work week for Joan.

**17. (A)** Miguel's salary included $(0.02)(25)$ or \$0.50 plus $(0.03)(25)$ or \$0.75 plus $(0.04)(50) = \$2.00$ plus \$5.00, for a total of \$8.25. Martin received \$10.00.

**18. (C)** In triangle $ABC$, $\angle C$ is inscribed in the semicircle and is therefore a right angle. $ABC$ is a 30–60–90 triangle. Therefore, $AB$ is the hypotenuse, and the side opposite the 30° angle $= \dfrac{1}{2}AB = \dfrac{1}{2}y$. Since $x = \dfrac{1}{2}y$, $2x = y$.

**19. (B)** $\sqrt{\dfrac{1}{9} + \dfrac{1}{16}} = \sqrt{\dfrac{16}{144} + \dfrac{9}{144}} = \sqrt{\dfrac{25}{144}} = \dfrac{5}{12}$

$\sqrt{\dfrac{1}{16}} + \sqrt{\dfrac{1}{9}} = \dfrac{1}{4} + \dfrac{1}{3} = \dfrac{7}{12}$

$\dfrac{7}{12} > \dfrac{5}{12}$

**20. (A)**   $3 - 2x < 9$
$\quad\quad -2x < 6$ (Subtraction)
$\quad\quad -x < 3$ (Division by 2)
$\quad\quad\quad x > -3$ (Division by $-1$ [the sign is reversed for division by a negative number])

**21. (A)**   Since $a$ and $b$ have negative values:
$\quad a - b = -|a| + |b|$, and
$\quad a + b = -|a| - |b|$
$\quad + |b| > -|b|$

**22. (B)**   Since $x$ and $y$ have positive values:
$\quad \dfrac{x}{y} > 2$ becomes
$\quad x > 2y$ (Multiplication by positive $y$)

**23. (C)**   $a = 180° - 150° = 30°$
$\quad b = 180° - 30° = 150°$
$\quad a + b \quad = 180°$ (Column A)
$\quad 30° + 150° = 180°$ (Column B)

**24. (C)**   $\dfrac{1}{x} = \sqrt{0.09} = 0.3 = \dfrac{3}{10}$
$\quad \dfrac{1}{x} = \dfrac{3}{10}$
$\quad x = \dfrac{10}{3} = 3\dfrac{1}{3}$

**25. (A)**   $a + c = 180$ (supplementary angles)
$\quad a + b < 180$ (The sum of the measures in degrees of the angles of a triangle is 180°.)

# 7    Practice SAT Exam

You are now about to take a major step in preparing yourself to handle an actual SAT. Before you is a practice test patterned after current published SATs. Up to now, you've concentrated on specific areas and on general testing techniques. You've mastered testing tips and worked on practice exercises. Now you have a chance to test yourself before you walk in that test center door.

This Practice SAT resembles the actual SAT in format, in difficulty, and in content. When you take it, take it as if it were the actual SAT.

### Build Your Stamina

Don't start and stop and take time out for a soda or for an important phone call. To do well on the SAT, you have to focus on the test, the test, and nothing but the test for hours at a time. Most high school students have never had to sit through a three-hour examination before they take their first SAT. To survive a three-hour exam takes stamina, and, as marathon runners know, the only way to build stamina is to put in the necessary time.

### Refine Your Skills

You know how to maximize your score by tackling easy questions first and by eliminating wrong answers whenever you can. Put these skills into practice. If you find yourself spending too much time on any one question, skip it and move on. Remember to check frequently to make sure you are answering the questions in the right spots. This is a great chance for you to get these skills down pat.

### Take a Deep Breath—and Smile!

It's hard to stay calm when those around you are tense, and you're bound to run into some pretty tense people when you take the SAT. So you may experience a slight case of "exam nerves" on the big day. Don't worry about it.

1. Being keyed up for an examination isn't always bad: you may outdo yourself because you are so worked up.

2. Total panic is unlikely to set in: you know too much.

You know you can handle a three-hour test.

You know you can handle the sorts of questions you'll find on the SAT.

You know you can omit several questions and still score high. Answer only 50–60% of the questions correctly and you'll still get an average or better than average score (and dozens of solid, well-known colleges are out there right now, looking for serious students with just that kind of score). Answer more than that correctly and you should wind up with a superior score.

### Make Your Practice Pay—Approximate the Test

1. Complete the entire Practice Test at one sitting.

2. Use a clock or timer.

3. Allow precisely 30 minutes for each section. (If you have time left over, review your answers or recheck the way you've marked your answer sheet.)

4. After each section, give yourself a five-minute break.

5. Allow no talking in the test room.

6. Work rapidly without wasting time.

# ANSWER SHEET

### Section 1

1. Ⓐ Ⓑ Ⓒ Ⓓ Ⓔ
2. Ⓐ Ⓑ Ⓒ Ⓓ Ⓔ
3. Ⓐ Ⓑ Ⓒ Ⓓ Ⓔ
4. Ⓐ Ⓑ Ⓒ Ⓓ Ⓔ
5. Ⓐ Ⓑ Ⓒ Ⓓ Ⓔ
6. Ⓐ Ⓑ Ⓒ Ⓓ Ⓔ
7. Ⓐ Ⓑ Ⓒ Ⓓ Ⓔ
8. Ⓐ Ⓑ Ⓒ Ⓓ Ⓔ
9. Ⓐ Ⓑ Ⓒ Ⓓ Ⓔ
10. Ⓐ Ⓑ Ⓒ Ⓓ Ⓔ
11. Ⓐ Ⓑ Ⓒ Ⓓ Ⓔ
12. Ⓐ Ⓑ Ⓒ Ⓓ Ⓔ
13. Ⓐ Ⓑ Ⓒ Ⓓ Ⓔ
14. Ⓐ Ⓑ Ⓒ Ⓓ Ⓔ
15. Ⓐ Ⓑ Ⓒ Ⓓ Ⓔ
16. Ⓐ Ⓑ Ⓒ Ⓓ Ⓔ
17. Ⓐ Ⓑ Ⓒ Ⓓ Ⓔ
18. Ⓐ Ⓑ Ⓒ Ⓓ Ⓔ
19. Ⓐ Ⓑ Ⓒ Ⓓ Ⓔ
20. Ⓐ Ⓑ Ⓒ Ⓓ Ⓔ
21. Ⓐ Ⓑ Ⓒ Ⓓ Ⓔ
22. Ⓐ Ⓑ Ⓒ Ⓓ Ⓔ
23. Ⓐ Ⓑ Ⓒ Ⓓ Ⓔ
24. Ⓐ Ⓑ Ⓒ Ⓓ Ⓔ
25. Ⓐ Ⓑ Ⓒ Ⓓ Ⓔ

26. Ⓐ Ⓑ Ⓒ Ⓓ Ⓔ
27. Ⓐ Ⓑ Ⓒ Ⓓ Ⓔ
28. Ⓐ Ⓑ Ⓒ Ⓓ Ⓔ
29. Ⓐ Ⓑ Ⓒ Ⓓ Ⓔ
30. Ⓐ Ⓑ Ⓒ Ⓓ Ⓔ
31. Ⓐ Ⓑ Ⓒ Ⓓ Ⓔ
32. Ⓐ Ⓑ Ⓒ Ⓓ Ⓔ
33. Ⓐ Ⓑ Ⓒ Ⓓ Ⓔ
34. Ⓐ Ⓑ Ⓒ Ⓓ Ⓔ
35. Ⓐ Ⓑ Ⓒ Ⓓ Ⓔ
36. Ⓐ Ⓑ Ⓒ Ⓓ Ⓔ
37. Ⓐ Ⓑ Ⓒ Ⓓ Ⓔ
38. Ⓐ Ⓑ Ⓒ Ⓓ Ⓔ
39. Ⓐ Ⓑ Ⓒ Ⓓ Ⓔ
40. Ⓐ Ⓑ Ⓒ Ⓓ Ⓔ
41. Ⓐ Ⓑ Ⓒ Ⓓ Ⓔ
42. Ⓐ Ⓑ Ⓒ Ⓓ Ⓔ
43. Ⓐ Ⓑ Ⓒ Ⓓ Ⓔ
44. Ⓐ Ⓑ Ⓒ Ⓓ Ⓔ
45. Ⓐ Ⓑ Ⓒ Ⓓ Ⓔ
46. Ⓐ Ⓑ Ⓒ Ⓓ Ⓔ
47. Ⓐ Ⓑ Ⓒ Ⓓ Ⓔ
48. Ⓐ Ⓑ Ⓒ Ⓓ Ⓔ
49. Ⓐ Ⓑ Ⓒ Ⓓ Ⓔ
50. Ⓐ Ⓑ Ⓒ Ⓓ Ⓔ

## ANSWER SHEET

### Section 2

1. Ⓐ Ⓑ Ⓒ Ⓓ Ⓔ
2. Ⓐ Ⓑ Ⓒ Ⓓ Ⓔ
3. Ⓐ Ⓑ Ⓒ Ⓓ Ⓔ
4. Ⓐ Ⓑ Ⓒ Ⓓ Ⓔ
5. Ⓐ Ⓑ Ⓒ Ⓓ Ⓔ
6. Ⓐ Ⓑ Ⓒ Ⓓ Ⓔ
7. Ⓐ Ⓑ Ⓒ Ⓓ Ⓔ
8. Ⓐ Ⓑ Ⓒ Ⓓ Ⓔ
9. Ⓐ Ⓑ Ⓒ Ⓓ Ⓔ
10. Ⓐ Ⓑ Ⓒ Ⓓ Ⓔ
11. Ⓐ Ⓑ Ⓒ Ⓓ Ⓔ
12. Ⓐ Ⓑ Ⓒ Ⓓ Ⓔ
13. Ⓐ Ⓑ Ⓒ Ⓓ Ⓔ
14. Ⓐ Ⓑ Ⓒ Ⓓ Ⓔ
15. Ⓐ Ⓑ Ⓒ Ⓓ Ⓔ
16. Ⓐ Ⓑ Ⓒ Ⓓ Ⓔ
17. Ⓐ Ⓑ Ⓒ Ⓓ Ⓔ
18. Ⓐ Ⓑ Ⓒ Ⓓ Ⓔ
19. Ⓐ Ⓑ Ⓒ Ⓓ Ⓔ
20. Ⓐ Ⓑ Ⓒ Ⓓ Ⓔ
21. Ⓐ Ⓑ Ⓒ Ⓓ Ⓔ
22. Ⓐ Ⓑ Ⓒ Ⓓ Ⓔ
23. Ⓐ Ⓑ Ⓒ Ⓓ Ⓔ
24. Ⓐ Ⓑ Ⓒ Ⓓ Ⓔ
25. Ⓐ Ⓑ Ⓒ Ⓓ Ⓔ
26. Ⓐ Ⓑ Ⓒ Ⓓ Ⓔ
27. Ⓐ Ⓑ Ⓒ Ⓓ Ⓔ
28. Ⓐ Ⓑ Ⓒ Ⓓ Ⓔ
29. Ⓐ Ⓑ Ⓒ Ⓓ Ⓔ
30. Ⓐ Ⓑ Ⓒ Ⓓ Ⓔ
31. Ⓐ Ⓑ Ⓒ Ⓓ Ⓔ
32. Ⓐ Ⓑ Ⓒ Ⓓ Ⓔ
33. Ⓐ Ⓑ Ⓒ Ⓓ Ⓔ
34. Ⓐ Ⓑ Ⓒ Ⓓ Ⓔ
35. Ⓐ Ⓑ Ⓒ Ⓓ Ⓔ
36. Ⓐ Ⓑ Ⓒ Ⓓ Ⓔ
37. Ⓐ Ⓑ Ⓒ Ⓓ Ⓔ
38. Ⓐ Ⓑ Ⓒ Ⓓ Ⓔ
39. Ⓐ Ⓑ Ⓒ Ⓓ Ⓔ
40. Ⓐ Ⓑ Ⓒ Ⓓ Ⓔ
41. Ⓐ Ⓑ Ⓒ Ⓓ Ⓔ
42. Ⓐ Ⓑ Ⓒ Ⓓ Ⓔ
43. Ⓐ Ⓑ Ⓒ Ⓓ Ⓔ
44. Ⓐ Ⓑ Ⓒ Ⓓ Ⓔ
45. Ⓐ Ⓑ Ⓒ Ⓓ Ⓔ
46. Ⓐ Ⓑ Ⓒ Ⓓ Ⓔ
47. Ⓐ Ⓑ Ⓒ Ⓓ Ⓔ
48. Ⓐ Ⓑ Ⓒ Ⓓ Ⓔ
49. Ⓐ Ⓑ Ⓒ Ⓓ Ⓔ
50. Ⓐ Ⓑ Ⓒ Ⓓ Ⓔ

# ANSWER SHEET

### Section 3

1. Ⓐ Ⓑ Ⓒ Ⓓ Ⓔ
2. Ⓐ Ⓑ Ⓒ Ⓓ Ⓔ
3. Ⓐ Ⓑ Ⓒ Ⓓ Ⓔ
4. Ⓐ Ⓑ Ⓒ Ⓓ Ⓔ
5. Ⓐ Ⓑ Ⓒ Ⓓ Ⓔ
6. Ⓐ Ⓑ Ⓒ Ⓓ Ⓔ
7. Ⓐ Ⓑ Ⓒ Ⓓ Ⓔ
8. Ⓐ Ⓑ Ⓒ Ⓓ Ⓔ
9. Ⓐ Ⓑ Ⓒ Ⓓ Ⓔ
10. Ⓐ Ⓑ Ⓒ Ⓓ Ⓔ
11. Ⓐ Ⓑ Ⓒ Ⓓ Ⓔ
12. Ⓐ Ⓑ Ⓒ Ⓓ Ⓔ
13. Ⓐ Ⓑ Ⓒ Ⓓ Ⓔ
14. Ⓐ Ⓑ Ⓒ Ⓓ Ⓔ
15. Ⓐ Ⓑ Ⓒ Ⓓ Ⓔ
16. Ⓐ Ⓑ Ⓒ Ⓓ Ⓔ
17. Ⓐ Ⓑ Ⓒ Ⓓ Ⓔ
18. Ⓐ Ⓑ Ⓒ Ⓓ Ⓔ
19. Ⓐ Ⓑ Ⓒ Ⓓ Ⓔ
20. Ⓐ Ⓑ Ⓒ Ⓓ Ⓔ
21. Ⓐ Ⓑ Ⓒ Ⓓ Ⓔ
22. Ⓐ Ⓑ Ⓒ Ⓓ Ⓔ
23. Ⓐ Ⓑ Ⓒ Ⓓ Ⓔ
24. Ⓐ Ⓑ Ⓒ Ⓓ Ⓔ
25. Ⓐ Ⓑ Ⓒ Ⓓ Ⓔ

26. Ⓐ Ⓑ Ⓒ Ⓓ Ⓔ
27. Ⓐ Ⓑ Ⓒ Ⓓ Ⓔ
28. Ⓐ Ⓑ Ⓒ Ⓓ Ⓔ
29. Ⓐ Ⓑ Ⓒ Ⓓ Ⓔ
30. Ⓐ Ⓑ Ⓒ Ⓓ Ⓔ
31. Ⓐ Ⓑ Ⓒ Ⓓ Ⓔ
32. Ⓐ Ⓑ Ⓒ Ⓓ Ⓔ
33. Ⓐ Ⓑ Ⓒ Ⓓ Ⓔ
34. Ⓐ Ⓑ Ⓒ Ⓓ Ⓔ
35. Ⓐ Ⓑ Ⓒ Ⓓ Ⓔ
36. Ⓐ Ⓑ Ⓒ Ⓓ Ⓔ
37. Ⓐ Ⓑ Ⓒ Ⓓ Ⓔ
38. Ⓐ Ⓑ Ⓒ Ⓓ Ⓔ
39. Ⓐ Ⓑ Ⓒ Ⓓ Ⓔ
40. Ⓐ Ⓑ Ⓒ Ⓓ Ⓔ
41. Ⓐ Ⓑ Ⓒ Ⓓ Ⓔ
42. Ⓐ Ⓑ Ⓒ Ⓓ Ⓔ
43. Ⓐ Ⓑ Ⓒ Ⓓ Ⓔ
44. Ⓐ Ⓑ Ⓒ Ⓓ Ⓔ
45. Ⓐ Ⓑ Ⓒ Ⓓ Ⓔ
46. Ⓐ Ⓑ Ⓒ Ⓓ Ⓔ
47. Ⓐ Ⓑ Ⓒ Ⓓ Ⓔ
48. Ⓐ Ⓑ Ⓒ Ⓓ Ⓔ
49. Ⓐ Ⓑ Ⓒ Ⓓ Ⓔ
50. Ⓐ Ⓑ Ⓒ Ⓓ Ⓔ

# ANSWER SHEET

### Section 4

1. Ⓐ Ⓑ Ⓒ Ⓓ Ⓔ
2. Ⓐ Ⓑ Ⓒ Ⓓ Ⓔ
3. Ⓐ Ⓑ Ⓒ Ⓓ Ⓔ
4. Ⓐ Ⓑ Ⓒ Ⓓ Ⓔ
5. Ⓐ Ⓑ Ⓒ Ⓓ Ⓔ
6. Ⓐ Ⓑ Ⓒ Ⓓ Ⓔ
7. Ⓐ Ⓑ Ⓒ Ⓓ Ⓔ
8. Ⓐ Ⓑ Ⓒ Ⓓ Ⓔ
9. Ⓐ Ⓑ Ⓒ Ⓓ Ⓔ
10. Ⓐ Ⓑ Ⓒ Ⓓ Ⓔ
11. Ⓐ Ⓑ Ⓒ Ⓓ Ⓔ
12. Ⓐ Ⓑ Ⓒ Ⓓ Ⓔ
13. Ⓐ Ⓑ Ⓒ Ⓓ Ⓔ
14. Ⓐ Ⓑ Ⓒ Ⓓ Ⓔ
15. Ⓐ Ⓑ Ⓒ Ⓓ Ⓔ
16. Ⓐ Ⓑ Ⓒ Ⓓ Ⓔ
17. Ⓐ Ⓑ Ⓒ Ⓓ Ⓔ
18. Ⓐ Ⓑ Ⓒ Ⓓ Ⓔ
19. Ⓐ Ⓑ Ⓒ Ⓓ Ⓔ
20. Ⓐ Ⓑ Ⓒ Ⓓ Ⓔ
21. Ⓐ Ⓑ Ⓒ Ⓓ Ⓔ
22. Ⓐ Ⓑ Ⓒ Ⓓ Ⓔ
23. Ⓐ Ⓑ Ⓒ Ⓓ Ⓔ
24. Ⓐ Ⓑ Ⓒ Ⓓ Ⓔ
25. Ⓐ Ⓑ Ⓒ Ⓓ Ⓔ

26. Ⓐ Ⓑ Ⓒ Ⓓ Ⓔ
27. Ⓐ Ⓑ Ⓒ Ⓓ Ⓔ
28. Ⓐ Ⓑ Ⓒ Ⓓ Ⓔ
29. Ⓐ Ⓑ Ⓒ Ⓓ Ⓔ
30. Ⓐ Ⓑ Ⓒ Ⓓ Ⓔ
31. Ⓐ Ⓑ Ⓒ Ⓓ Ⓔ
32. Ⓐ Ⓑ Ⓒ Ⓓ Ⓔ
33. Ⓐ Ⓑ Ⓒ Ⓓ Ⓔ
34. Ⓐ Ⓑ Ⓒ Ⓓ Ⓔ
35. Ⓐ Ⓑ Ⓒ Ⓓ Ⓔ
36. Ⓐ Ⓑ Ⓒ Ⓓ Ⓔ
37. Ⓐ Ⓑ Ⓒ Ⓓ Ⓔ
38. Ⓐ Ⓑ Ⓒ Ⓓ Ⓔ
39. Ⓐ Ⓑ Ⓒ Ⓓ Ⓔ
40. Ⓐ Ⓑ Ⓒ Ⓓ Ⓔ
41. Ⓐ Ⓑ Ⓒ Ⓓ Ⓔ
42. Ⓐ Ⓑ Ⓒ Ⓓ Ⓔ
43. Ⓐ Ⓑ Ⓒ Ⓓ Ⓔ
44. Ⓐ Ⓑ Ⓒ Ⓓ Ⓔ
45. Ⓐ Ⓑ Ⓒ Ⓓ Ⓔ
46. Ⓐ Ⓑ Ⓒ Ⓓ Ⓔ
47. Ⓐ Ⓑ Ⓒ Ⓓ Ⓔ
48. Ⓐ Ⓑ Ⓒ Ⓓ Ⓔ
49. Ⓐ Ⓑ Ⓒ Ⓓ Ⓔ
50. Ⓐ Ⓑ Ⓒ Ⓓ Ⓔ

# ANSWER SHEET

### Section 5

1. Ⓐ Ⓑ Ⓒ Ⓓ Ⓔ
2. Ⓐ Ⓑ Ⓒ Ⓓ Ⓔ
3. Ⓐ Ⓑ Ⓒ Ⓓ Ⓔ
4. Ⓐ Ⓑ Ⓒ Ⓓ Ⓔ
5. Ⓐ Ⓑ Ⓒ Ⓓ Ⓔ
6. Ⓐ Ⓑ Ⓒ Ⓓ Ⓔ
7. Ⓐ Ⓑ Ⓒ Ⓓ Ⓔ
8. Ⓐ Ⓑ Ⓒ Ⓓ Ⓔ
9. Ⓐ Ⓑ Ⓒ Ⓓ Ⓔ
10. Ⓐ Ⓑ Ⓒ Ⓓ Ⓔ
11. Ⓐ Ⓑ Ⓒ Ⓓ Ⓔ
12. Ⓐ Ⓑ Ⓒ Ⓓ Ⓔ
13. Ⓐ Ⓑ Ⓒ Ⓓ Ⓔ
14. Ⓐ Ⓑ Ⓒ Ⓓ Ⓔ
15. Ⓐ Ⓑ Ⓒ Ⓓ Ⓔ
16. Ⓐ Ⓑ Ⓒ Ⓓ Ⓔ
17. Ⓐ Ⓑ Ⓒ Ⓓ Ⓔ
18. Ⓐ Ⓑ Ⓒ Ⓓ Ⓔ
19. Ⓐ Ⓑ Ⓒ Ⓓ Ⓔ
20. Ⓐ Ⓑ Ⓒ Ⓓ Ⓔ
21. Ⓐ Ⓑ Ⓒ Ⓓ Ⓔ
22. Ⓐ Ⓑ Ⓒ Ⓓ Ⓔ
23. Ⓐ Ⓑ Ⓒ Ⓓ Ⓔ
24. Ⓐ Ⓑ Ⓒ Ⓓ Ⓔ
25. Ⓐ Ⓑ Ⓒ Ⓓ Ⓔ

26. Ⓐ Ⓑ Ⓒ Ⓓ Ⓔ
27. Ⓐ Ⓑ Ⓒ Ⓓ Ⓔ
28. Ⓐ Ⓑ Ⓒ Ⓓ Ⓔ
29. Ⓐ Ⓑ Ⓒ Ⓓ Ⓔ
30. Ⓐ Ⓑ Ⓒ Ⓓ Ⓔ
31. Ⓐ Ⓑ Ⓒ Ⓓ Ⓔ
32. Ⓐ Ⓑ Ⓒ Ⓓ Ⓔ
33. Ⓐ Ⓑ Ⓒ Ⓓ Ⓔ
34. Ⓐ Ⓑ Ⓒ Ⓓ Ⓔ
35. Ⓐ Ⓑ Ⓒ Ⓓ Ⓔ
36. Ⓐ Ⓑ Ⓒ Ⓓ Ⓔ
37. Ⓐ Ⓑ Ⓒ Ⓓ Ⓔ
38. Ⓐ Ⓑ Ⓒ Ⓓ Ⓔ
39. Ⓐ Ⓑ Ⓒ Ⓓ Ⓔ
40. Ⓐ Ⓑ Ⓒ Ⓓ Ⓔ
41. Ⓐ Ⓑ Ⓒ Ⓓ Ⓔ
42. Ⓐ Ⓑ Ⓒ Ⓓ Ⓔ
43. Ⓐ Ⓑ Ⓒ Ⓓ Ⓔ
44. Ⓐ Ⓑ Ⓒ Ⓓ Ⓔ
45. Ⓐ Ⓑ Ⓒ Ⓓ Ⓔ
46. Ⓐ Ⓑ Ⓒ Ⓓ Ⓔ
47. Ⓐ Ⓑ Ⓒ Ⓓ Ⓔ
48. Ⓐ Ⓑ Ⓒ Ⓓ Ⓔ
49. Ⓐ Ⓑ Ⓒ Ⓓ Ⓔ
50. Ⓐ Ⓑ Ⓒ Ⓓ Ⓔ

## ANSWER SHEET

### Section 6

1. Ⓐ Ⓑ Ⓒ Ⓓ Ⓔ
2. Ⓐ Ⓑ Ⓒ Ⓓ Ⓔ
3. Ⓐ Ⓑ Ⓒ Ⓓ Ⓔ
4. Ⓐ Ⓑ Ⓒ Ⓓ Ⓔ
5. Ⓐ Ⓑ Ⓒ Ⓓ Ⓔ
6. Ⓐ Ⓑ Ⓒ Ⓓ Ⓔ
7. Ⓐ Ⓑ Ⓒ Ⓓ Ⓔ
8. Ⓐ Ⓑ Ⓒ Ⓓ Ⓔ
9. Ⓐ Ⓑ Ⓒ Ⓓ Ⓔ
10. Ⓐ Ⓑ Ⓒ Ⓓ Ⓔ
11. Ⓐ Ⓑ Ⓒ Ⓓ Ⓔ
12. Ⓐ Ⓑ Ⓒ Ⓓ Ⓔ
13. Ⓐ Ⓑ Ⓒ Ⓓ Ⓔ
14. Ⓐ Ⓑ Ⓒ Ⓓ Ⓔ
15. Ⓐ Ⓑ Ⓒ Ⓓ Ⓔ
16. Ⓐ Ⓑ Ⓒ Ⓓ Ⓔ
17. Ⓐ Ⓑ Ⓒ Ⓓ Ⓔ
18. Ⓐ Ⓑ Ⓒ Ⓓ Ⓔ
19. Ⓐ Ⓑ Ⓒ Ⓓ Ⓔ
20. Ⓐ Ⓑ Ⓒ Ⓓ Ⓔ
21. Ⓐ Ⓑ Ⓒ Ⓓ Ⓔ
22. Ⓐ Ⓑ Ⓒ Ⓓ Ⓔ
23. Ⓐ Ⓑ Ⓒ Ⓓ Ⓔ
24. Ⓐ Ⓑ Ⓒ Ⓓ Ⓔ
25. Ⓐ Ⓑ Ⓒ Ⓓ Ⓔ

26. Ⓐ Ⓑ Ⓒ Ⓓ Ⓔ
27. Ⓐ Ⓑ Ⓒ Ⓓ Ⓔ
28. Ⓐ Ⓑ Ⓒ Ⓓ Ⓔ
29. Ⓐ Ⓑ Ⓒ Ⓓ Ⓔ
30. Ⓐ Ⓑ Ⓒ Ⓓ Ⓔ
31. Ⓐ Ⓑ Ⓒ Ⓓ Ⓔ
32. Ⓐ Ⓑ Ⓒ Ⓓ Ⓔ
33. Ⓐ Ⓑ Ⓒ Ⓓ Ⓔ
34. Ⓐ Ⓑ Ⓒ Ⓓ Ⓔ
35. Ⓐ Ⓑ Ⓒ Ⓓ Ⓔ
36. Ⓐ Ⓑ Ⓒ Ⓓ Ⓔ
37. Ⓐ Ⓑ Ⓒ Ⓓ Ⓔ
38. Ⓐ Ⓑ Ⓒ Ⓓ Ⓔ
39. Ⓐ Ⓑ Ⓒ Ⓓ Ⓔ
40. Ⓐ Ⓑ Ⓒ Ⓓ Ⓔ
41. Ⓐ Ⓑ Ⓒ Ⓓ Ⓔ
42. Ⓐ Ⓑ Ⓒ Ⓓ Ⓔ
43. Ⓐ Ⓑ Ⓒ Ⓓ Ⓔ
44. Ⓐ Ⓑ Ⓒ Ⓓ Ⓔ
45. Ⓐ Ⓑ Ⓒ Ⓓ Ⓔ
46. Ⓐ Ⓑ Ⓒ Ⓓ Ⓔ
47. Ⓐ Ⓑ Ⓒ Ⓓ Ⓔ
48. Ⓐ Ⓑ Ⓒ Ⓓ Ⓔ
49. Ⓐ Ⓑ Ⓒ Ⓓ Ⓔ
50. Ⓐ Ⓑ Ⓒ Ⓓ Ⓔ

# SECTION 1

### 45 Questions—30 Minutes

For each question in this section, choose the best answer and blacken the corresponding space on the answer sheet.

Each question below consists of a word in capital letters, followed by five lettered words or phrases. Choose the word or phrase that is most nearly <u>opposite</u> in meaning to the word in capital letters. Since some of the questions require you to distinguish fine shades of meaning, consider all the choices before deciding which is best.

Example:

GOOD:  (A) sour  (B) bad  (C) red  (D) hot  (E) ugly

Ⓐ ● Ⓒ Ⓓ Ⓔ

1. FLOURISH:  (A) darken  (B) waste away  (C) beckon
   (D) endure  (E) bring back
2. TOLERATE:  (A) refuse to bear  (B) act wrongly
   (C) take seriously  (D) use foolishly  (E) shout angrily
3. ENHANCE:  (A) retreat  (B) loathe  (C) detract  (D) pursue
   (E) convert
4. SPIRITED:  (A) remote  (B) unanimated  (C) unimaginative
   (D) insincere  (E) awkward
5. HEFTY:  (A) frail  (B) liquid  (C) feminine  (D) quick
   (E) undisturbed
6. PURIFY:  (A) resolve  (B) desire  (C) pollute
   (D) discriminate  (E) agitate
7. SAGE:  (A) upright  (B) foolish  (C) cheerful  (D) deliberate
   (E) unconcerned

8. ENACT: (A) improvise   (B) defy   (C) suffer   (D) externalize
   (E) repeal

9. DISMANTLE: (A) reassure   (B) kindle   (C) equip
   (D) impede   (E) suppose

10. CLEMENCY: (A) stupidity   (B) filth   (C) lack of money
    (D) lack of mercy   (E) slowness

11. MITIGATE: (A) disarm   (B) worsen   (C) predict   (D) initiate
    (E) compensate

12. SURREPTITIOUS: (A) sugary   (B) monotonous   (C) rash
    (D) open   (E) wholesome

13. CORPULENCE: (A) energetic nature   (B) spiritual bent
    (C) juvenile behavior   (D) untidiness   (E) slenderness

14. METICULOUS: (A) careless   (B) shapeless   (C) transient
    (D) intrepid   (E) dogmatic

15. PROCLIVITY: (A) fear of interference   (B) contradiction in terms
    (C) lack of inclination   (D) need for reassurance
    (E) position of strength

---

Each sentence below has one or two blanks, each blank indicating
that something has been omitted. Beneath the sentence are five
lettered words or sets of words. Choose the word or set of words
that <u>best</u> fits the meaning of the sentence as a whole.

Example:

Although its publicity has been ----, the film itself is intelligent,
well-acted, handsomely produced, and altogether ----.

(A) tasteless..respectable   (B) extensive..moderate
   (C) sophisticated..amateur   (D) risqué..crude
      (E) perfect..spectacular

**16.** Despite the ---- of the materials with which he worked, many of
Tiffany's glass masterpieces have survived for over seventy years.

(A) beauty
(B) translucence
(C) abundance
(D) majesty
(E) fragility

**17.** Although similar to mice in many physical characteristics, voles may
be ---- mice by the shortness of their tails.

(A) distinguished from
(B) classified with
(C) related to
(D) categorized as
(E) enumerated with

**18.** Because he saw no ---- to the task assigned him, he worked at it in a
very ---- way.

(A) function..systematic
(B) method..dutiful
(C) purpose..diligent
(D) end..rigid
(E) point..perfunctory

**19.** The herb Chinese parsley is an example of what we mean by an
acquired taste: Westerners who originally ---- it eventually come to ----
its flavor in Oriental foods.

(A) relish..enjoy
(B) dislike..welcome
(C) savor..abhor
(D) ignore..detest
(E) discern..recognize

**20.** Although the doctor's words were ----, the patient's family hoped
against hope for a ---- of the disease.

(A) discouraging..resurgence
(B) disheartening..remission
(C) inaudible..report
(D) reassuring..transfusion
(E) authoritative..diagnosis

Each passage below is followed by questions based on its content. Answer all questions following a passage on the basis of what is <u>stated</u> or <u>implied</u> in that passage.

To the world when it was half a thousand years younger, the outlines of all things seemed more clearly marked than to us. The contrast between suffering and joy, between adversity and
*Line* happiness, appeared more striking. All experience had yet to
(5) the minds of men the directness and absoluteness of the pleasure and pain of child-life. Every event, every action, was still embodied in expressive and solemn forms, which raised them to the dignity of a ritual. For it was not merely the great facts of birth, marriage, and death which, by their sacredness,
(10) were raised to the rank of mysteries; incidents of less importance, like a journey, a task, a visit, were equally attended by a thousand formalities: benedictions, ceremonies, formulae.

Calamities and indigence were more afflicting than at
(15) present; it was more difficult to guard against them, and to find solace. Illness and health presented a more striking contrast; the cold and darkness of winter were more real evils. Honors and riches were relished with greater avidity and contrasted more vividly with surrounding misery. We, at the present day,
(20) can hardly understand the keenness with which a fur coat, a good fire on the hearth, a soft bed, a glass of wine, were formerly enjoyed.

Then, again, all things in life were of a proud or cruel publicity. Lepers sounded their rattles and went about in
(25) processions, beggars exhibited their deformity and their misery in churches. Every order and estate, every rank and profession, was distinguished by its costume. The great lords never moved about without a glorious display of arms and liveries, exciting fear and envy. Executions and other public acts of
(30) justice, hawking, marriages and funerals, were all announced by cries and processions, songs and music. The lover wore the

colors of his lady; companions the emblem of their
confraternity; parties and servants the badges or blazon of
their lords. Between town and country, too, the contrast was
*(35)* very marked. A medieval town did not lose itself in extensive
suburbs of factories and villas; girded by its walls, it stood
forth as a compact whole, bristling with innumerable turrets.
However tall and threatening the houses of noblemen or
merchants might be, in the aspect of the town the lofty mass
*(40)* of the churches always remained dominant.

The contrast between silence and sound, darkness and light,
like that between summer and winter, was more strongly
marked than it is in our lives. The modern town hardly knows
silence or darkness in their purity, nor the effect of a solitary
*(45)* light or a single distant cry.

All things presenting themselves to the mind in violent
contrasts and impressive forms, lent a tone of excitement and
of passion to everyday life and tended to produce the
perpetual oscillation between despair and distracted joy,
*(50)* between cruelty and pious tenderness which characterizes life
in the Middle Ages.

**21.** The author's main purpose in this passage is best defined as an
attempt to show how

(A) extremes of feeling and experience marked the Middle Ages
(B) the styles of the very poor and the very rich complemented each
other
(C) twentieth century standards of behavior cannot be applied to the
Middle Ages
(D) the Middle Ages developed out of the Dark Ages
(E) the medieval spirit languished five hundred years ago

**22.** According to the passage, surrounding an activity with formalities
makes it

(A) less important
(B) more dignified
(C) less expensive
(D) more indirect
(E) less solemn

23. To the author, the Middle Ages seem to be all of the following EXCEPT

   (A) harsh and bleak
   (B) festive and joyful
   (C) dignified and ceremonious
   (D) passionate and turbulent
   (E) routine and boring

24. According to the passage, well above the typical medieval town there towered

   (A) houses of worship
   (B) manufacturing establishments
   (C) the mansions of the aristocracy
   (D) great mercantile houses
   (E) walled suburbs

25. The author's use of the term "formulae" (line 13) could best be interpreted to mean which of the following?

   (A) set forms of words for rituals
   (B) mathematical rules or principles
   (C) chemical symbols
   (D) nourishment for infants
   (E) prescriptions for drugs

It is a most miserable thing to feel ashamed of home. There may be black ingratitude in the thing, and the punishment may be retributive and well deserved; but, that it is a miserable thing, I can testify.

Home had never been a very pleasant place to me, because of my sister's temper. But Joe had sanctified it and I believed in it. I had believed in the best parlor as a most elegant salon; I had believed in the front door, as a mysterious portal of the Temple of State whose solemn opening was attended with a sacrifice of roast fowls; I had believed in the kitchen as a chaste though not magnificent apartment; I had believed in the forge as the glowing road to manhood. Now, it was all coarse and common, and I would not have had Miss Havisham and Estella see it on any account.

Once, it had seemed to me that when I should at last roll up my shirt sleeves and go into the forge, Joe's 'prentice, I should be distinguished and happy. Now the reality was in my hold, I only felt that I was dusty with the dust of small coal, and that I had a weight upon my daily remembrance to which the anvil was a feather. There have been occasions in my later life (I suppose as in most lives) when I have felt for a time as if a thick curtain had fallen on all its interest and romance, to shut me out from anything save dull endurance any more. Never has that curtain dropped so heavy and blank, as when my way in life lay stretched out straight before me through the newly-entered road of apprenticeship to Joe.

I remember that at a later period of my "time," I used to stand about the churchyard on Sunday evenings, when night was falling, comparing my own perspective with the windy marsh view, and making out some likeness between them by thinking how flat and low both were, and how on both there came an unknown way and a dark mist and then the sea. I was quite as dejected on the first working-day of my apprenticeship as in that after time; but I am glad to know that I never breathed a murmur to Joe while my indentures lasted. It is about the only thing I *am* glad to know of myself in that connection.

For, though it includes what I proceed to add, all the merit of what I proceed to add was Joe's. It was not because I was faithful, but because Joe was faithful, that I never ran away and went for a soldier or a sailor. It was not because I had a strong sense of the virtue of industry, but because Joe had a strong sense of the virtue of industry, that I worked with tolerable zeal against the grain. It is not possible to know how far the influence of any amiable honest-hearted duty-going man flies out into the world; but it is very possible to know how it has touched one's self in going by, and I know right well that any good that intermixed itself with my apprenticeship came of plain contented Joe, and not of restless aspiring discontented me.

26. The passage as a whole is best described as

   (A) an analysis of the reasons behind a change in attitude
   (B) an account of a young man's reflections on his emotional state
   (C) a description of a young man's awakening to the harsh conditions of working class life
   (D) a defense of a young man's longings for romance and glamor
   (E) a criticism of young people's ingratitude to their elders

27. It may be inferred from the passage that the young man has been apprenticed to a

    (A) cook
    (B) forger
    (C) coal miner
    (D) blacksmith
    (E) grave digger

28. In the passage, Joe is portrayed most specifically as

    (A) distinguished
    (B) virtuous
    (C) independent
    (D) homely
    (E) coarse

29. According to the passage, the narrator gives himself a measure of credit for

    (A) working diligently despite his unhappiness
    (B) abandoning his hope of a military career
    (C) keeping his menial position secret from Miss Havisham
    (D) concealing his despondency from Joe
    (E) surrendering his childish beliefs

30. The passage suggests that the narrator's increasing discontent with his home during his apprenticeship was caused by

    (A) a new awareness on his part of how his home would appear to others
    (B) the increasing heaviness of the labor involved
    (C) the unwillingness of Joe to curb his sister's temper
    (D) the narrator's lack of an industrious character
    (E) a combination of simple ingratitude and sinfulness

Select the word or set of words that <u>best</u> completes each of the following sentences.

31. We were distressed by these inexplicable ---- from his generally ---- taste.

    (A) departures..execrable
    (B) lapses..flawless
    (C) deviations..questionable
    (D) results..faulty
    (E) variations..unusual

32. Because they did not accept his basic ----, they were ---- by his argument.

    (A) assumption..convinced
    (B) motivation..confused
    (C) bias..impressed
    (D) premise..unconvinced
    (E) supposition..justified

33. Pain is the body's early warning system: loss of ---- in the extremities leaves a person ---- injuring himself unwittingly.

    (A) agony..incapable of
    (B) sensation..vulnerable to
    (C) consciousness..desirous of
    (D) feeling..habituated to
    (E) movement..prone to

34. She was ---- her accomplishments and properly unwilling to ---- them before her friends.

    (A) excited by..parade
    (B) immodest about..discuss
    (C) deprecatory about..flaunt
    (D) uncertain of..concede
    (E) unaware of..conceal

35. Despite their ---- of Twain's *Huckleberry Finn* for its stereotyped portrait of the slave Jim, even the novel's ---- agreed it was a masterpiece of American prose.

   (A) admiration..critics
   (B) denunciation..supporters
   (C) criticism..detractors
   (D) defense..censors
   (E) praise..advocates

---

Each question below consists of a related pair of words or phrases, followed by five lettered pairs of words or phrases. Select the lettered pair that best expresses a relationship similar to that expressed in the original pair.

Example:

YAWN : BOREDOM ::   (A) dream : sleep
   (B) anger : madness   (C) smile : amusement
   (D) face : expression   (E) impatience : rebellion

Ⓐ Ⓑ ● Ⓓ Ⓔ

---

36. SIGNATURE : PORTRAIT ::   (A) title : novel
   (B) negative : photograph   (C) autograph : celebrity
   (D) postscript : letter   (E) byline : article

37. BREEZE : TORNADO ::   (A) ice : floe   (B) trickle : gusher
   (C) conflagration : flame   (D) river : stream   (E) eruption : volcano

38. ARCHIVES : RECORDS ::   (A) catalog : shelves   (B) aviary : birds
   (C) thread : spindle   (D) clothes : shoes   (E) pedestal : statue

39. ENVELOP : SURROUND ::   (A) efface : confront   (B) house : dislodge
   (C) loiter : linger   (D) distend : struggle   (E) ascend : agree

40. INDIFFERENT : CONCERN ::   (A) intrepid : bravery
   (B) arrogant : modesty   (C) unbigoted : tolerance
   (D) unnatural : emotion   (E) variable : change

41. DILETTANTE : DABBLE ::   (A) coquette : flirt   (B) gymnast : exercise
   (C) soldier : drill   (D) embezzler : steal   (E) benefactor : donate

42. BARREN : FECUND ::   (A) dry : parched   (B) naked : sinful
   (C) hackneyed : original   (D) incessant : continuous
   (E) impetuous : rash

**43.** SLANDER:DEFAMATORY :: (A) fraud:notorious
(B) tenet:devotional    (C) elegy:sorrowful    (D) edict:temporary
(E) exhortation:cautionary

**44.** SLOUGH:SKIN :: (A) shed:hair    (B) polish:teeth
(C) shade:eyes    (D) tear:ligaments    (E) remove:tonsils

**45.** HYPERBOLIC:EXAGGERATED :: (A) metabolic:restrained
(B) choleric:fitful    (C) capricious:whimsical
(D) idiomatic:impersonal    (E) melancholy:bemused

---

IF YOU FINISH BEFORE TIME IS
CALLED, YOU MAY CHECK YOUR
WORK ON THIS SECTION ONLY. DO     **STOP**
NOT WORK ON ANY OTHER SECTION
IN THE TEST.

---

---

## SECTION 2

### 25 Questions—30 Minutes

<u>Directions:</u> In this section solve each problem, using any available space on the page for scratchwork. Then decide which is the best of the choices given and blacken the corresponding space on the answer sheet.

The following information is for your reference in solving some of the problems.

Circle of radius $r$:
Area $= \pi r^2$;
Circumference $= 2 \pi r$

   The number of degrees of arc in a circle is 360.

   The measure in degrees of a straight angle is 180.

Triangle: The sum of the measures in degrees of the angles of a triangle is 180.

If $\angle CDA$ is a right angle, then

(1) area of $\triangle ABC =$
$$\frac{AB \times CD}{2}$$

(2) $AC^2 = AD^2 + DC^2$

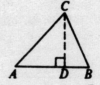

<u>Definitions of symbols:</u>

| | |
|---|---|
| $=$ is equal to | $\leq$ is less than or equal to |
| $\neq$ is unequal to | $\geq$ is greater than or equal to |
| $<$ is less than | $\parallel$ is parallel to |
| $>$ is greater than | $\perp$ is perpendicular to |

<u>Note:</u> Figures which accompany problems in this test are intended to provide information useful in solving the problems. They are drawn as accurately as possible EXCEPT when it is stated in a specific problem that its figure is not drawn to scale. All figures lie in a plane unless otherwise indicated. All numbers used are real numbers.

1. If $\dfrac{6}{5} = \dfrac{x}{6}$ then $x =$

   (A) $\dfrac{5}{6}$

   (B) $\dfrac{5}{36}$

   (C) $7\dfrac{1}{5}$

   (D) $7\dfrac{1}{2}$

   (E) $36$

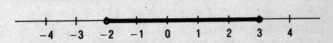

2. Which inequality is represented by the graph above?

   (A) $-2 < x \leq 3$
   (B) $2 < x < 3$
   (C) $2 < x = 3$
   (D) $2 > x > 3$
   (E) $-2 > x \leq 3$

3. The average of two numbers is $K$. If one number is equal to $M$, the other number is equal to

   (A) $2M - K$

   (B) $\dfrac{-2M + K}{2}$

   (C) $\dfrac{2M - K}{2}$

   (D) $\dfrac{M + K}{2}$

   (E) $2K - M$

4. A woman purchases 4 lbs. of peaches priced at 80¢ per lb. What change does she receive from a ten-dollar bill?

   (A) $3.20
   (B) $7.20
   (C) $7.80
   (D) $6.80
   (E) $9.20

   ___

   Note: Figure not drawn to scale.

5. In this diagram, what is the value of $a$?

   (A) 30
   (B) 33
   (C) 36
   (D) 39
   (E) 40

   ___

6. What fraction must be added to $\frac{3}{5}, \frac{1}{4}, \frac{1}{10}, \frac{1}{2}$ to give an average of exactly $\frac{3}{10}$?

   (A) $\frac{1}{20}$

   (B) $\frac{2}{3}$

   (C) $\frac{6}{5}$

   (D) $\frac{29}{20}$

   (E) $\frac{3}{2}$

7. In the marathon, runners #149 to #201 were given blue identification tags. Others were given red tags. How many runners were given blue tags?

   (A) 50
   (B) 51
   (C) 52
   (D) 53
   (E) 54

8. The wey of Scotland is equivalent to 40 bushels. How many weys are there in 4 bushels?

   (A) $\dfrac{1}{10}$
   (B) 1
   (C) 10
   (D) 44
   (E) 160

9. In triangle $ABC$, angle $BAC$ has a measure of 60 degrees and side $AB$ = side $AC$ = 6 inches. What is the length of side $BC$ (in inches)?

   (A) 3
   (B) 6
   (C) 9
   (D) 12
   (E) cannot be determined from the information given

10. A man earns $d$ dollars each week and spends $s$ dollars a week. In how many weeks will he have $Q$ dollars?

   (A) $d - s$
   (B) $\dfrac{Q}{d - s}$
   (C) $d - Q$
   (D) $\dfrac{d - s}{Q}$
   (E) $\dfrac{d - Q}{s}$

11. In a Quiz Program, $\frac{1}{3}$ of the contestants were eliminated in the first round. In the next round, $\frac{1}{2}$ of the remainder were eliminated. What fraction of the original number were in the third round?

(A) $\frac{1}{6}$

(B) $\frac{1}{5}$

(C) $\frac{1}{3}$

(D) $\frac{1}{2}$

(E) $\frac{2}{3}$

12. If is defined to equal $\frac{ab}{c}$ and $-\frac{1}{x}=0$, then $x=$

(A) $\frac{ab}{c}$   (B) $\frac{ac}{b}$   (C) $\frac{c}{ab}$   (D) $\frac{bc}{a}$   (E) $\frac{a}{bc}$

13. If $\dfrac{x^2 + 4x + 6}{x^2 + 3x + 7} = 1$, then $x =$

(A) 0

(B) $-1$

(C) 1

(D) $\frac{7}{6}$

(E) 6

**14.** A manufacturer finds that 0.4% of his production is defective and not suitable for marketing. How many articles of each 1000 produced will be rejected?

(A)  4
(B)  14
(C)  40
(D)  140
(E)  400

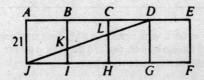

**15.** In the figure above, *ABIJ, BCHI, CDGH,* and *DEFG* are congruent rectangles. If *AJ* = 21, then *KI* =

(A)  3
(B)  5.25
(C)  7
(D)  10.5
(E)  14

**16.** If $\dfrac{1}{x} + \dfrac{1}{x} = 6$, then $x =$

(A)  $\dfrac{1}{6}$

(B)  $\dfrac{1}{3}$

(C)  $\dfrac{1}{2}$

(D)  2
(E)  3

17. An automobile travels at the rate of 50 miles per hour on the Pennsylvania Turnpike. How many minutes will it take to travel $\frac{2}{5}$ of a mile at this rate?

    (A) 0.2
    (B) 0.48
    (C) 2.2
    (D) 13.5
    (E) 22

18. A trailer carries 3, 4, or 5 crates on a trip. Each crate weighs no less than 125 lbs. and no more than 250 lbs. What is the minimum weight (in lbs.) of the crates on a single trip?

    (A) 375
    (B) 600
    (C) 625
    (D) 750
    (E) 1250

19. The area of a circle with radius $r$ is equal to the area of a rectangle with base $b$. Find the altitude of the rectangle in terms of $\pi$, $r$, and $b$.

    (A) $\sqrt{\pi r}$
    (B) $\dfrac{2\pi r}{b}$
    (C) $\pi r^2 b$
    (D) $\dfrac{\pi r^2}{b}$
    (E) $\dfrac{\pi r^2}{b^2}$

**20.** A girl keeps a record of time she spends practicing her music. On
Monday she spends $1\frac{1}{4}$ hours; on Tuesday and Wednesday she spends
2 hours each day; on Thursday she spends $1\frac{3}{4}$ hours. How many
hours will she have to spend practicing for the rest of the week in
order to have an average of exactly 90 minutes each day?

(A) $1\frac{1}{2}$

(B) 2

(C) $2\frac{1}{2}$

(D) $3\frac{1}{2}$

(E) 4

**21.** To raise $500 for a charitable organization a school plans a musical
festival with expenses of $250. What is the minimum number of
tickets at 75 cents each that will have to be sold to reach this goal?

(A) 100
(B) 300
(C) 334
(D) 1000
(E) 1500

**22.** If the side of a square is increased by 150%, by what % is the area
increased?

(A) 125
(B) 225
(C) 300
(D) 525
(E) 625

**23.** A circle whose center is the point ($-$ 2, 6) is tangent to the $x$-axis. The coordinates of the point of tangency are

    (A) (0, 6)
    (B) ($-$2, 0)
    (C) (0, $-$2)
    (D) (6, 0)
    (E) ($-$2, $-$2)

---

**24.** What are the coordinates of the midpoint of the line segment joining point $A$ ($-5$, $-4$) and point $B$ (3, $-2$)?

    (A) ($-1$, $-3$)
    (B) (1, 3)
    (C) ($-2$, $-6$)
    (D) ($-1$, $-6$)
    (E) ($-2$, $-3$)

---

**25.** The length of the line segment joining the points whose coordinates are ($-4$, 3) and (2, $-5$) is

    (A) 4
    (B) 5
    (C) 7
    (D) 10
    (E) 20

IF YOU FINISH BEFORE TIME IS CALLED, YOU MAY CHECK YOUR WORK ON THIS SECTION ONLY. DO NOT WORK ON ANY OTHER SECTION IN THE TEST.  **STOP**

## SECTION 3 TEST OF STANDARD WRITTEN ENGLISH

50 Questions — 30 Minutes

The questions in this section measure skills that are important to
writing well. In particular, they test your ability to recognize and
use language that is clear, effective, and correct according to the
requirements of standard written English, the kind of English
found in most college textbooks.

Directions:   The following sentences contain problems in grammar, usage, diction (choice of words), and idiom.

Some sentences are correct.
No sentence contains more than one error.

You will find that the error, if there is one, is underlined and lettered. Assume that elements of the sentence that are not underlined are correct and cannot be changed. In choosing answers,
follow the requirements of standard written English.

If there is an error, select the <u>one underlined part</u> that must be
changed to make the sentence correct and blacken the corresponding space on your answer sheet.

If there is no error, blacken answer space Ⓔ.
   EXAMPLE:

The region has a climate <u>so severe that</u> plants
                              A

<u>growing</u> there rarely <u>had been</u> more than twelve inches
    B                      C

<u>high</u>. <u>No error</u>
  D      E

SAMPLE ANSWER
Ⓐ Ⓑ ● Ⓓ Ⓔ

1. His salary is lower than a caretaker. No error
   $\overline{\text{A}}$ $\overline{\text{B}}$ $\overline{\text{C}}$ $\overline{\text{D}}$ $\overline{\text{E}}$

2. Not one of the children has ever sang in public before. No error
   $\overline{\text{A}}$ $\overline{\text{B}}$ $\overline{\text{C}}$ $\overline{\text{D}}$ $\overline{\text{E}}$

3. The book must be old, for it's cover is torn. No error
   $\overline{\text{A}}$ $\overline{\text{B}}$ $\overline{\text{C}}$ $\overline{\text{D}}$ $\overline{\text{E}}$

4. Neither the players nor the trainer were in the locker room when the
   $\overline{\text{A}}$ $\overline{\text{B}}$ $\overline{\text{C}}$ $\overline{\text{D}}$
   thief broke in. No error
   $\overline{\text{E}}$

5. We have come to the conclusion that we can end hostilities in
   $\overline{\text{A}}$
   that area of the world by providing food to both sides, bringing the
   $\overline{\text{B}}$
   opposing forces to the negotiation table, and to guarantee financial
   $\overline{\text{C}}$ $\overline{\text{D}}$
   aid to both sides once peace is established. No error
   $\overline{\text{E}}$

6. I should like you and him to attend my birthday party on Saturday
   $\overline{\text{A}}$ $\overline{\text{B}}$ $\overline{\text{C}}$
   afternoon. No error
   $\overline{\text{D}}$ $\overline{\text{E}}$

7. Neither you nor I can realize the affect his behavior will have on his
   $\overline{\text{A}}$ $\overline{\text{B}}$ $\overline{\text{C}}$ $\overline{\text{D}}$
   chances for promotion. No error
   $\overline{\text{E}}$

8. In order to conserve valuable gasoline, motorists had ought to check
   $\overline{\text{A}}$ $\overline{\text{B}}$
   their speedometers while driving along the highways; it is very easy
   $\overline{\text{C}}$ $\overline{\text{D}}$
   to exceed 55 miles per hour while driving on open roads. No error
   $\overline{\text{E}}$

9. He awaited final instructions about giving the reward to whoever
   $\overline{\text{A}}$ $\overline{\text{B}}$ $\overline{\text{C}}$
   had found the lost dog. No error
   $\overline{\text{D}}$ $\overline{\text{E}}$

10. The ancient <u>concept</u> <u>where</u> the sun <u>revolves</u> around the earth was
               A     B               C

     contradicted <u>by</u> Copernicus. <u>No error</u>
             D               E

11. Reggie <u>Jackson's</u> three home runs in the final game of the 1977
              A

     World Series <u>proved</u> that <u>few</u> players in the game deserved more
                B       C

     respect than <u>him</u>. <u>No error</u>
               D     E

12. The <u>apparently</u> <u>obvious</u> solution to the problem <u>was overlooked by</u>
              A       B                         C

     <u>many</u> of the contestants. <u>No error</u>
      D                   E

13. The Senate Committee <u>investigating</u> the Watergate affair <u>was</u>
                            A                        B

     <u>surprised</u> to hear that conversations in the Oval Office <u>is being</u>
      C                                      D

     recorded on tape by order of President Nixon. <u>No error</u>
                                         E

14. <u>Without</u> a <u>moment</u> delay, the computer <u>began</u> to print out the <u>answer</u>
         A        B                         C             D

     to the problem. <u>No error</u>
                   E

15. I <u>cannot hardly</u> believe your <u>story</u>; it <u>seems</u> <u>so</u> incredible. <u>No error</u>
            A                B        C  D               E

16. Writing a beautiful <u>sonnet</u> is <u>as much</u> an achievement as <u>to finish</u> a
                      A      B                    C

     400-page novel. <u>No error</u>
       D            E

17. <u>Today's</u> program on public television <u>consisting</u> of a play and a
          A                            B

     telecast of a live performance <u>from</u> the stage of the Metropolitan
         C                      D

     Opera House. <u>No error</u>
               E

18. Of the two candidates for this government position, John is the most
    $\overline{\quad}$ A                                                          $\overline{\quad}$ B

    qualified because of his experience in the field. No error
    $\overline{\quad}$ C $\quad$ $\overline{\quad}$ D                          $\overline{\quad}$ E

19. Diligence and honesty, as well as being intelligent, are qualities which
    $\overline{\quad}$ A $\quad$ $\overline{\quad}$ B $\quad$ $\overline{\quad}$ C

    I look for when I interview applicants. No error
    $\overline{\quad}$ D                                      $\overline{\quad}$ E

20. Dashing across the campus, John tried to overtake the instructor
    $\overline{\quad}$ A $\quad$ $\overline{\quad}$ B $\quad$ $\overline{\quad}$ C

    who had forgotten his briefcase. No error
    $\overline{\quad}$ D                                   $\overline{\quad}$ E

21. Jane, Mary, and Richard play musical instruments, but only the latter
    $\overline{\quad}$ A                                                 $\overline{\quad}$ B $\quad$ $\overline{\quad}$ C $\quad$ $\overline{\quad}$ D

    has real talent. No error
    $\overline{\quad}$ E

22. Rebecca Jones is one of the nurses' aides who have been so helpful
    $\overline{\quad}$ A $\quad$ $\overline{\quad}$ B $\quad$ $\overline{\quad}$ C $\quad$ $\overline{\quad}$ D

    to the staff. No error
    $\overline{\quad}$ E

23. After he had drank the warm milk, he began to feel sleepy and
    $\overline{\quad}$ A $\quad$ $\overline{\quad}$ B                             $\overline{\quad}$ C

    decided to go to bed. No error
    $\overline{\quad}$ D                           $\overline{\quad}$ E

24. The colorful dressed natives and the strange architecture made the
    $\overline{\quad}$ A $\quad$ $\overline{\quad}$ B                                                    $\overline{\quad}$ C

    traveler realize he was now in a new world. No error
    $\overline{\quad}$ D                                                        $\overline{\quad}$ E

25. After conferring with John Brown and Mary Smith, I have decided
    $\overline{\quad}$ A

    that she is better qualified than him to edit the school newspaper.
    $\overline{\quad}$ B $\quad$ $\overline{\quad}$ C                    $\overline{\quad}$ D

    No error
    $\overline{\quad}$ E

Directions: In each of the following sentences, some part or all of the sentence is underlined. Below each sentence you will find five ways of phrasing the underlined part. Select the answer that produces the most effective sentence, one that is clear and exact, without awkwardness or ambiguity, and blacken the corresponding space on your answer sheet. In choosing answers, follow the requirements of standard written English. Choose the answer that best expresses the meaning of the original sentence.

Answer (A) is always the same as the underlined part. Choose answer (A) if you think the original sentence needs no revision.

EXAMPLE:

Laura Ingalls Wilder published her first book <u>and she was sixty-five years old then</u>.

(A)   and she was sixty-five years old then
(B)   when she was sixty-five years old
(C)   at age sixty-five years old
(D)   upon reaching sixty-five years
(E)   at the time when she was sixty-five

SAMPLE ANSWER

26.  <u>If he was to decide to go to college,</u> I, for one, would recommend that he plan to go to Yale.

(A)   If he was to decide to go to college,
(B)   If he were to decide to go to college,
(C)   Had he decided to go to college,
(D)   In the event that he decides to go to college,
(E)   Supposing he was to decide to go to college,

27.  <u>Except for you and I, everyone brought</u> a present to the party.

(A)   Except for you and I, everyone brought
(B)   With the exception of you and I, everyone brought
(C)   Except for you and I, everyone had brought
(D)   Except for you and me, everyone brought
(E)   Except for you and me, everyone had brought

28. When one reads the poetry of the 17th-century, you find a striking contrast between the philosophy of the Cavalier poets such as Suckling and the attitude of the Metaphysical poets such as Donne.

    (A) When one reads the poetry of the 17th-century, you find
    (B) When you read the poetry of the 17th-century, one finds
    (C) When one reads the poetry of the 17th-century, he finds
    (D) If one reads the poetry of the 17th-century, you find
    (E) As you read the poetry of the 17th-century, one finds

29. Because of his broken hip, John Jones <u>has not and possibly never will be able to run</u> the mile again.

    (A) has not and possibly never will be able to run
    (B) has not and possibly will never be able to run
    (C) has not been and possibly never would be able to run
    (D) has not and possibly never would be able to run
    (E) has not been able to run and possibly never will be able to run

30. <u>Had I realized how close</u> I was to failing, I would not have gone to the party.

    (A) Had I realized how close
    (B) If I would have realized how close
    (C) Had I had realized how close
    (D) When I realized how close
    (E) If I realized how close

31. Having finished the marathon in record-breaking time, <u>the city awarded him its Citizen's Outstanding Performance Medal.</u>

    (A) the city awarded him its Citizen's Outstanding Performance Medal.
    (B) the city awarded the Citizen's Outstanding Performance Medal to him.
    (C) he was awarded the Citizen's Outstanding Performance Medal by the city.
    (D) the Citizen's Outstanding Performance Medal was awarded to him.
    (E) he was awarded by the city with the Citizen's Outstanding Performance Medal.

**32.** The football team's winning it's first game of the season excited the student body.

 (A) The football team's winning it's first game of the season
 (B) The football team having won it's first game of the season
 (C) The football team's having won it's first game of the season
 (D) The football team's winning its first game of the season
 (E) The football team winning it's first game of the season

**33.** Anyone interested in the use of computers can learn much if you have access to a Radio Shack TRS-80 or a Pet Microcomputer.

 (A) if you have access to
 (B) if he has access to
 (C) if access is available to
 (D) by access to
 (E) from access to

**34.** No student had ought to be put into a situation where he has to choose between his loyalty to his friends and his duty to the class.

 (A) No student had ought to be put into a situation where
 (B) No student had ought to be put into a situation in which
 (C) No student should be put into a situation where
 (D) No student ought to be put into a situation in which
 (E) No student ought to be put into a situation where

**35.** Being a realist, I could not accept his statement that supernatural beings had caused the disturbance.

 (A) Being a realist,
 (B) Since I am a realist,
 (C) Being that I am a realist,
 (D) Being as I am a realist,
 (E) Realist that I am,

**36.** The reason I came late to class today is because the bus broke down.

 (A) I came late to class today is because
 (B) why I came late to class today is because
 (C) I was late to school today is because
 (D) that I was late to school today is because
 (E) I came late to class today is that

37. I have to make dinner, wash the dishes, do my homework, and then <u>relaxing</u>.

    (A) to make dinner, wash the dishes, do my homework, and then relaxing.
    (B) to make dinner, washing the dishes, do my homework, and then relax.
    (C) to make dinner, wash the dishes, doing my homework and then relaxing.
    (D) to prepare dinner, wash the dishes, do my homework, and then relaxing.
    (E) to make dinner, wash the dishes, do my homework and then relax.

38. The climax <u>occurs when he asks who's</u> in the closet.

    (A) occurs when he asks who's
    (B) is when he asks whose
    (C) occurs when he asks whose
    (D) is when he asks who'se
    (E) occurs when he asked who's

39. The grocer <u>hadn't hardly any of those kind</u> of canned goods.

    (A) hadn't hardly any of those kind
    (B) hadn't hardly any of those kinds
    (C) had hardly any of those kind
    (D) had hardly any of those kinds
    (E) had scarcely any of those kind

40. <u>Having stole the money, the police searched the thief.</u>

    (A) Having stole the money, the police searched the thief.
    (B) Having stolen the money, the thief was searched by the police.
    (C) Having stolen the money, the police searched the thief.
    (D) Having stole the money, the thief was searched by the police.
    (E) Being that he stole the money, the police searched the thief.

---

<u>Note</u>: The remaining questions are like those at the beginning of the section.

Directions:  For each sentence in which you find an error, select the one underlined part that must be changed to make the sentence correct and blacken the corresponding space on your answer sheet.

If there is no error, blacken answer space Ⓔ.

EXAMPLE:

The region has a climate <u>so severe that</u> plants
                              A

<u>growing there</u> rarely <u>had been</u> more than twelve inches
    B                          C

<u>high</u>. <u>No error</u>
  D      E

SAMPLE ANSWER

Ⓐ Ⓑ ● Ⓓ Ⓔ

---

**41.** Either of the two boys who <u>sing</u> in the chorus <u>are</u> capable of taking
        <u>A</u>                  <u>B</u>                      <u>C</u>

the job of <u>understudy</u> to the star. <u>No error</u>
              D                              E

**42.** By the time I <u>reached</u> the bank, the doors <u>were closed</u>; I
        <u>A</u>          B                          C

<u>could not cash</u> my check. <u>No error</u>
    D                          E

**43.** If anyone <u>calls</u> while we are in conference, tell <u>them</u> I will return the
        <u>A</u>      <u>B</u>                  <u>C</u>              <u>D</u>

call after the meeting. <u>No error</u>
                          E

**44.** The <u>principal</u> of equal justice for all <u>is</u> one of the <u>cornerstones</u> of our
            A                          B          C

<u>democratic</u> way of life. <u>No error</u>
    D                          E

**45.** <u>Except</u> for <u>you and me</u>, no one else <u>knows</u> about this plan. <u>No error</u>
        A          B  C                  D                          E

46. Neither the earthquake or the subsequent fire was able to destroy the
                 A             B       C  D
    spirit of the city dwellers. No error
                         E

47. My plane was grounded for thirty minutes, which made me miss my
               A               B        C  D
    connecting flight at Atlanta. No error
                       E

48. I might of passed if I had done my homework, but I had to go to
      A            B            C    D
    work. No error
         E

49. The customer had scarcely enough money to pay the clerk at the
        A       B    C                   D
    checkout counter. No error
                  E

50. I have lived in this house for three years, but I now live in a different
      A                             B    C
    neighborhood. No error
      D      E

---

IF YOU FINISH BEFORE TIME IS CALLED,
YOU MAY CHECK YOUR WORK ON THIS
SECTION ONLY. DO NOT WORK ON ANY    **STOP**
OTHER SECTION IN THE TEST.

# SECTION 4

### 40 Questions—30 Minutes

For each question in this section, choose the best answer and blacken the corresponding space on the answer sheet.

---

Each question below consists of a word in capital letters, followed by five lettered words or phrases. Choose the word or phrase that is most nearly <u>opposite</u> in meaning to the word in capital letters. Since some of the questions require you to distinguish fine shades of meaning, consider all the choices before deciding which is best.

Example:

GOOD: (A) sour   (B) bad   (C) red
(D) hot   (E) ugly

Ⓐ ● Ⓒ Ⓓ Ⓔ

---

1. FLEXIBLE: (A) massive   (B) unbending   (C) elderly
   (D) probable   (E) remarkable
2. AMPLIFY: (A) oppose   (B) irritate   (C) satisfy   (D) diminish
   (E) deceive
3. RECKLESS: (A) powerful   (B) unkind   (C) cautious
   (D) anonymous   (E) plentiful
4. AGITATOR: (A) lunatic   (B) peacemaker   (C) wise investor
   (D) gifted amateur   (E) accurate reporter
5. ARBITRARY: (A) beneficial   (B) popular   (C) reasonable
   (D) minute   (E) competitive
6. GULLIBLE: (A) able to succeed   (B) willing to spend
   (C) ready to listen   (D) hard to fool   (E) aiming to please
7. PROFANE: (A) act impolite   (B) ward off danger   (C) sanctify
   (D) congregate   (E) smother

8. INDIGENOUS: (A) foreign (B) unpatriotic (C) exhausted
(D) impudent (E) shallow

9. PUSILLANIMITY: (A) righteousness (B) immensity
(C) courage (D) insularity (E) prevalence

10. EVANESCENCE: (A) lack of thought (B) need for assistance
(C) innocuousness (D) permanence (E) negligence

---

Each sentence below has one or two blanks, each blank indicating
that something has been omitted. Beneath the sentence are five
lettered words or sets of words. Choose the word or set of words
that <u>best</u> fits the meaning of the sentence as a whole.

Example:

Although its publicity has been ----, the film itself is intelligent,
well-acted, handsomely produced, and altogether ----.

(A) tasteless..respectable (B) extensive..moderate
(C) sophisticated..amateur (D) risqué..crude
(E) perfect..spectacular

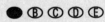

---

11. Either the Polynesian banquets at Waikiki are ----, or the one I visited
was a poor example.

(A) delicious
(B) impeccable
(C) overrated
(D) untasted
(E) unpopular

12. Lee, who refrained from excesses in his personal life, differed
markedly from Grant, who ---- notorious drinking bouts with his
cronies.

(A) deprecated
(B) minimized
(C) indulged in
(D) shunned
(E) compensated for

13. The college librarian initiated a new schedule of fines for overdue books with the ----, if not the outright encouragement, of the faculty library committee.

   (A) skepticism
   (B) acquiescence
   (C) scorn
   (D) applause
   (E) disapprobation

14. He was habitually so docile and ---- that his friends could not understand his sudden outburst against his employers.

   (A) complacent
   (B) incorrigible
   (C) truculent
   (D) erratic
   (E) hasty

15. In the absence of native predators to stop their spread, imported deer ---- to such an inordinate degree that they overgrazed the countryside and ---- the native vegetation.

   (A) thrived..threatened
   (B) propagated..cultivated
   (C) suffered..abandoned
   (D) flourished..scrutinized
   (E) dwindled..eliminated

---

Each question below consists of a related pair of words or phrases, followed by five lettered pairs of words or phrases. Select the lettered pair that best expresses a relationship similar to that expressed in the original pair.

Example:

YAWN : BOREDOM :: (A) dream : sleep
   (B) anger : madness   (C) smile : amusement
      (D) face : expression   (E) impatience : rebellion

Ⓐ Ⓑ ● Ⓓ Ⓔ

---

16. BRAKE : AUTOMOBILE :: (A) pad : helicopter   (B) ship : fleet
   (C) reins : horse   (D) helmet : motorcycle   (E) boot : saddle

17. AREA:SQUARE :: (A) diagonal:rectangle   (B) volume:cube
    (C) angle:triangle   (D) radius:circle   (E) base:cylinder

18. TALLY:VOTES :: (A) census:population   (B) taxation:revenue
    (C) government:laws   (D) team:athletes
    (E) election:candidates

19. TERMITE:WOOD :: (A) moth:wool   (B) silkworm:silk
    (C) oyster:shell   (D) anthracite:coal   (E) terrace:stone

20. CEASE-FIRE:HOSTILITIES :: (A) alimony:divorce
    (B) battery:missiles   (C) lull:storm   (D) bonfire:kindling
    (E) apology:insult

21. COLLEAGUES:PROFESSION :: (A) kinsfolk:family
    (B) spectators:game   (C) exiles:country   (D) rivals:team
    (E) passengers:subway

22. INTEREST:USURY :: (A) concern:disregard   (B) thrift:prodigality
    (C) debit:credit   (D) frugality:parsimony   (E) pleasure:utility

23. CACOPHONY:EAR :: (A) calligraphy:eye   (B) piquancy:taste
    (C) stench:nose   (D) tracheotomy:throat   (E) retina:eye

24. EULOGY:PRAISE :: (A) elegy:death   (B) slander:disparagement
    (C) paean:anger   (D) reproof:confirmation   (E) satire:vanity

25. EMBROIL:STRIFE :: (A) chafe:restriction   (B) embarrass:pride
    (C) emulate:model   (D) annul:marriage   (E) imperil:danger

---

Each passage below is followed by questions based on its content.
Answer all questions following a passage on the basis of what is
<u>stated</u> or <u>implied</u> in that passage.

---

It is no secret that I am not one of those naturalists who
suffer from cities, or affect to do so, nor do I find a city unnatural or
uninteresting, or a rubbish heap of follies. It has always seemed to me
there is something more than mechanically admirable about a train
that arrives on time, a fire department that comes when you call it, a
light that leaps into the room at a touch, and a clinic that will fight for
the health of a penniless man and mass for him the agencies of mercy,
the X-ray, the precious radium, the anesthetics and the surgical skill.
For, beyond any pay these services receive, stands out the pride in

perfect performance. And above all, I admire the noble impersonality of civilization that does not inquire where the recipient stands on religion or politics or race. I call this beauty, and I call it spirit—not some mystical soulfulness that nobody can define, but the spirit of man, that has been a million years a-growing.

26. The tone of the author can best be described as

    (A) impersonal    (B) humble    (C) tolerant
       (D) assertive    (E) mystical

27. The author's primary purpose in this passage is to

    (A) defend cities against their detractors
    (B) expose the deficiency of free urban services
    (C) question the affectations of other naturalists
    (D) explore the influence of mysticism on city life
    (E) compare the advantages of urban and rural life

28. The aspect of city life most commendable to this author is its

    (A) punctuality
    (B) free benefits
    (C) impartial service
    (D) mechanical improvement
    (E) health clinics

29. The author implies that efficient operation of public utilities is

    (A) needlessly expensive
    (B) of no special interest
    (C) admired by most naturalists
    (D) mechanically commendable
    (E) spiritual in quality

      Scattered around the globe are more than 100 small regions of isolated volcanic activity known to geologists as hot spots. Unlike most of the world's volcanoes, they are not always found at the boundaries of the great drifting plates that make up the earth's surface; on the contrary, many of them lie deep in the interior of a plate. Most of the hot spots move only slowly, and in some cases the movement of the plates past them has left trails of extinct volcanoes. The hot spots and their volcanic trails are milestones that mark the passage of the plates.

That the plates are moving is now beyond dispute. Africa and South America, for example, are receding from each other as new material is injected into the sea floor between them. The complementary coastlines and certain geological features that seem to span the ocean are reminders of where the two continents were once joined. The relative motion of the plates carrying these continents has been constructed in detail, but the motion of one plate with respect to another cannot readily be translated into motion with respect to the earth's interior. It is not possible to determine whether both continents are moving (in opposite directions) or whether one continent is stationary and the other is drifting away from it. Hot spots, anchored in the deeper layers of the earth, provide the measuring instruments needed to resolve the question. From an analysis of the hot-spot population it appears that the African plate is stationary and that it has not moved during the past 30 million years.

The significance of hot spots is not confined to their role as a frame of reference. It now appears that they also have an important influence on the geophysical processes that propel the plates across the globe. When a continental plate comes to rest over a hot spot, the material welling up from deeper layers creates a broad dome. As the dome grows it develops deep fissures; in at least a few cases the continent may rupture entirely along some of these fissures, so that the hot spot initiates the formation of a new ocean. Thus just as earlier theories have explained the mobility of the continents, so hot spots may explain their mutability.

**30.** According to the passage, which of the following statements indicate that Africa and South America once adjoined one another?

 I. They share certain common topographic traits.
 II. Their shorelines are physical counterparts.
 III. The African plate has been stable for 30 million years.

 (A) I only　(B) II only　(C) I and II only
 (D) II and III only　(E) I, II, and III

31. According to the passage, the hot spot theory eventually may prove useful in interpreting

   (A) the boundaries of the plates
   (B) the depth of the ocean floor
   (C) the relative motion of the plates
   (D) current instruments of measurement
   (E) major changes in continental shape

32. The author regards the theory of plate movement as

   (A) controversial
   (B) irrefutable
   (C) tangential
   (D) dubious
   (E) unwarranted

Certitude is not the test of certainty. We have been cocksure of many things that were not so. If I may quote myself again, property, friendship, and truth have a common
Line root in time. One cannot be wrenched from the rocky crevices
(5) into which one has grown for many years without feeling that one is attacked in one's life. What we most love and revere generally is determined by early associations. I love granite rocks and barberry bushes, no doubt because with them were my earliest joys that reach back through the past eternity of
(10) my life. But while one's experience thus makes certain preferences dogmatic for oneself, recognition of how they came to be so leaves one able to see that others, poor souls, may be equally dogmatic about something else. And this again means skepticism. Not that one's belief or love does not
(15) remain. Not that we would not fight and die for it if important—we all, whether we know it or not, are fighting to make the kind of world that we should like—but that we have learned to recognize that others will fight and die to make a different world, with equal sincerity of belief. Deep-seated
(20) preferences cannot be argued about—you cannot argue a man into liking a glass of beer—and therefore, when differences are sufficiently far-reaching, we try to kill the other man rather than let him have his way. But that is perfectly consistent with admitting that, so far as appears, his grounds are just as good
(25) as ours.

33. With which of the following statements would the author be most likely to agree?

    I. The degree of assurance we feel about an issue is directly proportional to the truth of that issue.

    II. Early associations determine later preferences to a considerable degree.

    III. Knowing why we have certain preferences destroys our faith in their worth.

        (A) I only    (B) II only    (C) III only
        (D) I and II    (E) II and III

34. The author uses the phrase "wrenched from the rocky crevices into which one has grown" (lines 4–5) to describe disturbing

    (A) trenches in wartime
    (B) grave sites
    (C) fixed preferences
    (D) belief in an afterlife
    (E) barberry leaves

35. The reference to the glass of beer (line 21) is introduced primarily to

    (A) make an abstract assertion concrete
    (B) introduce a note of impatience
    (C) illustrate the power of alcohol
    (D) demonstrate the author's preferences
    (E) weaken the argument for skepticism

      Of the poetry of the United States different opinions have been entertained, and prejudice on the one side, and partiality on the other, have equally prevented a just and rational
*Line* estimate of its merits. Abroad, our literature has fallen under
(5) unmerited contumely from those who were but slenderly acquainted with the subject on which they professed to decide; and at home, it must be confessed that the swaggering and pompous pretensions of many have done not a little to provoke and excuse the ridicule of foreigners. Either of these
(10) extremes exerts an injurious influence on the cause of letters in our country. To encourage exertion and embolden merit to come forward, it is necessary that they should be acknowledged and rewarded—few will have the confidence to solicit what has been withheld from claims as strong as theirs,

*(15)* or the courage to tread a path which presents no prospect but
the melancholy wrecks who have gone before them. National
gratitude—national pride—every high and generous feeling
that attaches us to the land of our birth, or that exalts our
character as individuals, ask of us that we should foster the
*(20)* infant literature of our country, and that genius and industry,
employing their efforts to hasten its perfection, should receive
from our hands, that celebrity which reflects as much honor on
the nation which confers it as on those to whom it is
extended. On the other hand, it is not necessary for these
*(25)* purposes, it is even detrimental to bestow on mediocrity the
praise due to excellence, and still more so is the attempt to
persuade ourselves and others into an admiration of the faults
of favorite writers. We make but a contemptible figure in the
eyes of the world, and set ourselves up as objects of pity to
*(30)* our posterity, when we affect to rank the poets of our own
country with those mighty masters of song who have
flourished in Greece, Italy and Britain.

**36.** The author's main purpose in writing this passage is to

    (A) assert the greatness of our poetry
    (B) answer foreign critics who sneer at American literature
    (C) deplore the lack of good writing in this country
    (D) discuss the need for encouraging our writers appropriately
    (E) deplore the extravagant claims made on behalf of American
        authors

**37.** By the phrase "the melancholy wrecks who have gone before them"
(line 16), the author of the passage most probably means

    (A) shipwrecked vessels on transatlantic crossings
    (B) damaged national pride
    (C) underappreciated authors of previous generations
    (D) Greek, Italian, and British masters of song
    (E) writers of elegies, odes, and laments

38. The author would most likely agree with all of the following statements
EXCEPT

   (A) American literature is less mature than its European counterpart.
   (B) Foreign critics possess a wide knowledge of American verse.
   (C) It is both pretentious and self-defeating to overrate minor poets.
   (D) Americans need to create a literary climate that nourishes artists.
   (E) Many gifted poets languish in undeserved obscurity.

39. The author's attitude toward the state of American poetry is primarily
one of

   (A) fascinated curiosity
   (B) bitter disillusionment
   (C) pretended indifference
   (D) passionate chauvinism
   (E) measured enthusiasm

40. As used in line 5, "contumely" most likely means

   (A) praise
   (B) evaluation
   (C) rudeness
   (D) domination
   (E) publication

IF YOU FINISH BEFORE TIME IS
CALLED, YOU MAY CHECK YOUR
WORK ON THIS SECTION ONLY. DO
NOT WORK ON ANY OTHER SECTION
IN THE TEST.

**STOP**

# SECTION 5

## 35 Questions—30 Minutes

Directions: In this section solve each problem, using any available space on the page for scratchwork. Then decide which is the best of the choices given and blacken the corresponding space on the answer sheet.

The following information is for your reference in solving some of the problems.

Circle of radius $r$:

Area $= \pi r^2$;

Circumference $= 2\pi r$

The number of degrees of arc in a circle is 360.

The measure in degrees of a straight angle is 180.

Triangle: The sum of the measures in degrees of the angles of a triangle is 180.

If $\angle CDA$ is a right angle, then

(1) area of $\triangle ABC =$
$$\frac{AB \times CD}{2}$$

(2) $AC^2 = AD^2 + DC^2$

Definitions of symbols:

| | |
|---|---|
| $=$ is equal to | $\leq$ is less than or equal to |
| $\neq$ is unequal to | $\geq$ is greater than or equal to |
| $<$ is less than | $\parallel$ is parallel to |
| $>$ is greater than | $\perp$ is perpendicular to |

Note: Figures that accompany problems in this test are intended to provide information useful in solving the problems. They are drawn as accurately as possible EXCEPT when it is stated in a specific problem that its figure is not drawn to scale. All figures lie in a plane unless otherwise indicated. All numbers used are real numbers.

1. An architect uses a scale of $\frac{1}{4}$ inch to a foot. If the dimensions of a room as represented on the plans of a house are $4\frac{1}{4}$ inches by $3\frac{3}{4}$ inches, the actual dimensions in feet are

   (A) $8\frac{1}{2} \times 9\frac{1}{2}$
   (B) $17 \times 15$
   (C) $34 \times 30$
   (D) $51 \times 45$
   (E) $68 \times 60$

2. What was the grade a student received on his first examination if the grades on his other examinations were 50%, 70%, and 90%, and his average on the four was 75%?

   (A) 60
   (B) 65
   (C) 75
   (D) 80
   (E) 90

3. Four equal circles of diameter one foot touch at four points as shown in the figure below. What is the area of the shaded portion (in feet)?

   (A) $1 - \frac{\pi}{4}$
   (B) $1 - \pi$
   (C) $1 - 4\pi$
   (D) $\pi$
   (E) $\frac{\pi}{4}$

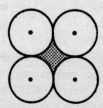

**4.** If $4y - x - 10 = 0$ and $3x = 2y$, then $xy =$

(A) $\dfrac{2}{3}$

(B) 1

(C) $1\dfrac{1}{3}$

(D) 5

(E) 6

---

**5.** A train traveling 30 miles per hour for 2 hours covers the same distance as a train traveling 60 miles per hour for how many hours?

(A) $\dfrac{1}{3}$

(B) $\dfrac{1}{2}$

(C) 1

(D) 2

(E) 3

---

**6.** A man works $a$ times as fast as any one of his helpers. If the man does a job in $h$ hours, how many hours are required for $w$ helpers to do the job?

(A) $\dfrac{ah}{w}$

(B) $\dfrac{aw}{h}$

(C) $\dfrac{w}{ah}$

(D) $awh$

(E) $\dfrac{a}{wh}$

---

**7.** If $x = 2z + 3$ and $y = 4z^2$, what is the value of $y$ in terms of $x$?

(A) $x + 3$

(B) $\dfrac{(x + 3)^2}{4}$

(C) $\dfrac{(x - 3)^2}{4}$

(D) $(x - 3)^2$

(E) $2(x - 3)^2$

---

Questions 8-27 each consist of two quantities, one in Column A and one in Column B. You are to compare the two quantities and on the answer sheet blacken space

A if the quantity in Column A is greater;

B if the quantity in Column B is greater;

C if the two quantities are equal;

D if the relationship cannot be determined from the information given.

**AN E RESPONSE WILL NOT BE SCORED.**

---

Notes:

1. In certain questions, information concerning one or both of the quantities to be compared is centered above the two columns.

2. In a given question, a symbol that appears in both columns represents the same thing in Column A as it does in Column B.

3. Letters such as $x$, $n$, and $k$ stand for real numbers.

| | EXAMPLES | | Answers |
|---|---|---|---|
| | Column A | Column B | |
| E1. | $2 \times 6$ | $2 + 6$ | ● Ⓑ Ⓒ Ⓓ Ⓔ |
| E2. | $x°$ $y°$ $180 - x$ | $y$ | Ⓐ Ⓑ ● Ⓓ Ⓔ |
| E3. | $p - q$ | $q - p$ | Ⓐ Ⓑ Ⓒ ● Ⓔ |

| | Column A | Column B |
|---|---|---|
| **8.** | 105% of 25 | 26 |

$$\frac{48}{x} = 4$$

| | Column A | Column B |
|---|---|---|
| **9.** | 16⅔% of 72 | $x$ |

| | Column A | Column B |
|---|---|---|
| **10.** | $\left(\dfrac{1}{3}\right)^2$ | $\left(\dfrac{1}{2}\right)^2$ |

$$a > b$$
$$c < b$$

| | Column A | Column B |
|---|---|---|
| **11.** | $b$ | 0 |

|  | Column A | Column B |
|---|---|---|

$$x = -y$$

**12.** $\quad x + y \qquad\qquad\qquad\qquad 0$

---

**13.** The time required to cover $\frac{1}{2}$ mile traveling at 20 miles per hour

The time required to cover $\frac{1}{3}$ mile traveling at 30 miles per hour

---

**14.** The number of revolutions made by the wheel of a bicycle (diameter of $\frac{7}{\pi}$ feet) covering a distance of 70 feet

The number of revolutions made by the wheel of a motorcycle (diameter of $\frac{10}{\pi}$ feet) covering a distance of 100 feet

---

$$X + Y + Z = 350$$
$$X + Y = 100$$

**15.** $\qquad\qquad Z \qquad\qquad\qquad\qquad\qquad X$

---

Distance from $X$ to $Y$ = 3 miles
Distance from $Y$ to $Z$ = 2 miles

**16.** Distance from $X$ to $Z \qquad\qquad$ Distance from $X$ to $Y$

---

$$9x^2 = y$$

**17.** $\qquad\qquad x \qquad\qquad\qquad\qquad\qquad y$

---

| Column A | Column B |
|----------|----------|

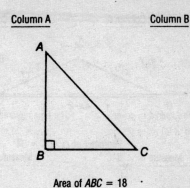

Area of *ABC* = 18

**18.**  *AB*  ⟂  *BC*

---

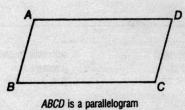

*ABCD* is a parallelogram

**19.**  *AD* + *BC*  |  *AB* + *DC*

---

**20.**  $\dfrac{2}{\sqrt{2}}$  |  $\sqrt{2}$

---

**21.**  Ratio of $\dfrac{1}{2}$ to $\dfrac{1}{3}$  |  Ratio of $\dfrac{1}{3}$ to $\dfrac{1}{2}$

---

**22.**  *x*  |  $\dfrac{2x + 1}{2}$

---

Column A                               Column B

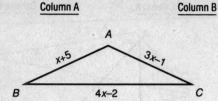

Perimeter of △ ABC = 34

23.     Measure of ∠ BAC              Measure of ∠ ABC

---

$$9x^2 = y$$

24.              x                              y

---

25. arithmetic mean              arithmetic mean
    (average) of                   (average) of
    2, 3, x                        3, 4, x

---

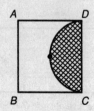

ABCD is a square and the shaded
area is a semicircle.

26. Ratio of the shaded area to the          $\dfrac{\pi}{8}$
    area of the square

---

Column A                              Column B

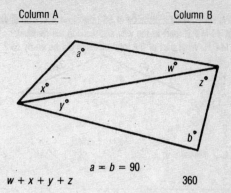

$a = b = 90$

27.        $w + x + y + z$                    360

---

Solve each of the remaining problems in this section using any available space for scratchwork. Then decide which is the best of the choices given and blacken the corresponding space on the answer sheet.

---

28. How many 5-gallon cans of milk will be needed to fill 120 pint bottles?

   (A) 3
   (B) 6
   (C) 9
   (D) 12
   (E) 24

---

29. In the figure below, the area of circle $O = 9\pi$. What is the area of ABCD?

   (A) 24
   (B) 30
   (C) 35
   (D) 36
   (E) 48

**30.** Mr. Walker covered a distance of 55 miles in 4 hours by driving his car at 40 M.P.H. part of the way and walking the remainder of the way at 5 M.P.H. What part of the total distance did he go by car?

(A) $\dfrac{3}{11}$

(B) $\dfrac{8}{11}$

(C) $\dfrac{1}{8}$

(D) $\dfrac{3}{8}$

(E) $\dfrac{1}{3}$

**31.** At a masquerade party the judges eliminate $\dfrac{1}{4}$ of the eligible contestants after each half hour. If 256 contestants were present at the party, how many would still be eligible for a prize after two hours?

(A) 0

(B) 16

(C) 32

(D) 64

(E) 81

**32.** A man owned $\dfrac{5}{8}$ of an interest in a house. He sold $\dfrac{1}{5}$ of his interest, at cost, for $1000. What is the total value of the house?

(A) $3000

(B) $5000

(C) $6000

(D) $8000

(E) $9000

33. A salesman sold a book at 105% of the marked price instead of
discounting the marked price by 5%. If he sold the book for $4.20,
what was the price for which he should have sold the book?

    (A) $3.40
    (B) $3.80
    (C) $4.20
    (D) $4.40
    (E) $4.60

34. After several tryouts 20% of a football squad was discharged. The
coach then had 32 players. How many players were on the squad at
first?

    (A) 24
    (B) 26
    (C) 39
    (D) 40
    (E) 80

35. If the sum of a set of odd integers is exactly zero, which of the
following would always be true?

    I. The product of integers in the set is zero.
    II. The average of the set is zero.
    III. The number of integers in the set is an even number.

    (A) I only    (B) II only    (C) I and II only    (D) II and III only
    (E) I, II, and III

IF YOU FINISH BEFORE TIME IS
CALLED, YOU MAY CHECK YOUR
WORK ON THIS SECTION ONLY. DO          **STOP**
NOT WORK ON ANY OTHER SECTION
IN THE TEST.

## SECTION 6

### 25 Questions—30 Minutes

---

Directions: In this section solve each problem, using any available space on the page for scratchwork. Then decide which is the best of the choices given and blacken the corresponding space on the answer sheet.

The following information is for your reference in solving some of the problems.

Circle of radius $r$:
Area $= \pi r^2$;
Circumference $= 2\pi r$
   The number of degrees of arc in a circle is 360.
   The measure in degrees of a straight angle is 180.

Triangle: The sum of the measures in degrees of the angles of a triangle is 180.

If $\angle CDA$ is a right angle, then

(1) area of $\triangle ABC = \dfrac{AB \times CD}{2}$

(2) $AC^2 = AD^2 + DC^2$

Definitions of symbols:

| | |
|---|---|
| $=$ is equal to | $\leq$ is less than or equal to |
| $\neq$ is unequal to | $\geq$ is greater than or equal to |
| $<$ is less than | $\parallel$ is parallel to |
| $>$ is greater than | $\perp$ is perpendicular to |

Note: Figures that accompany problems in this test are intended to provide information useful in solving the problems. They are drawn as accurately as possible EXCEPT when it is stated in a specific problem that its figure is not drawn to scale. All figures lie in a plane unless otherwise indicated. All numbers used are real numbers.

1. Of 25 tulip bulbs that are planted each year, from 20 to 22 produce flowers each year. What is the maximum percentage of flowers produced in any one year?

   (A) 12
   (B) 20
   (C) 22
   (D) 80
   (E) 88

---

2. $\frac{a}{b} = c$; $b = c$; $b =$

   (A) $\frac{a}{2}$
   (B) $\sqrt{a}$
   (C) $a$
   (D) $2a$
   (E) $a^2$

---

3. John and James painted a barn for $100. If John worked 8 days and James worked 12 days, how much should James receive for his work?

   (A) $32
   (B) $40
   (C) $60
   (D) $75
   (E) $80

---

4. If each of a man's three sons works one eighth as fast as he does, and the man does a job in three hours, how many hours does it take his sons working together to do the job?

   (A) 5
   (B) 6
   (C) 7
   (D) 8
   (E) 9

5. A chicken farmer has 750 eggs. Four percent of the eggs are cracked and 5% of the remainder are found to be defective after candling. How many eggs can he sell on the market?

(A) 300
(B) 450
(C) 675
(D) 684
(E) 720

6. The area of the shaded portion below is

(A) $2r^2(4 - \pi)$
(B) $2r^2(2 - 2\pi)$
(C) $2r^2(\pi - 4)$
(D) $2r^2(\pi - 2)$
(E) $r^2(2 - \pi)$

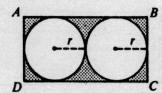

7. A department store offers a typewriter for $72 instead of the list price of $90. What is the rate of discount for this item?

(A) 2%
(B) 5%
(C) 18%
(D) 20%
(E) 25%

8. A man left $5,000.00 to his three sons. For every dollar Abraham received, Benjamin received $1.50 and Charles received $2.50. How much money was left to Benjamin?

(A) $750
(B) $1000
(C) $1100
(D) $1500
(E) $3000

9. The El Capitan of the Santa Fe travels a distance of 152.5 miles from La Junta to Garden City in two hours. What is the average speed in M.P.H.?

   (A) 15.25
   (B) 31.5
   (C) 30.5
   (D) 71
   (E) 76.3

10. A man travels for 5 hours at an average rate of 40 M.P.H. He develops some motor trouble and returns to his original starting point in 10 hours. What was his average rate, in miles per hour, on the return trip?

    (A) 10
    (B) 15
    (C) 20
    (D) 26.6
    (E) 40

11. How many square units are there in the shaded triangle below?

    (A) 4
    (B) 6
    (C) 8
    (D) 9
    (E) 12

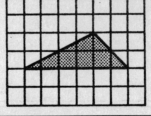

12. In the figure below, if $AE \perp ED$, $CD \perp ED$, and $DC \perp CB$, then $AB =$

    (A) 8
    (B) 13
    (C) 14
    (D) 15
    (E) 17

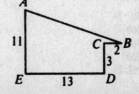

**13.** If a carload contains from 12 to 18 crates, what is the least number of crates contained in 4 carloads?

    (A)  24
    (B)  36
    (C)  48
    (D)  60
    (E)  72

---

**14.** Of the values 45.9, 49.5, 59.4, and $x$ (where $x$ is more than 45), which of the following CANNOT possibly be the average?

    (A)  45
    (B)  55
    (C)  56
    (D)  550
    (E)  555

---

**15.** What is the length of the line segment joining the points whose coordinates are $(-2, -7)$ and $(6, 8)$?

    (A)  4
    (B)  5
    (C)  $7\frac{1}{2}$
    (D)  $8\frac{1}{2}$
    (E)  17

---

**16.** A line segment has one endpoint at $(3, -2)$, and its midpoint at $(2, -5)$. The coordinates of the other endpoint of the line segment are

    (A)  $(1, -8)$
    (B)  $(5, -7)$
    (C)  $(1, -3)$
    (D)  $(1, 8)$
    (E)  $(-1, 8)$

---

**17.** The locus of points 2 inches from a given line and 3 inches from a point on that line is exactly

(A) 1 point
(B) 2 points
(C) 3 points
(D) 4 points
(E) 5 points

---

**18.** Which of the following is greater than $\frac{1}{4}$?

(A) 0.04
(B) $\left(\frac{1}{4}\right)^2$
(C) $\frac{1}{0.04}$
(D) $(0.04)^2$
(E) none of these

---

**19.** If  is defined as $ad - bc$ and

$$\begin{array}{|cc|} a & b \\ d & c \end{array} - x = 0, \text{ then } x =$$

(A) $ad - ac$
(B) $bc + ad$
(C) $-bc$
(D) $bc - ad$
(E) $ad - bc$

---

**20.** If $\frac{3}{4} + \frac{5}{n} = \frac{19}{12}$, then $n =$

(A) 4
(B) 6
(C) 8
(D) 10
(E) 12

**21.** $2.4 \sqrt{\dfrac{x^4 y^2}{16} + \dfrac{y^2 x^4}{9}} =$

    (A) $xy$

    (B) $xy^2$

    (C) $x^2 y$

    (D) $x\sqrt{y}$

    (E) $y\sqrt{x}$

---

**22.** How long is the shadow of a 35-foot tree, if a 98-foot tree casts a 42-foot shadow at the same time?

    (A) 8

    (B) 9

    (C) 12

    (D) 13

    (E) 15

---

**23.** The square below is divided into 9 equal smaller squares. If the perimeter of the large square is 4, then the perimeter of a small square is

    (A) $\dfrac{1}{3}$

    (B) $\dfrac{1}{4}$

    (C) $\dfrac{4}{3}$

    (D) $\dfrac{9}{4}$

    (E) $\dfrac{4}{9}$

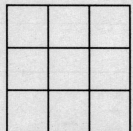

---

**24.** If the area of rectangle $R$ with altitude 4 feet is equal to the area of square $S$, which has a perimeter of 24 feet, then the perimeter of rectangle $R$ equals

(A)  9 feet
(B)  16 feet
(C)  24 feet
(D)  26 feet
(E)  36 feet

---

**25.** In an egg box with a dozen eggs, some are white and some are brown eggs. Each of the following could be the ratio of white eggs to brown eggs EXCEPT

(A)  1:1
(B)  2:1
(C)  3:1
(D)  5:1
(E)  10:1

IF YOU FINISH BEFORE TIME IS
CALLED, YOU MAY CHECK YOUR
WORK ON THIS SECTION ONLY. DO      **STOP**
NOT WORK ON ANY OTHER SECTION
IN THE TEST.

## Answer Key

### Section 1 Verbal

| | | | | | | | | | |
|---|---|---|---|---|---|---|---|---|---|
| 1. B | 10. D | 19. B | 28. B | 37. B |
| 2. A | 11. B | 20. B | 29. D | 38. B |
| 3. C | 12. D | 21. A | 30. A | 39. C |
| 4. B | 13. E | 22. B | 31. B | 40. B |
| 5. A | 14. A | 23. E | 32. D | 41. A |
| 6. C | 15. C | 24. A | 33. B | 42. C |
| 7. B | 16. E | 25. A | 34. C | 43. C |
| 8. E | 17. A | 26. B | 35. C | 44. A |
| 9. C | 18. E | 27. D | 36. E | 45. C |

### Section 2 Math

| | | | | |
|---|---|---|---|---|
| 1. C | 6. A | 11. C | 16. B | 21. D |
| 2. A | 7. D | 12. C | 17. B | 22. D |
| 3. E | 8. A | 13. C | 18. A | 23. B |
| 4. D | 9. B | 14. A | 19. D | 24. A |
| 5. A | 10. B | 15. C | 20. D | 25. D |

### Section 3 Test of Standard Written English

| | | | | |
|---|---|---|---|---|
| 1. D | 11. D | 21. D | 31. C | 41. C |
| 2. C | 12. E | 22. E | 32. D | 42. C |
| 3. C | 13. D | 23. B | 33. B | 43. D |
| 4. C | 14. B | 24. A | 34. D | 44. A |
| 5. D | 15. A | 25. D | 35. A | 45. E |
| 6. E | 16. C | 26. B | 36. E | 46. A |
| 7. B | 17. B | 27. D | 37. E | 47. B |
| 8. B | 18. B | 28. C | 38. A | 48. A |
| 9. E | 19. B | 29. E | 39. D | 49. E |
| 10. B | 20. E | 30. A | 40. B | 50. A |

**Section 4 Verbal**

| | | | | |
|---|---|---|---|---|
| 1. B | 9. C | 17. B | 25. E | 33. B |
| 2. D | 10. D | 18. A | 26. D | 34. C |
| 3. C | 11. C | 19. A | 27. A | 35. A |
| 4. B | 12. C | 20. C | 28. C | 36. D |
| 5. C | 13. B | 21. A | 29. E | 37. C |
| 6. D | 14. A | 22. D | 30. C | 38. B |
| 7. C | 15. A | 23. C | 31. E | 39. E |
| 8. A | 16. C | 24. B | 32. D | 40. C |

**Section 5 Math**

| | | | | |
|---|---|---|---|---|
| 1. B | 8. A | 15. D | 22. B | 29. D |
| 2. E | 9. C | 16. D | 23. A | 30. B |
| 3. A | 10. B | 17. D | 24. D | 31. E |
| 4. E | 11. D | 18. D | 25. B | 32. D |
| 5. C | 12. C | 19. D | 26. C | 33. B |
| 6. A | 13. A | 20. C | 27. B | 34. D |
| 7. D | 14. C | 21. A | 28. A | 35. D |

**Section 6 Math**

| | | | | |
|---|---|---|---|---|
| 1. E | 6. A | 11. B | 16. A | 21. C |
| 2. B | 7. D | 12. E | 17. D | 22. E |
| 3. C | 8. D | 13. C | 18. C | 23. C |
| 4. D | 9. E | 14. A | 19. E | 24. D |
| 5. D | 10. C | 15. E | 20. B | 25. E |

## Answer Explanations

### Section 1 Verbal

1. **(B)** To *flourish* is to flower or to increase in prosperity. Its opposite is to *waste away* or decay.
   Context Clue: Think of "a flourishing community."

2. **(A)** To *tolerate* something is to endure or bear it. The opposite of *tolerate* is to *refuse to bear*.
   Context Clue: "How can she tolerate such behavior?"

3. **(C)** To *enhance* something is to advance or increase it. Its opposite is to *detract*.
   Context Clue: Think of "enhancing your self-image."

4. **(B)** *Spirited* means lively, full of spirit. Its opposite is *unanimated*, lacking life.
   Context Clue: Think of "a spirited performance."

5. **(A)** *Hefty* means big and burly. Its opposite is *frail* (slight; delicate).
   Context Clue: Think of "a hefty truck driver."

6. **(C)** *Purify* means to cleanse or make pure. Its opposite is *pollute*.
   Context Clue: Think of "purifying the atmosphere."

7. **(B)** *Sage* means perceptive and wise. Its opposite is *foolish*.
   Context Clue: Think of "sage advice."

8. **(E)** To *enact* is to make something into law. The opposite of enact is *repeal*. When you repeal a law, you revoke it or take it back.
   Context Clue: "The Senate enacts legislation."

9. **(C)** To *dismantle* is to remove coverings or equipment. The opposite of dismantle is *equip*.
   Context Clue: Think of "dismantling the sound system after a concert."

10. **(D)** *Clemency* is leniency or mercy. The opposite of *clemency* is a *lack of mercy*.
    Context Clue: "The prisoner asked the judge for clemency."

11. **(B)** To *mitigate* is to lessen in intensity or make less severe; its opposite is to *worsen*.
    Context Clue: Think of "mitigating the pain."

12. **(D)** *Surreptitious* means secret; done by stealth. Its opposite is *open* or *aboveboard*.
    Context Clue: "He glanced surreptitiously at his classmate's paper."

13. **(E)** *Corpulence* is largeness or bulkiness of body; excessive fatness. Its opposite is *slenderness*.
    Context Clue: Think of "fighting a tendency to corpulence."

14. **(A)** *Meticulous* means painstaking; very careful. Its opposite is sloppy or careless.
    Context Clue: "She did a meticulous job."

**15. (C)** A *proclivity* is a leaning toward or inclination to something. Its opposite is *lack of inclination*.

Context Clue: Think of "a proclivity for driving fast cars."

**16. (E)** Tiffany's works of art have survived in spite of their *fragility* (tendency to break).

Remember to watch for signal words that link one part of the sentence to another. The use of "despite" in the opening phrase sets up a contrast. *Despite* signals you that Tiffany's glass works were unlikely candidates to survive for several decades.

(Contrast Signal)

**17. (A)** Voles are similar to mice; however, they are also different from them, and may be *distinguished from* them.

Note how the use of "although" in the opening phrase sets up the basic contrast here.

(Contrast Signal)

**18. (E)** Feeling that a job was *pointless* might well lead you to perform it in a *perfunctory* (indifferent or mechanical) manner.

Remember, watch for signal words that link one part of the sentence to another. The use of "because" in the opening clause is a cause signal.

(Cause and Effect Signal)

**19. (B)** To acquire a taste for something, you must originally not have that taste or even *dislike* it; you acquire the taste by growing to like or *welcome* it.

Note how the second clause of the sentence serves to clarify what is meant by the term "acquired taste."

(Examples)

**20. (B)** The doctor's words are *disheartening* (discouraging); logically, the family should lose hope. Instead, they cling to the hope of a *remission* (lessening of the symptoms of a disease).

Note how the use of "although" sets up the contrast.

(Contrast Signal)

**21. (A)** The opening paragraph, with its talk of clearly marked outlines and contrasts "between suffering and joy," and the concluding sentence, with its mentions of "violent contrasts" and "the perpetual oscillation between despair and joy" emphasize the author's main idea: the Middle Ages were marked by extremes.

Choice B is incorrect. Though the author depicts aspects of the lives of the very rich and the very poor, he does not stress the notion that their styles complemented one another.

Choice C is incorrect. The author's concern is for the Middle Ages, not for the twentieth century.

Choices D and E are incorrect. They are unsupported by the text.

Remember, when asked to find the main idea, be sure to check the opening and summary sentences of each paragraph.

(Main Idea)

22. **(B)** The cloaking of minor activities (journeys, visits, etc.) with forms (line 7) "raised them to the dignity of a ritual"; in other words, the forms (fixed or formal ways of doing things) made the acts more dignified.

Choices A, C, D, and E are incorrect. They are not supported by the passage.

Remember, when asked about specific details in the passage, spot key words in the question and scan the passage to find them (or their synonyms).

Key Word: formalities.

(Specific Details)

23. **(E)** In cataloging the extremes of medieval life, the author in no way suggests the Middle Ages were *boring*.

Choice A is incorrect. The author suggests the Middle Ages were harsh and bleak; he portrays them as cold and miserable.

Choice B is incorrect. The author portrays the Middle Ages as festive and joyful; he says they were filled with vivid pleasures and proud celebrations.

Choice C is incorrect. The author portrays the Middle Ages as filled with ceremony and ritual.

Choice D is incorrect. The author portrays the Middle Ages as passionate and turbulent; he mentions the "tone of excitement and of passion" in everyday life.

(Specific Details)

24. **(A)** The last sentence of the third paragraph states that the lofty churches, the houses of worship, towered above the town. The churches always "remained dominant."

When asked about specific details, spot the key words in the question and scan the passage to find them (or their variants).

Key Words: above, towered.

(Specific Details)

25. **(A)** The linking of "formulae" with "ceremonies" (formal series of acts) and "benedictions" (words of blessing) suggests that these formulae are most likely *set forms of words for rituals.*

Note how the use of the colon suggests that all three words that follow are examples of "formalities."

(Word from Context)

26. **(B)** The opening lines indicate that the narrator is reflecting on his feelings. Throughout the passage he uses words like "miserable," "ashamed," and "discontented" to describe his emotional state.

Choice A is incorrect. The narrator does not analyze or dissect a change in attitude; he describes a continuing attitude.

Choice C is incorrect. The passage gives an example of emotional self-awareness, not of political consciousness.

Choice D is incorrect. The narrator condemns rather than defends the longings that brought him discontentment.

Choice E is incorrect. The narrator criticizes himself, not young people in general.

(Main Idea)

27. **(D)** The references to the forge and the anvil support Choice D. None of the other choices are suggested by the passage.

Remember, when asked to make inferences, base your answers on what the passage implies, not what it states directly.

(Inference)

28. **(B)** Note the adjectives used to describe Joe: "faithful," "industrious," "kind." These are virtues, and Joe is fundamentally virtuous.

Choice A is incorrect. Joe is plain and hardworking, not eminent and distinguished.

Choice C is incorrect. The passage portrays not Joe but the narrator as desiring to be independent.

Choice D is incorrect. It is unsupported by the passage.

Choice E is incorrect. The narrator thinks his life is coarse; he thinks Joe is virtuous.

(Specific Details)

29. **(D)** In the last two sentences of the fourth paragraph the narrator manages to say something good about his youthful self: "I am glad to know I never breathed a murmur to Joe." He gives himself credit for concealing his despondency.

Choices A and B are incorrect. The narrator gives Joe all the credit for his having worked industriously and for his not having run away to become a soldier.

Choices C and E are incorrect. They are unsupported by the passage.

(Specific Details)

30. **(A)** Choice A is supported by the last sentence of the second paragraph in which the narrator states he "would not have had Miss Havisham and Estella see (his home) on any account."

Choices B and C are incorrect. Nothing in the passage suggests either might be the case.

Choice D is incorrect. Though the narrator may not show himself as hard-working, nothing in the passage suggests laziness led to his discontent.

Choice E is incorrect. Nothing in the passage suggests that sinfulness has prompted his discontent. In addition, although ingratitude may play a part in his discontent, shame of his background plays a part far greater.

(Inference)

**31. (B)** For us to be distressed by his *lapses,* his usual taste must be extremely good or even *flawless* so that the lapses or deviations would be bad.

(Examples)

**32. (D)** An argument is *unconvincing* if you don't agree to all its *premises.* Remember, watch for signal words that link one part of the sentence to another. The use of "Because" in the opening clause is a cause signal.

(Cause and Effect Signal)

**33. (B)** Pain is a *sensation.* Losing the ability to feel pain would leave the body *vulnerable,* or defenseless, lacking its usual warnings against impending bodily harm.

Note how the second clause serves to clarify or explain what is meant by pain's being an "early warning system."

(Definition)

**34. (C)** If she *deprecated* her accomplishments (diminished them or saw nothing praiseworthy in them), she would show her unwillingness to boast about them or *flaunt* them.

Note the use of *properly* to describe her unwillingness to do something. This suggests that the second missing word would have negative associations.

(Definition)

**35. (C)** A stereotyped or oversimplified portrait of a slave would lead sensitive readers to *criticize* it for dismissing the issue of slavery so casually. Thus, they normally would be *detractors* of the novel. However, *Huckleberry Finn* is such a fine work that even its critics acknowledge its greatness.

Signal words are helpful here. *Despite* in the first clause implies a contrast, and *even* in the second clause implies that the subjects somewhat reluctantly agree that the novel is a masterpiece.

(Contrast Signal)

**36. (E)** A *signature* on a *portrait* establishes who painted it. A *byline* on an *article* establishes who wrote it.

(Function)

**37. (B)** Just as a *breeze* is a less intense wind than a *tornado* (violent windstorm), a *trickle* is a less intense outpouring of liquid than a *gusher.*

(Degree of Intensity)

**38. (B)** *Records* are kept in *archives; birds* are kept in an *aviary* (bird house).

(Location)

**39. (C)** *Envelop* and *surround* are synonyms; *loiter* and *linger* (hang back) are synonyms also.

(Synonyms)

**40. (B)** Someone *indifferent* is uncaring or unconcerned; he is lacking in *concern*. Someone *arrogant* is proud and immodest; he is lacking in *modesty*.

(Antonym Variant)

**41. (A)** A *dilettante* is not serious about his art; he merely *dabbles*. A *coquette* is not serious about her affairs of the heart; she merely *flirts*.

(Definition)

**42. (C)** *Barren* (unable to produce offspring; infertile) and *fecund* (fertile) are antonyms, as are *hackneyed* (trite) and *original*.

(Antonyms)

**43. (C)** *Slander* is by its nature *defamatory* (injurious to one's reputation); an *elegy* (poem or song of mourning) is by nature *sorrowful*.

(Defining Characteristic)

**44. (A)** A snake *sloughs* or casts off its dead *skin*; people and animals *shed* their unneeded *hair*.

(Function)

**45. (C)** *Hyperbolic* and *exaggerated* are synonyms. So are *capricious* (unpredictable; fanciful) and *whimsical*.

(Synonyms)

## SECTION 2 MATH

**1. (C)** Crossmultiply: $5x = 36$
$$x = 7\frac{1}{5}$$

**2. (A)** The thickened line between $-2$ and $3$ represents all the numbers whose points (coordinates) are on that line. The open circle at $-2$ indicates that $-2$ is not part of the set while the solid circle indicates that $3$ is a member of the set. Thus, the inequality shown is all numbers more than $-2$ and less than or equal to $3$.

**3. (E)** Since the average is $K$ the sum of the two numbers is $2K$. Since one number is $M$ the other number is $2K - M$.

**4. (D)** At 80¢ per lb. the cost of 4 lbs. is $3.20. The change is $10.00 − $3.20 or $6.80

**5. (A)**
$$10x° + 8x° = 180$$
$$18x° = 180$$
$$x° = 10$$
$$5x° + 10x° + a° = 180$$
$$50 + 100 + a° = 180$$
$$a° = 30$$

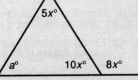

6. **(A)** To attain an average of $\frac{3}{10}$, the sum of the five fractions must be

   $5\left(\frac{3}{10}\right)$ or $\frac{15}{10}$

   $\frac{3}{5} + \frac{1}{4} + \frac{1}{10} + \frac{1}{2}$

   $\frac{12}{20} + \frac{5}{20} + \frac{2}{20} + \frac{10}{20} = \frac{29}{20}$

   The sum of the four fractions $= \frac{29}{20}$

   The fraction to be added must be $\frac{15}{10} - \frac{29}{20}$ or, $\frac{30}{20} - \frac{29}{20} = \frac{1}{20}$

7. **(D)** The difference between 201 and 149 is 52 but the number of integers from 149 to 201 is 53.

8. **(A)** This is a direct proportion.

   Let $x$ = number of weys in 4 bushels

   $\frac{\text{Wey}}{\text{Bushel}} = \frac{1}{40} = \frac{x}{4}$

   $40x = 4$

   $x = \frac{4}{40}$ or $\frac{1}{10}$

9. **(B)** Since angle $A$ has a measure of 60° and $AB = AC$, $ABC$ is an equilateral triangle and $BC = 6$.

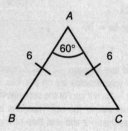

10. **(B)** In one week the man saves $(d - s)$ dollars.

    To save $Q$ dollars it will take $\frac{Q}{d - S}$ weeks.

11. **(C)** After the first round, $\frac{2}{3}$ of the original number were in the second round. One-half of the $\frac{2}{3}$ were eliminated and $\frac{1}{2}$ of the $\frac{2}{3}$ or $\frac{1}{3}$ of the original number would be eligible for the third round.

**12. (C)**

$$\frac{ab}{c} - \frac{1}{x} = 0$$
$$\frac{ab}{c} = \frac{1}{x}$$
$$abx = c$$
$$x = \frac{c}{ab}$$

**13. (C)**

$$x^2 + 4x + 6 = x^2 + 3x + 7$$
$$4x + 6 = 3x + 7 \quad \text{(subtract } x^2\text{)}$$
$$x + 6 = 7 \quad\quad \text{(subract } 3x\text{)}$$
$$x = 1 \quad\quad\quad \text{(subtract 6)}$$

**14. (A)** 0.4% of 1000 will be rejected

$$0.4\% = \frac{0.4}{100} = \frac{4}{1000}$$
$$\frac{4}{1000} \cdot \frac{1000}{1} = 4$$

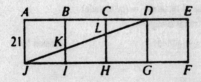

**15. (C)** In triangle *DJG*, *KI* is parallel to *LH* is parallel to *DG* cutting off equal segments *JI*, *IH*, *HG*. Triangle *JKI* is similar to triangle *DJG*.

$$\frac{(KI)}{(DG)} = \frac{(JI)}{(JG)}$$
$$\frac{(KI)}{21} = \frac{1}{3} \text{ (since } JI = IH = HG \text{ and } AJ = DG = 21)$$
$$3(KI) = 21 \text{ (product of means equals product of extremes)}$$
$$KI = 7 \text{ (divide by 3)}$$

**16. (B)**

$$\frac{1}{x} + \frac{1}{x} = 6$$
$$1 + 1 = 6x$$
$$2 = 6x$$
$$\frac{1}{3} = x$$

**17. (B)** This is a direct proportion.

Let $x$ = number of minutes required to travel $\frac{2}{5}$ of a mile

$$\frac{\text{Distance (miles)}}{\text{Time (minutes)}} = \frac{50}{60} = \frac{\frac{2}{5}}{x}$$

$50x = \left(\frac{2}{5}\right)(60)$ (product of means equals product of extremes)

$50x = 24$

$x = \frac{24}{50}$ or 0.48

**18. (A)** The minimum number of crates on a trip = 3
The minimum weight of a crate = 125 lbs.
Minimum weight of crates on a trip = 375 lbs.

**19. (D)** Area of circle = $\pi(\text{radius})^2$
Area of circle = $\pi r^2$
Area or rectangle = $\pi r^2$ \qquad (given)
Area of rectangle = (base)(altitude)
Area of rectangle = $(b)$(altitude)
$\pi r^2 = (b)$(altitude)
$\dfrac{\pi r^2}{b}$ = altitude \qquad (division by $b$)

**20. (D)** To have an average of 90 minutes (or $1\frac{2}{2}$ hours) per day, the total time spent practicing for the week must equal $(7)\left(1\frac{1}{2}\right)$ or $10\frac{1}{2}$ hours. From Monday to Thursday the girl has practiced $1\frac{1}{4} + 2 + 2 + 1\frac{3}{4}$ or 7 hours. She must therefore spend $3\frac{1}{2}$ additional hours practicing for the rest of the week.

**21. (D)** To raise $500 in addition to the expenses of $250 the school must receive $750 for tickets. At 75 cents per ticket they must sell $\dfrac{\$750}{\$0.75}$ or 1000 tickets.

**22. (D)**  Let $s$ = side of original square

$s + 150\%s$ or $s + 1\frac{1}{2}s$ or $2\frac{1}{2}s$ or $\frac{5}{2}s$ = side of new square

Area of square = (side)²

Area of original square = $(s)^2$ or $s^2$

Area of new square = $\left(\dfrac{5s}{2}\right)^2$ or $\dfrac{25s_2}{4}$ or $6\frac{1}{4}s^2$

Area of new square is $6\frac{1}{4}s^2$ (or 625%$s^2$)

Area of original square is $1s^2$ (or 100%$s^2$)

Increase = 525% or $s^2$

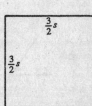

**23. (B)**  Observe that the point of tangency is at $(-2, 0)$. Radius $OT$ is $\perp$ to the $x$-axis since a radius is $\perp$ to a tangent at the point of contact. Thus $OT$ is parallel to the $y$-axis and point $T$, like point $O$, is two units to the left of the $y$-axis. Thus $x = -2$. Since the point $T$ lies on the $x$-axis, $y = 0$. The coordinates of the point of tangency, point $T$, are $(-2, 0)$.

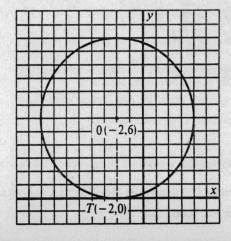

**24. (A)** Let $M$ be the midpoint of $AB$

$x$-midpoint $= \dfrac{x_1 + x_2}{2}$

$x_m = \dfrac{-5 + 3}{2} = \dfrac{-2}{2}$

$\phantom{x_m} = -1$

$y$-midpoint $= \dfrac{y_1 + y_2}{2}$

$y_m = \dfrac{-4 - 2}{2} = \dfrac{-6}{2}$

$\phantom{y_m} = -3$

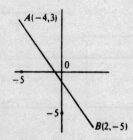

**25. (D)** Use the distance formula

$d = \sqrt{(x_1 - x_2)^2 + (y_1 - y_2)^2}$

In this case, $x_1 = -4$, $x_2 = 2$, $y_1 = 3$, $y_2 = -5$

$d = \sqrt{(-4 - 2)^2 + [3 - (-5)]^2}$

$d = \sqrt{(-6)^2 + (3 + 5)^2}$

$d = \sqrt{(-6)^2 + (8)^2}$

$d = \sqrt{36 + 64}$

$d = \sqrt{100}$

$d = 10$

The distance between the points is 10.

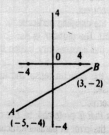

### Section 3 Test of Standard Written English

1. **(D)** Lack of parallel structure. Change *lower than a caretaker* to *lower than that of a caretaker.*
2. **(C)** Error in tense. Change *has sang* to *has sung.*
3. **(C)** Error in punctuation. Change *it's* to *its.*
4. **(C)** Error in agreement. Change *were* to *was.*
5. **(D)** Lack of parallel structure. Change *to guarantee* to *guaranteeing.*
6. **(E)** Sentence is correct.
7. **(B)** Error in diction. Change *affect* to *effect.*
8. **(B)** Error in diction. Change *had ought* to *ought.*
9. **(E)** Sentence is correct.
10. **(B)** Misuse of an adverbial clause when an adjective clause is needed. Change *where* to *that.*
11. **(D)** Error in case. Change *him* to *he.*
12. **(E)** Sentence is correct.
13. **(D)** Errors in tense and agreement. Change *is* to *were.*
14. **(B)** Error in case. Change *moment* to *moment's.*
15. **(A)** Double negative. Change *cannot* to *can.*
16. **(C)** Lack of parallel structure. Change *to finish* to *finishing.*
17. **(B)** Incomplete sentence. Change *consisting* to *consists.*
18. **(B)** Incorrect use of the superlative. Change *most* to *more.*
19. **(B)** Lack of parallel structure. Change *being intelligent* to *intelligence.*
20. **(E)** Sentence is correct.
21. **(D)** Error in diction. Change *latter* to *last.*
22. **(E)** Sentence is correct.
23. **(B)** Error in verb. Change *had drank* to *had drunk.*
24. **(A)** Misuse in adjective instead of adverb. Change *colorful* to *colorfully.*
25. **(D)** Error in case. Change *him* to *he.*
26. **(B)** This corrects the misuse of the subjunctive.
27. **(D)** This corrects the error in the case of the pronoun. Choice (E) corrects the error in case but introduces an error in tense.
28. **(C)** The improper use of the pronouns *one* and *you* is corrected in choice (C).
29. **(E)** The omission of the past participle *been* is corrected in choice (E).
30. **(A)** The clause is correct.
31. **(C)** This corrects the dangling participle.
32. **(D)** Misuse of word. The pronoun is *its.*
33. **(B)** This corrects the unnecessary switch in the pronouns, *anyone—you.*
34. **(D)** This corrects the error in tense and in the use of adjective and adverbial clauses.
35. **(A)** Sentence is correct.
36. **(E)** *The reason is that* is preferable to *The reason is because.*
37. **(E)** This corrects the error in parallel structure.

**38.** **(A)** Sentence is correct.

**39.** **(D)** This corrects the double negative (*hadn't hardly*) and the misuse of *those* with *kind*.

**40.** **(B)** This corrects the dangling participle and the misuse of *stole* for *stolen*.

**41.** **(C)** Error in agreement. Change *are* to *is*.

**42.** **(C)** Error in sequence of tenses. Change *were closed* to *had been closed*.

**43.** **(D)** Error in agreement. Change *them* to *him*.

**44.** **(A)** Error in diction. Change *principal* to *principle*.

**45.** **(E)** Sentence is correct.

**46.** **(A)** Error in diction. Change *or* to *nor*.

**47.** **(B)** Vague antecedent of pronoun. Change *minutes, which* to *minutes. This delay.*

**48.** **(A)** Error in diction. Change *might of* to *might have*.

**49.** **(E)** Sentence is correct.

**50.** **(A)** Error in tense. Change *have lived* to *lived*.

### Section 4 Verbal

**1.** **(B)** *Flexible* means pliable, able to be twisted or bent without breaking. Its opposite is *unbending*.
Word Parts Clue: *Flex-* means bend; *-ible* means able. *Flexible* means able to be bent.
Context Clue: Think of "flexible rules."

**2.** **(D)** To *amplify* is to enlarge or expand. Its opposite is to lessen or *diminish*.
Word Parts Clue: *Ample* means abundant, plentiful; more than adequate in size or scope.
To amplify something is to further increase its size or scope.

**3.** **(C)** *Reckless* means careless, thoughtless, foolhardy. Its opposite is *cautious* or careful.
Context Clue: Think of "reckless driving."

**4.** **(B)** An *agitator* stirs things up. A *peacemaker* calms things down.
Context Clue: Think of "troublesome agitators."

**5.** **(C)** *Arbitrary* means capricious, unreasonable, unsupported. Its opposite is *reasonable*.
Context Clue: Think of "making arbitrary demands."

**6.** **(D)** *Gullibility* is the quality of being easily cheated or fooled. Its opposite is *hardness to fool*.
Word Parts Clue: A *gull* is a dupe or fool.

**7.** **(C)** To *profane* something is to treat it with irreverence, to desecrate or debase it. Its opposite is to *sanctify* it or make it holy.
Context Clue: Think of "profaning a holy place."

**8. (A)** *Indigenous* means native. Its opposite is *foreign* or alien.
Context Clue: Think of "plants indigenous to Florida," "indigenous inhabitants."

**9. (C)** *Pusillanimity* means cowardliness, faint-heartedness, timidity. Its opposite is *courage*.

**10. (D)** *Evanescence* is the quality of being transient, fleeting, impermanent. Its opposite is *permanence* or durability.
Context Clue: Think of "the evanescence of a rainbow."
Word Parts Clue: *Van-* is related to vanish. *Evanescence* is the process of vanishing.

**11. (C)** The sentence implies that Polynesian banquets are usually reputed to be good. The speaker was disappointed by the banquet. Two possibilities exist: either this banquet was a poor one, or the banquets in general are *overrated* (too highly valued).
Note how the "either . . . or" structure sets up a contrast between the two clauses.
(Contrast Signal)

**12. (C)** Since Lee avoided or refrained from excesses, Grant, his opposite, must have *indulged in* or satisfied his taste for excesses.
The key words in this sentence are "differed markedly." They set up the contrast between the two men.
Note that you are looking for a word that suggests Grant enjoyed drinking. Therefore, you can eliminate any word that suggests he disliked or disapproved of it. Choices A, B, and D all suggest dislike or disapproval. Only Choice C or Choice E can be correct.
(Contrast Pattern)

**13. (B)** The librarian has the committee's *acquiescence* or agreement; they assent but do not go so far as to encourage or spur on the librarian. Their support is of a lesser degree.
Note how the "with the . . . if not the" structure signals that the two nouns must differ in meaning to some degree.
Remember, before you look at the choices, read the sentence and think of a word that makes sense.
Likely Words: agreement, permission, consent, approval.

**14. (A)** His friends could not understand his outburst because he was usually submissive *(docile)* and satisfied *(complacent)*.
Remember to watch for signal words that link one part of the sentence to another. The presence of *and* linking items in a series indicates that the missing word may be a synonym or near-synonym for the other linked words. In this case, *docile* and *complacent* are near-synonyms.
(Support Signal)

**15. (A)** With no enemies to stop their spread, the deer must have done well or *thrived*. They did so extremely well that they "overgrazed" or ate too much grass. This *threatened* (was bad for) the vegetation.

Note how the "so . . . that" structure signals cause and effect. Remember, in double-blank sentences, go through the answer choices, testing the *first* words in each choice and eliminating those that don't fit. You can immediately eliminate Choices C and E.

(Cause and Effect Signal)

**16. (C)** A *brake* slows or stops an *automobile*. *Reins* slow or stop a *horse*.

(Function)

**17. (B)** *Area* measures the size of a *square*. *Volume* measures the size of a *cube*.

(Defining Characteristic)

**18. (A)** A *tally* is a recorded account of *votes*. A *census* is a recorded account of *population*.

Beware Eye-Catchers: Choice E is incorrect. An election is a choice among candidates; it is not a recorded account of candidates.

(Definition)

**19. (A)** A *termite* feeds on (and eats away) *wood*. In its larval stage, a *moth* feeds on (and eats away) *wool*.

Beware Eye-Catchers: Choice B is incorrect. A silkworm makes silk; it does not feed on it.

(Function)

**20. (C)** A *cease-fire* is a temporary pause in *hostilities* (acts of warfare). A *lull* is a temporary pause in a *storm*.

(Defining Characteristic)

**21. (A)** *Colleagues* (professional associates) share a common *profession*. *Kinsfolk* (relatives) share a common *family*.

(Defining Characteristic)

**22. (D)** *Usury* (exorbitant interest) is an excessive or extreme form of *interest*. *Parsimony* (miserliness; excessive thrift) is an excessive or extreme form of *frugality* (economy; thrift). Use the process of elimination to improve your guessing odds. The word pairs in Choices A, B, and C are all antonyms. Since they all belong to the same analogy type, none of the three can be the correct answer. Eliminate all three.

(Degree of Intensity)

**23. (C)** *Cacophony* (harsh discordant sound) is distasteful to the *ear*. A *stench* (foul smell) is distasteful to the *nose*.

Remember, if more than one answer appears to fit the relationship in your sentence, look for a narrower approach. "Cacophony is perceived by the ear" is too general a framework. It would fit both Choice A and Choice C.

(Defining Characteristic)

**24. (B)** A *eulogy* is an expression of *praise*. A *slander* (statement damaging someone's reputation) is an expression of *disparagement* (depreciation, scorn).

Beware Eye-Catchers: Choice A is incorrect. An elegy is an expression of sorrow over a death. It is not an expression of death.

(Definition)

25. **(E)** To *embroil* someone is to involve him in conflict or *strife*. To *imperil* someone is to involve him in peril or *danger*.

(Defining Characteristic)

26. **(D)** The author makes strong positive statements about cities ("I call this beauty . . . I call it spirit"); he is *assertive*.

Choice A is incorrect. The author admires the impersonality of civilization; he himself is not emotionally uninvolved or impersonal.

Choice B is incorrect. The author is not self-effacing or humble as he states his beliefs.

Choice C is incorrect. The author admires tolerance—lack of concern about "religion or politics or race." However, his tone is not tolerant.

Choice E is incorrect. The author is scornful of "mystical soulfulness." He himself is not mystical.

Remember, when asked to determine the author's attitude or tone, look for words that convey emotion or paint pictures.

(Attitude/Tone)

27. **(A)** This passage is a defense of cities. By differentiating himself from naturalists who criticize cities, the author establishes himself as one who defends cities.

Choice B is incorrect. The author discusses the good points about free urban services, not their bad points or deficiencies.

Choice C is incorrect. The author discusses other naturalists' faults only in passing. Questioning them is not his main purpose.

Choice D is incorrect. It is not supported by the passage.

Choice E is incorrect. The author never touches on rural life.

(Main Idea)

28. **(C)** The use of the phrase "and above all" in the next to last sentence emphasizes the author's appreciation of the impersonal or *impartial service*.

Choices A, B, and E are incorrect. While the author admires these different attributes, they are not the aspects of city life he finds *most* commendable.

Choice D is incorrect. It is unsupported by the passage.

(Specific Details)

29. **(E)** In the last sentence, the author associates the impersonal provision of city services—public utilities—with the spirit of man. Thus, to operate these public utilities efficiently is to perform a service that is *spiritual* as well as practical.

Choice A is incorrect. The author is not complaining about the cost of services.

Choice B is incorrect. The author is interested in this efficient operation.

Choice C is incorrect. The author implies the opposite.

Choice D is incorrect. The author calls this efficient operation *more than* mechanically admirable; it is *spiritually* admirable.

(Inference)

**30. (C)** Choice C is correct. You can arrive at it by the process of elimination.

Statement I is correct. There are "certain geographical features that seem to span the ocean." These indicate the continents were once joined. Therefore, you can eliminate Choices B and D.

Statement II is correct. The "complementary coastlines" are *physical counterparts*. This indicates the continents were once joined. Therefore, you can eliminate Choice A.

Statement III is not correct. Though it is true that the African plate has been stable for ages, this fact is not stated as proof that Africa and South America once were joined. Therefore, you can eliminate Choice E.

Only Choice C is left. It is the correct answer.

(Specific Details)

**31. (E)** The concluding sentence of the passage states that hot spots someday "may explain (the continents') mutability," their tendency to change in shape, even break apart and form a new ocean.

Choice A is incorrect. Hot spots are seldom located near the boundaries of plates. Thus, they would be unlikely to provide useful information about plate boundaries.

Choice B is incorrect. It is unsupported by the passage.

Choice C is incorrect. Hot spots have proved useful in studying the *respective* motion of the plates, not their relative motion.

Choice D is incorrect. According to the passage, hot spots have served as measuring instruments in determining the respective motion of the plates. They have not been used to interpret instruments of measurement.

(Specific Details)

**32. (B)** In the first sentence of the second paragraph, the author states that the movement of the plates is "now beyond dispute": there is no question that they move. In other words, in his opinion the theory of plate movement is *irrefutable* (unable to be proven wrong).

Choices A, D, and E are incorrect. Something that is beyond dispute is no longer *controversial*, or considered *dubious* (doubtful) or *unwarranted* (unjustified).

Choice C is incorrect. The theory of plate movement is central to the author's discussion, not *tangential* (digressive).

(Specific Details)

**33. (B)** Choice B is correct. You can arrive at it by the process of elimination. The author would disagree with Statement I. According to lines 1–2,

"We have been cocksure of many things that were not so." The confidence or degree of assurance we feel about an issue is *not necessarily* related to the issue's truth. Therefore, you can eliminate Choices A and D.

The author would agree with Statement II. Lines 6–7 state that "what we most love and revere generally is determined by early associations." Therefore, you can eliminate Choice C.

The author would disagree with Statement III. Even though we realize that everyone's grounds for belief "are just as good as ours," our belief or faith still remains (lines 14–15). Knowing why we have preferences does not destroy our faith in their worth. Therefore, you can eliminate Choice E.

Only Choice B is left. It is the correct answer.

(Inference)

**34. (C)** Throughout the passage the author is discussing our long-term fixed preferences. To give us a sense of what it is like to disturb such deep-seated feelings, he creates an image of tearing up a tough mountain plant whose roots go deep into the rock.

(Technique)

**35. (A)** In lines 19–20, the author states firmly that "deep-seated preferences cannot be argued about." Then, to support his opinion, the author gives a common everyday example: "you cannot argue a man into liking a glass of beer." The author substitutes a concrete physical act *(liking a glass of beer)* for an abstract phrase *(deep-seated preference)*.

(Technique)

**36. (D)** The author's primary purpose is to convince people of the need to influence the cause of letters in our country positively. Throughout the passage he argues that we should foster the literature of our country, praising the good and criticizing the bad.

Choice A is incorrect. The author stresses that our infant literature cannot stand comparison with the literary masterpieces of Britain, Italy, and Greece (lines 28–32).

Choice B is incorrect. It is insufficiently broad. While the author rebukes the foreign critics, he also rebukes American boasters who overpraise American verse (lines 7–9).

Choice C is incorrect. The author asserts that we should reward American literary "genius and industry" (lines 20–24) and condemns those who scorn our literature.

Choice E is incorrect. It is insufficiently broad. While the author rebukes those who overrate American authors, he also rebukes the prejudiced foreign critics who underrate them.

(Main Idea)

**37. (C)** The author states that few writers are confident enough to believe their work can win them fame when they see other writers' work, work just as good as theirs, ignored. Few writers are brave enough to stick to a career that has destroyed generations of American writers before them. These ignored writers of previous generations are the *melancholy wrecks* American writers see—the only "prospect before them."

Remember, when asked to give the meaning of an unfamiliar word, look for nearby context clues.

(Word from Context)

**38. (B)** The author does not suggest that foreign critics possess a wide knowledge of American verse: they are "but slenderly acquainted" with it.

Choice A is incorrect. The author refers to the "infant literature of our country" and compares it unfavorably with the works of Europe's "mighty masters of song." This implies that he would agree *American literature is less mature* than European.

Choice C is incorrect. The author states that it is "detrimental to bestow on mediocrity the praise due to excellence" (lines 25–26). Doing so makes us "a contemptible figure" to others. This implies that the author would agree it is *pretentious* (self-important; pompous and conceited) and *self-defeating* to do so.

Choice D is incorrect. The author's main point is that Americans need to create an environment that nourishes writers.

Choice E is incorrect. Lines 13–16 indicate both that not every worthy artist is bold enough to come forward with his work and that many who do come forward receive no reward. The writer might well agree that many gifted poets languish in obscurity.

**39. (E)** While the author is enthusiastic about the prospects for poetry in America, he is not excessive in his enthusiasm. Instead, he measures out both praise and blame judiciously. His attitude is one of *measured enthusiasm*.

Choice A is incorrect. He is interested, not *fascinated;* objective, not full of wonder.

Choice B is incorrect. The author is hopeful that the climate for literature in America will improve. He is not *bitter and disillusioned.*

Choice C is incorrect. The author makes no pretence of being unconcerned. He clearly cares about American poetry.

Choice D is incorrect. *Chauvinism* means blind patriotism, excessive devotion to American poetry not because it is good but simply because it is American. That is not the author's attitude.

Remember, when asked to determine the author's attitude or tone, look for words that convey emotion or paint pictures.

(Attitude/Tone)

**40. (C)** The opening sentence sets up a contrast between the prejudice against American literature shown by foreigners and the over-enthusiasm shown by Americans. The second sentence continues this contrast. *Contumely* (rude language, insults) in the second sentence balances *prejudice* in the first: it is a negative word.

(Word from Context)

## Section 5 Math

**1. (B)** Let $x$ = actual length of the room

$$\frac{\text{Dimensions on drawing (inches)}}{\text{Actual dimensions (feet)}} = \frac{\frac{1}{4}}{1} = \frac{4\frac{1}{4}}{x}$$

$$\frac{1}{4}x = 4\frac{1}{4}$$

$$\frac{1}{4}x = \frac{17}{4}$$

$$x = 17 \quad \text{(multiply by 4)}$$

Let $y$ = actual width of the room

Using proportion above

$$\frac{\frac{1}{4}}{1} = \frac{3\frac{3}{4}}{y}$$

$$\frac{1}{4}y = 3\frac{3}{4}$$

$$\frac{1}{4}y = \frac{15}{4}$$

$$y = 15 \quad \text{(multiply by 4)}$$

Actual dimensions 17′ × 15′

**2. (E)** If average of four examinations was 75%, the sum of all examination marks was (75%) (4) or 300%

Sum of three examinations is 50 + 70 + 90 or 210%

Therefore the first examination grade was 90%

**3. (A)** Draw *ABCD*. Area of shaded portion equals area of square *ABCD*

minus the 4 equal sectors. Each sector equals $\frac{1}{4}$ of the circle. The

sum of the 4 sectors equals 1 circle. Therefore the area of the shaded portion equals the area of square *ABCD* minus the area of one circle.

*AB* = 2 radii = 1 foot

Area of square = $(AB)^2 = (1)^2 = 1$ square foot

Area of circle = $\pi r^2$

Diameter = 1 foot; Radius = $\frac{1}{2}$ foot

Area of circle = $\pi\left(\frac{1}{2}\right)^2 = \frac{1}{4}\pi$

Area of shaded portion = $1 - \frac{1}{4}\pi$ or $1 - \frac{\pi}{4}$

4. **(E)**   $4y - x - 10 = 0$
$$4y = x + 10$$
$$2y = 3x \quad \text{(given)}$$
$$4y = 6x \quad \text{(multiply by 2)}$$
$$6x = x + 10 \quad \text{(things equal to the same thing are equal to each other)}$$
$$5x = 10 \quad \text{(subtract } x\text{)}$$
$$x = 2 \quad \text{(divide by 5)}$$
$$3x = 2y \quad \text{(given)}$$
$$6 = 2y \quad \text{(substitute value of } x\text{)}$$
$$y = 3 \quad \text{(divide by 2)}$$
$$xy = 6 \quad \text{(substitute values of } x \text{ and } y\text{)}$$

5. **(C)**   You are not expected to do any time-consuming computations to get the correct answer. Consider that the speed is doubled and therefore the time required to cover the same distance would be halved.

6. **(A)**   If the man can do this job in $h$ hours each of the helpers will take $ah$ hours to do the job. Let $x$ = number of hours required by $w$ helpers to do the job. This is an inverse proportion.

$$\frac{1 \text{ helper}}{w \text{ helpers}} = \frac{x \text{ hours}}{ah \text{ hours}}$$
$$wx = ah \quad \text{(product of means equals product of extremes)}$$
$$x = \frac{ah}{w} \quad \text{(divide by } w\text{)}$$

7. **(D)**   $x = 2z + 3$
$$x - 3 = 2z$$
$$(x - 3)^2 = 4z^2 \quad \text{(square both sides of the equation)}$$
Since $y = 4z^2$
$$y = (x - 3)^2$$

8. **(A)**   100% of 25 = 25; 5% of 25 = 5
$$105\% \text{ of } 25 = 26.25$$

9. **(C)**    $4x = 48; x = 12$
$16\frac{2}{3}\% = \frac{1}{6}; \frac{1}{6}$ of $72 = 12$

10. **(B)**    $\left(\frac{1}{3}\right)^2 = \frac{1}{9}$ and $\left(\frac{1}{2}\right)^2 = \frac{1}{4} \cdot \frac{1}{4} > \frac{1}{9}$.

11. **(D)**    The value of $b$ may be negative, positive, or equal to zero.

12. **(C)**    Substitute $x = -y$ in $x + y = 0$. Then $-y + y = 0$.

13. **(A)**    Time $= \dfrac{\text{Distance}}{\text{Rate}}$

Time $= \dfrac{\frac{1}{2}\text{mile}}{20 \text{ miles per hour}} = \dfrac{1}{4}$ hour

Time $= \dfrac{\frac{1}{3}\text{mile}}{30 \text{ miles per hour}} = \dfrac{1}{90}$ hour

14. **(C)**    $\dfrac{\text{Distance}}{\text{Circumference}}$ = number of revolutions

Circumference $= \pi D$

Circumference $= (\pi) \cdot \dfrac{7}{\pi} = 7$

Circumference $= (\pi) \cdot \dfrac{10}{(\pi)} = 10$

$\dfrac{70 \text{ feet}}{7 \text{ feet}} = 10$ revolutions (Column A)

$\dfrac{100 \text{ feet}}{10 \text{ feet}} = 10$ revolutions (Column B)

15. **(D)**    If $X + Y = 100$; then $100 + Z = 350$ and $Z = 250$
However since $Y$ could be either positive or negative, $X$ could be either greater than or less than 250.

16. **(D)**    If $Y$ is at the center of both circles, then $Z$ could be anywhere on the circumference of the circle with radius $= 2$ and $X$ could be at any point on the circumference with radius $= 3$. There are many possibilities for the location of $X$ in respect to the location of $Z$.

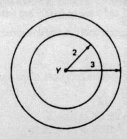

**17. (D)** If $x$ is $> 1$, $x^2$ will be greater than 1, and $y$ will be greater than $x$ since $y = 9x^2$. However, if $x$ is a small positive number, say $x = .01$, $x^2$ will equal $.0001$ and $y$ will be $.0009$ and therefore less than $x$.

**18. (D)** From the information given, we can only deduce that $\frac{1}{2}$ the product of these two values equals 18.

**19. (D)** We may conclude only that $AD = BC$ and $AB = DC$

**20. (C)** In Column A, $\dfrac{2}{\sqrt{2}} \cdot \dfrac{\sqrt{2}}{\sqrt{2}} = \dfrac{2\sqrt{2}}{2} = \sqrt{2}$.

**21. (A)** Column A: $\dfrac{\frac{1}{2}}{\frac{1}{3}} = \dfrac{1}{2} \div \dfrac{1}{3} = \dfrac{1}{2} \cdot \dfrac{3}{1} = \dfrac{3}{2} = 1\dfrac{1}{2}$.

Column B: $\dfrac{\frac{1}{3}}{\frac{1}{2}} = \dfrac{1}{3} \div \dfrac{1}{2} = \dfrac{1}{3} \cdot \dfrac{2}{1} = \dfrac{2}{3}$.

$$1\dfrac{1}{2} > \dfrac{2}{3}$$

**22. (B)** In Column B, $\dfrac{2x + 1}{2} = \dfrac{2x}{2} + \dfrac{1}{2} = x + \dfrac{1}{2}$.

$$x + \dfrac{1}{2} > x$$

**23. (A)** 
$$x + 5 + 3x - 1 + 4x - 2 = 34$$
$$8x + 2 = 34$$
$$8x = 32$$
$$x = 4$$
$$BC = 4x - 2 = 14$$
$$AC = 3x - 1 = 11$$
$$BC > AC$$

Therefore the measure of $\angle BAC >$ the measure of $\angle ABC$.

**24. (D)** If $x > 1$, $x^2$ will be greater than 1 and $y$ will be greater than $x$, since $y = 9x^2$. However, if $x$ is a small positive number, say $x = 0.01$, $x^2$ will equal $0.0001$ and $y$ will be $0.0009$ and therefore less than $x$.

**25. (B)** Since $x$ appears in both columns do not consider $x$ in calculating the averages.

Column A: $\dfrac{5}{2} = 2\dfrac{1}{2}$

Column B: $\dfrac{7}{2} = 3\dfrac{1}{2}$

$$3\dfrac{1}{2} > 2\dfrac{1}{2}$$

**26. (C)**   Let $s$ = the side of the square

$s^2$ = area of the square

$\dfrac{s}{2}$ = radius of semicircle

$\dfrac{\pi r^2}{2}$ = area of semicircle

$\dfrac{\pi\left(\dfrac{s}{2}\right)^2}{2}$ = area of semicircle

$\dfrac{\pi\dfrac{s^2}{4}}{2}$ or $\dfrac{\pi s^2}{8}$ = area of semicircle

The ratio of shaded area to area of square is $\dfrac{\dfrac{\pi s^2}{8}}{s^2} = \dfrac{\pi s^2}{8} \cdot \dfrac{1}{s^2} = \dfrac{\pi}{8}$

**27. (B)**   Since $a = 90$, then $x + w = 90$

Since $b = 90$, then $y + z = 90$

$w + x + y + z = 180$

**28. (A)**   5 gallons = 20 quarts = 40 pints

$\dfrac{120 \text{ pint bottles}}{40 \text{ pints in each can}} = 3 \text{ cans}$

**29. (D)**   Area of circle = $\pi r^2$

Area of circle = $9\pi$

$\pi r^2 = 9\pi$

$r^2 = 9$   (divide by $\pi$)

$r = 3$

$AB$ (side of square) = $2r$ or $6$

Area of square = (side)$^2$ or $(6)^2$ or $36$

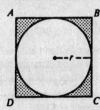

**30. (B)**   Let $x$ = distance covered by driving car

$55 - x$ = distance covered by walking

Rate riding = 40 M.P.H.

Rate walking = 5 M.P.H.

$\dfrac{\text{Distance}}{\text{Rate}} = \text{Time}$

Time driving car $= \dfrac{x}{40}$

Time walking $= \dfrac{55 - x}{5}$

Total time $= 4$ hours (given)

$\dfrac{x}{40} + \dfrac{55 - x}{5} = 4$

$x + 8(55 - x) = 160$   (multiply by 40)

$x + 440 - 8x = 160$

$-7x = -280$

$7x = 280$

$x = 40$   (distance covered by driving car)

$\dfrac{\text{Distance covered by driving car}}{\text{Total distance}} = \dfrac{40}{55} = \dfrac{8}{11}$

31. **(E)** At the end of the first half hour $\dfrac{1}{4}$ of 256 or 64 contestants are eliminated and 192 remain eligible. At the end of the first hour $\dfrac{1}{4}$ of 192 or 48 contestants are eliminated and 144 remain eligible. After one and one-half hours $\dfrac{1}{4}$ of 144 or 36 contestants are eliminated and 108 remain eligible. After two hours $\dfrac{1}{4}$ of 108 or 27 contestants are eliminated and 81 contestants remain eligible.

32. **(D)** The man sold $\dfrac{1}{5}$ of $\dfrac{5}{8}$ or $\dfrac{1}{8}$ of the property. Since this represents $1000, then $\dfrac{8}{8}$ (the whole) has a value of $8000.

33. **(B)** Let $x =$ Marked Price

$\dfrac{105x}{100} = \$4.20$

$105x = 420$       (product of means equals product of the extremes)

$x = \$4.00$       (division by 105)

$4.00 less 5% discount $= \$3.80$

34. **(D)** Let $x =$ number of players who were on the squad at first

$x - 20\%$ of $x = 32$

$x - .2x = 32$

$10x - 2x = 320$ (multiply by 10)

$8x = 320$

$x = 40$

**35. (D)** (1) Since no integer is zero (all are odd) the product of these integers cannot be zero.

(2) Since the sum is zero, the average must be zero.

(3) The sum of all the negative integers must be the negative of the sum of all the positive integers in order for the total sum to be zero. If there is an even number of positive (odd) integers, their sum will be even and there will also have to be an even number of negative (odd) integers to balance this sum. If there is an odd number of positive (odd) integers, their sum will be odd and there will also have to be an odd number of negative (odd) integers to balance this sum. In either case the total number of positive and negative integers will be even.

## Section 6 Math

**1. (E)** The maximum number of bulbs that produce flowers = 22

$$\frac{22}{25} \times 100 = \text{Per cent that produce flowers}$$

$$\frac{22}{\underset{5}{\cancel{25}}} \times \frac{\overset{4}{\cancel{100}}}{1} = 88\%$$

**2. (B)** $\dfrac{a}{b} = c$

$b = c$

$b = \dfrac{a}{b}$   (things equal to the same thing are equal to each other)

$b^2 = a$   (multiply by $b$)

$b = \sqrt{a}$ (extract square root)

**3. (C)** The total number of days required to paint the barn was 20 days.

James worked $\dfrac{12}{20}$ or $\dfrac{3}{5}$ of the total days.

He should receive $\dfrac{3}{5}$ of $100 or $60.

**4. (D)** Each son takes 8 times as much time as the father (or 24 hours each). With the three sons working it would take $\dfrac{1}{3}$ the time or $\dfrac{1}{3}$ of 24 = 8 hours.

**5. (D)** 4% of 750 or (0.04) (750) or 30 eggs cracked.

750 − 30 = 720 eggs remaining.
5% of 720 or (0.05) (720) or 36 eggs were found to be defective after candling.
720 − 36 = 684 eggs that can be sold.

**6. (A)** Area of shaded portion equals area of rectangle *ABCD* minus area of the two circles.

Length of rectangle equals four radii (4*r*)
Width of rectangle equals two radii (2*r*)
Area of rectangle = (base)(altitude)
Area of rectangle = (4*r*)(2*r*) or 8*r*²
Area of one circle = $\pi r^2$
Area of two circles = $2\pi r^2$
Area of shaded portion = $8r^2 - 2\pi r^2$
Or, $2r^2(4 - \pi)$ (factoring)

**7. (D)** List Price − Discount = Selling Price
$90 − Discount = $72
Discount = $18
$$\frac{\text{Discount}}{\text{List Price}} \times 100 = \text{Rate of Discount}$$
$$\frac{18}{90} \times 100 = 20\%$$

**8. (D)** For every $5 left by the father Benjamin received $1.50.
Benjamin received $\frac{\$1.50}{\$5.00}$ or $\frac{3}{10}$ of the money left.
$\frac{3}{10}$ of $5000 (amount left by father) = $1500

**9. (E)** Distance = 152.5 miles
Time = 2 hours
$$\frac{\text{Distance}}{\text{Time}} = \text{Average speed}$$
$$\frac{152.5}{2} = 76.25 \text{ or } 76.3 \text{ miles per hour}$$

**10. (C)** Distance = (Rate)(Time)
Distance = (40 M.P.H.)(5 hours)
Distance (one way) = 200 miles
$$\text{Average rate for return trip} = \frac{\text{Distance}}{\text{Time}}$$
$$\text{Average rate for return trip} = \frac{200 \text{ miles}}{10 \text{ hours}}$$
or 20 miles per hour

**11. (B)** Area of triangle $= \dfrac{1}{2}$ (base)(altitude)

Area of triangle $= \dfrac{1}{2}$ (6 units)(2 units)

Area of triangle = 6 square units

**12. (E)** Draw $CF$ parallel to $DE$ forming rectangle $FEDC$.

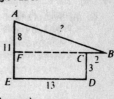

$FC = ED = 13$

$FB = FC + CB$

$FB = 13 + 2$ or $15$

$FE = CD = 3$

$AF = AE - FE$

$AF = 11 - 3$ or $8$

In right triangle $AFB$,

$(AB)^2 = (AF)^2 + (FB)^2$ (Pythagorean theorem)

$(AB)^2 = (8)^2 + (15)^2$

$(AB)^2 = 64 + 225$

$(AB)^2 = 289$

$\quad AB = 17$ \qquad (extract square root)

**13. (C)** The least number of crates in a carload is 12. The least number in 4 carloads is (4)(12) or 48.

**14. (A)** Since $x$ equals more than 45, each of the four values is more than 45 and the average of the numbers cannot possibly be 45.

**15. (E)** We are given the points whose coordinates are $(-2, -7)$ and $(6, 8)$. We are required to find the distance between these points.

We use the distance formula:

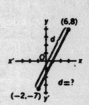

$d = \sqrt{(x_1 - x_2)^2 + (y_1 - y_2)^2}$

In this case, $x_1 = -2$, $x_2 = 6$,

$y_1 = -7$, $y_2 = 8$

$d = \sqrt{(-2 - 6)^2 + (-7 - 8)^2}$

$d = \sqrt{(-8)^2 + (-15)^2}$

$d = \sqrt{64 + 225}$

$d = \sqrt{289}$

$d = 17$

**16. (A)** Let the coordinates of the other end-point of the line segment be $(a, b)$.

$x_m = \dfrac{x_1 + x_2}{2}$

In this case, $x_m = 2$, $x_1 = 3$, and $x_2 = a$.

$2 = \dfrac{3 + a}{2}$

$4 = 3 + a,\ a = 4 - 3$

$a = 1$

$y_m = \dfrac{y_1 + y_2}{2}$

In this case, $y_m = -5$, $y_1 = -2$, and $t_2 = b$.

$$-5 = \frac{-2 + b}{2}$$

$$-10 = -2 + b,\ b = -10 + 2$$

$$b = -8$$

**17. (D)** The locus of points 2 inches from line $AB$ consists of two parallel lines, $P_1 P_2$ and $P_{-3} P_{-4}$. The locus of points 3 inches from point $C$ is a cirlce with $C$ as center and 3 inches as radius.

Points $P_1, P_2, P_3, P_4$ are both
2 inches from $AB$ and 3 inches from $C$

**18. (C)** $0.04 = 4\%$

$$\left(\frac{1}{4}\right)^2 = \frac{1}{16} = 6\frac{1}{4}\%$$

$$\frac{1}{0.04} = \frac{100}{4} = 25 = 2500\%$$

$$(0.04)^2 = 0.0016 = 0.16\%$$

Answer $= \dfrac{1}{0.04}$

**19. (E)** If $ad - bc - x = 0$, then $ad - bc = x$.

**20. (B)** $\dfrac{3}{4} + \dfrac{5}{n} = \dfrac{19}{12}$

$$\frac{3}{4} + \frac{5}{n} = \frac{19}{12}\ \text{(multiply by } 12n)$$

$$9n + 60 = 19n$$

$$-10n = -60$$

$$10n = 60$$

$$n = 6$$

**21. (C)** $2.4 \sqrt{\dfrac{x^4 y^2}{16} + \dfrac{y^2 x^4}{9}}$

$2.4 \sqrt{\dfrac{9x^4 y^2 + 16y^2 x^4}{144}}$   (144 is L.C.D.)

$2.4 \sqrt{\dfrac{25x^4 y^2}{144}}$      (combine fractions)

$2.4 \left(\dfrac{5x^2 y}{12}\right)$      (extract square root)

$\dfrac{12x^2 y}{12}$      (multiply)

$x^2 y$      (cancellation)

**22.** **(E)** Let $x$ = length of shadow of 35 foot tree.

$$\frac{\text{Length of object (feet)}}{\text{Length of shadow (feet)}} = \frac{35}{x} = \frac{98}{42}$$

$98x = (35)(42)$ (product of means equals product of extremes)

$98x = 1470$

$\quad x = 15 \quad$ (division by 98)

**23.** **(C)** Mark up the diagram. Each side of the small square = $\frac{1}{3}$ and $4(\frac{1}{3}) = \frac{4}{3}$.

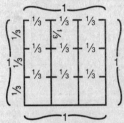

**24.** **(D)** Since the perimeter of the square is 24, each side is 6 and its area is 36. Since the area of $R$ is also 36 and its altitude is 4, its base is 9 (note this is incorrect choice A). The perimeter of $R$ is $(2)(4) + (2)(9)$ or 26 feet. Choice (E) gives the area of $R$. Choice (B) fails to consider $R$ a rectangle. Choice (C) assumes that the base of $R$ equals the side of the square.

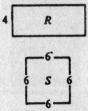

**25.** **(E)** A ratio of 10:1 would be true for 11 eggs.

(A) is possible with a combination of 6 and 6.
(B) is possible with a combination of 8 and 4.
(C) is possible with a combination of 9 and 3.
(D) is possible with a combination of 10 and 2.

Observe that the possible combinations yield sums of 12, the dozen.